W9-AFI-675

WITHDRAWN

CHE GUEVARA

GUERRILLA WARFARE

WITH AN INTRODUCTION AND
CASE STUDIES BY
BRIAN LOVEMAN AND
THOMAS M. DAVIES, JR.

UNIVERSITY OF NEBRASKA PRESS
LINCOLN AND LONDON

Copyright 1985 by the
University of Nebraska Press

Guerrilla Warfare, by Che Guevara, copyright © 1961 by
Monthly Review Press; reprinted by permission of Monthly
Review Press.

"Guerrilla Warfare: A Method," by Che Guevara, is reprinted
by permission of the MIT Press from *Che: Selected Works of
Ernesto Guevara,* edited and with an introduction by Rolando
E. Bonachea and Nelson P. Valdés (Cambridge, Mass.: MIT
Press, 1969), copyright © 1969 by The Massachusetts Insti-
tute of Technology.

Library of Congress Cataloging in Publication Data
Guevara, Ernesto, 1928–1967.
    Guerrilla warfare.
    Translation of: La guerra de guerrillas.
    Reprint. Originally published: New York : Monthly Review
Press, 1961.
    Includes bibliographical references and index.
    1. Guerrilla warfare—Case studies. 2. Latin America—His-
tory—1948–   . I. Loveman, Brian. II. Davies, Thomas M.
III. Title.
U240.G8313   1985   355.4'25   84–13162
ISBN 0-8032-2116-9
ISBN 0-8032-7010-0 (pbk.)

CONTENTS

ACKNOWLEDGMENTS

In the course of compiling this volume, we were greatly aided by many people. Professors Ernst Griffin, Edwin Lieuwen, Frederick Nunn, Robert Oppenheimer, Gonzalo Palacios, David Scott Palmer, and Louis Terrell all read and commented on the manuscript and each contributed immensely to the final product without in any way bearing responsibility for remaining deficiencies. Our students William Armstrong, Phillip Burke, Richard Swain, and Michael Stanfield likewise read the manuscript and made many valuable suggestions from the user's perspective. The excellent maps were prepared by Barbara Aguado and Lorissa Boxer.

We are also indebted to Betsy Gautsch and Teddy Ralph, who patiently typed and retyped the essays, and to Veva Link, Kirsten Barstad-Mulvey, Lidia Ramírez, and Grace Thomas, who proofread, retyped, and copied parts of the manuscript. Kirsten Barstad-Mulvey and Michael Stanfield prepared the index.

Finally, as always, we could never have completed this work without the love and support of our wives, Sharon Loveman and Tita Davies, and our children, Taryn, Mara, Carly, Ben, and Ryan Loveman, and Jennifer Davies.

PREFACE

The publication of *Guerrilla Warfare* in 1960 marked a dramatic moment in Latin American history and in U.S.–Latin American relations. In this landmark book the author, Ernesto "Che" Guevara, declared war against the incumbent regimes throughout Latin America and against U.S. imperialism. Che proclaimed for all to hear that through guerrilla warfare the dictatorships of Central America and the Caribbean would be destroyed and that Cuba would be a vanguard force in the war for liberation.

Almost immediately the new Cuban revolutionary government that had taken power in January 1959 began to provide training and small amounts of military assistance to would-be insurrectionists in the Western Hemisphere. Che Guevara took personal control and participated actively in the Cuban efforts to inspire "new Cubas" in Latin America. In response, the United States and most Latin American governments created a vast military counterinsurgency apparatus to destroy the nascent guerrilla organizations and established an "Alliance for Progress" to undermine support for revolutionary movements in the region. Indeed, in many respects, it may be said that the last quarter century of United States foreign policy toward Latin America has consisted essentially of defeating the threat, the legacy, the legend of Ernesto "Che" Guevara—the most important martyr of revolutionary struggle in Latin America in the twentieth century.

Born into a middle-class Argentine family in 1928, Ernesto "Che" Guevara overcame frailty in infancy and chronic asthma to become one of the twentieth century's most glorified fighters—a symbol of the power of human volition and determination. Evolving gradually in his student days from an intense Argentine nationalist into a believer in the unity of anti-imperialist struggle in Latin America, Guevara traveled as an itinerant throughout Latin America. Working the grape harvests in Argentina, as a security guard in Chile's northern mines, as a male nurse aboard an Argentine freighter, in a leper colony in the Amazon region, and as a truck driver and dishwasher, Guevara experienced at first hand the poverty and misery of Latin America's masses in the early 1950s.[1]

In March 1953, he received a medical degree in Argentina, but less than four months later he again took to traveling throughout the continent. After spending time in Bolivia, Ecuador, and Panama, Guevara walked and hitchhiked to Guatemala. In Guatemala, he lived through the U.S.-sponsored counterrevolution that ousted President Jacobo Arbenz. He met a number of Peruvian Apristas and other leftist Latin American political exiles who dreamed of social revolution.[2] He also met Cubans who belonged to the "26th of July Movement," led by Fidel Castro and named after the 1953 assault by Fidel's group on the Moncada Barracks in Cuba.

After the overthrow of Arbenz, Guevara took refuge in the Argentine embassy; shortly thereafter he went to Mexico. There he renewed his association with members of the "26th of July Movement," including Castro's younger brother, Raul. Eventually Fidel Castro invited Guevara, now nicknamed "Che" (for his typically Argentine habit of calling his friends, and ending his sentences with "Che"—meaning "friend" or "buddy"), to join the expeditionary force as a fighter-doctor. Trained by former Spanish Civil War general and guerrilla fighter Alberto Bayo, the eighty-two-man force left Mexico for Cuba on the now celebrated "yacht" *Granma*. Of these eighty-two, perhaps twenty reached the Sierra Maestra after encounters with dictator Fulgencio Batista's troops. From this unlikely beginning, the guerrilla fighters sparked a popular insurrection that finally caused Batista to flee the island in January 1959.

The success of the Cuban revolution generated enthusiastic emulation in other parts of Latin America. Che Guevara, now one of the heroes of the revolutionary victory, proclaimed the desirability and feasibility of adapting the Cuban guerrilla strategy to the overthrow of tyranny in the rest of Latin America. In January 1959, Guevara's "Social Projections of the Rebel Army" linked the success of the guerrillas to the organization of the urban working classes and the peasantry against the Cuban dictatorship. For Che, guerrilla warfare involved political as well as military struggle, thereby making student, peasant, and worker organizations potentially "subversive" in the eyes of incumbent governments. By April 1961, his essay "Cuba: Historical Exception or Vanguard in the Anticolonial Struggle?" clearly identified the enemy of the peoples of Latin America as "the great phenomenon of imperialism with its sequel of puppet governments in each country and mercenary armies, disposed to defend each puppet." He also proclaimed emphatically the objectives of his efforts and those of the guerrillas he inspired: to create "the subjective conditions, of which the most important is the awareness of the possibility of victory over the imperial powers and their internal allies by taking the violent road."

From the time Che announced his intentions to export Cuba's revolution to its Latin American brethren, U.S. political and military policy concentrated on finding and destroying the threat of Guevarist-inspired guerrilla movements. After Che's death in 1967 at the hands of U.S.-trained Bolivian counterinsurgency forces, the legacy of revolutionary guerrilla warfare and the legend, even mystification, of Che, the heroic *guerrillero*, inspired new generations of revolutionaries from Mexico to Tierra del Fuego, while U.S. foreign policy continued to emphasize the eradication of Che's legacy.

More often defeated than victorious, the guerrilla movements of the 1960s and 1970s contributed to the establishment of repressive military regimes in much of Latin America. Seemingly successful in their counterinsurgency programs, U.S. and Latin American leaders celebrated the apparent demise of rural guerrilla movements in Central America and the northern tier of South America, as well as the defeat of urban guerrillas in Uruguay and Argentina. With harsh military regimes in control of the Southern Cone and more traditional dictatorships dominating most of Central America, the threat of "more Cubas" appeared defeated. By 1968 the Soviet Union, at least for the moment, clearly rejected the export of revolution. Even the Cubans—after designating 1968 the "Year of the Heroic Guerrilla"—subtly attacked Regis Debray's glorification of Che and the primacy of the guerrilla *foco* (small cadre of revolutionary fighters in the countryside) in *Revolution in the Revolution?* Although Fidel Castro never wavered from his commitment to assist Latin American revolutionaries, in 1969 reality seemed to dictate a more patient stance: "We will wait and watch as, one by one, those countries [in Latin America] break away from the past; as, one by one, they make their revolutions. . . . How long will we wait? . . . as long as necessary."

If guerrilla failures in the 1960s made the Cubans more cautious, it seemed almost as if Che Guevara's death and the repression of the guerrilla movements diverted the attention of U.S. policy makers and Latin American elites from the unchanging realities that Che had pointed to as "ideal conditions for the fight": wretched poverty in the countryside, persistence of the *latifundio* (the large rural estates that controlled most of the best agricultural land), intensifying urban squalor, and repressive, dictatorial political regimes.

Just as these "ideal conditions for the fight" persisted, so significant guerrilla movements reappeared in the 1970s and early 1980s. Sandinista revolutionaries overthrew the corrupt Somoza dynasty in Nicaragua and guerrilla fighters threatened the old order in El Salvador and Guatemala. After President Carter's refusal to rescue Somoza contributed to the insurrectionists' victory, the United States again reacted to the threat of guerrilla warfare—the legacy of Che Guevara—with support for counterinsurgency programs in El Salvador, Guatemala, and Honduras and covert CIA action against the new revolutionary government in Managua.

Ironically, as the political and military significance of guerrilla movements resurged in Central and South America, Che Guevara's *Guerrilla Warfare* went out of print in English. It is made available once more in the belief that students of Latin American history and politics—and U.S. policy makers—

cannot fully understand the origins or direction of present events in Latin America without studying the theoretical contribution to revolutionary literature and, perhaps more important, the inspiration that Che's example and *Guerrilla Warfare* have provided to Latin American revolutionaries since the 1960s. In a very real sense Che *vive*—Che lives—wherever guerrilla movements oppose incumbent regimes in Latin America.

In reprinting *Guerrilla Warfare*, we have included a brief introductory essay discussing Che's theoretical contribution to the revolutionary tradition and reviewing several major critiques of Guevara's thesis by other revolutionary theorists. We have provided, in addition, brief comparative surveys of the major Latin American rural-based guerrilla movements of the 1960s and the more recent revolutionary conflicts in Central America, including the victory of the Sandinistas in Nicaragua. In summarizing the experiences of these guerrilla movements, we consider in each case the extent to which their leadership, ideology, tactics, and politico-military experience conform to Che's vision. We also discuss the U.S. response in each case. Finally, a brief postscript provides an assessment of the impact of Che Guevara's ideas and of U.S. policy response to guerrilla movements in Latin America since 1959.[3]

Without understating Che's contribution to revolutionary theory, it is essential to remember that his inspiration and faith in ultimate victory was his major legacy to Latin American revolutionaries. Che asserted that the Cuban revolution had demonstrated that popular forces could win in war against the forces of repression. He further declared that it was not necessary to wait until all the conditions for revolution existed, but that the guerrillas could, themselves, create revolutionary conditions. His call to action, his proclamation of "invincibility"—the ultimate victory of revolutionary forces—whether correct or incorrect, continues to influence the course of Latin American history and international relations.

NOTES

1. For useful biographical material on Che Guevara and assessments of his intellectual contributions, see Rolando E. Bonachea and Nelson P. Valdés, *Che: Selected Works of Ernesto Guevara* (Cambridge, Mass.: MIT Press, 1969); John Gerassi, ed., *Venceremos: The Speeches and Writings of Ernesto Che Guevara* (London: Wiedenfeld and Nicholson, 1968); and Donald C. Hodges, *The Legacy of Che Guevara* (London: Thames and Hudson, 1977).

2. For discussion of the Guatemalan counterrevolution of 1954 and the Peruvian Apristas (APRA), see below, chapters on Guatemala and Peru.

3. Throughout this book we have attempted to refer in the notes to sources most likely to be available to students in university libraries. This often meant citing secondary rather than primary sources.

INTRODUCTION

GUERRILLA WARFARE, REVOLUTIONARY THEORY, AND REVOLUTIONARY MOVEMENTS IN LATIN AMERICA

Spanish peasants resisting Napoleon's early-nineteenth-century (1808–13) invasion of the Iberian Peninsula popularized the guerrilla fighter in modern military history. Hit-and-run attacks by Spanish irregulars supported by British and Portuguese troops and matériel introduced the *guerrilla*, or "little war," into military lexicon (by adding the diminutive suffix to the Spanish word for war, *guerra*).[1]

In historical perspective, however, these Spanish irregulars and armed civilians merely added to the numerous ancient, medieval, and more modern instance of military improvisation by the weak against the strong, by small unconventional units against larger conventional forces. In recent time, most guerrilla warriors, like their Spanish predecessors, have been part of wider international confrontations and clashes of competing ideologies—even if their banners remained strictly nationalist or restorationist. Guerrillas, partisans, irregulars, resistance groups, terrorists, armed revolutionists, social bandits—whatever the immediate terminology—always do better if they can rely on external assistance and strong ideological, nationalist, or religious motivation against an "evil" enemy.

Guerrilla wars have often frustrated incumbent regimes or armies of military occupation; and frustration breeds brutality and repression. French repression of entire Spanish towns in the Napoleonic Wars proved as little successful, militarily, as

British efforts against the Boers in South Africa and the Jews in Palestine early in the twentieth century, or U.S. tactics in Vietnam in the 1960s and 1970s. As one British observer of the Boer War commented in 1901: "If there is one certain education to be drawn from past experience it is that guerrilla tactics, when carved out by a resourceful and persistent enemy, have invariably led to a protracted struggle, during which the invading armies against which they fought have suffered a series of minor disasters and regrettable incidents."[2]

Historically, guerrilla operations have contributed to or even led (1) resistance to foreign invasion and occupation; (2) the attainment of political or socioeconomic concessions from incumbent regimes; (3) the overthrow of unpopular governments; (4) wars of national liberation or decolonization; and (5) the creation of new political entities. As in the Spanish case, favorable terrain; hit-and-run tactics; refusal to risk defeat in pitched battles; support from international allies; safe base areas, or "sanctuary"; and reliance upon the local population for support in the form of provisions, intelligence, and personnel have combined to deny the politico-military advantage to superior forces in a variety of nineteenth- and twentieth-century wars.[3]

Although guerrilla-type military operations considerably antedate explicit theoretical treatment of guerrilla strategies, whether strictly military or as instruments of political movements, the great Prussian military strategist Karl von Clausewitz's classic *On War* enumerates five general conditions for successful irregular warfare "in coordination with operations carried out by a regular army, both actions according to an overall plan."

1. The war must be carried on in the interior of the country.
2. The war cannot hinge upon a single battle.
3. The theater of war must extend over a considerable area.
4. The national character must support the war.
5. The terrain must be irregular, difficult, inaccessible.

According to Clausewitz:

> Militia and armed civilians cannot and should not be employed against the main force of the enemy, or even against sizable units.

They should not try to crack the core, but only nibble along the surface and on the edges. They should rise in provinces lying to one side of the main theater of war, which the invader does not enter in force, in order to draw these areas entirely from his grasp. These storm clouds forming on his flanks should also follow to the rear of his advance. . . . The enemy has no other means with which to oppose the actions of armed civilians than the dispatching of numerous detachments to escort his convoys, to occupy posts, defiles, bridges, etc. Just as the first efforts of the people will be insignificant, so these detachments will be weak, because he is afraid of dividing his forces too much. It is on these small units that the spark of popular war really catches fire; at some points, the enemy is overpowered by sheer numbers, courage and enthusiasm grow, and the intensity of the struggle increases until the culmination comes, which will decide the entire issue.[4]

For the most part, this assessment of guerrilla activities is reiterated in Che Guevara's *Guerrilla Warfare*. Che refers to guerrilla warfare as "a phase that does not offer in itself opportunities to arrive at complete victory." Like Clausewitz, he accepts the premise that the ultimate objective of modern warfare (including guerrilla warfare "as its steady growth acquires the characteristics of a regular army") is "to win, to annihilate the enemy." Che also emphasizes the critical nature of favorable terrain, operations in the hinterland, and popular support. At the same time, however, Che Guevara categorically rejected Clausewitz's assertion that guerrillas can succeed only as support units for conventional forces, insisting rather on the catalytic role of the guerrilla which leads eventually to victory by a "people's army."[5]

If Clausewitz's formulation is a classic expression of guerrilla tactics as part of modern warfare, T. E. Lawrence is often credited with the first theoretical contribution to understanding guerrilla warfare as a *political* movement furthered through unconventional tactics rather than as a military tactic supplementary to conventional warfare. Lawrence's experience as leader of Arab irregulars supported by the British opposing the Turks in World War I convinced him that guerrilla warfare could not be fought without its own set of rules. According to Lt. Col. Frederick Wilkins, T. E. Lawrence "almost converted the tactics of guerrilla warfare into a science and claimed that no enemy could occupy a country employing guerrilla warfare unless every acre of land could be occupied with troops." Wilkins elaborates:

In *Seven Pillars of Wisdom* Lawrence explained the plan that eventually defeated the Turks in Arabia. "In the Turkish Army materials were scarce and precious, men more plentiful than equipment . . . the aim should be to destroy not the army but the materials." Eventually 35,000 Turkish casualties resulted from the new change in methods, but they were incidental to the attack on enemy material. The plan was to convince the Turks they couldn't stay, rather than to drive them out.

Using English demolition specialists Lawrence had the Arabs blow up railway bridges and tunnels, cut rails, harass fortified railway stations. Medina was no longer the primary objective; the railway to the city was the target. Isolated posts and garrisons were threatened, so that the Turks reinforced them. No further attacks were made, as the heavily reinforced garrison sat about and ate up their rations. In a short time the Turkish troops had additional supply problems. No open battles were allowed by Lawrence. Whenever the enemy concentrated to crush the rebellion, he had his tribesmen scatter and avoid raids. Lulled into a false feeling of security, the Turkish forces would resume their garrison positions — whereupon the raids would start again.

The Turkish position gradually became impossible in Arabia. Garrisons withered and the effectiveness of the Turkish field force was largely on paper. Lawrence even wanted to keep it in being in Arabia, as the necessity for feeding the scattered units placed a heavy drain on the already burdened enemy supply system. As they had local success the Arab tribes were gradually joined into one unit, or such was the plan.[6]

Che Guevara's *Guerrilla Warfare* incorporates the insights of Lawrence as well as Clausewitz. Like Lawrence, Guevara understood fully that the most significant immediate impact of guerrillas need not be military. Rather, by maintaining systematic pressure on isolated enemy posts as well as supply convoys and communications by striking from any point of the compass, at any time, "the guerrilla eroded the strength and morale of the enemy forces." Similarly, energetic political work among the local population developed invaluable military intelligence networks and sources of material support and personnel while winning over or solidifying popular support for the insurgent cause. Thus, guerrilla warfare provided an ideal instrument for revolutionary political struggle when confronted by superior military forces.

Che's original contributions on tactical and operational matters, beyond discussion of the initial stages of guerrilla organization and suburban or urban guerrilla warfare, are very limited. In contrast, the very mundaneness of Guevara's discussion of the importance to guerrilla fighters of soap, tobacco, books, and "war industries" highlights, in a fashion characteristic of military treatises, the role of individual human beings as historical actors who determine the outcome of warfare and revolutionary struggle. Che's *Guerrilla Warfare* thus reaffirms the value of human commitment and volition, the importance of individual will and action. No better example of this is his romantic generalization from the Cuban reality that, given suitable operating terrain, land hunger, enemy injustices, and the like, a hard core of thirty to fifty men is enough to initiate armed revolution in any country of Latin America. Although the U.S. response to the Cuban experience made the realization of Che's vision unlikely, his optimistic view exceeded greatly the assessment of guerrilla capabilities by earlier military theorists.

Just as *Guerrilla Warfare* followed in the general tradition of military theory on irregular warfare, so it consciously adapted the Marxist-Leninist contributions to this tradition.[7] Lenin specifically accepted tactical flexibility in the revolutionary struggle as well as the concept of "protracted revolutionary conflict."

Lenin's position on partisan warfare, *Partisan skaya voina*, originally appeared October 13, 1906, in *Proletariat*. He emphatically accepted partisan war, terrorism, and robbery to support the revolution: "Marxism does not tie the movement to any particular combat method. It recognizes the possibility that struggle may assume the most variegated forms. For that matter, Marxism does not 'invent' those forms of struggle. It merely organizes the tactics of strife and renders them suitable for general use. . . . Marxism never will reject any particular combat method, let alone reject it forever."[8] Lenin's formulation is not totally compatible with the scope of guerrilla warfare as conceived by Che Guevara. Lenin does, nevertheless, discuss the importance of adapting revolutionary tactics to conditions, emphasizing that "one must *learn* how to wage war. . . . Marxism asks that the various types of struggle be analyzed within their historical framework. To discuss conflict outside of its historical and concrete setting is to misunderstand elementary dialectic materialism. At various junctures of economic evolution, and depending on changing political, national, cultural, social and other conditions, differing types of struggle may become important and even predominant.[9]

Lenin also introduced the concept of protracted revolutionary war under circumstances when

the uprising cannot assume the traditional form of a single blow limited to a very short time and a very small area . . . [and] it is natural and unavoidable that the uprising assume the higher and more complicated form of a protracted civil war enmeshing the entire country. Such a war must be conceived as a series of a few big battles, separated by comparatively long intervals, and a large number of small engagements, which take place during these interim periods. . . . then the task of social democracy is to create organizations most suitable to leading masses both in the big battles and, so far as practical, in smaller actions. . . . The [Party] must educate and prepare its organizations in such a way that they will not fail to exploit opportunities through which the strengths of the opponent can be sapped.[10]

Although Lenin viewed irregular warfare as secondary to educational mass organization and other "combat methods," he emphasized, as did Guevara later, that objective and subjective historical conditions determine the appropriate forms of struggle. This "flexibility" in Leninist theory allowed Che Guevara to identify closely with Marxist ideals while departing considerably from the strict Leninist position on the role of the vanguard party in the revolutionary struggle.

Stalin combined Lenin's theoretical formulations with his own career as a guerrilla fighter in the Caucasus Mountains to add *Marxism and the National Question* to Marxist literature on guerrilla warfare. Under Stalin's direction, Soviet doctrine on guerrilla warfare expanded with *The Russian Partisan Directive of 1933*. This contribution stressed the political, economic, and psychological significance of guerrilla operations in addition to the strictly military objectives.

During the Russian resistance to the German armies at Moscow in 1941–42, partisans infiltrated German lines, disrupted supply movements, and coordinated their actions with Soviet conventional forces, on the traditional Clausewitzian model. Whereas the guerrillas coordinated their actions with Soviet conventional forces, the guerrilla forces maintained their own chain of command which reached to Stalin himself.[11] Thus, the Russian experience with partisan warfare during both the revolutionary era and World War II convinced Soviet leaders of the military, political, and psychological value of irregular warfare *under the appropriate historical conditions.* Later support for wars of national liberation by insurgents in colonial and neocolonial Asia and Africa or Latin America flowed logically from the basic premises of the Marxist-Leninist tradition and the praxis of revolutionary experience.

Lenin, Trotsky, and Stalin all accepted partisan warfare as an instrument of revolutionary struggle directed by the urban-based vanguard cadres. In China, Mao Tse-Tung systematized and attempted to universalize the *rural-based* guerrilla strategy that finally proved successful in the Communist victory in that country.[12] Drawing upon classic Chinese military writings as well as upon Western military theorists such as Clausewitz, Mao connected Marxist-Leninist political theory and the Chinese experience with the concept of protracted war.[13] In particular, he stressed that political mobilization constituted "the most fundamental condition for winning the war." Political education, initiating the construction of socialism through the creation of new political values and behavior, became an integral aspect of revolutionary warfare. Citing Clausewitz, Lenin, Stalin, and numerous commentaries on the Soviet experience, Mao blended the classic military, revolutionary Marxist, and Chinese experiences—just as Che Guevara would later add the Cuban experience in *Guerrilla Warfare.*

What is basic guerrilla strategy? Guerrilla strategy must be based primarily on alertness, mobility, and attack. It must be adjusted to the enemy situation, the terrain, the existing lines of communication, the relative strengths, the weather, and the situation of the people.

In guerrilla warfare, select the tactic of seeming to come from the east and attacking from the west; avoid the solid, attack the hollow; attack; withdraw; deliver a lightning blow, seek a lightning decision. When guerrillas engage a stronger enemy, they withdraw when he advances; harass him when he stops; strike him when he is weary; pursue him when he withdraws. In guerrilla strategy, the enemy's rear, flanks, and other vulnerable spots are his vital points, and there he must be harassed, attacked, dispersed, exhausted and annihilated. Only in this way can guerrillas carry out their mission of independent guerrilla action and coordination with the effort of the regular armies.[14]

Mao's initial observations go little beyond Clausewitz. He adds, however, a sophisticated, non-Western conception of the role of time and space in protracted warfare and embellishes the yin-yang concept, or the principle of "unity of opposites." According to this formulation, protracted guerrilla warfare is made possible, in part, by exchanging space (territory) for time. Time means survival of the guerrillas, harassment of the enemy, obtaining popular support for the insurgents, and political education of the revolutionary forces. Territory is not important so long as the first rule—survival—is maintained and the enemy placed under constant, unpredictable pressure.

Essential to the yin-yang theory is that strength conceals weakness, while within weakness there is strength. According to the translator of his work, Mao derives from this postulate that

it is a weakness of guerrillas that they operate in small groups that can be wiped out in a matter of minutes. But because they do operate in small groups, they can move rapidly and secretly into the vulnerable rear of the enemy.

In conventional tactics, dispersion of forces invites destruction; in guerrilla war, this very tactic is desirable both to confuse the enemy and to preserve the illusion that the guerrillas are ubiquitous.

It is often a disadvantage not to have heavy infantry weapons available, but the very fact of having to transport them has until recently tied conventional columns to roads and well-used tracks. The guerrilla travels light and travels fast. He turns the hazards of terrain to his advantage and makes an ally of tropical rains, heavy snow, intense heat, and freezing cold. Long night marches are difficult and dangerous, but the darkness shields his approach to an unsuspecting enemy.

In every apparent disadvantage, some advantage is to be found. The converse is equally true: In each apparent advantage lie the seeds of disadvantage. The yin is not wholly yin, nor the yang wholly yang. . . .

Guerrilla tactical doctrine may be summarized in four Chinese characters pronounced "Sheng Tung, Chi Hsi," which mean "Uproar (in the) East; Strike (in the) West." Here we find expressed the all-important principles of distraction on the one hand and concentration on the other; to fix the enemy's attention and to strike where and when he least anticipates the blow.

Guerrillas are masters of the arts of simulation and dissimulation; they create pretenses and simultaneously disguise or conceal their true semblance. Their tactical concepts, dynamic and flexible, are not cut to any particular pattern. But Mao's first law of war, to preserve oneself and destroy the enemy, is always governing.[15]

Mao Tse-Tung not only insisted on a flexible guerrilla strategy and the ultimate political objectives of guerrilla warfare, but like Che Guevara later, in regard to the Cuban revolution, was convinced that the example of the Chinese revolution would have broader implications. If Che Guevara essentially limited his focus (in the early 1960s) to Latin America, Mao dreamed always of the worldwide influence of China's experience: "Historical experience is written in iron and blood. We must point out that the guerrilla campaigns being waged in China today are a page in history that has no precedent. Their influence will not be confined solely to China in her present anti-Japanese war but will be worldwide."[16]

Following in the Maoist tradition, the Vietnamese general Vo Nguyen Giap drew lessons from the history of the Vietnamese resistance to the French and Japanese to extend the international revolutionary appeal of a "people's war," "protracted war," and anti-imperialist struggle. It is clear from the following passages from his *People's War, People's Army*, that General Giap relied heavily on Mao:

The Vietnamese people's war . . . had to be hard and long lasting in order to succeed in creating conditions for victory. Conceptions born of impatience and aimed at obtaining speedy victory could only be gross errors. It was necessary to accumulate thousands of small victories and to turn them into one great success, gradually altering the balance of forces, transforming our weakness into power, and carrying off final victory.

We contented ourselves with attacking when success was certain, refusing to give battle likely to incur losses to us, or to engage in hazardous actions. In the Vietnamese theater of operations, this method carried off great victories. . . .

The strategy of long-term war and the principle of expansion from guerrilla to regular war were successful. . . . Such were the basic strategy and tactics of the people's war in a small and backward agricultural country under the leadership of our Party.[17]

Giap, like Lenin and Mao, insisted upon the close tie between the vanguard party and its military instrument, the guerrillas: "Right at the founding of our army, the first armed groups and platoons had their Party groups and branches. The platoons had their political commissars. As soon as they were formed, the regiments had political commissars. The method of the Party committee taking the lead and the commander allotting the work also took shape from the very first days. Officers were provided with handbooks, *The Political Commissar's Book* or *Political Work in the Army*."[18] This emphasis on the priority of a political vanguard, in the form of the Communist party, to direct the revolutionary struggle would be a significant difference between Lenin, Mao, Giap, and other traditional Marxist-Leninists and the generation of Latin American revolutionaries influenced by Che Guevara.

THE CONTRIBUTIONS OF *GUERRILLA WARFARE*

Che Guevara's *Guerrilla Warfare* consists largely of practical prescriptions concerning the organization, equipment, supply, personal qualities, and modus operandi of the guerrilla band. In most respects it goes very little beyond the strategic and tactical observations of Mao and Giap. At another level, though, Guevara's work is much more than a simple field manual or blueprint for tactical operations. Above all else, it is a call to action intended to stimulate the creation of the "subjective conditions" and to intensify the "objective conditions" requisite to the revolution proclaimed by Lenin and other Marxist philosophers and social theorists of the twentieth century.

Guerrilla Warfare is a tactical guide for overcoming the inertia of leftist forces, particularly the traditional Communist parties in Latin America in the 1960s. It asserts that the Cuban example demonstrates that (1) victory against the repressive incumbent regimes is possible through armed struggle, and (2) armed struggle, on the Cuban example, should initially take the form of guerrilla movements based in the countryside, mountains, forests, or jungles of the hinterland. Thus *Guerrilla Warfare* is essentially a prescription of politico-military tactics appropriate for the moment.

Che's own eclectic, pragmatic Marxism is incompatible with a literalist interpretation of *Guerrilla Warfare*. Guevara consistently rejected the notion that there is only one correct method for making revolution in Latin America. Rather, guerrilla warfare served as one means whereby, under then-existing conditions, Latin American revolutionaries could further Che's goal of successful socialist revolution.

Guerrilla Warfare is predicated upon a firm commitment to socialist revolution through armed struggle directed by a revolutionary vanguard. Che's belief that socialism could be achieved only through destruction of the prevailing repressive military-bureaucratic apparatus of the capitalist states in Latin America raised the question of means, not ends. This is made clear by Che's later elaboration of themes introduced in *Guerrilla Warfare* and his ongoing concern to discover through revolutionary praxis the correct methods of achieving socialism.[19] For Che—as for Marx and Lenin—revolution entailed the creation of a new human consciousness, a new Communist consciousness, as an essential component of the new revolutionary society, in which individual human beings overcome the legacy of capitalist alienation.[20]

In this sense, any serious discussion of *Guerrilla Warfare* must begin by recognizing that Che Guevara's ultimate objectives were the destruction of the *ancien régime*, the establishment of socialism in Latin America, and the worldwide transformation of human society into the Communist vision outlined by Marxist theory.

In *Guerrilla Warfare*, Che essentially limited the applicability of the tactic of guerrilla warfare to "Caribbean-type" dictatorships (exemplified by Batista in Cuba, Trujillo in the Dominican Republic, Somoza in Nicaragua). These Caribbean-type dictatorships were personalist, authoritarian regimes lacking any credible appearance of constitutional legality. Arbitrary rule and routine repression of opposition movements left little hope for peaceful reform through elections or legislative checks on the executive. Guevara explicitly rejected "the guerrilla outbreak" in those cases where formal democracies, however fraudulent, masked the domination of capitalist class rules, "since the possibilities of peaceful struggle have not yet been exhausted."

In 1961 Che modified this position, arguing that all of Latin America had the objective conditions for revolution. Only the subjective condition—awareness of the possibility of victory over imperialism and its internal allies—was lacking. This could be created by the armed struggle itself.[21] The small cadre of revolutionary fighters in the countryside, or *foco*, would create this subjective condition by igniting the spark of rural-based revolution. As elaborated later by Regis Debray, Guevara's method of revolution became known as *foquismo* and was harshly criticized by traditional Marxists, Trotskyists, and, later (into the 1970s and 1980s), proponents of more sophisticated politico-military strategies of "protracted popular warfare" and guerrilla-induced popular insurrection.[22]

Two years later, Che fundamentally altered his original thesis regarding the impossibility of overthrowing the "oligarchic dictatorship" in "Guerrilla Warfare: A Method." Although he reiterated the three lessons of the Cuban revolution and reemphasized that guerrilla warfare was a strategic prescription, "a method for achieving a purpose," he now clearly extended the applicability of the guerrilla strategy to the struggle against the formal democratic regimes of Latin America, those that had periodic elections, political parties, and civilian governments. Relying on Lenin's characterization of the bourgeois state in *The State and Revolution* and Lenin's support for revolutionary civil wars in *The Military Program of the Proletarian Revolution,* Che argued the necessity of forcing these "oligarchic dictatorships" to unmask themselves. Guer-

rilla struggle, he asserted, leaves the capitalist state no choice
but to bare its repressive character:

> The equilibrium between oligarchic dictatorship and the popular
> pressure must be changed. The dictatorship tries to function without
> resorting to force. Thus, we must try to oblige the dictatorship to resort
> to violence, thereby unmasking its true nature as the dictatorship of
> the reactionary social classes. This event will deepen the struggle to
> such an extent that there will be no retreat from it. The performance of
> the people's forces depends on the task of forcing the dictatorship to a
> decision—to retreat or unleash the struggle—thus beginning the
> stage of long-range armed action.[23]

To date (1984), no guerrilla movement in Latin America has
overcome a formal democratic regime. However, the response
to these movements by certain elements of the Latin American
political elite and the character of U.S. military and economic
assistance certainly contributed to the destruction of formal
democratic systems in Brazil (1964), Argentina (1966), Peru
(1968), Chile (1973), and Uruguay (1973). In all these countries
military dictatorships justified their governments and programs on grounds of the threat of internal subversion and "Cas-
tro-Communist" politico-military movements. Guerrilla activities in the 1960s and 1970s in Central America, Venezuela,
Colombia, and Bolivia also intensified the repressive actions
of military and police forces as well as increasing military
participation (without absolute domination) in national
politics.[24]

For Che Guevara such temporary failures, resulting from the
"Alliance for Progress," counterinsurgency programs, and the
repressive responses of Latin American elites, were to be expected. Echoing Lenin's prediction of the ultimate transition
from socialism to Communism, Che declared his faith in ultimate victory: "The outcome of today's struggles does not matter. It does not matter in the final count that one or two movements were temporarily defeated because what is definite is
the decision to struggle which matures every day, the consciousness of the need for revolutionary change, and the certainty that is is possible."[25]

Che proclaimed for all to hear that the revolutionary struggle could not avoid direct confrontation with the United States. If the government of the United States defined Guevara as a dangerous enemy, it did so on the basis of Che's own unmistaken declaration of war:

Within the over-all struggle on a continental scale, the battles which are now taking place are only episodes—but they have already furnished their martyrs, who will figure in the history of our America as having given their necessary quota of blood in this last stage of the fight for the total freedom of man. . . . America, a forgotten continent in the world's more recent liberation struggles, which is now beginning to make itself heard through the Tricontinental in the voice of the vanguard of its peoples, the Cuban Revolution, has before it a task of much greater relevance: to create a second or a third Vietnam, or the second and third Vietnam of the world.[26]

Thus, by 1967, Che Guevara had come to view the guerrilla *foco* in each Latin American nation, the "hard core of thirty to fifty men," as an expendable element in a "long war," a "cruel war," against the "imperialist soldiers."

GUERRILLA WARFARE AND LATIN AMERICAN GUERRILLA MOVEMENTS

Che Guevara's writing, speeches, and renewed involvement in guerrilla movements in Africa and Latin America generated bitter, violent, and sectarian disputes within the Latin American political left. Theoretical critiques of *Guerrilla Warfare* and of the "Guevarist line" contrasted markedly with Guevara's own pragmatic, antidogmatic, eclectic—indeed sometimes careless—adaptations of Marxist-Leninist theory to the Latin American context (in Che's words, "We offer an outline, not a bible").

Guevara's primary message was that "the duty of revolutionaries is to make revolution," and that the guerrilla *foco* was part of the struggle to defeat imperialism—the last stage of capitalism—in world confrontation. The Latin American left, however, seemed intent on pursuing sectarian quarrels over the correct tactics for making revolution in individual Latin American nations. These theoretical disputes fragmented the revolutionary movements within particular Latin American nations as well as the continental revolutionary forces.

Some of the major theoretical issues raised for Marxist-Leninist revolutionaries in Latin America by the so-called "Guevarist line" included: (1) the role of the vanguard party, if any, and its relationship to the guerrilla *foco*; (2) relative emphasis on the various forms of class struggle (mass organization, labor conflict, general strikes, armed struggle, etc.); (3) comparative importance of rural and urban political and armed struggle, that is, the best "strategic terrain"; (4) relationships between revolutionary forces, bourgeois political parties, and the traditional Communist parties in Latin America; and (5) alternative conceptions of the "continental war of liberation."[27]

Many Trotskyist critics found fault with what they termed the "Guevarist adventurist line." Peter Camejo, for example, relying on "literalist" Leninism, laments most of all the lack of a central role for the vanguard party in the Guevarist scheme and the Guevarist failure to do the necessary "political work" for the revolution.

How should the masses be organized? How should revolutionists answer the maneuvers of the ruling class? Guevarism offers no strategy or program for the class struggle as a whole. The fundamental error of Guevarism is that it reduces all of politics to a technical military problem by turning a tactic, guerrilla warfare, into a strategy. The need to build a mass revolutionary party is seen as irrelevant by the Guevarists and they generally oppose building such a party.

What have been the results of his approach? With the victory of the Cuban revolution a whole new generation was attracted to revolutionary ideas. This new vanguard, however, abstained from the effort to win the masses away from the influence of the populist and Stalinist formations. Instead it devoted itself to the establishment of guerrilla fronts. The masses were left in the hands of the reformists.[28]

Old-line Communists (pro-Soviet, official Communist parties) in Latin America also resisted the Guevarist thesis. Accustomed as they were to "class alliances" and "peaceful means of class struggle" (elections, labor organization, propaganda, etc.), Communist leaders feared both the lack of control over guerrilla *focos* and the repressive responses of the Latin American regimes. However, ideological-tactical clashes within particular Communist parties led to significant splits. For example, in Venezuela, Douglas Bravo (former member of the Venezuelan Communist Party's political bureau and leader of the Fuerzas Armadas de Liberación Nacional) rejected the authority and the "mass line" of the party. He affirmed:

We are pacifists, but understand us well, we are not the kind of pacifists you find here, like those who oppose the development of the armed struggle. We are fighters who want a peace that is in a sense broader and more profound; as fighters for and lovers of peace, as men striving for a new world, we take up arms. . . . But it must be quite obvious—and everyone must be made objectively aware of this—that the conditions in which the semi-colonial and colonial peoples dominated by North American imperialism and by powerful oligarchies live, make it materially impossible to achieve [the desired] changes through electoral means, through peaceful means.[29]

In response, the Venezuelan Communist Party (PCV) expelled Douglas Bravo. Fidel Castro then bitterly attacked the PCV, which categorically rejected Castro's "claim to be the one who alone decides what is and what is not revolutionary in Latin America. In Venezuela this question is a matter between the PCV and its people, and no one else."[30]

A similar split, or more accurately, a series of splits, occurred in Guatemala from 1962 to 1968. In April of 1967, César Montes, a member of the Politburo of the Guatemalan Communist Party (PGT) until January 1968, declared:

The fact that some communists are in the FAR [Rebel Armed Forces] does not mean that our movement functions as the armed arm of any party. The FAR is not the armed arm of the PGT. Ours is a broad, patriotic movement with a very simple program: We Guatemalans want to be able to control ourselves without any foreign military, economic, or political intervention. We are creating the people's organization for the revolutionary war; within the guerrilla, is the germ of the great people's army which ultimately will be able to offer a power alternative.[31]

The break between the FAR and the PGT in Guatemala led to the resignation of 50 percent of the PGT's central committee and 40 percent of its politburo. In March of 1968 the PGT central committee responded with a statement designed to clarify the relationship between vanguard functions and guerrilla struggle.

. . . we should promote political struggle both among the masses, in order to win them over definitively, and in the solution of national problems, pinpointing and combating the vices of the regime and the system. We should promote class struggle in all fields—economic, political, and cultural—on the basis of a minimum program incorporating the struggle against unemployment, for a general rise in the wages, against the high cost of living, against the crisis in the country, against the violation of the rights of man, for social freedom, in defense of sovereignty. We should support the concrete demands of the women, students and young people in general, support the popular forces in the conflicts that break out, and above all, mobilize all strata of the population, organize them and draw them into the struggle.[32]

This effort to clarify the role of the party failed to reconcile the FAR to the Communists' reluctance to commit themselves fully to armed struggle.

Literalist interpretation and emulation of the Cuban experience brought little immediate success, but not even Che's death in Bolivia dissuaded the militant *foquistas.* Accused by more orthodox Marxist-Leninists and the local Communist parties of neglecting the daily struggle of the working class, of rejecting organizational and trade union agitation, and of relying exclusively upon military attacks on the incumbent regime, groups such as the Bolivian Army of National Liberation (ELN) insisted that, in the insurrectionary stages, the revolution had no indispensable need for a vanguard party. In response, orthodox Communists in Latin America simply recalled the "early" Che Guevara who, in *Guerrilla Warfare,* had recognized the need for "political work" before a guerrilla *foco* could hope to succeed. Thus, the Communist party of El Salvador added the following remarks as part of an epilogue to the Salvadoran edition of *El Diario de Che en Bolivia (Che's Bolivian Diary):*

Che has taught us in his *Guerrilla Warfare* that armed struggle can only arise and be developed after political struggle, as a means of attaining power, has been exhausted. . . .
    If Che Guevara and Fidel Castro later changed their views on guer-

rilla war and came to originate the theory of the armed *foco* as the source of the revolutionary process, whether it be a *foco* established from within a country or one planted from without, this is a phenomenon that may be explained in terms of complex causes rooted in the social composition of the Cuban revolutionary vanguard and in the development of the Cuban Revolution after the seizure of power. . . .

As all revolutionaries, we desire the least suffering for our people, and we would seize the possibility of peaceful triumph for the revolution with all our strength if that should appear possible in practice; but, as revolutionaries, we are also realists who believe that such an eventuality is not likely for Latin American countries in general and that only exceptionally could a peaceful transformation take place in our continent. In asserting our disagreement with the strategy of the guerrilla *foco*, we are not, therefore, expressing opposition to armed struggle in order to take power, nor are we even questioning all forms of guerrilla warfare. We question only one form: the guerrilla *foco*.[33]

Gradually, after Che Guevara's death, revolutionary movements as varied as the urban Tupamaro guerrillas in Uruguay, the ELN in Bolivia, the Argentine Montoneros, and the Chilean Left Revolutionary Movement sought to overcome the "false dilemma." Thus in "Party or *Foco*: A False Dilemma" (1971), the Tupamaros concluded that the "*foco* is a method of struggle, not a political apparatus like the Vanguard Party. Revolutionaries need not, therefore, choose between the two but could combine them."[34] Nevertheless, the debates and conflict persisted within the revolutionary left.

In a sense Che Guevara himself sought to reconcile these opposing views by insisting in his writing and through his actions that the duty of revolutionaries was to *make revolution*. He elaborated the role of the vanguard in directing the construction of socialism and emphasized the necessity of immediate armed struggle. To overcome the status quo, he asserted, revolutionary theory must be formulated and reformulated according to concrete historical conditions and in the light of social forces in particular societies. His writings and speeches made clear that he could take no pleasure from an insurgency that attained political power but lacked the political vision to establish a socialist society.

As in Venezuela and Guatemala, however, many revolutionaries in the rest of Latin America inspired by Guevarismo and the Cuban revolution became more and more intolerant of anything but the commitment to immediate armed struggle directed by the guerrilla cadres themselves. With this in mind, Che Guevara concluded his message to the Tricontinental in 1967 with a plea for tolerance in tactical disagreements combined with uncompromising dedication to the ultimate strategic objective: Communist victory. He also seemed almost to anticipate his impending death and called upon others to follow in his path: "Our every action is a battle cry against imperialism and a call for the people's unity against the great enemy of mankind: the United States of America. Whenever death may surprise us it will be welcome, provided that this, our battle cry, reach some receptive ear, that another hand be extended to take up our weapons, and that other men come forward to intone our funeral dirge with the staccato of machine guns and new cries of battle and victory."[35]

If, in this message to the Tricontinental, Che Guevara wrote his own epitaph, it was an epitaph that continues to inspire the "staccato singing of the machine-guns" throughout Latin America.

THE RESPONSE OF THE UNITED STATES
TO *GUERRILLA WARFARE*

Che Guevara's declaration of war against the United States, capitalism, and imperialism did not fall on deaf ears. Interpreted by U.S. foreign policy makers and military strategists as a part of a broad international Communist offensive, Guevara's writing and the Cuban revolution became the object of intense intellectual, doctrinal, and military concerns. When Nikita Khrushchev proclaimed Soviet support for "wars of national liberation" in January of 1961, U.S. State Department officialdom declared that "the military arm of Mr. Khrushchev's . . . doctrine is, clearly, guerrilla warfare. . . . we have, indeed, begun to take the problem of guerrilla warfare seriously."[36]

Before the Cuban revolution, U.S. security policy toward Latin America focused primarily on hemispheric defense from external aggression.[37] Indeed, in adopting the Mutual Security

Act of 1959, Congress specifically used language reaffirming this policy commitment, stipulating that "internal security requirements shall not, unless the President determines otherwise, be the basis for military assistance programs to the American Republics."[38] Even if, in practice, U.S. military assistance bolstered repressive regimes in Central America, the Caribbean, and South America, U.S. policy did not officially proclaim that support for incumbent governments against internal opposition constituted the principal purpose of the military assistance program.

The Cuban revolution and *Guerrilla Warfare* dramatically altered U.S. foreign policy toward Latin America and the rationale, character, and operation of the military assistance programs. Following analyses by a number of Kennedy administration intellectuals, including Walt W. Rostow and Roger Hillsman, official U.S. policy came to be predicated upon certain basic assumptions concerning the timing and international significance of guerrilla insurgency in Latin America.[39] Simplified, these premises were as follows:

1. The nations of Africa, Asia, and Latin America are experiencing a process of modernization and social change.
2. This process of modernization of traditional society is disruptive and potentially revolutionary.
3. Most modernizing nations have relatively weak governments, highly vulnerable to subversion and guerrilla warfare. Even popular governments are hard-pressed to mobilize the resources necessary to combat military insurgency and to meet the social and economic demands of modernization.
4. Modernization, therefore, provides opportunities for highly disciplined Communist insurgents to take advantage of the "difficult transitional moments" in the modernization process.
5. Communists, thus, are the "scavengers of the modernization process," and Communism is best understood as a "disease of the transition to modernization."
6. Under these conditions, the central task of the United States is "to protect the independence of the revolutionary process" in the Third World by assisting these nations in their

struggle against the "scavengers of the modernization process"—international Communism.

Rostow asserted that "despite all the Communist talk of American imperialism, we are committed, by the nature of our system, to support the course of national independence," adding, "We are determined to help destroy this international disease; that is, guerrilla war designed, initiated, and supplied, and led from outside an independent nation. . . . A guerrilla war mounted from outside a transitional nation, is a crude act of international vandalism. There will be no peace in the world if the international community accepts the outcome of a guerrilla war, mounted from outside a nation, as tantamount to a free election."[40]

By early 1961, the dramatic change in U.S. foreign policy toward Latin America, imposed by the threat of "more Cubas," reverberated throughout the country with the words of President John F. Kennedy. Adopting Rostow's conception of Communism as a "disease of the transition to modernization" spread through "international vandalism," President Kennedy made clear the new administation's view of international conflict:

Power is the hallmark of this offensive—power and discipline and deceit. The legitimate discontent of yearning peoples is exploited. The legitimate trappings of self-determination are employed. But, once in power, all talk of discontent is repressed—all self-determination disappears—and the promise of a revolution of hope is betrayed, as in Cuba, into a reign of terror. . . . The message of Cuba, of Laos, of the rising din of Communist voices in Asia and Latin America—these messages are all the same. . . . Now it should be clear . . . that our security may be lost piece by piece, country by country, without the firing of a single missile or the crossing of a single border.[41]

Two years later, after the unsuccessful invasion of the Bay of Pigs and confrontation with the Soviet Union over its installation of offensive missiles in Cuba, President Kennedy reiterated his administration's commitment to eradicating the threat of Communist subversion by providing whatever assistance was necessary to combat the guerrilla forces in Latin America:

"The American states must be ready to come to the aid of any government requesting aid to prevent a takeover aligned to the policies of foreign Communism rather than to an internal desire for change. My own country is prepared to do this. We in this hemisphere must also use every resource at our command to prevent the establishment of another Cuba in this hemisphere."[42]

In line with this new perception of inter-American relations, the Kennedy administration adopted a multipronged strategy to counter the "systematic attempt by the Communists to impose a serious disease on those societies attempting the transition to modernization." To alleviate the conditions that spawn the "Communist disease," President Kennedy proposed an "Alliance for Progress"—numerous programs of U.S. public and private economic assistance and investment in Latin America over the next decade. To meet the immediate guerrilla threat, the Kennedy administration adopted a variety of military training, supply, and operational assistance programs, combined with "civic action"—an effort to win or regain the support of the local population for incumbent regimes through public works, health care, and local support activities carried out by Latin American *military* forces.

THE ALLIANCE FOR PROGRESS

President Kennedy initiated the Alliance for Progress with great fanfare in August of 1961 at the Punta del Este Conference in Uruguay.[43] In theory, a ten-year commitment of twenty billion dollars in public and private U.S. funds for economic and social development in Latin America would be accompanied by internal reforms (land, tax, and electoral reforms; housing and education programs; public works, etc.) throughout the region. According to Secretary of State Dean Rusk, this program would support "the prospects of peaceful change through constructive, democratic processes as an alternative to change through the destructive extremism offered by the Communists."[44]

In short, the Alliance for Progress was a U.S. response to the

Cuban revolution and the threat posed by *Guerrilla Warfare*. The U.S. recognized the accuracy of Che Guevara's observations on the objective conditions of misery, poverty, and oppression that made all of Latin America vulnerable to revolutionary warfare. To alleviate these conditions, at least enough to buy time for incumbent regimes and allow defeat of the guerrilla movements, the U.S. government intended to promote social and economic reform. The Alliance for Progress would be a prophylactic; it would allow for "progress" (reform)—or the perception of "progress"—by stifling the idea that a new society must be based upon revolutionary change.

Looking back at the years 1961–71, it is clear that the Alliance for Progress failed to achieve most of its social and economic objectives. Nevertheless, in some nations, U.S.-supported programs certainly contributed to improvements in education, public health, and housing programs, as well as, to a more limited degree, in land tenure and rural social conditions.[45] It also contributed to the expansion of government programs in rural and urban Latin America while raising the expectations of millions of peasants and urban workers for a better life. When these expectations could not be satisfied, widespread popular frustration placed more severe pressure on the political regimes of the region.

Latin America elites bitterly resisted U.S. intrusions into domestic policy making, particularly where the Alliance for Progress threatened centuries-old privileges and the very basis of political power: the system of large rural estates. Even if both Rostow and Che Guevara had accurately pointed to the misery of the countryside and the oppression of rural labor as a source of support for insurgency, the Latin American political and social elites would not relinquish to reform what they were willing to wage war to preserve. The United States found only reluctant allies in its Alliance and could promote very little "progress" as intensified rural-urban migration created growing rings of misery around every Latin American capital. Food production stagnated in much of the region, unemployment increased, and reformist regimes gave way to repressive military dictatorships. Summarizing the dilemmas of the first five years of the Alliance for Progress, Simon Hanson noted that the rate of economic growth dropped sharply from the average for 1950–55 and 1955–60 and the change in the growth rate per capita was even more adverse. . . . the distribution of income became even more unsatisfactory as the gap between the rich and poor widened appreciably. . . . a very heavy proportion of the disbursements went to military regimes which had overthrown constitutional governments, and at the end of the period, with almost half of the population of the area under military rule, a significant portion of the aid was going *not* to assist "free men and free governments" but rather to hold in power regimes to which the people had lost their freedom."[46]

MILITARY ASSISTANCE, COUNTERINSURGENCY, AND CIVIC ACTION

Although the Alliance for Progress largely failed to achieve its social and economic goals, the military and civic action programs experienced great immediate success. From 1962 to 1972, no guerrilla movement in Latin America replicated the Cuban experience. Indeed, in 1967, U.S.-trained and -supported forces in Bolivia even captured and killed Che Guevara, the very symbol of revolutionary guerrilla warfare.

U.S. military and security policy toward Latin America after 1961 represented a critical departure from pre–Cuban revolution programs. From World War II until 1960, U.S.–Latin American mutual security policies underwent considerable change, but never did Latin America have a high priority in U.S. strategic planning or defense policy. Congressional failure to act on the Truman administration's proposals for a continuing postwar program of hemispheric military cooperation discouraged Latin American military leaders as well as incumbent governments in Latin America. As in the past, these governments turned to Europe for military matériel and training. Only in 1949 did the new Mutual Defense Assistance Act permit Latin American acquisition of selected, typically obsolete war matériel, oriented often toward coastal defense.

The outbreak of war in Korea in 1950 induced U.S. policy makers to reassert the need for "self-help and mutual aid for defense of the continent."[47] From 1951 to 1961, with variations from country to country, and not without considerable congressional debate in the United States, U.S. military assistance to Latin America was premised upon supporting the Latin American military establishments for their role in defense of the Western Hemisphere. Less dramatic, but perhaps more important, this continuous military cooperation allowed U.S. personnel to establish good personal relationships with Latin American military leaders. The great political value of these contacts was repeatedly emphasized by U.S. policy makers in testimony before Congress and in private discussions. Thus, in 1962, Defense Secretary Robert McNamara testified before a Senate committee:

Probably the greatest return on our military assistance investment dollar comes from the training of selected officers and key specialists at our military schools and training centers in the United States and overseas. These students are handpicked by their own countries to become instructors when they return home. They are the coming leaders in the nations, the men that will have the know-how and impart it to their own forces. I need not dwell on the value of having in positions of leadership men who have firsthand knowledge of how Americans do things and how they think. . . . Each of these men will receive an exposure to democracy at work, to the traditions and philosophies of our Government, and I think he will go back to his nation with a far better understanding of democracy and its possible application to this particular nation than he had before he became a student in one of our schools.[48]

As indicated above, as late as 1959, Congress and government officials had still emphasized hemispheric defense in the military assistance programs financed by the United States. The Mutual Security Act of 1959, which amended the previous legislation of 1954–58, provided for two basic limitations:
1. Military equipment and materials would be furnished to the other American republics only to further missions relating directly to the common defense of the Western Hemisphere which were found by the president to be important to the security of the United States.
2. Internal security requirements would not, unless the president determined otherwise, be the basis for military assistance programs to American republics.
With regard to the second limitation, Congress had deleted the

word "normally" from the old legislation regulating the provision of military assistance and required a specific determination by the president in each case where military assistance involved primary attention to internal security.

With the success of Fidel Castro in Cuba and the 1961 change of administrations in Washington, the policy focus of U.S. military assistance programs shifted emphatically from hemispheric defense to internal security and counterinsurgency. The military component of the Alliance for Progress—counterinsurgency and civic action—received overriding attention from the Kennedy administration. In June 1961, Secretary of State Dean Rusk explained the basis of the new U.S.–Latin American policy and argued that the increased threats of subversion in Latin America justified deletion of congressional requirements for "special determination" of need for internal security programs. Such restrictions, he believed, were "too large an impediment to swift action."[49] A week later, Secretary of Defense Robert McNamara repeated the new policy direction: "Our objective . . . is to provide the means for local military establishments, with the support and cooperation of local populations, to guard against external covert intrusion and internal subversion designed to create dissidence and insurrection."[50]

Latin American policy was now clearly a part of the cold war. The United States considered "wars of national liberation" and guerrilla movements to be integral elements in an international conflict with the Soviet Union. If Che Guevara declared war on worldwide imperialism, the United States and its Latin American allies were prepared to meet the challenge of "international Communism."[51]

Despite the Kennedy administration's dire warnings of the Communist threat, Congress did not easily accede to its requests for increased authority, increased funding, and deletion of congressional oversight of the military assistance programs. With the passage of Public Law 87-135 (September 4, 1961), however, Congress changed the avowed purpose of military assistance to Latin America from hemispheric defense to the maintenance of internal security. In addition, Section 505(b) of that law provided authorization for civic action—

type programs, a new focus of U.S.-Latin American policy that remained constant into the early 1970s.[52]

The addition of civic action programs to counterinsurgency represented a political response to Che Guevara's call for political warfare. Although civic action programs originated conceptually as far back as 1951, only with the Kennedy administration did civic action, as part of internal security programs, enter the diplomatic and congressional lexicon.[53] Through civic action programs, military assistance could create popular support for Latin American military establishments as these groups contributed to local construction, education, health, and security programs. In turn, the local population would be weaned from the guerrillas, provide military intelligence for the official military forces, and attach their hopes and loyalties to the incumbent regime.

What United States policy makers never understood, however, was that civic action programs were anathema to most senior military officers in Latin America. First, building roads, bridges, latrines, irrigation and water works, sewer systems, schools, and the like requires that soldiers engage in manual labor. For centuries most Spanish (and therefore Spanish-American) military officers have viewed manual labor as demeaning, fit only for women and infidels and, later, Indians and blacks. As one Peruvian general angrily asked one of the authors in the late 1960s: "What does your ambassador think we are—a bunch of Indians?"

Second, it must be remembered that most Latin American nations are divided into military zones or regions with a senior-ranking general in command of each. These zones are as important politically as they are militarily, and the political power of each general depends upon both his zone's proximity to the national capital and the general's ability to mobilize the men under his command rapidly in the event of a national political crisis or attempted coup d'état. Scattering troops around the countryside to engage in civic action projects represents a real threat to each general's political influence.

Nevertheless, while never popular with Latin American military elites, civic action programs become a significant part of the military assistance–counterinsurgency programs funded by the U.S. Congress in the mid-1960s. If nothing else, these programs recognized the political basis for revolutionary guerrilla warfare as outlined by Che Guevara. Civic action sought to take the guerrilla "fish" out of water, to deprive them of the essential cooperation of the local population. Such programs also represented a response to Rostow's central thesis: Socioeconomic alleviation by incumbent regimes of the crisis of modernization would deprive insurgents of the conditions that make possible popular mobilization for revolutionary struggle.

Coincident with the intellectual and high-level policy response to events in Cuba, *Guerrilla Warfare*, and insurgency in Latin America, the reorganized U.S. Southern Command assumed coordination of counterinsurgency programs, arms sales and transfers, and military training programs, and augmented military advisory assistance groups. The Agency for International Development also contributed to the new programs with training for police in counterinsurgency programs and "interrogation" techniques. Across Latin America, a massive U.S.-supported counterinsurgency apparatus moved into action against the threat of "more Cubas" in the hemisphere.[54]

In contrast, Soviet policy proved much less militant than the Soviet rhetoric applauding wars of national liberation would suggest. The high cost of subsidizing the Cuban revolution's social and economic initiatives made clear the practical limits to Soviet military and economic aid in Latin America. Willing to extend moral support and small amounts of military assistance, often via Cuba, the Soviets nonetheless attempted to minimize their risks in the Western Hemisphere and to sustain the more cautious official Communist parties throughout the region. Thus, the Soviet Union, through Cuba, could extend cold war policies to the U.S. sphere of influence at relatively little cost, even when Cuban and Soviet objectives and methods conflicted.[55] Latin America became a tactical conflict on the international chessboard, its peoples the victims of both sides who sacrificed pawns to obtain more important goals.

U.S. politico-military programs achieved great immediate success in confronting insurgency in Latin America and in buttressing some incumbent regimes in the region. For example, U.S. assistance greatly enhanced the capabilities of reformist regimes in Venezuela (1959–80) and Chile (1964–70). In other cases, however, defeat of the guerrilla movements became secondary to the new political role of self-appointed military saviors in Latin America. Adaptation of Rostow's analysis by military intellectuals led to conclusions incompatible with the Kennedy vision of constructive democratic reform. Following the formulations of Brazilian General Golbery do Couto e Silva and like-minded military professionals, military elites in Brazil, Bolivia, Peru, Argentina, Chile, Uruguay—and, later, Central America—concluded that only a military regime could confront the dual challenges of modernization and the threat to national security posed by Communist insurgency.

In the short run, both U.S. policy makers and Che Guevara failed. Instead of either "many Vietnams" or "constructive democratic reform," the U.S. and Latin American responses to Che Guevara's anti-imperialist struggle gave birth to military governments and terrorist regimes that frequently adopted as public policy institutionalized torture, repression, and anti-politics—the rejection of "politics" with its conflicts among political parties or personalist factions and in its place the establishment of long-term military rule.[56]

Thus, the legacy of Che Guevara and *Guerrilla Warfare* is not only the revolutionary struggle of the 1960s and 1970s, not only the 1979 victory of the Sandinistas in Nicaragua, but also the antipolitical and terrorist regimes that have seized power in much of Latin America since 1964. Some may see it as confirmation of Che Guevara's 1963 prediction that the "oligarchic dictatorships," or formal democracies, would give way to more repressive dictatorships under the pressure of guerrilla *focos* and revolutionary struggle—the necessary "unmasking" of the "oligarchic dictatorships."

Others, however, prefer Che's original formulation in *Guerrilla Warfare* limiting the applicability of the guerrilla strategy to Caribbean-style dictatorships. In either case, the Cuban example, along with Che Guevara's *Guerrilla Warfare* and later writings, fundamentally altered the course of Latin American history, of U.S. foreign policy, of international politics, and, for both better and worse, the human condition in Latin America.

The influence of the Cuban revolution and of Che Guevara

continues to be felt in the 1980s in Central America, the Caribbean, Colombia, Chile, Peru, Argentina, and Bolivia, where Che met his death at the hands of those he declared his enemies. Even if he should be proved wrong on the ultimate defeat of imperialism and the ultimate victory of socialism, those who follow in his path continue to shape the course of national and international events.

NOTES

1. For a detailed description of Napoleon's Iberian campaign, see Michael Glover, *Legacy of Glory* (New York: Charles Scribner's Sons, 1971).
2. J. B. Firth, "The Guerrillas in History," *Fortnightly Review* 70 (1901): 803.
3. For surveys of the history and tactics of guerrilla warfare, see Lt. Col. Frederick Wilkin, U.S. Army (retired), "Guerrilla Warfare," *U.S. Naval Institute Proceedings,* March 1954; Franklin M. Osanka, ed., *Modern Guerrilla Warfare* (New York: Free Press of Glencoe, 1962); Peter Paret and John W. Shy, *Guerrillas in the 1960s* (New York: Praeger, 1962); Lt. Col. T. N. Greene, ed., *The Guerrilla and How to Fight Him* (New York: Praeger, 1966); Major (USAF) John S. Pustay, *Counterinsurgency Warfare* (New York: Free Press, 1965); Robert B. Asprey, *War in the Shadows: The Guerrilla in History*, vols. 1–2 (Garden City, N.Y.: Doubleday, 1975); Gerard Chaliand, *Guerrilla Strategies: An Historical Anthology from the Long March to Afghanistan* (Berkeley: University of California Press, 1982). For the theoretical contributions and historical insights of one of the twentieth century's greatest politico-military guerrilla leaders (heading the Cypriot resistance to the British in the 1950s), see George Grivas, *The Memoirs of General Grivas*, ed. Charles Foley (New York: Frederick A. Praeger, 1964); George Grivas, *General Grivas on Guerrilla Warfare*, trans. A. S. Pallis (New York: Frederick A. Praeger, 1965).
4. Quoted in Paret and Shy, *Guerrillas in the 1960s*, pp. 13–14.
5. See below, "Guerrilla Warfare: A Method."
6. "Guerrilla Warfare," in Osanka, *Modern Guerrilla Warfare*, p. 6. See also T. E. Lawrence, *Revolt in the Desert* (New York: Doran, 1927); idem, *Seven Pillars of Wisdom* (New York: Doubleday &

Co., 1935); and A. P. Wevell, *The Palestine Campaigns* (London: Constable, 1928).

7. The discussion that follows relies in part on Pustay, *Counterinsurgency Warfare*, especially chapter 3.

8. Translated by Regine Elder from volume 10 of the third edition of *Sochineniya* and from volume 10 of the German *Saemtliche Werke*. Originally published in *Orbis*, Summer 1958, and reprinted in Osanka, *Modern Guerrilla Warfare*, pp. 65–79.

9. Ibid., p. 75.

10. Ibid.. p. 78.

11. Brooks McClure, "Russia's Hidden Army," *Infantry Journal* (July–August 1949), reprinted in Osanka, *Modern Guerrilla Warfare*, pp. 80–99.

12. "Strategic Problems of China's Revolutionary War" (1936); "Strategic Problems in the Anti-Japanese Guerrilla War" (1938); "On the Protracted War" (1938). For a discussion of these writings, see Edward Katzenbach, Jr., and Gene Z. Hanrahan, "The Revolutionary Strategy of Mao Tse-Tung," *Political Science Quarterly*, September 1955, reprinted in Osanka, *Modern Guerrilla Warfare*, pp. 131–46.

13. See the commentary by Brig. Gen. Samuel B. Griffith, USMC (Ret.), in his translation of Mao's *Yu Chi Chan* as *On Guerrilla Warfare* (New York: Praeger, 1961).

14. Quoted ibid., p. 46.

15. Ibid., p. 26.

16. Ibid., p. 65.

17. Quoted in Pustay, *Counterinsurgency*, pp. 41–42; Greene, *The Guerrilla*, pp. 151–52. See also General Vo Nguyen Giap, "Inside the Vietminh," in Greene, *The Guerrilla*, pp.147–77.

18. Greene, *The Guerrilla*, pp. 163–64.

19. See, in particular, "Cuba: Exceptional Case or Vanguard in the Struggle against Colonialism?" *Verde Olivo*, April 9, 1961, pp. 22–29.

20. See "Socialism and Man in Cuba," in Rolando E. Bouachea and Nelson P. Valdés, *Che: Selected Works of Ernesto Guevara* (Cambridge, Mass.: MIT Press, 1969), p. 161.

21. Che Guevara, "Cuba: Exceptional Case or Vanguard in the Struggle against Colonialism?" *Obras, 1957–1967* (Havana, 1970), 2:410–11, cited in Donald C. Hodges, ed., *The Legacy of Che Guevara: A Documentary Study* (London: Thomas & Hudson, 1977), pp. 79–83.

22. See Regis Debray, *Revolution in the Revolution?* (New York: Monthly Review Press, 1967); Guillermo Lora, *Foquismo y Rev-*

olución (La Paz, 1971); Leo Huberman and Paul Sweezy, *Regis Debray and the Latin American Revolution* (New York: Monthly Review Press, 1968); Abraham Guillén, "Lecciones de la Guerrilla LatinoAmericana," in Donald C. Hodges and Abraham Guillén, *Revaloración de la Guerrilla Urbana* (Mexico, D.F.: El Caballito, 1977), pp. 69–130. For Debray's critical reassessment of his own earlier writing, see *A Critique of Arms,* trans. Rosemary Sheed (New York: Penguin, 1977), especially volume 1, where Debray says, "The guerrilla *foco* is, if you like, the Party in khaki" and "the *foquismo* of the sixties was . . . Leninism in a hurry" (pp. 169, 170).

23. See below, "Guerrilla Warfare: A Method."
24. Richard Gott, *Guerrilla Movements in Latin America* (Garden City, N.Y.: Doubleday, 1971); James Kohl and John Litt, eds., *Urban Guerrilla Warfare in Latin America* (Cambridge: MIT Press, 1974); Luis Mercier Vega, *Guerrillas in Latin America* (New York: Praeger, 1969); and William E. Ratliff, *Castroism and Communism in Latin America, 1959–1976: The Varieties of Marxist-Leninist Experience* (Washington, D.C.: American Enterprise Institute for Public Policy Research, 1976).
25. See below, "Guerrilla Warfare: A Method."
26. See below, "Message to the Tricontinentals."
27. For a variety of interpretations of Guevarism, see Hodges, *The Legacy of Che Guevara.* See also Michael Lowy, *The Marxism of Che Guevara* (New York: Monthly Review Press, 1973). The most influential propagator of *Guevarism* (and, some argue, the most important distorter) is Regis Debray in *Revolution in the Revolution?*
28. Peter Camejo, *Guevara's Guerrilla Strategy: A Critique and Some Proposals* (New York: Pathfinder Press, 1972), pp. 16–21.
29. Quoted in Mercier Vega, *Guerrillas in Latin America,* p. 219.
30. See ibid., p. 224.
31. See interview with Eduardo Galeano in *Guatemala: Clave de latinoamérica* (Montevideo, 1967), quoted in Ratliff, *Castroism and Communism,* p. 113.
32. Quoted in ibid., p. 115.
33. Quoted in Hodges, *The Legacy of Che Guevara,* p. 102.
34. Quoted in ibid., p. 36.
35. See below, "Message to the Tricontinental."
36. Walt W. Rostow, "Countering Guerrilla Attack," in Osanka, *Modern Guerrilla Warfare,* pp. 464–71. Also reprinted in Greene, *The Guerrilla,* as "Guerrilla Warfare in Underdeveloped Areas," pp. 54–61, and in *Army Magazine,* September 1961. Rostow, a foreign policy adviser, made the basic arguments in this article in

a speech to the graduating class of the Counter-guerrilla Course of the Army Special Warfare Center at Fort Bragg, North Carolina, in 1961.

37. For a summary of U.S. military assistance to Latin America from the 1920s to the early 1960s, see Raymond Estep, *United States Military Aid to Latin America* (Maxwell Air Force Base, Alabama, Documentary Research Division, Aerospace Studies Institute, Air University, 1966). Estep reviews World War II lend-lease and postwar programs, and appends summaries of World War II military cooperation with individual Latin American nations.

38. *Mutual Security Act of 1959,* Senate Hearings, pt. 2, p. 708. See also the *Mutual Security Act of 1959,* Senate Report no. 412, pp. 11–12, in which Congress attempted to tighten restrictions on military aid for internal security.

39. See Roger Hilsman, "Internal War: The New Communist Tactic," in Greene, *The Guerrilla,* pp. 22–36. Also reprinted in Osanka, *Modern Guerrilla Warfare,* pp. 452–63. This report was released by the U.S. Department of State on August 10, 1961, at which time Hilsman was serving as director of intelligence and research in the Department of State.

40. Rostow, "Countering Guerrilla Attack," in Osanka, *Modern Guerrilla Warfare,* pp. 467–69.

41. *Department of State Bulletin,* May 8, 1961, p. 660.

42. Ibid., December 9, 1963, p. 903. For descriptions and analyses of the U.S.-supported invasion of Cuba in 1961, see Peter Wyden, *Bay of Pigs* (New York: Simon & Schuster, 1979); Arthur Schlesinger, *A Thousand Days* (Boston: Houghton Mifflin, 1965); Haynes Johnson, *The Bay of Pigs* (New York: W. W. Norton, 1964); and David Wise and Thomas B. Ross, *The Invisible Government* (New York: Random House, 1964). For efforts to analyze the Cuban missile crisis, see Graham T. Allison, *Essence of Decision* (Boston: Little, Brown, & Co., 1971); Robert A. Divine, ed., *The Cuban Missile Crisis* (Chicago: Quadrangle Books, 1971); John Plank, ed., *Cuba and the U.S.: The Long Range Prospects* (Washington, D.C.: Brookings Institution, 1967); Robert F. Kennedy, *Thirteen Days: A Memoir of the Cuban Missile Crisis* (New York: Norton, 1969); U.S. Congress, House of Representatives, Committee on Appropriations, Subcommittee on Department of Defense Appropriations, Hearings, 88th Cong., 1st sess., 1963; U.S. Congress Senate, Committee on Armed Services, Preparedness Investigating Subcommittee, *Interim Report on Cuban Military Build-up,* 88th Cong., 1st sess., 1963; Elie Abel, *The Missile Crisis* (New York: J. B. Lippincott, 1965).

43. See "Declaration of Punta del Este, 1961" and "The Charter of

Punta del Este: Establishing an Alliance for Progress within the Framework of Operation Pan America," in *InterAmerican Relations* (printed for the use of the Committee on Foreign Affairs), 92d Cong., 2d sess., October 10, 1972, pp. 165–80.

44. Speech in *Department of State Bulletin*, September 12, 1966, p. 367.

45. The original objectives of the Alliance for Progress were so ambitious as to practically guarantee failure. See "The Charter of Punta del Este."

46. Simon C. Hanson, *Five Years of the Alliance for Progress* (Washington, D.C.: InterAmerican Affairs Press, 1967), p. 1.

47. *First Report to Congress on the Mutual Security Program*, December 31, 1951 (Washington, D.C.: Government Printing Office, 1952), p. 39.

48. *Foreign Assistance Act*, 1962, Senate Hearings, pp. 61, 77.

49. *Information and Guidance—Military Assistance Program,* 5th ed. (1960), p. 58; *The Mutual Security Act of 1959*, Senate Report no. 4005, pp. 11–12.

50. International Development and Security Act, *House Hearings*, pt. 1, p. 73, as cited in Estep, *United States Military Aid*, p. 75.

51. Ibid., and Senate Hearings, 1959, pt, 2, p. 594, in Estep, United States Military Aid. Acting Assistant Secretary of State Symberley Coen testified before the House Foreign Affairs Committee: "It is clear from such Communist tactics that the immediate threat to Latin America is not the threat of overt aggression toward which we have primarily directed our military aid programs in the past years. . . . You will find that the program submitted this year reflects our awareness of, and places unprecedented emphasis in, the newly demonstrated threat of successful Communist intervention. Such intervention which may at times seem essentially internal, is actually a menacing form of indirect aggression." *International Development and Security Act*, House Hearings, pt. 1, p. 425, ibid.; Senate Hearings, 1959, pt. 2, p. 780, ibid. Secretary of Defense McNamara continued to reiterate this theme into the late 1960s. See, e.g., *Foreign Assistance and Related Agencies Appropriations for 1967*, Hearing before a Subcommittee of the Committee on Appropriations, 89th Cong., 1st sess., 1967, pp. 605–6.

52. See, e.g., Raymond J. Barrett, "The Development Process and Stability Operations," in Brian Loveman and Thomas M. Davies, Jr., *The Politics of Antipolitics* (Lincoln: University of Nebraska Press, 1978), p. 153, reprinted from *Military Review* 50, no. 2 (November 1972): 58–68.

53. Raymond Estep (*United States Military Aid*, p. 74) summarizes
the background to civic action as follows: "U.S. interest in the
subject of internal security manifested itself on many occasions in
congressional committee rooms beginning with Lt. Gen. Bolte's
declaration in 1951 that the Joint Chiefs of Staff would favor allo-
cating to Venezuela 'such things as armored cars or tear gas grenades and so on, to provide for the policing work and internal
security against subversion or sabotage if Venezuela could
guarantee the 'uninterrupted' flow of oil from the Maracaibo
area.'" Estep goes on to review the history of congressional-
executive conflict and debate over military assistance during the
next fifteen years. See *Mutual Security Act of 1951*, Senate Hearings, p. 397; *Mutual Security Act of 1958*, Senate Hearings,
pp. 62–63; *Mutual Security Appropriations for 1959*, House
Hearings, p. 1096; *Mutual Security Act of 1959*, Senate Hearings,
pt. 2, p. 708; *Mutual Security Act of 1959*, Senate Hearings, pt. 1,
pp. 217, 219. In 1959, Congress moved to tighten the restrictions
on aid that might be used for internal security purposes by reword-
ing the legislation of 1958 to read: "Internal security requirements
shall not, unless the President determines otherwise, be the basis
for military assistance programs to American Republics." See *The*
Mutual Security Act of 1959, Senate Report no. 412, pp. 11–12.

54. A thorough leftist critique of these programs, including discus-
sion of the role of South Com, U.S. Army School of the Americas,
U.S. Army Infantry and Ranger School (Fort Benning, Georgia);
Civil Affairs and Military Government School (Fort Gordon, Geor-
gia); John F. Kennedy School of Military Assistance (Fort Bragg,
North Carolina); U.S. Army Command and General Staff College
(Fort Leavenworth, Kansas); West Point Inter-American Defense
College (Washington, D.C.); and Mobile Training Teams, along
with Air Force and Navy programs, can be found in "U.S. Training
Programs for Foreign Military Personnel," North American Con-
gress on Latin America (NACLA), *NACLA Latin American and*
Empire Report 10, no. 1 (January 1976). See also "The Politics of
U.S. Arms Sales to Latin America," *NACLA Latin American and*
Empire Report 9, no. 2 (March 1975); Michael T. Klare and Cynth-
ia Arnson, *Supplying Repression: U.S. Support for Authoritarian*
Regimes Abroad (Washington, D.C.: Institute for Policy Studies,
1981); and John Saxe-Fernández, "A Latin American Perspective
on the Latin American Military and Pax Americana," in Loveman
and Davies, *The Politics of Antipolitics*, pp. 162–69; John Saxe-
Fernández, *Proyecciones hemisféricas de la Pax americana*
(Lima: Instituto de Estudios Peruanos, 1971).

55. For a cogent discussion of Soviet Latin American policy in the years following the Cuban revolution and the Cuban missile crisis, see Herbert S. Dinerstein, "Soviet Policy in Latin America," *American Political Science Review* 61, no. 1 (March 1967): 80–90.

56. For a fuller description of antipolitics, see Loveman and Davies, *The Politics of Antipolitics.* In some cases, notably Peru, and to a lesser extent Ecuador, "military populism" rather than military terrorist regimes emerged from the confrontation between guerrilla movements and counterinsurgency programs. Though still "antipolitical" in character, these regimes adopted less repressive and more reformist policies. See David Scott Palmer, "Reformist Military Rule in Peru, 1968–1980," in Robert Wesson, ed., *New Military Politics in Latin America* (New York: Hoover Institution/Stanford University, Praeger, 1982), pp. 131–49; Kevin J. Middlebrook and David Scott Palmer, *The Military and Political Development: Lessons from Peru* (Beverly Hills: Sage Publications, 1975).

CHE GUEVARA

GUERRILLA WARFARE

THE AUTHORIZED TRANSLATION

Translated from the Spanish by J. P. MORRAY

CONTENTS

DEDICATION

TO

CAMILO

*T*he author would like to claim for this work the approval of Camilo Cienfuegos, who was to have read and corrected it when another destiny intervened.[1] These lines and those which follow may be considered the homage of the Rebel Army to its grand captain, to the greatest guerrilla chief that this revolution produced, to a perfect revolutionary and a fraternal friend. Camilo was the companion of a hundred battles, the intimate counselor of Fidel in difficult moments of the war, the stoic fighter who always made of sacrifice an instrument for steeling his own character and forging the morale of his troops. I believe he would have approved of this manual wherein our guerrilla experiences are synthesized, because it is the product of life itself. But he added to the skeleton of words here presented the inner vitality of his temperament, his intelligence and his audacity, all these in such an exact measure as rarely appears in persons of history.

But Camilo should not be seen as an isolated hero performing marvelous feats only on the impulse of his individual genius, but rather as a true part of the peo-

[1] Camilo Cienfuegos was lost at sea during an airplane flight from Camaguey to Havana on October 28, 1959.

ple that formed him, as it always forms its heroes, martyrs, and leaders, by selection in a rigorous struggle.

I do not know if Camilo had heard of Danton's maxim for revolutionary movements, "Audacity, audacity, and more audacity." At any rate, he practiced it in his action and added to it other qualities necessary in a guerrilla fighter: a faculty for precise and rapid analysis of situations and forehanded thought about problems to be resolved in the future.

These lines, which serve as the homage of the author and of a whole people to our hero, will not attempt to provide his biography or even to relate any anecdotes about him. Camilo was the subject of a thousand anecdotes; he created them naturally wherever he went. To his ease of manner, always appreciated by the people, he added a personality that naturally and almost unconsciously put the stamp of Camilo on everything connected with him. Few men have succeeded in leaving on every action such a distinctive personal mark. As Fidel has said, he did not have culture from books; he had the natural intelligence of the people who had chosen him out of thousands for a privileged position on account of the audacity of his blows, his tenacity, intelligence, and unequaled devotion. Camilo practiced loyalty like a religion; he was its votary, both in his personal loyalty to Fidel, who embodied as no one else the will of the people, and in his loyalty to the people themselves. The people and Fidel march united; and thus joined were the devotions of the invincible guerrilla fighter.

Who killed him?

We should rather ask: Who destroyed his body? Because men like him continue to live with the people. Their life does not end so long as the people do not will it.

The enemy succeeded in killing him, because there are no safe airplanes; because pilots cannot acquire all the experience necessary; because, overburdened with work, Camilo wished to be in Havana quickly. His own character killed him, too. Camilo did not measure danger; he used it for a diversion, mocked it, lured, toyed, and played with it. In his mentality as guerrilla fighter a plan was not to be postponed on account of a cloud.

It happened after a whole people had come to know him, admire him, and love him. It could have happened earlier, and his history would be the simple one of a guerrilla captain. "There will be many Camilos," said Fidel; and I can add, there were Camilos, Camilos who finished their lives before completing the magnificent circle that carried Camilo into history. Camilo and the other Camilos (those who did not arrive and those who will come) are the index of the forces of the people. They are the highest expression which a nation produces in a time of war for the defense of its purest ideals, fought with faith in the achievement of its noblest ends.

Let us not try to classify him, to capture him in a mold, that is, kill him. Let us leave him thus, in general lines, without attributing to him a precise social and economic ideology which he never completely defined. Let us emphasize that there was not a soldier to be compared to Camilo in this war of liberation. A thorough revolutionary, a man of the people, a product of this revolution that the Cuban nation made for itself, through his head never passed the lightest shadow of weariness or discouragement. Camilo, the guerrilla warrior, who made this or that thing "something of Camilo," who put his precise and indelible mark on the Cuban Revolution, is a permanent and daily inspiration. He belongs to those others who did not arrive and to those who are to come.

In his continual and immortal renewal, Camilo is the monument of the people.

GUERRILLA WARFARE

CHAPTER I

GENERAL PRINCIPLES

OF GUERRILLA WARFARE

1. ESSENCE OF GUERRILLA WARFARE

*T*he armed victory of the Cuban people over the Batista dictatorship was not only the triumph of heroism as reported by the newspapers of the world; it also forced a change in the old dogmas concerning the conduct of the popular masses of Latin America. It showed plainly the capacity of the people to free themselves by means of guerrilla warfare from a government that oppresses them.

We consider that the Cuban Revolution contributed three fundamental lessons to the conduct of revolutionary movements in America. They are:

(1) Popular forces can win a war against the army.

(2) It is not necessary to wait until all conditions for making revolution exist; the insurrection can create them.

(3) In underdeveloped America the countryside is the basic area for armed fighting.

Of these three propositions the first two contradict the defeatist attitude of revolutionaries or pseudo-revolutionaries who remain inactive and take refuge in the pretext that against a professional army nothing can be done, who sit down to wait until in some mechanical way all necessary objective and subjective conditions are given without working to accelerate them. As these problems were formerly a subject of discussion in Cuba, until facts settled the question, they are probably still much discussed in America.

Naturally, it is not to be thought that all conditions for revolution are going to be created through the impulse given to them by guerrilla activity. It must always be kept in mind that there is a necessary minimum without which the establishment and consolidation of the first center is not practicable. People must see clearly the futility of maintaining the fight for social goals within the framework of civil debate. When the forces of oppression come to maintain themselves in power against established law, peace is considered already broken.

In these conditions popular discontent expresses itself in more active forms. An attitude of resistance finally crystallizes in an outbreak of fighting, provoked initially by the conduct of the authorities.

Where a government has come into power through some form of popular vote, fraudulent or not, and maintains at least an appearance of constitutional legality, the guerrilla outbreak cannot be promoted, since the possibilities of peaceful struggle have not yet been exhausted.

The third proposition is a fundamental of strategy. It ought to be noted by those who maintain dogmatically that the struggle of the masses is centered in city movements, entirely forgetting the immense participation of the country people in the life of all the underdeveloped parts of America. Of course the struggles of the city masses of organized workers should not be underrated; but their real possibilities of engaging in armed struggle must be carefully analyzed where the guarantees which customarily adorn our constitutions are suspended or ignored. In these conditions the illegal workers' movements face enormous dangers. They must function secretly without arms. The situation in the open country is not so difficult. There, in places beyond the reach of the repressive forces, the inhabitants can be supported by the armed guerrillas.

We will later make a careful analysis of these three conclusions that stand out in the Cuban revolutionary experience. We emphasize them now at the beginning of this work as our fundamental contribution.

Guerrilla warfare, the basis of the struggle of a people to redeem itself, has diverse characteristics, different facets, even though the essential will for liberation remains the same. It is obvious—and writers on the theme have said it many times—that war responds to a certain series of scientific laws; whoever ignores them will go down to defeat. Guerrilla warfare as a phase of war must be ruled by all of these; but besides, because of its special aspects, a series of corollary laws must also be recognized in order to carry it forward. Though geographical and social conditions in each country determine the mode and particular forms that guerrilla warfare will take, there are general laws that hold for all fighting of this type.

Our task at the moment is to find the basic principles of this kind of fighting and the rules to be followed by peoples seeking liberation; to develop theory from facts; to generalize and give structure to our experience for the profit of others.

Let us first consider the question: who are the combatants in guerrilla warfare? On one side we have a group composed of the oppressor and his agents, the professional army, well armed and disciplined, in many cases receiving foreign help as well as the help of the bureaucracy in the employ of the oppressor. On the other side are the people of the nation or region involved. It is important to emphasize that guerrilla warfare is a war of the masses, a war of the people. The guerrilla band is an armed nucleus, the fighting vanguard of the people. It draws its great force from the mass of the people themselves. The guerrilla band is not to be considered inferior to the army against which it fights simply because it is inferior in fire power. Guerrilla warfare is used by the side which is supported by a majority but which possesses a much smaller number of arms for use in defense against oppression.

The guerrilla fighter needs full help from the people of the area. This is an indispensable condition. This is clearly seen by considering the case of bandit gangs that operate in a region. They have all the characteristics of a guerrilla army, homogeneity, respect for the leader, valor, knowledge of the ground, and, often, even good understanding of the tactics to be employed. The only thing missing is support of the people; and, inevitably, these gangs are captured and exterminated by the public force.

Analyzing the mode of operation of the guerrilla band, seeing its form of struggle and understanding its base in the masses, we can answer the question: why does the guerrilla fighter fight? We must come to the inevitable conclusion that the guerrilla fighter is a social reformer, that he takes up arms responding to the angry protest of the people against their oppressors, and that he fights in order to change the social system that keeps all his unarmed brothers in ignominy and misery. He launches himself against the conditions of the reigning institutions at a particular moment and dedicates himself with all the vigor that circumstances permit to breaking the mold of these institutions.

When we analyze more fully the tactic of guerrilla warfare, we will see that the guerrilla fighter needs to have a good knowledge of the surrounding countryside, the paths of entry and escape, the possibilities of speedy maneuver, good hiding places; naturally also, he must count on the support of the people. All this indicates that the guerrilla fighter will carry out his action in wild places of small population. Since in these places the struggle of the people for reforms is aimed primarily and almost exclusively at changing the social form of land ownership, the guerrilla fighter is above all an agrarian revolutionary. He interprets the desires of the great peasant mass to be owners of land, owners of their means of production, of their animals, of all that which they have long yearned to call their own, of that which constitutes their life and will also serve as their cemetery.

It should be noted that in current interpretations there are two different types of guerrilla warfare, one of which—a struggle complementing great regular armies such as was the case of the Ukrainian fighters in the Soviet Union—does not enter into this analysis. We are interested in the other type, the case of an armed group engaged in struggle against the constituted power, whether colonial or not, which establishes itself as the only base and which builds itself up in rural areas. In all such cases, whatever the ideological aims that may inspire the fight, the economic aim is determined by the aspiration toward ownership of land.

The China of Mao begins as an outbreak of worker groups in the South, which is defeated and almost annihilated. It succeeds in establishing itself and begins its advance only when, after the long march from Yenan, it takes up its base in rural territories and makes agrarian reform its fundamental goal. The struggle of Ho Chi Minh is based in the rice-growing peasants, who are oppressed by the French colonial yoke; with this force it is going forward to the defeat of the colonialists. In both cases there is a framework of patriotic war against the Japanese invader, but the economic basis of a fight for the land has not disappeared. In the case of Algeria, the grand idea of Arab nationalism has its economic counterpart in the fact that nearly all of the arable land of Algeria is utilized by a million French settlers. In some countries, such as Puerto Rico, where the special conditions of the island have not permitted a guerrilla outbreak, the nationalist spirit, deeply wounded by the discrimination that is daily practiced, has as its basis the aspiration of the peasants (even though many of them are already a proletariat) to recover the land that the Yankee invader seized from them. This same central idea, though in different forms, inspired the small farmers, peasants, and slaves of the eastern estates of Cuba to close ranks and defend together the right to possess land during the thirty-year war of liberation.[2]

Taking account of the possibilities of development of guerrilla warfare, which is transformed with the increase in the operating potential of the guerrilla band into a war of positions, this type of warfare, despite its special character, is to be considered as an embryo, a prelude, of the other. The possibilities of growth of the guerrilla band and of changes in the mode of fight until conventional warfare is reached, are as great as the possibilities of defeating the enemy in each of the different battles, combats, or skirmishes that take place. Therefore, the fundamental principle is that no battle, combat, or skirmish is to be fought unless it will be won. There is a malevolent definition that says: "The guerrilla fighter is the Jesuit of warfare." By this is indicated a quality of secretiveness, of treachery, of surprise that is obviously an essential element of guerrilla warfare. It is a special kind of Jesuitism, naturally prompted by circumstances, which necessitates acting at certain moments in ways different from the romantic and sporting conceptions with which we are taught to believe war is fought.

[2] The war fought by Cubans for independence from Spain began in 1868 and ended in 1898, with a period of peace from 1878 to 1895.

War is always a struggle in which each contender tries to annihilate the other. Besides using force, they will have recourse to all possible tricks and stratagems in order to achieve the goal. Military strategy and tactics are a representation by analysis of the objectives of the groups and of the means of achieving these objectives. These means contemplate taking advantage of all the weak points of the enemy. The fighting action of each individual platoon in a large army in a war of positions will present the same characteristics as those of the guerrilla band. It uses secretiveness, treachery, and surprise; and when these are not present, it is because vigilance on the other side prevents surprise. But since the guerrilla band is a division unto itself, and since there are large zones of territory not controlled by the enemy, it is always possible to carry out guerrilla attacks in such a way as to assure surprise; and it is the duty of the guerrilla fighter to do so.

"Hit and run" some call this scornfully, and this is accurate. Hit and run, wait, lie in ambush, again hit and run, and thus repeatedly, without giving any rest to the enemy. There is in all this, it would appear, a negative quality, an attitude of retreat, of avoiding frontal fights. However, this is consequent upon the general strategy of guerrilla warfare, which is the same in its ultimate end as is any warfare: to win, to annihilate the enemy.

Thus it is clear that guerrilla warfare is a phase that does not afford in itself opportunities to arrive at complete victory. It is one of the initial phases of warfare and will develop continuously until the guerrilla army in its steady growth acquires the characteristics of a regular army. At that moment it will be ready to deal final blows to the enemy and to achieve victory. Triumph will always be the product of a regular army, even though its origins are in a guerrilla army.

Just as the general of a division in a modern war

does not have to die in front of his soldiers, the guerrilla fighter, who is general of himself, need not die in every battle. He is ready to give his life, but the positive quality of this guerrilla warfare is precisely that each one of the guerrilla fighters is ready to die, not to defend an ideal, but rather to convert it into reality. This is the basis, the essence of guerrilla fighting. Miraculously, a small band of men, the armed vanguard of the great popular force that supports them, goes beyond the immediate tactical objective, goes on decisively to achieve an ideal, to establish a new society, to break the old molds of the outdated, and to achieve, finally, the social justice for which they fight.

Considered thus, all these disparaged qualities acquire a true nobility, the nobility of the end at which they aim; and it becomes clear that we are not speaking of distorted means of reaching an end. This fighting attitude, this attitude of not being dismayed at any time, this inflexibility when confronting the great problems in the final objective is also the nobility of the guerrilla fighter.

2. GUERRILLA STRATEGY

In guerrilla terminology, strategy is understood as the analysis of the objectives to be achieved in the light of the total military situation and the overall ways of reaching these objectives.

To have a correct strategic appreciation from the point of view of the guerrilla band, it is necessary to analyze fundamentally what will be the enemy's mode of action. If the final objective is always the complete destruction of the opposite force, the enemy is confronted in the case of a civil war of this kind with the standard task: he will have to achieve the total destruction of each one of the components of the guerrilla band. The guerrilla fighter, on the other hand, must analyze the resources which the enemy has for trying to achieve that outcome: the means in men, in mobility, in popular support, in armaments, in capacity of leadership on which he can count. We must make our own strategy adequate on the basis of these studies, keeping in mind always the final objective of defeating the enemy army.

There are fundamental aspects to be studied: the armament, for example, and the manner of using this armament. The value of a tank, of an airplane in a fight of this type must be weighed. The arms of the enemy, his ammunition, his habits must be considdered; because the principal source of provision for the guerrilla force is precisely in enemy armaments. If there is a possibility of choice, we should prefer the same type as that used by the enemy, since the greatest problem of the guerrilla band is the lack of ammunition, which the opponent must provide.

After the objectives have been fixed and analyzed, it is necessary to study the order of the steps leading to the achievement of the final objective. This should be planned in advance, even though it will be modified and adjusted as the fighting develops and unforeseen circumstances arise.

At the outset, the essential task of the guerrilla fighter is to keep himself from being destroyed. Little by little it will be easier for the members of the guerrilla band or bands to adapt themselves to their form of life and to make flight and escape from the forces that are on the offensive an easy task, because it is performed daily. When this condition is reached, the guerrilla, having taken up inaccessible positions out of reach of the enemy, or having assembled forces that deter the enemy from attacking, ought to proceed to the gradual weakening of the enemy. This will be carried out at first at those points nearest to the points of active warfare against the guerrilla band

and later will be taken deeper into enemy territory, attacking his communications, later attacking or harassing his bases of operations and his central bases, tormenting him on all sides to the full extent of the capabilities of the guerrilla forces.

The blows should be continuous. The enemy soldier in a zone of operations ought not to be allowed to sleep; his outposts ought to be attacked and liquidated systematically. At every moment the impression ought to be created that he is surrounded by a complete circle. In wooded and broken areas this effort should be maintained both day and night; in open zones that are easily penetrated by enemy patrols, at night only. In order to do all this the absolute cooperation of the people and a perfect knowledge of the ground is necessary. These two necessities affect every minute of the life of the guerrilla fighter. Therefore, along with centers for study of present and future zones of operations, intensive popular work must be undertaken to explain the motives of the revolution, its ends, and to spread the incontrovertible truth that victory of the enemy against the people is finally impossible. *Whoever does not feel this undoubted truth cannot be a guerrilla fighter.*

This popular work should at first be aimed at securing secrecy; that is, each peasant, each member of the society in which action is taking place, will be asked not to mention what he sees and hears; later, help will be sought from inhabitants whose loyalty to the revolution offers greater guarantees; still later, use will be made of these persons in missions of contact, for transporting goods or arms, as guides in the zones familiar to them; still later, it is possible to arrive at organized mass action in the centers of work, of which the final result will be the general strike.

The strike is a most important factor in civil war, but in order to reach it a series of complementary conditions are necessary which do not always exist and which very rarely come to exist spontaneously. It is necessary to create these essential conditions, basically by explaining the purposes of the revolution and by demonstrating the forces of the people and their possibilities.

It is also possible to have recourse to certain very homogeneous groups, which must have shown their efficacy previously in less dangerous tasks, in order to make use of another of the terrible arms of the guerrilla band, sabotage. It is possible to paralyze entire armies, to suspend the industrial life of a zone, leaving the inhabitants of a city without factories, without light, without water, without communications of any kind, without being able to risk travel by highway except at certain hours. If all this is achieved, the morale of the enemy falls, the morale of his combatant units weakens, and the fruit ripens for plucking at a precise moment.

All this presupposes an increase in the territory included within the guerrilla action, but an excessive increase of this territory is to be avoided. It is essential always to preserve a strong base of operations and to continue strengthening it during the course of the war. Within this territory, measures of indoctrination of the inhabitants of the zone should be utilized; measures of quarantine should be taken against the irreconcilable enemies of the revolution; all the purely defensive measures, such as trenches, mines, and communications, should be perfected.

When the guerrilla band has reached a respectable power in arms and in number of combatants, it ought to proceed to the formation of new columns. This is an act similar to that of the beehive when at a given moment it releases a new queen, who goes to another region with a part of the swarm. The mother hive with the most notable guerrilla chief will stay in the less dangerous places, while the new columns will penetrate other enemy territories following the cycle already described.

A moment will arrive in which the territory occupied by the columns is too small for them; and in the advance toward regions solidly defended by the enemy, it will be necessary to confront powerful forces. At that instant the columns join, they offer a compact fighting front, and a war of positions is reached, a war carried on by regular armies. However, the former guerrilla army cannot cut itself off from its base, and it should create new guerrilla bands behind the enemy acting in the same way as the original bands operated earlier, proceeding thus to penetrate enemy territory until it is dominated.

It is thus that guerrillas reach the stage of attack, of the encirclement of fortified bases, of the defeat of reinforcements, of mass action, ever more ardent, in the whole national territory, arriving finally at the objective of the war: victory.

3. GUERRILLA TACTICS

In military language, tactics are the practical methods of achieving the grand strategic objectives.

In one sense they complement strategy and in another they are more specific rules within it. As means, tactics are much more variable, much more flexible than the final objectives, and they should be adjusted continually during the struggle. There are tactical objectives that remain constant throughout a war and others that vary. The first thing to be considered is the adjusting of guerrilla action to the action of the enemy.

The fundamental characteristic of a guerrilla band is mobility. This permits it in a few minutes to move far from a specific theatre and in a few hours far even from the region, if that becomes necessary; permits it constantly to change front and avoid any type of encirclement. As the circumstances of the war require, the guerrilla band can dedicate itself exclusively to fleeing from an encirclement which is the enemy's only way of forcing the band into a decisive fight that could be unfavorable; it can also change the battle into a counter-encirclement (small bands of men are presumably surrounded by the enemy when suddenly the enemy is surrounded by stronger contingents; or men located in a safe place serve as a lure, leading to the encirclement and annihilation of the entire troops and supply of an attacking force). Characteristic of this war of mobility is the so-called minuet, named from the analogy with the dance: the guerrilla bands encircle an enemy position, an advancing column, for example; they encircle it completely from the four points of the compass, with five or six men in each place, far enough away to avoid being encircled themselves; the fight is started at any one of the points, and the army moves toward it; the guerrilla band then retreats, always maintaining visual contact, and initiates its attack from another point. The army will repeat its action and the guerrilla band the same. Thus, successively, it is possible to keep an enemy column immobilized, forcing it to expend large quantities of ammunition and weakening the morale of its troops without incurring great dangers.

This same tactic can be applied at nighttime, closing in more and showing greater aggressiveness, because in these conditions counter-encirclement is much more difficult. Movement by night is another important characteristic of the guerrilla band, enabling it to advance into position for an attack and, where the danger of betrayal exists, to mobilize in new territory. The numerical inferiority of the guerrilla makes it necessary that attacks always be carried out by surprise; this great advantage is what permits the guerrilla fighter to inflict losses on the enemy without suffering losses. In a fight between a hundred men on one side and ten on the other, losses are not equal where there is one casualty on each side. The enemy loss is always reparable; it amounts to only one percent of his effectives. The loss of the guerrilla band requires more time to be repaired because it involves a soldier of high specialization and is ten percent of the operating forces.

A dead soldier of the guerrillas ought never to be left with his arms and his ammunition. The duty of every guerrilla soldier whenever a companion falls is to recover immediately these extremely precious elements of the fight. In fact, the care which must be taken of ammunition and the method of using it are further characteristics of guerrilla warfare. In any combat between a regular force and a guerrilla band it is always possible to know one from the other by their different manner of fire: a great amount of firing on the part of the regular army, sporadic and accurate shots on the part of the guerrillas.

Once one of our heroes, now dead, had to employ his machine guns for nearly five minutes, burst after burst, in order to slow up the advance of enemy soldiers. This fact caused considerable confusion in our forces, because they assumed from the rhythm of fire that that key position must have been taken by the enemy, since this was one of the rare occasions where departure from the rule of saving fire had been called for because of the importance of the point being defended.

Another fundamental characteristic of the guerrilla soldier is his flexibility, his ability to adapt himself to all circumstances, and to convert to his service all of the accidents of the action. Against the rigidity of classical methods of fighting, the guerrilla fighter invents his own tactics at every minute of the fight and constantly surprises the enemy.

In the first place, there are only elastic positions, specific places that the enemy cannot pass, and places of diverting him. Frequently the enemy, after easily overcoming difficulties in a gradual advance, is surprised to find himself suddenly and solidly detained without possibilities of moving forward. This is due to the fact that the guerrilla-defended positions, when they have been selected on the basis of a careful study of the ground, are invulnerable. It is not the number of attacking soldiers that counts, but the number of defending soldiers. Once that number has been placed there, it can nearly always hold off a battalion with success. It is a major task of the chiefs to choose well the moment and the place for defending a position without retreat.

The form of attack of a guerrilla army is also different; starting with surprise and fury, irresistible, it suddenly converts itself into total passivity.

The surviving enemy, resting, believes that the attacker has departed; he begins to relax, to return to the routine life of the camp or of the fortress, when suddenly a new attack bursts forth in another place, with the same characteristics, while the main body of the guerrilla band lies in wait to intercept reinforcements. At other times an outpost defending the camp will be suddenly attacked by the guerrilla, dominated, and captured. The fundamental thing is surprise and rapidity of attack.

Acts of sabotage are very important. It is necessary to distinguish clearly between sabotage, a revolutionary and highly effective method of warfare, and terrorism, a measure that is generally ineffective and indiscriminate in its results, since it often makes victims of innocent people and destroys a large number of lives that would be valuable to the revolution. Terrorism should be considered a valuable tactic when it is used to put to death some noted leader of the oppressing forces well known for his cruelty, his efficiency in repression, or other quality that makes his elimination useful. But the killing of persons of small importance is never advisable, since it brings on an increase of reprisals, including deaths.

There is one point very much in controversy in opinions about terrorism. Many consider that its use, by provoking police oppression, hinders all more or less legal or semiclandestine contact with the masses and makes impossible unification for actions that will be necessary at a critical moment. This is correct; but it also happens that in a civil war the repression by the governmental power in certain towns is already so great that, in fact, every type of legal action is suppressed already, and any action of the masses that is not supported by arms is impossible. It is therefore necessary to be circumspect in adopting methods of this type and to consider the consequences that they may bring for the revolution. At any rate, well-managed sabotage is always a very effective arm, though it should not be employed to put means of production out of action, leaving a sector of the population paralyzed (and thus without work) unless this paralysis affects the normal life of the society. It is ridiculous to carry out sabotage against a soft-drink factory, but it is absolutely correct and advisable to carry out sabotage against a power plant. In the first case, a certain number of workers are put out of a job but nothing is done to modify the rhythm of industrial life; in the second case, there will again be displaced workers, but this is entirely justified by the paralysis of the life of the region. We will return to the technique of sabotage later.

One of the favorite arms of the enemy army, supposed to be decisive in modern times, is aviation. Nevertheless, this has no use whatsoever during the period that guerrilla warfare is in its first stages, with small concentrations of men in rugged places. The utility of aviation lies in the systematic destruction of visible and organized defenses; and for this there must be large concentrations of men who construct these defenses, something that does not exist in this type of warfare. Planes are also potent against marches by columns through level places or places without cover; however, this latter danger is easily avoided by carrying out the marches at night.

One of the weakest points of the enemy is transportation by road and railroad. It is virtually impossible to maintain a vigil yard by yard over a transport line, a road, or a railroad. At any point a considerable amount of explosive charge can be planted that will make the road impassable; or by exploding it at the moment that a vehicle passes, a considerable loss in lives and materiel to the enemy is caused at the same time that the road is cut.

The sources of explosives are varied. They can be brought from other zones; or use can be made of bombs seized from the dictatorship, though these do not always work; or they can be manufactured in secret laboratories within the guerrilla zone. The technique of setting them off is quite varied; their manufacture also depends upon the conditions of the guerrilla band.

In our laboratory we made powder which we used as a cap, and we invented various devices for exploding the mines at the desired moment. The ones that gave the best results were electric. The first mine that we exploded was a bomb dropped from an aircraft of the dictatorship. We adapted it by inserting various caps and adding a gun with the trigger pulled by a cord. At the moment that an enemy truck passed, the weapon was fired to set off the explosion.

These techniques can be developed to a high degree. We have information that in Algeria, for example, tele-explosive mines, that is, mines exploded by radio at great distances from the point where they are located, are being used today against the French colonial power.

The technique of lying in ambush along roads in order to explode mines and annihilate survivors is one of the most remunerative in point of ammunition and arms. The surprised enemy does not use his ammunition and has no time to flee; so with a small expenditure of ammunition large results are achieved.

As blows are dealt the enemy, he also changes his tactics, and in place of isolated trucks, veritable motorized columns move. However, by choosing the ground well, the same result can be produced by breaking the column and concentrating forces on one vehicle. In these cases the essential elements of guerrilla tactics must always be kept in mind. These are: perfect knowledge of the ground; surveillance and foresight as to the lines of escape; vigilance over all the secondary roads that can bring support to the point of attack; intimacy with people in the zone so as to have sure help from them in respect to supplies, transport, and temporary or permanent hiding places if it becomes necessary to leave wounded companions behind; numerical superiority at a chosen point of action; total mobility; and the possibility of counting on reserves.

If all these tactical requisites are fulfilled, surprise attack along the lines of communication of the enemy yields notable dividends.

A fundamental part of guerrilla tactics is the treatment accorded the people of the zone. Even the treatment accorded the enemy is important; the norm to be followed should be an absolute inflexibility at the time of attack, an absolute inflexibility toward all the despicable elements that resort to informing and assassination, and clemency as absolute as possible toward the enemy soldiers who go into the fight performing or believing that they perform a military duty. It is a good policy, so long as there are no considerable bases of operations and invulnerable places, to take no prisoners. Survivors ought to be set free. The wounded should be cared for with all possible resources at the time of the action. Conduct toward the civil population ought to be regulated by a large respect for all the rules and traditions of the people of the zone, in order to demonstrate effectively, with deeds, the moral superiority of the guerrilla fighter over the oppressing soldier. Except in special situations, there ought to be no execution of justice without giving the criminal an opportunity to clear himself.

4. WARFARE ON FAVORABLE GROUND

As we have already said, guerrilla fighting will not always take place in country most favorable to the employment of its tactics; but when it does, that is, when the guerrilla band is located in zones difficult to reach, either because of dense forests, steep mountains, impassable deserts or marshes, the general tactics, based on the fundamental postulates of guerrilla warfare, must always be the same.

An important point to consider is the moment for making contact with the enemy. If the zone is so thick, so difficult that an organized army can never reach it, the guerrilla band should advance to the regions where the army can arrive and where there will be a possibility of combat.

As soon as the survival of the guerrilla band has been assured, it should fight; it must constantly go out from its refuge to fight. Its mobility does not have to be as great as in those cases where the ground is unfavorable; it must adjust itself to the capabilities of the enemy, but it is not necessary to be able to move as quickly as in places where the enemy can concentrate a large number of men in a few minutes. Neither is the nocturnal character of this warfare so important; it will be possible in many cases to carry out daytime operations, especially mobilizations by day, though subjected to enemy observation by land and air. It is also possible to persist in a military action for a much longer time, above all in the mountains; it is possible to undertake battles of long duration with very few men, and it is very probable that the arrival of enemy reinforcements at the scene of the fight can be prevented.

A close watch over the points of access is, however, an axiom never to be forgotten by the guerrilla fighter. His aggressiveness (on account of the difficulties that the enemy faces in bringing up reinforcements) can be greater, he can approach the enemy more closely, fight much more directly, more frontally and for a longer time, though these rules may be qualified by various circumstances, such, for example, as the amount of ammunition.

Fighting on favorable ground and particularly in the mountains presents many advantages but also the inconvenience that it is difficult to capture in a single operation a considerable quantity of arms and ammunition, owing to the precautions that the enemy takes in these regions. (The guerrilla soldier must never forget the fact that it is the enemy that must serve as his source of supply of ammunition and arms.) But much more rapidly than in unfavorable ground the guerrilla band will here be able to "dig in," that is, to form a base capable of engaging in a war of positions, where small industries may be installed as they are needed, as well as hospitals, centers for education and training, storage facilities, organs of propaganda, etc., adequately protected from aviation or from long-range artillery.

The guerrilla band in these conditions can number

many more personnel; there will be noncombatants and perhaps even a system of training in the use of the arms that eventually are to fall into the power of the guerrilla army.

The number of men that a guerrilla band can have is a matter of extremely flexible calculation adapted to the territory, to the means available of acquiring supplies, to the mass flights of oppressed people from other zones, to the arms available, to the necessities of organization. But, in any case, it is much more practicable to establish a base and expand with the support of new combatant elements.

The radius of action of a guerrilla band of this type can be as wide as conditions or the operations of other bands in adjacent territory permit. The range will be limited by the time that it takes to arrive at a zone of security from the zone of operation; assuming that marches must be made at night, it will not be possible to operate more than five or six hours away from a point of maximum security. Small guerrilla bands that work constantly at weakening a territory can go farther away from the zone of security.

The arms preferable for this type of warfare are long-range weapons requiring small expenditure of bullets, supported by a group of automatic or semi-automatic arms. Of the rifles and machine guns that exist in the markets of the United States, one of the best is the M-1 rifle, called the Garand. However, this should be used only by people with some experience, since it has the disadvantage of expending too much ammunition. Medium-heavy arms, such as tripod machine guns, can be used on favorable ground, affording a greater margin of security for the weapon and its personnel, but they ought always to be a means of repelling an enemy and not for attack.

An ideal composition for a guerrilla band of 25 men would be: 10 to 15 single-shot rifles and about 10 automatic arms between Garands and hand ma-

chine guns, including light and easily portable automatic arms, such as the Browning or the more modern
Belgian FAL and M-14 automatic rifles. Among the
hand machine guns the best are those of nine millimeters, which permit a larger transport of ammunition. The simpler its construction the better, because
this increases the ease of switching parts. All this
must be adjusted to the armament that the enemy
uses, since the ammunition that he employs is what
we are going to use when his arms fall into our
hands. It is practically impossible for heavy arms to
be used. Aircraft cannot see anything and cease to
operate; tanks and cannons cannot do much owing
to the difficulties of advancing in these zones.

A very important consideration is supply. In general, the zones of difficult access for this very reason
present special problems, since there are few peasants,
and therefore animal and food supplies are scarce.
It is necessary to maintain stable lines of communication in order to be able always to count on a minimum of food, stockpiled, in the event of any disagreeable development.

In this kind of zone of operations the possibilities
of sabotage on a large scale are generally not present;
with the inaccessibility goes a lack of constructions,
telephone lines, aqueducts, etc., that could be damaged by direct action.

For supply purposes it is important to have animals, among which the mule is the best in rough country. Adequate pasturage permitting good nutrition is
essential. The mule can pass through extremely hilly
country impossible for other animals. In the most difficult situations it is necessary to resort to transport
by men. Each individual can carry twenty-five kilograms for many hours daily and for many days.

The lines of communication with the exterior
should include a series of intermediate points manned
by people of complete reliability, where products

can be stored and where contacts can go to hide themselves at critical times. Internal lines of communication can also be created. Their extension will be determined by the stage of development reached by the guerrilla band. In some zones of operations in the recent Cuban war, telephone lines of many kilometers of length were established, roads were built, and a messenger service maintained sufficient to cover all zones in a minimum of time.

There are also other possible means of communication, not used in the Cuban war but perfectly applicable, such as smoke signals, signals with sunshine reflected by mirrors, and carrier pigeons.

The vital necessities of the guerrillas are to maintain their arms in good condition, to capture ammunition, and, above everything else, to have adequate shoes. The first manufacturing efforts should therefore be directed toward these objectives. Shoe factories can initially be cobbler installations that replace half-soles on old shoes, expanding afterwards into a series of organized factories with a good average daily production of shoes. The manufacture of powder is fairly simple; and much can be accomplished by having a small laboratory and bringing in the necessary materials from outside. Mined areas constitute a grave danger for the enemy; large areas can be mined for simultaneous explosion, destroying up to hundreds of men.

5. WARFARE ON UNFAVORABLE GROUND

In order to carry on warfare in country that is not very hilly, lacks forests, and has many roads, all the fundamental requisites of guerrilla warfare must be observed; only the forms will be altered. The quantity, not the quality, of guerrilla warfare will change. For example, following the same order as before, the mobility of this type of guerrilla should be extraordinary; strikes should be made preferably at night; they should be extremely rapid but the guerrilla should move to places different from the starting point, the farthest possible from the scene of action, assuming that there is no place secure from the repressive forces that the guerrilla can use as its garrison.

A man can walk between 30 and 50 kilometers during the night hours; it is possible also to march during the first hours of daylight, unless the zones of operation are closely watched or there is danger that people in the vicinity, seeing the passing troops, will notify the pursuing army of the location of the guerrilla band and its route. It is always preferable in these cases to operate at night with the greatest possible silence both before and after the action; the first hours of night are best. Here too there are exceptions to the general rule, since at times the dawn hours will be preferable. It is never wise to habituate the enemy to a certain form of warfare; it is necessary to vary constantly the places, the hours, and the forms of operation.

We have already said that the action cannot endure for long, but must be rapid; it must be of a high degree of effectiveness, last a few minutes, and be followed by an immediate withdrawal. The arms employed here will not be the same as in the case of actions on favorable ground; a large quantity of automatic weapons is to be preferred. In night attacks marksmanship is not the determining factor, but rather concentration of fire; the more automatic arms firing at short distance, the more possibilities there are of annihilating the enemy.

Also, the use of mines in roads and the destruction of bridges are tactics of great importance. Attacks by the guerrilla will be less aggressive so far as the persistence and continuation are concerned, but they can be very violent, and they can utilize different arms, such as mines and the shotgun. Against open vehicles heavily loaded with men, which is the usual method of transporting troops, and even against closed vehicles that do not have special defenses— against buses, for example—the shotgun is a tremendous weapon. A shotgun loaded with large shot is the most effective. This is not a secret of guerrilla fighters; it is used also in big wars. The Americans used shotgun platoons armed with high-quality weapons and bayonets for assaulting machine-gun nests.

There is an important problem to explain, that of ammunition; this will almost always be taken from the enemy. It is therefore necessary to strike blows where there will be the absolute assurance of restoring the ammunition expended, unless there are large reserves in secure places. In other words, an annihilating attack against a group of men is not to be undertaken at the risk of expending all ammunition without being able to replace it. Always in guerrilla tactics it is necessary to keep in mind the grave problem of procuring the war materiel necessary for continuing the fight. For this reason guerrilla arms ought to be the same as those used by the enemy, except for weapons such as revolvers and shotguns, for which the ammunition can be obtained in the zone itself or in the cities.

The number of men that a guerrilla band of this type should include does not exceed ten to fifteen. In forming a single combat unit it is of great importance always to consider the limitations on numbers: ten, twelve, fifteen men can hide anywhere and at the same time can help each other in putting up a powerful resistance to the enemy. Four or five would perhaps be too small a number, but when the number exceeds ten the possibility that the enemy will discover them in their camp or on the march is much greater.

Remember that the velocity of the guerrilla band on the march is equal to the velocity of its slowest man. It is more difficult to find uniformity of marching speed with twenty, thirty, or forty men than with ten. And the guerrilla fighter on the plain must be fundamentally a runner. Here the practice of hitting and running acquires its maximum use. The guerrilla bands on the plain suffer the enormous inconvenience of being subject to a rapid encirclement and of not having sure places where they can set up a firm resistance; therefore they must live in conditions of absolute secrecy for a long time, since it would be dangerous to trust any neighbor whose fidelity is not perfectly established. The reprisals of the enemy are so violent, usually so brutal, inflicted not only on the head of the family but frequently on the women and children as well, that pressure on individuals lacking firmness may result at any moment in their giving way and revealing information as to where the guerrilla band is located and how it is operating. This would immediately produce an encirclement with consequences always disagreeable, although not necessarily fatal. When conditions, the quantity of arms, and the state of insurrection of the people call for an increase in the number of men, the guerrilla band should be divided. If it is necessary, all can rejoin at a given moment to deal a blow, but in such a way that immediately afterwards they can disperse toward separate zones, again divided into small groups of ten, twelve, or fifteen men.

It is entirely feasible to organize whole armies under a single command and to assure respect and obedience to this command without the necessity of being in a single group. Therefore the election of the guerrilla chiefs and the certainty that they coordinate ideologically and personally with the overall chief of the zone are very important.

The bazooka is a heavy weapon that can be used by

the guerrilla band because of its easy portability and operation. Today the rifle-fired anti-tank grenade can replace it. Naturally, it will be a weapon taken from the enemy. The bazooka is ideal for firing on armored vehicles, and even on unarmored vehicles that are loaded with troops, and for taking small military bases of few men in a short time; but it is important to point out that not more than three shells per man can be carried, and this only with considerable exertion.

As for the utilization of heavy arms taken from the enemy, naturally nothing is to be scorned. But there are weapons such as the tripod machine gun, the heavy fifty-millimeter machine gun, etc., that, when captured, can be utilized with a willingness to lose them again. In other words, in the unfavorable conditions that we are now analyzing, a battle to defend a heavy machine gun or other weapon of this type cannot be allowed; they are simply to be used until the tactical moment when they must be abandoned. In our Cuban war of liberation, to abandon a weapon constituted a grave offense, and there was never any case where the necessity arose. Nevertheless, we mention this case in order to explain clearly the only situation in which abandonment would not constitute an occcasion for reproaches. On unfavorable ground, the guerrilla weapon is the personal weapon of rapid fire.

Easy access to the zone usually means that it will be habitable and that there will be a peasant population in these places. This facilitates supply enormously. Having trustworthy people and making contact with establishments that provide supplies to the population, it is possible to maintain a guerrilla band perfectly well without having to devote time or money to long and dangerous lines of communication. Also it is well to reiterate that the smaller the number of men the easier it will be to procure food for them. Essential supplies such as bedding, waterproof material, mosquito netting, shoes, medicines, and food will be found directly in the zone, since they are things of daily use by its inhabitants.

Communications will be much easier in the sense of being able to count on a larger number of men and more roads; but they will be more difficult as a problem of security for messages between distant points, since it will be necessary to rely on a series of contacts that have to be trusted. There will be the danger of an eventual capture of one of the messengers, who are constantly crossing enemy zones. If the messages are of small importance, they should be oral; if of great importance, code writing should be used. Experience shows that transmission by word of mouth greatly distorts any communication.

For these same reasons manufacture will have much less importance, at the same time that it would be much more difficult to carry it out. It will not be possible to have factories making shoes or arms. Practically speaking, manufacture will have to be limited to small shops, carefully hidden, where shotgun shells can be recharged and mines, simple grenades, and other minimum necessities of the moment manufactured. On the other hand, it is possible to make use of all the friendly shops of the zone for such work as is necessary.

This brings us to two consequenes that flow logically from what has been said. One of them is that the favorable conditions for establishing a permanent camp in guerrilla warfare are inverse to the degree of productive development of a place. All favorable conditions, all facilities of life normally induce men to settle; but for the guerrilla band the opposite is the case. The more facilities there are for social life, the more nomadic, the more uncertain the life of the guerrilla fighter. These really are the results of one and the same principle. The title of this section is "War on Unfavorable Ground," because everything that is favorable to human life, communications, urban and semi-urban concentrations of large numbers of people, land easily worked by machine, all these place the guerrilla fighter in a disadvantageous situation.

The second conclusion is that if guerrilla fighting must include the extremely important factor of work on the masses, this work is even more important in the unfavorable zones, where a single enemy attack can produce a catastrophe. Indoctrination should be continuous, and so should be the struggle for unity of the workers, of the peasants, and of other social classes that live in the zone, in order to achieve toward the guerrilla fighters a maximum homogeneity of attitude. This task with the masses, this constant work at the huge problem of relations of the guerrilla band with the inhabitants of the zone, must also govern the attitude to be taken toward the case of an individual recalcitrant enemy soldier: he should be eliminated without hesitation when he is dangerous. In this respect the guerrilla band must be drastic. Enemies cannot be permitted to exist within the zone of operations in places that offer no security.

6. SUBURBAN WARFARE

If during the war the guerrilla bands close in on cities and penetrate the surrounding country in such a way as to be able to establish themselves in conditions of some security, it will be necessary to give these suburban bands a special education, or rather, a special organization.

It is fundamental to recognize that a suburban guerrilla band can never spring up of its own accord. It will be born only after certain conditions necessary for its survival have been created. Therefore, the suburban guerrilla will always be under the direct orders of chiefs located in another zone. The function of this guerrilla band will not be to carry out independent actions but to coordinate its activities with overall strategic plans in such a way as to support the action of larger groups situated in another area, contributing specifically to the success of a fixed tactical objective, without the operational freedom of guerrilla bands of the other types. For example, a suburban band will not be able to choose among the operations of destroying telephone lines, moving to make attacks in another locality, and surprising a patrol of soldiers on a distant road; it will do exactly what it is told. If its function is to cut down telephone poles or electric wires, to destroy sewers, railroads, or water mains, it will limit itself to carrying out these tasks efficiently.

It ought not to number more than four or five men. The limitation on numbers is important, because the suburban guerrilla must be considered as situated in exceptionally unfavorable ground, where the vigilance of the enemy will be much greater and the possibilities of reprisals as well as of betrayal are increased enormously. Another aggravating circumstance is that the suburban guerrilla band cannot depart far from the places where it is going to operate. To speed of action and withdrawal there must be added a limitation on the distance of withdrawal from the scene of action and the need to remain totally hidden during the daytime. This is a nocturnal guerrilla band in the extreme, without possibilities of changing its manner of operating until the insurrection is so far advanced that it can take part as an active combatant in the siege of the city.

The essential qualities of the guerrilla fighter in this situation are discipline (perhaps in the highest degree of all) and discretion. He cannot count on more than two or three friendly houses that will provide food; it is almost certain that an encirclement in these conditions will be equivalent to death. Weapons, furthermore, will not be of the same kind as those of the other groups. They will be for personal defense, of the type that do not hinder a rapid flight or betray a secure hiding place. As their armament the band ought to have not more than one carbine or one sawed-off shotgun, or perhaps two, with pistols for the other members.

They will concentrate their action on prescribed sabotage and never carry out armed attacks, except by surprising one or two members or agents of the enemy troops.

For sabotage they need a full set of instruments. The guerrilla fighter must have good saws, large quantities of dynamite, picks and shovels, apparatus for lifting rails, and, in general, adequate mechanical equipment for the work to be carried out. This should be hidden in places that are secure but easily accessible to the hands that will need to use it.

If there is more than one guerrilla band, they will all be under a single chief who will give orders as to the necessary tasks through contacts of proven trustworthiness who live openly as ordinary citizens. In certain cases the guerrilla fighter will be able to maintain his peacetime work, but this is very difficult. Practically speaking, the suburban guerrilla band is a group of men who are already outside the law, in a condition of war, situated as unfavorably as we have described.

The importance of a suburban struggle has usually been underestimated; it is really very great. A good operation of this type extended over a wide area paralyzes almost completely the commercial and industrial life of the sector and places the entire population in a situation of unrest, of anguish, almost of impatience for the development of violent events that will relieve the period of suspense. If from the first moment of the war, thought is taken for the future possibility of this type of fight and an organization of specialists started, a much more rapid action will be assured, and with it a saving of lives and of the priceless time of the nation.

CHAPTER II

THE

GUERRILLA

BAND

1. THE GUERRILLA FIGHTER: SOCIAL REFORMER

We have already described the guerrilla fighter as one who shares the longing of the people for liberation and who, once peaceful means are exhausted, initiates the fight and converts himself into an armed vanguard of the fighting people. From the very beginning of the struggle he has the intention of destroying an unjust order and therefore an intention, more or less hidden, to replace the old with something new.

We have also already said that in the conditions that prevail, at least in America and in almost all countries with deficient economic development, it is the countryside that offers ideal conditions for the fight. Therefore the foundation of the social structure that the guerrilla fighter will build begins with changes in the ownership of agrarian property.

The banner of the fight throughout this period will be agrarian reform. At first this goal may or may not be completely delineated in its extent and limits; it may simply refer to the age-old hunger of the peasant for the land on which he works or wishes to work.

The conditions in which the agrarian reform will be realized depend upon the conditions which existed before the struggle began, and on the social depth of the struggle. But the guerrilla fighter, as a person conscious of a role in the vanguard of the people, must have a moral conduct that shows him to be a true priest of the reform to which he aspires. To the stoicism imposed by the difficult conditions of warfare should be added an austerity born of rigid self-control that will prevent a single excess, a single slip, whatever the circumstances. The guerrilla soldier should be an ascetic.

As for social relations, these will vary with the development of the war. At the beginning it will not be possible to attempt any changes in the social order.

Merchandise that cannot be paid for in cash will be paid for with bonds; and these should be redeemed at the first opportunity.

The peasant must always be helped technically, economically, morally, and culturally. The guerrilla fighter will be a sort of guiding angel who has fallen into the zone, helping the poor always and bothering the rich as little as possible in the first phases of the war. But this war will continue on its course; contradictions will continuously become sharper; the moment will arive when many of those who regarded the revolution with a certain sympathy at the outset will place themselves in a position diametrically opposed; and they will take the first step into battle against the popular forces. At that moment the guerrilla fighter should act to make himself into the standard bearer of the cause of the people, punishing every betrayal with justice. Private property should acquire in the war zones its social function. For example, excess land and livestock not essential for the maintenance of a wealthy family should pass into the hands of the people and be distributed equitably and justly.

The right of the owners to receive payment for possessions used for the social good ought always to be respected; but this payment will be made in bonds ("bonds of hope," as they were called by our teacher, General Bayo,[3] referring to the common interest that is thereby established between debtor and creditor).

The land and property of notorious and active enemies of the revolution should pass immediately into the hands of the revolutionary forces. Furthermore, taking advantage of the heat of the war—those moments in which human fraternity reaches its highest intensity—all kinds of cooperative work, as much as the mentality of the inhabitants will permit, ought to be stimulated.

The guerrilla fighter as a social reformer should not only provide an example in his own life but he ought also constantly to give orientation in ideological problems, explaining what he knows and what he wishes to do at the right time. He will also make use of what he learns as the months or years of the war strengthen his revolutionary convictions, making him more radical as the potency of arms is demonstrated, as the outlook of the inhabitants becomes a part of his spirit and of his own life, and as he understands the justice and the vital necessity of a series of changes, of which the theoretical importance appeared to him before, but devoid of practical urgency.

This development occurs very often, because the initiators of guerrilla warfare, or rather the directors of guerrilla warfare, are not men who have bent their backs day after day over the furrow. They are men who understand the necessity for changes in the social treatment accorded peasants, without having suffered in the usual case this bitter treatment in their own per-

[3] Colonel Alberto Bayo, a Cuban veteran of guerrilla warfare in Spain, served as instructor of the forces assembled by Fidel Castro in Mexico for training prior to the invasion of Cuba in December 1956.

sons. It happens then (I am drawing on the Cuban experience and enlarging it) that a genuine interaction is produced between these leaders, who with their acts teach the people the fundamental importance of the armed fight, and the people themselves who rise in rebellion and teach the leaders these practical necessities of which we speak. Thus, as a product of this interaction between the guerrilla fighter and his people, a progressive radicalization appears which further accentuates the revolutionary characteristics of the movement and gives it a national scope.

2. THE GUERRILLA FIGHTER AS COMBATANT

The life and activities of the guerrilla fighter, sketched thus in their general lines, call for a series of physical, mental, and moral qualities needed for adapting oneself to prevailing conditions and for fulfilling completely any mission assigned.

To the question as to what the guerrilla soldier should be like, the first answer is that he should preferably be an inhabitant of the zone. If this is the case, he will have friends who will help him; if he belongs to the zone itself, he will know it (and this knowledge of the ground is one of the most important factors in guerrilla warfare); and since he will be habituated to local peculiarities he will be able to do better work, not to mention that he will add to all this the enthusiasm that arises from defending his own people and fighting to change a social regime that hurts his own world.

The guerrilla combatant is a night combatant; to say this is to say at the same time that he must have all the special qualities that such fighting requires. He must be cunning and able to march to the place of attack across plains or mountains without anybody's noticing him, and then to fall upon the enemy, taking advantage of the factor of surprise which deserves to be emphasized again as important in this type of fight. After causing panic by this surprise, he should launch himself into the fight implacably without permitting a single weakness in his companions and taking advantage of every sign of weakness on the part of the enemy. Striking like a tornado, destroying all, giving no quarter unless the tactical circumstances call for it, judging those who must be judged, sowing panic among the enemy combatants, he nevertheless treats defenseless prisoners benevolently and shows respect for the dead.

A wounded enemy should be treated with care and respect unless his former life has made him liable to a death penalty, in which case he will be treated in accordance with his deserts. What can never be done is to keep prisoners, unless a secure base of operations, invulnerable to the enemy, has been established. Otherwise, the prisoner will become a dangerous menace to the security of the inhabitants of the region or to the guerrilla band itself because of the information that he can give upon rejoining the enemy army. If he has not been a notorious criminal, he should be set free after receiving a lecture.

The guerrilla combatant ought to risk his life whenever necessary and be ready to die without the least sign of doubt; but, at the same time, he ought to be cautious and never expose himself unnecessarily. All possible precautions ought to be taken to avoid a defeat or an annihilation. For this reason it is extremely important in every fight to maintain vigilance over all the points from which enemy reinforcements may arrive and to take precautions against an encirclement, the consequences of which are usually not physically disastrous but which damages morale by causing a loss of faith in the prospects of the struggle.

However, he ought to be audacious, and, after carefully analyzing the dangers and possibilities in an action, always ready to take an optimistic attitude toward circumstances and to see reasons for a favorable decision even in moments when the analysis of the adverse and favorable conditions does not show an appreciable positive balance.

To be able to survive in the midst of these conditions of life and enemy action, the guerrilla fighter must have a degree of adaptability that will permit him to identify himself with the environment in which he lives, to become a part of it, and to take advantage of it as his ally to the maximum possible extent. He also needs a faculty of rapid comprehension and an instantaneous inventiveness that will permit him to change his tactics according to the dominant course of the action.

These faculties of adaptability and inventiveness in popular armies are what ruin the statistics of the warlords and cause them to waver.

The guerrilla fighter must never for any reason leave a wounded companion at the mercy of the enemy troops, because this would be leaving him to an almost certain death. At whatever cost he must be removed from the zone of combat to a secure place. The greatest exertions and the greatest risks must be taken in this task. The guerrilla soldier must be an extraordinary companion.

At the same time he ought to be close-mouthed. Everything that is said and done before him should be kept strictly in his own mind. He ought never to permit himself a single useless word, even with his own comrades in arms, since the enemy will always try to introduce spies into the ranks of the guerrilla band in order to discover its plans, location, and means of life.

Besides the moral qualities that we have mentioned, the guerrilla fighter should possess a series of very important physical qualities. He must be indefatigable. He must be able to produce another effort at the moment when weariness seems intolerable. Profound conviction, expressed in every line of his face, forces him to take another step, and this not the last one, since it will be followed by another and another and another until he arrives at the place designated by his chiefs.

He ought to be able to endure extremities, to withstand not only the privations of food, water, clothing, and shelter to which he is subjected frequently, but also the sickness and wounds that often must be cured by nature without much help from the surgeon. This is all the more necessary because usually the individual who leaves the guerrilla zone to recover from sickness or wounds will be assassinated by the enemy.

To meet these conditions he needs an iron constitution that will enable him to resist all these adversities without falling ill and to make of his hunted animal's life one more factor of strength. With the help of his natural adaptability, he becomes a part of the land itself where he fights.

All these considerations bring us to ask: what is the ideal age for the guerrilla fighter? These limits are always very difficult to state precisely, because individual and social peculiarities change the figure. A peasant, for example, will be much more resistant than a man from the city. A city dweller who is accustomed to physical exercise and a healthy life will be much more efficient than a man who has lived all his life behind a desk. But generally the maximum age of combatants in the completely nomadic stage of the guerrilla struggle ought not to exceed forty years, although there will be exceptional cases, above all among the peasants. One of the heroes of our struggle, Comandante Crescencio Perez, entered the Sierra at 65 years of age and was immediately one of the most useful men in the troop.

We might also ask if the members of the guerrilla band should be drawn from a certain social class. It has already been said that this social composition ought to be adjusted to that of the zone chosen for the center of operations, which is to say that the combatant nucleus of the guerrilla army ought to be made up of peasants. The peasant is evidently the best soldier; but the other strata of the population are not by any means to be excluded nor deprived of the opportunity to fight for a just cause. Individual exceptions are also very important in this respect.

We have not yet fixed the lower limit of age. We believe that minors less than sixteen years of age ought not to be accepted for the fight, except in very special circumstances. In general these young boys, nearly children, do not have sufficient development to bear up under the work, the weather, and the suffering to which they will be subjected.

The best age for a guerrilla fighter varies between 25 and 35 years, a stage in which the life of most persons has assumed definite shape. Whoever sets out at that age, abandoning his home, his children, and his entire world, must have thought well of his responsibility and reached a firm decision not to retreat a step. There are extraordinary cases of children who as combatants have reached the highest ranks of our rebel army, but this is not the usual case. For every one of them who displayed great fighting qualities, there were tens who ought to have been returned to their homes and who frequently constituted a dangerous burden for the guerrilla band.

The guerrilla fighter, as we have said, is a soldier who carries his house on his back like the snail; therefore, he must arrange his knapsack in such a way that the smallest quantity of utensils will render the greatest possible service. He will carry only the indispensable, but he will take care of it at all times as something fundamental and not to be lost except in extremely adverse situations.

His armament will also be only that which he can carry on his own. Reprovisioning is very difficult, above all with bullets. To keep them dry, always to keep them clean, to count them one by one so that none is lost; these are the watchwords. And the gun ought always to be kept clean, well greased, and with the barrel shining. It is advisable for the chief of each group to impose some penalty or punishment on those who do not maintain their armaments in these conditions.

People with such notable devotion and firmness must have an ideal that sustains them in the adverse conditions that we have described. This ideal is simple, without great pretensions, and in general does not go very far; but it is so firm, so clear that one will give his life for it without the least hesitation. With almost all peasants this ideal is the right to have and work a piece of land of their own and to enjoy just social treatment. Among workers it is to have work, to receive an adequate wage as well as just social treatment. Among students and professional people more abstract ideas such as liberty are found to be motives for the fight.

This brings us to the question: what is the life of the guerrilla fighter like? His normal life is the long hike. Let us take as an example a mountain guerrilla fighter located in wooded regions under constant harassment by the enemy. In these conditions the guerrilla band moves during daylight hours, without eating, in order to change its position; when night arrives, camp is set up in a clearing near a water supply according to a routine, each group assembling in order to eat in common; at dusk the fires are lighted with whatever is at hand.

The guerrilla fighter eats when he can and everything he can. Sometimes fabulous feasts disappear in the gullet of the combatant; at other times he fasts for two or three days without suffering any diminution in his capacity for work.

His house will be the open sky; between it and his

hammock he places a sheet of waterproof nylon and beneath the cloth and hammock he places his knapsack, gun, and ammunition, which are the treasures of the guerrilla fighter. At times it is not wise for shoes to be removed, because of the possibility of a surprise attack by the enmey. Shoes are another of his precious treasures. Whoever has a pair of them has the security of a happy existence within the limits of the prevailing circumstances.

Thus, the guerrilla fighter will live for days without approaching any inhabited place, avoiding all contact that has not been previously arranged, staying in the wildest zones, knowing hunger, at times thirst, cold, heat; sweating during the continuous marches, letting the sweat dry on his body and adding to it new sweat without any possibility of regular cleanliness (although this also depends somewhat upon the individual disposition, as does everything else).

During the recent war, upon entering the village of El Uvero following a march of sixteen kilometers and a fight of two hours and forty-five minutes in a hot sun (all added to several days passed in very adverse conditions along the sea with intense heat from a boiling sun) our bodies gave off a peculiar and offensive odor that repelled anyone who came near. Our noses were completely habituated to this type of life; the hammocks of guerrilla fighters are known for their characteristic, individual odor.

In such conditions breaking camp ought to be done rapidly, leaving no traces behind; vigilance must be extreme. For every ten men sleeping there ought to be one or two on watch, with the sentinels being changed continually and a sharp vigil being maintained over all entrances to the camp.

Campaign life teaches several tricks for preparing meals, some to help speed their preparation; others to add seasoning with little things found in the forest; still others for inventing new dishes that give a more varied character to the guerrilla menu, which is composed mainly of roots, grains, salt, a little oil or lard, and, very sporadically, pieces of the meat of some animal that has been slain. This refers to the life of a group operating in tropical sectors.

Within the framework of the combatant life, the most interesting event, the one that carries all to a convulsion of joy and puts new vigor in everybody's steps, is the battle. The battle, climax of the guerrilla life, is sought at an opportune moment either when an enemy encampment sufficiently weak to be annihilated has been located and investigated; or when an enemy column is advancing directly toward the territory occupied by the liberating force. The two cases are different.

Against an encampment the action will be a thin encirclement and fundamentally will become a hunt for the members of the columns that come to break the encirclement. An entrenched enemy is never the favorite prey of the guerrilla fighter; he prefers his enemy to be on the move, nervous, not knowing the ground, fearful of everything and without natural protections for defense. Whoever is behind a parapet with powerful arms for repelling an offensive will never be in the plight, however bad his situation, of a long column that is attacked suddenly in two or three places and cut. If the attackers are not able to encircle the column and destroy it totally, they will retire prior to any counteraction.

If there is no possibility of defeating those entrenched in a camp by means of hunger or thirst or by a direct assault, the guerrilla ought to retire after the encirclement has yielded its fruits of destruction in the relieving columns. In cases where the guerrilla column is too weak and the invading column too strong, the action should be concentrated upon the vanguard. There should be a special preference for this tactic, whatever the hoped-for result, since after the

leading ranks have been struck several times, thus dif-
fusing among the soldiers the news that death is constantly occurring to those in the van, the reluctance to
occupy those places will provoke nothing less than mu-
tiny. Therefore, attacks ought to be made on that
point even if they are also made at other points of the
column.

The facility with which the guerrilla fighter can perform his function and adapt himself to the environment will depend upon his equipment. Even though
joined with others in small groups, he has individual
characteristics. He should have in his knapsack, besides his regular shelter, everything necessary to survival in case he finds himself alone for some time.

In giving the list of equipment we will refer essentially to that which should be carried by an individual
located in rough country at the beginning of a war,
with frequent rainfall, some cold weather, and harassment by the enemy; in other words, we place ourselves
in the situation that existed at the beginning of the
Cuban war of liberation.

The equipment of the guerrilla fighter is divided
into the essential and the accessory. Among the first is
a hammock. This provides adequate rest; it is easy to
find two trees from which it can be strung; and, in
cases where one sleeps on the ground, it can serve as
a mattress. Whenever it is raining or the ground is wet,
a frequent occurrence in tropical mountain zones, the
hammock is indispensable for sleeping. A piece of waterproof nylon cloth is its complement. The nylon
should be large enough to cover the hammock when
tied from its four corners, and with a line strung
through the center to the same trees from which the
hammock hangs. This last line serves to make the nylon into a kind of tent by raising a center ridge and
causing it to shed water.

A blanket is indispensable, because it is cold in the
mountains at night. It is also necessary to carry a gar-

HAMMOCK WITH A NYLON ROOF.

ment such as a jacket or coat which will enable one to bear the extreme changes of temperature. Clothing should consist of rough work trousers and shirt, which may or may not be of a uniform cloth. Shoes should be of the best possible construction and also, since without good shoes marches are very difficult, they should be one of the first articles laid up in reserve.

Since the guerrilla fighter carries his house in his knapsack, the latter is very important. The more primitive types may be made from any kind of sack carried by two ropes; but those of canvas found in the market or made by a harness maker are preferable. The guerrilla fighter ought always to carry some personal food besides that which the troop carries or consumes in its camps. Indispensable articles are: lard or oil, which is necessary for fat consumption; canned goods, which should not be consumed except in circumstances where food for cooking cannot be found or when there are too many cans and their weight impedes the march; preserved fish, which has great nutritional value; condensed milk, which is also nourishing, particularly on account of the large quantity of sugar that it contains; some sweet for its good taste. Powdered milk can also be carried. Sugar is another essential part of the supplies, as is salt, without which life becomes sheer martyrdom, and something that serves to season the meals, such as onion, garlic, etc., according to the characteristics of the country. This completes the category of the essentials.

The guerrilla fighter should carry a plate, knife, and fork, camping style, which will serve all the various necessary functions. The plate can be camping or military type or a pan that is usable for cooking anything from a piece of meat to a "malanga" or a potato, or for brewing tea or coffee.

To care for the rifle, special greases are necessary; and these must be carefully administered—sewing machine oil is very good if there is no special oil available. Also needed are cloths that will serve for cleaning the arms frequently and a rod for cleaning the gun inside, something that ought to be done often. The ammunition belt can be of commercial type or homemade, according to the circumstances, but it ought to be so made that not a single bullet will be lost. Ammunition is the basis of the fight without which everything else would be in vain; it must be cared for like gold.

A canteen or a bottle for water is essential, since it will frequently be necessary to drink in a situation where water is not available. Among medicines, those of general use should be carried: for example, penicillin or some other type of antibiotic, preferably the types taken orally, carefully closed; medicines for lowering fever, such as aspirin; and others adapted to treating the endemic diseases of the area. These may be tablets against malaria, sulfas for diarrhea, medicines against parasites of all types; in other words, fit the medicine to the characteristics of the region. It is advisable in places where there are poisonous animals to carry appropriate injections. Surgical instruments will complete the medical equipment. Small personal items for taking care of less important injuries should also be included.

A customary and extremely important comfort in the life of the guerrilla fighter is a smoke, whether cigars, cigarettes, or pipe tobacco; a smoke in moments of rest is a great friend to the solitary soldier. Pipes are useful, because they permit using to the extreme all tobacco that remains in the butts of cigars and cigarettes at time of scarcity. Matches are extremely important, not only for lighting a smoke, but also for starting fires; this is one of the great problems in the forest in rainy periods. It is preferable to carry both matches and a lighter, so that if the lighter runs out of fuel, matches remain as a substitute.

Soap should be carried, not only for personal cleanliness, but for washing eating utensils, because intestinal infections or irritations are frequent and can be caused by spoiled food left on dirty cooking ware. With this set of equipment, the guerrilla fighter can be assured that he will be able to live in the forest under adverse conditions, no matter how bad, for as long as is necessary to dominate the situation.

There are accessories that at times are useful and others that constitute a bother but are very useful. The compass is one of these; at the outset this will be used a great deal in gaining orientation, but little by little knowledge of the country will make it unnecessary. In mountainous regions a compass is not of much use, since the route it indicates will usually be cut off by impassable obstacles. Another useful article is an extra nylon cloth for covering all equipment when it rains. Remember that rain in tropical countries is continuous during certain months and that water is the enemy of all the things that the guerrilla fighter must carry: food, ammunition, medicine, paper, and clothing.

A change of clothing can be carried, but this is usually a mark of inexperience. The usual custom is to carry no more than an extra pair of pants, eliminating extra underwear and other articles, such as towels. The life of the guerrilla fighter teaches him to conserve his energy in carrying his knapsack from one place to another, and he will, little by little, get rid of everything that does not have essential value.

In addition to a piece of soap, useful for washing utensils as well as for personal cleanliness, a toothbrush and paste should be carried. It is worthwhile also to carry a book, which will be exchanged with other members of the band. These books can be good biographies of past heroes, histories, or economic geographies, preferably of the country, and works of general character that will serve to raise the cultural level of the soldiers and discourage the tendency toward gambling or other undesirable forms of passing the time. There are periods of boredom in the life of the guerrilla fighter.

Whenever there is extra space in the knapsack, it ought to be used for food, except in those zones where the food supply is easy and sure. Sweets or food of lesser importance complementing the basic items can be carried. Crackers can be one of these, although they occupy a large space and break up into crumbs. In thick forests a machete is useful; in very wet places a small bottle of gasoline or light resinous wood, such as pine, for kindling will make firebuilding easier when the wood is wet.

A small notebook and pen or pencil for taking notes and for letters to the outside or communication with other guerrilla bands ought always to be a part of the guerrilla fighter's equipment. Pieces of string or rope should be kept available; these have many uses. Also needles, thread, and buttons for clothing. The guerrilla fighter who carries this equipment will have a solid house on his back, rather heavy but furnished to assure a comfortable life during the hardships of the campaign.

3. ORGANIZATION OF A GUERRILLA BAND

No rigid scheme can be offered for the organization of a guerrilla band; there will be innumerable differences according to the environment in which it is to operate. For convenience of exposition we will suppose that our experience has a universal application, but it should be kept in mind always that there will possibly be new forms that comport better with the particular characteristics of a given armed group.

The size of the component units of the guerrilla force is one of the most difficult problems to deal with: there will be different numbers of men and different compositions of the troop, as we have already explained. Let us suppose a force situated in favorable ground, mountainous, with conditions not so bad as to necessitate perpetual flight, but not so good as to afford a base of operations. The combat units of an armed force thus situated ought to number not more than one hundred and fifty men, and even this number is rather high; ideal would be a unit of about one hundred men. This constitutes a column, and in the Cuban organization is commanded by a comandante. It should be remembered that in our war the grades of corporal and sergeant were omitted because they were considered reminiscent of the tyranny.[4]

On this premise, the comandante commands this whole force of one hundred to one hundred fifty men; and there will be as many captains as there are groups of thirty to forty men. The captain has the function of directing and unifying his platoon, making it fight almost always as a unit and looking after the distribution of men and the general organization. In guerrilla warfare, the squad is the functional unit. Each squad, made up of approximately eight to twelve men, is commanded by a lieutenant, who performs for his group functions analogous to those of the captain, to whom he must always be in constant subordination.

The operational tendency of the guerrilla band to function in small groups makes the squad the true unit. Eight to ten men are the maximum that can act as a unit in a fight in these conditions: therefore, the squad, which will frequently be separated from the captain even though they fight on the same front, will operate under the orders of its lieutenant; there are exceptions, of course. A squad should not be broken up nor kept dispersed at times when there is no fighting. Each squad and platoon should know who the immediate successor is in case the chief falls, and these persons should be sufficiently trained to be able to take over their new responsibilities immediately.

One of the fundamental problems of the troop is food supply; in this everyone from the last man to the chief must be treated alike. This acquires a high importance, not only because of the chronic shortage of supplies, but also because meals are the only events that take place daily. The troops, who have a keen sense of justice, measure the rations with a sharp eye; the least favoritism for anyone ought never to be

---

[4] Fulgencio Batista first came to power in Cuba as a result of a "sergeants' revolt" against Gerardo Machado in 1933.

permitted. If in certain circumstances the meal is served to the whole column, a regular order should be established and observed strictly, and at the same time the quantity and quality of food given to each one ought to be carefully checked. In the distribution of clothing the problem is different, these being articles of individual use. Here two considerations prevail: first, the demand for necessities of those who need them, which will almost always be greater than the supply; and, second, the length of service and merits of each one of the applicants. The length of service and merits, something very difficult to fix exactly, should be noted in special booklets by one assigned this responsibility under the direct supervision of the chief of the column. The same should be said about other articles that become available and are of individual rather than collective utility. Tobacco and cigarettes ought to be distributed according to the general rule of equal treatment for everybody.

This task of distribution should be a specifically assigned responsibility. It is preferable that the persons designated be attached directly to the command. The command performs, therefore, administrative tasks of liaison which are very important, as well as all the other special tasks that are necessary. Officers of the greatest intelligence ought to be in it. Soldiers attached to the command ought to be alert and of maximum dedication, since their burdens will usually be greater than those borne by the rest of the troop. Nevertheless, they can have no special treatment at mealtime.

Each guerrilla fighter carries his complete equipment; there is also a series of implements of use to the group that should be equitably distributed within the column. For this, too, rules can be established, depending upon the number of unarmed persons in the troop. One system is to distribute all extra materiel, such as medicines, medical or dental or surgical instruments, extra food, clothing, general supplies, and heavy weapons equally among all platoons, which will then be responsible for their custody. Each captain will distribute these supplies among the squads, and each chief of squad will distribute them among his men. Another solution, which can be used when a part of the troop is not armed, is to create special squads or platoons assigned to transport; this works out well, since it leaves the soldier who already has the weight and responsibility of his rifle free of extra cargo. In this way danger of losing materiel is reduced, since it is concentrated; and at the same time there is an incentive for the porter to carry more and to carry better and to demonstrate more enthusiasm, since in this way he will win his right to a weapon in the future. These platoons will march in the rear positions and will have the same duties and the same treatment as the rest of the troop.

The tasks to be carried out by a column will vary according to its activities. If it is encamped, there will be special teams for keeping watch. These should be experienced, specially trained, and they should receive some special reward for this duty. This can consist of increased independence, or, if there is an excess of sweets or tobacco after proportional distribution to each column, something extra for the members of those units that carry out special tasks. For example, if there are one hundred men and one hundred and fifteen packages of cigarettes, the fifteen extra packs of cigarettes can be distributed among the members of the units referred to. The vanguard and the rearguard units, separated from the rest, will have special duties of vigilance; but, besides, each platoon ought to have such a watch of its own. The farther from the encampment the watch is maintained, the greater is the security of the group, especially when it is in open country.

The places chosen should be high, dominating a

wide area by day and difficult to approach by night. If the plan is to stay several days, it is worthwhile to construct defenses that will permit a sustained fire in case of an attack. These defenses can be obliterated when the guerrilla band moves, or they can be left if circumstances no longer make it necessary to hide the path of the column.

In places where permanent encampments are established, the defenses ought to be improved constantly. Remember that in a mountainous zone on ground carefully chosen, the only heavy arm that is effective is the mortar. Using roofs reinforced with materials from the region, such as wood, rocks, etc., it is possible to make good refuges which are difficult for the enemy forces to approach and which will afford protection from mortar shells for the guerrilla forces.

It is very important to maintain discipline in the camp, and this should have an educational function. The guerrilla fighters should be required to go to bed and get up at fixed hours. Games that have no social function and that hurt the morale of the troops and the consumption of alcoholic drinks should both be prohibited. All these tasks are performed by a commission of internal order elected from those combatants of greatest revolutionary merit. Another mission of these persons is to prevent the lighting of fires in places visible from a distance or that raise columns of smoke before nightfall; also to see that the camp is kept clean and that it is left in such a condition when the column leaves as to show no signs of passage, if this is necessary.

Great care must be taken with fires which leave traces for a long time. They must be covered with earth; papers, cans, and scraps of food should also be burned. During the march complete silence must prevail in the column. Orders are passed by gestures or by whispers that go from mouth to mouth until they reach the last man. If the guerrilla band is marching through unknown places, breaking a road, or being led by a guide, the vanguard will be approximately one hundred or two hundred meters or even more in front, according to the characteristics of the ground. In places where confusion may arise as to the route, a man will be left at each turning to await those who follow, and this will be repeated until the last man in the rearguard has passed. The rearguard will also be somewhat separated from the rest of the column, keeping a watch on the roads in the rear and trying to erase tracks of the troops as much as possible. If there is a road coming from the side that offers danger, it is necessary always to have a group keeping a watch on it until the last man has passed. It is more practical that each platoon utilize its own men for this special duty, with each having the obligation to pass the guard to members of the following platoon and then to rejoin his own unit; this process will be continued until the whole troop has passed.

The march should be uniform and in an established order, always the same. Thus it will always be known that Platoon #1 is the vanguard, followed by Platoon #2 and then Platoon #3, which may be the command; then #4, followed by the rearguard or Platoon #5 or other platoons that make up the column, always in the same order. In night marches silence should be even stricter and the distance between each combatant shorter, so that no one will get lost and make it necessary to shout and turn on lights. Light is the enemy of the guerrilla fighter at nighttime.

If all this marching has attack as its objective, then upon arriving at a given point, the point to which all will return after the objective has been accomplished, extra weight will be set down, such things as knapsacks and cooking utensils, for example, and each platoon will proceed with nothing more than its arms and fighting equipment. The point of attack should have been already studied by trustworthy people who have reconnoitered the ground and have observed the location of the enemy guards. The leaders, knowing the orientation of the base, the number of men that defend it, etc., will make the final plan for the attack and send combatants to their places, always keeping in mind that a good part of the troops should be assigned to intercept reinforcements. In cases where the attack upon the base is to be merely a diversion in order to provoke the sending of reinforcements along roads that can be easily ambushed, a man should communicate the result rapidly to the command as soon as the attack has been carried out, in order to break the encirclement, if necessary to prevent being attacked from the rear. In any case there must always be a watch on the roads that lead to the place of combat while the encirclement or direct attack is being carried out.

By night a direct attack is always preferable. It is possible to capture an encampment if there is enough drive and necessary presence of mind and if the risks are not excessive.

An encirclement requires waiting and taking cover, closing in steadily on the enemy, trying to harass him in every way, and, above all, trying to force him by fire to come out. When the circle has been closed to short range, the "Molotov cocktail" is a weapon of extraordinary effectiveness.[5] Before arriving at a range for the "cocktail," shotguns with a special charge can be employed. These arms, christened in our war with the name of "M-16," consist of a 16-calibre sawed-off shotgun with a pair of legs added in such a way that with the butt of the gun they form a tripod. The weapon will thus be mounted at an angle of about 45 degrees; this can be varied by moving the legs back and forth. It is loaded with an open shell from which

[5] A Molotov cocktail is a bottle containing three parts kerosene and one part motor oil. The bottle is sealed and wrapped in waste cotton, which is sprinkled with gasoline and ignited. When hurled against a target the bottle breaks and burning kerosene spreads a sheet of flame.

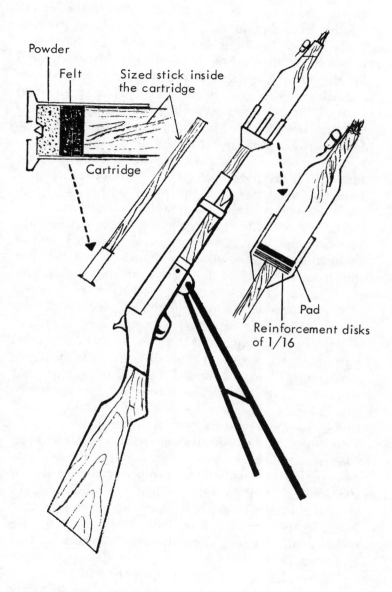

Powder

Felt

Sized stick inside
the cartridge

Cartridge

Pad

Reinforcement disks
of 1/16

ADAPTATION OF THE "MOLOTOV
COCKTAIL" TO A RIFLE.

all the shot has been removed. A cylindrical stick extending from the muzzle of the gun is used as the projectile. A bottle of gasoline resting on a rubber base is placed on the end of the stick. This apparatus will fire the burning bottles a hundred meters or more with a fairly high degree of accuracy. This is an ideal weapon for encirclements when the enemy has many wooden or inflammable material constructions; also for firing against tanks in hilly country.

Once the encirclement ends with a victory, or, having completed its objectives, is withdrawn, all platoons retire in order to the place where the knapsacks have been left, and normal life is resumed.

The nomadic life of the guerrilla fighter in this stage produces not only a deep sense of fraternity among the men but at times also dangerous rivalries between groups or platoons. If these are not channeled to produce beneficial emulation, there is a risk that the unity of the column will be damaged. The education of the guerrilla fighter is important from the very beginning of the struggle. This should explain to them the social purpose of the fight and their duties, clarify their understanding, and give them lessons in morale that serve to forge their characters. Each experience should be a new source of strength for victory and not simply one more episode in the fight for survival.

One of the great educational techniques is example. Therefore the chiefs must constantly offer the example of a pure and devoted life. Promotion of the soldier should be based on valor, capacity, and a spirit of sacrifice; whoever does not have these qualities in a high degree ought not to have responsible assignments, since he will cause unfortunate accidents at any moment.

The conduct of the guerrilla fighter will be subject to judgment whenever he approaches a house to ask for something. The inhabitants will draw favorable or unfavorable conclusions about the guerrilla band according to the manner in which any service or food or other necessity is solicited and the methods used to get what is wanted. The explanation by the chief should be detailed about these problems, emphasizing their importance; he should also teach by example. If a town is entered, all drinking of alcohol should be prohibited and the troops should be exhorted beforehand to give the best possible example of discipline. The entrances and exits to the town should be constantly watched.

The organization, combat capacity, heroism, and spirit of the guerrilla band will undergo a test of fire during an encirclement by the enemy, which is the most dangerous situation of the war. In the jargon of our guerrilla fighters in the recent war, the phrase "encirclement face" was given to the face of fear worn by someone who was frightened. The hierarchy of the deposed regime pompously spoke of its campaigns of "encirclement and annihilation." However, for a guerrilla band that knows the country and that is united ideologically and emotionally with its chief, this is not a particularly serious problem. It need only take cover, try to slow up the advance of the enemy, impede his action with heavy equipment, and await nightfall, the natural ally of the guerrilla fighter. Then with the greatest possible stealth, after exploring and choosing the best road, the band will depart, utilizing the most adequate means of escape and maintaining absolute silence. It is extremely difficult in these conditions at night to prevent a group of men from escaping the encirclement.

4. THE COMBAT

Combat is the most important drama in the guerrilla life. It occupies only a short time; nevertheless, these brilliant moments acquire an extraordinary importance, since each small encounter is a battle of a fundamental kind for the combatants.

We have already pointed out that an attack should be carried out in such a way as to give a guarantee of victory. In addition to general observations concerning the tactical function of attack in guerrilla warfare, the different characteristics that each action can present ought to be noted. We will refer initially, for purposes of description, to the type of fight carried out on favorable ground, because this is the original model of guerrilla warfare; and it is in this connection that certain principles must be examined before dealing with other problems through a study of practical experience. Warfare on the plain is always the result of an advance by the guerrilla bands consequent on their being strengthened and on changes in conditions; this implies an increase of experience on the part of the guerrilla and with it the possibility of using that experience to advantage.

In the first stage of guerrilla warfare, enemy columns will penetrate insurgent territory deeply; depending on the strength of these columns two different types of guerrilla attacks will be made. One of these, first in chronological order, is for a fixed number of months to cause systematic losses in the enemy's offensive capacity. This tactic is carried out on the vanguards. Unfavorable ground impedes flank defenses by the advancing columns; therefore, there must always be one point of the vanguard that, as it penetrates and exposes the lives of its components, serves to give security to the rest of the column. When men and reserves are insufficient and the enemy is strong, the guerrilla should always aim for the destruction of this vanguard point. The system is simple; only a certain coordination is necessary. At the moment when the vanguard appears at the selected place—the steepest possible—a deadly fire is let loose on them, after a convenient number of men have been allowed to penetrate. A small group must hold the rest of the column for some moments while arms, munitions, and equipment are being collected. The guerrilla soldier ought always to have in mind that his source of supply of arms is the enemy and that, except in special circumstances, he ought not to engage in a battle that will not lead to the capture of such equipment.

When the strength of the guerrilla band permits, a complete encirclement of the column will be carried out; or at least this impression will be given. In this case the guerrilla front line must be strong enough and well enough covered to resist the frontal assaults of the enemy, considering, naturally, both offensive power and combat morale. At the moment in which the enemy is detained in some chosen place, the rearguard guerrilla forces make an attack on the enemy's rear. Such a chosen place will have characteristics making a flank maneuver difficult; snipers, outnumbered, perhaps, by eight or ten times, will have the whole enemy column within the circle of fire. Whenever there are sufficient forces in these cases, all roads should be protected with ambushes in order to detain reinforcements. The encirclement will be closed gradually, above all at night. The guerrilla fighter knows the places where he fights, the invading column does not; the guerrilla fighter grows at night, and the enemy feels his fear growing in the darkness.

In this way, without too much difficulty, a column can be totally destroyed; or at least such losses can be inflicted upon it as to prevent its returning to battle and to force it to take a long time for regrouping.

When the force of the guerrilla band is small and it is desired above all to detain and slow down the advance of the invading column, groups of snipers fluctuating between two and ten should be distributed all around the column at each of the four cardinal points. In this situation combat can be begun, for example, on the right flank; when the enemy centers his action on that flank and fires on it, shooting will begin at that moment from the left flank; at another moment from the rearguard or from the vanguard; and so forth.

With a very small expenditure of ammunition it is possible to hold the enemy in check indefinitely.

The technique of attacking an enemy convoy or position must be adapted to the conditions of the place chosen for the combat. In general, the first attack on an encircled place should be made during night hours against an advance post, with surprise assured. A surprise attack carried out by skillful commandos can easily liquidate a position, thanks to the advantage of surprise. For a regular encirclement the paths of escape can be controlled with a few men and the roads of access defended with ambushes; these should be distributed in such a way that if one is unsuccessful, it falls back or simply withdraws, while a second remains, and so on successively. In cases where the surprise factor is not present, victory in an attempt to take an encampment will depend on the capacity of the encircling force to detain the attempts of the rescue columns. In these cases there will usually be support on the enemy's side by artillery, mortars, airplanes, and tanks. In favorable ground the tank is an arm of small danger; it must travel by roads that are narrow and is an easy victim of mines. The offensive capacity of these vehicles when in formation is here generally absent or reduced, since they must proceed in Indian file or at most two abreast. The best and surest weapon against the tank is the mine; but in a close fight, which may easily take place in steep places, the "Molotov cocktail" is an arm of extraordinary value. We will not talk yet of the bazooka, which for the guerrilla force is a decisive weapon but difficult to acquire, at least in the first stages. Against the mortar there is the recourse of a trench with a roof. The mortar is an arm of formidable potency when used against an encircled place; but on the other hand, against mobile attackers it loses its effectiveness unless it is used in large batteries. Artillery does not have great importance in this type of fight, since it has to be placed in locations of convenient access and it does not see the targets, which are constantly shifting. Aviation constitutes the principal arm of the oppressor forces, but its power of attack also is much reduced by the fact that its only targets are small trenches, generally hidden. Planes will be able to drop high-explosive or napalm bombs, both of which constitute inconveniences rather than true dangers. Besides, as the guerrilla draws as close as possible to the defensive lines of the enemy, it becomes very difficult for planes to attack these points of the vanguard effectively.

When encampments with wood or inflammable constructions are attacked, the "Molotov cocktail" is a very important arm at a short distance. At longer distances bottles with inflammable material with the fuse lighted can be launched from a sixteen-calibre shotgun, as described earlier.

Of all the possible types of mines, the most effective, although requiring the most technical capacity, is the remotely exploded mine; but contact, fuse, and above all electric mines with their lengths of cord are also extremely useful and constitute on mountainous roads defenses for the popular forces that are virtually invulnerable.

A good defense against armored cars along roads is to dig sloping ditches in such a way that the tank enters them easily and afterwards cannot get out, as the picture shows. These can easily be hidden from the enemy, especially at nighttime or when he has no infantry in advance of the tanks because of resistance by the guerrilla forces.

Another common form of advance by the enemy in

ANTI-TANK TRAP.

zones that are not too steep is in trucks that are more
or less open. The columns are headed by armored
vehicles and the infantry follows behind in trucks.
Depending upon the force of the guerrilla band it may
be possible to encircle the entire column, following
the general rules; or it can be split by attacking some
of the trucks and simultaneously exploding mines. It
is necessary to act rapidly in this case, seizing the
arms of the fallen enemy and retiring.

For an attack on open trucks, an arm of great importance which should be used with all its potential is the shotgun. A sixteen-calibre shotgun with large shot can sweep ten meters, nearly the whole area of the truck, killing some of the occupants, wounding others, and provoking an enormous confusion. Grenades, if they are available, are also excellent weapons for these cases.

For all these attacks surprise is fundamental because, at least at the moment of firing the first shot, it is one of the basic requirements of guerrilla warfare. Surprise is not possible if the peasants of the zone know of the presence of the insurgent army. For this reason all movements of attack should be made at night. Only men of proven discretion and loyalty can know of these movements and establish the contacts. The march should be made with knapsacks full of food, in order to be able to live two, three, or four days in the places of ambush.

The discretion of the peasants should never be trusted too much, first because there is a natural tendency to talk and to comment on events with other members of the family or with friends; and also because of the inevitable cruelty with which the enemy soldiers treat the population after a defeat. Terror can be sown, and this terror leads to someone's talking too much, revealing important information, in the effort to save his life.

In general, the place chosen for an ambush should be located at least one day's march from the habitual camp of the guerrilla band, since the enemy will almost always know its location more or less accurately.

We said before that the form of fire in a battle indicates the location of the opposing forces; on one side violent and rapid firing by the soldier of the line, who has the customary abundance of ammunition; on the other side the methodical, sporadic fire of the guerrilla fighter who knows the value of every bullet and who endeavors to expend it with a high degree of economy, never firing one shot more than necessary. It is not reasonable to allow an enemy to escape or to fail to use an ambush to the full in order to save ammunition, but the amount that is to be expended in determined circumstances should be calculated in advance and the action carried out according to these calculations.

Ammunition is the great problem of the guerrilla fighter. Arms can always be obtained. Furthermore, those which are obtained are not expended in guerrilla warfare, while ammunition is expended; also, generally, it is arms with their ammunition that are captured and never or rarely ammunition only. Each weapon that is taken will have its loads, but it cannot contribute to the others because there are no extras. The tactical principle of saving fire is fundamental in this type of warfare.

A guerrilla chief who takes pride in his role will never be careless about withdrawal. This should be timely, rapid, and carried out so as to save all the wounded and the equipment of the guerrilla, its knapsacks, ammunition, etc. The rebels ought never to be surprised while withdrawing, nor can they permit themselves the negligence of becoming surrounded. Therefore, guards must be posted along the chosen road at all places where the enemy army will eventually bring its troops forward in an attempt to close a circle; and there must be a system of communication that will permit rapid reports when a force tries to surround the rebels.

In the combat there must always be some unarmed men. They will recover the guns of companions who are wounded or dead, guns seized in battle or belonging to prisoners; they will take charge of the prisoners, of removing the wounded, and of transmission of messages. Besides, there ought to be a good corps of messengers with iron legs and a proven sense of responsibility who will give the necessary reports in the least possible time.

The number of men needed besides the armed combatants varies; but a general rule is two or three for each ten, including those who will be present at the scene of the battle and those who will carry out necessary tasks in the rearguard, keeping watch on the route of withdrawal and performing the messenger services mentioned above.

When a defensive type of war is being fought, that is to say, when the guerrilla band is endeavoring to prohibit the passage of an invasion column beyond a certain point, the action becomes a war of positions; but always at the outset it should have the factor of surprise. In this case, since trenches as well as other defensive systems that will be easily observable by the peasants are going to be used, it is necessary that these latter remain in the friendly zone. In this type of warfare the government generally establishes a blockade of the region, and the peasants who have not fled must go to buy their basic foods at establishments located outside the zones of guerrilla action. Should these persons leave the region at critical moments, such as those we are now describing, this would constitute a serious danger on account of the information that they could eventually supply to the enemy army. The policy of complete isolation must serve as the strategic principle of the guerrilla army in these cases.

The defenses and the whole defensive apparatus should be arranged in such a manner that the enemy vanguard will always fall into an ambush. It is very important as a psychological factor that the man in the vanguard will die without escape in every battle, because this produces within the enemy army a growing consciousness of this danger, until the moment arrives when nobody wants to be in the vanguard; and it is obvious that a column with no vanguard cannot move, since somebody has to assume that responsibility. Also encirclements can be carried out if these are expedient; or diversionary maneuvers such as flank attacks; or the enemy can simply be detained frontally. In every case, places which are susceptible of being utilized by the enemy for flank attacks should be fortified.

We are now assuming that more men and arms are available than in the combats described hitherto. It is evident that the blockade of all possible roads converging into a zone, which may be very numerous, requires a large personnel. The various kinds of traps and attacks against armored vehicles will be increased here, in order to give the greatest security possible to the systems of fixed trenches which can be located by the enemy. In general in this type of fight the order is to defend the positions unto death if necessary; and it is essential to assure the maximum possibilities of survival to every defender.

The more a trench is hidden from distant view, the better; above all, it is important to give it a cover so that mortar fire will be ineffective. Mortars of 60.1 or 85 millimeters, the usual campaign calibres, cannot penetrate a good roof made with simple materials from the region. This may be made from a base of wood, earth, and rocks covered with some camouflage material. An exit for escape in an extremity must always be constructed, so that the defender may get away with less danger.

The sketch below shows the form in which these defenses were constructed in the Sierra Maestra. They were sufficient to protect us from mortar fire.

This outline clearly indicates that fixed lines of fire do not exist. The lines of fire are something more or less theoretical; they are established at certain critical moments, but they are extremely elastic and permeable on both sides.

What does exist is a wide no man's land. But the

REFUGE AGAINST MORTAR FIRE.

characteristics of no man's land in guerrilla warfare are that it is inhabited by a civil population, and that this civil population collaborates in a certain measure with either of the two sides, even though in an overwhelming majority with the insurrectionary band. These people cannot be removed *en masse* from the zone on account of their numbers and because this would create problems of supply for either one of the contenders who tried to provide food for so many people. This no man's land is penetrated by periodic incursions (generally during the daytime) by the repressive forces and at night by the guerrilla forces. The guerrilla forces find there a maintenance base of great importance for their troops; this should be cared for in a political way, always establishing the best possible relations with the peasants and merchants.

In this type of warfare the tasks of those who do not carry arms, of those who are not direct combatants, are extremely important. We have already indicated some of the characteristics of liaison in places of combat; but liaison is an institution throughout the whole guerrilla organization. Liaison out to the most distant command or out to the most distant group of guerrilla fighters ought to be linked in such a way that messages will travel from one place to another via the most rapid system available in the region. This holds for regions of easy defense, that is to say, in favorable ground, as well as in unfavorable ground. A guerrilla band operating in unfavorable ground will not be able to use modern systems of communication, such as telegraph, roads, etc., except some radios located in military garrisons capable of being defended. If these fall into the hands of the enemy force, it is necessary to change codes and frequencies, a task that is rather troublesome.

In all these matters we are speaking from memory of things that occurred in our war of liberation. The daily and accurate report on all activities of the enemy is complemented with liaison. The system of espionage should be carefully studied, well worked out, and personnel chosen with maximum care. The harm that a counter-spy can do is enormous, but even without such an extreme case, the harm that can result from exaggerated information which misjudges the danger is very great. It is not probable that danger will be underrated. The tendency of people in the country is to overrate and exaggerate it. The same magic mentality that makes phantasms and various supernatural beings appear also creates monstrous armies where there is hardly a platoon or an enemy patrol. The spy ought to seem as neutral as possible, not known by the enemy to have any connection with the forces of liberation. This is not as difficult a task as it appears; many such persons are found in the course of the war: businessmen, professional men, and even clergymen can lend their help in this type of task and give timely information.

One of the most important characteristics of guerrilla warfare is the notable difference between the information that reaches the rebel forces and the information possessed by the enemy. While the latter must operate in regions that are absolutely hostile, finding sullen silence on the part of the peasants, the rebels have in nearly every house a friend or even a relative; and news is passed about constantly through the liaison system until it reaches the central command of the guerrilla force or of the guerrilla group that is in the zone.

When an enemy penetration occurs in territory that has become openly pro-guerrilla, where all the peasants respond to the cause of the people, a serious problem is created. The majority of peasants try to escape with the popular army, abandoning their children and their work; others even carry the whole family; some wait upon events. The most serious problem that an enemy penetration into guerrilla territory can provoke is that of a group of families finding themselves in a tight, at times desperate situation. Maximum help should be given to them, but they must be warned of the troubles that can follow upon a flight into inhospitable zones so far from their habitual places of livelihood, exposed to the hardships that usually befall in such cases.

It is not possible to describe any pattern of repression on the part of the enemies of the people. Although the general methods of repression are always the same, the enemies of the people act in a more or less intensely criminal fashion according to the specific social, historic, and economic circumstances of each place. There are places where the flight of a man into the guerrilla zone, leaving his family and his house, does not provoke any great reaction. There are others where this is enough to provoke the burning or seizure of his belongings, and still others where the flight will bring death to all members of his family. Adequate distribution and organization of the peasants who are going to be affected by an enemy advance must of course be arranged according to the habits that prevail in the war zone or country concerned.

Obviously preparations must be made to expel the enemy from such territory by moving against his supplies, completely cutting his lines of communication, destroying by means of small guerrilla bands his attempts to supply himself, and in general forcing him to devote large quantities of men to his supply problem.

In all these combat situations a very important factor is the correct utilization of reserves wherever battle begins. The guerrilla army, because of its characteristics, can rarely count on reserves, since it always strikes in such a way that the efforts of every individual are regulated and employed at something. Nevertheless, despite these characteristics it should have at some place men ready to respond to an unforeseen development, to detain a counter-offensive, or to take care of a situation at any moment. Within the organization of the guerrilla band, assuming that the conditions and possibilities of the moment permit, a utility platoon can be held in readiness, a platoon that should always go to the places of greatest danger. It can be christened the "suicide platoon" or something similar; this title in reality indicates its functions. This "suicide platoon" should be in every place where a battle is decided: in the surprise attacks upon the vanguard, in the defense of the most vulnerable and dangerous places, in a word, wherever the enemy threatens to break the stability of the line of fire. It ought to be made up strictly of volunteers. Entrance into this platoon should be regarded almost as a prize for merit. In time it becomes the favorite group of any guerrilla column, and the guerrilla fighter who wears its insignia enjoys the admiration and respect of all his companions.

5. BEGINNING, DEVELOPMENT, AND END OF A GUERRILLA WAR

We have now abundantly defined the nature of guerrilla warfare. Let us next describe the ideal development of such a war from its beginning as a rising by a single nucleus on favorable ground.

In other words, we are going to theorize once more on the basis of the Cuban experience. At the outset there is a more or less homogeneous group, with some arms, that devotes itself almost exclusively to hiding in the wildest and most inaccessible places, making little contact with the peasants. It strikes a fortunate blow and its fame grows. A few peasants, dispossessed of their land or engaged in a struggle to conserve it, and young idealists of other classes join the nucleus; it acquires greater audacity and starts to operate in inhabited places, making more contact with the people of the zone; it repeats attacks, always fleeing after making them; suddenly it engages in combat with some column or other and destroys its vanguard. Men continue to join it; it has increased in number, but its organization remains exactly the same; its caution diminishes, and it ventures into more populous zones.

Later it sets up temporary camps for several days; it abandons these upon receiving news of the approach of the enemy army, or upon suffering bombardments, or simply upon becoming suspicious that such risks have arisen. The numbers in the guerrilla band increase as work among the masses operates to make of each peasant an enthusiast for the war of liberation. Finally, an inaccessible place is chosen, a settled life is initiated, and the first small industries begin to be established: a shoe factory, a cigar and cigarette factory, a clothing factory, an arms factory, a bakery, hospitals, possibly a radio transmitter, a printing press, etc.

The guerrilla band now has an organization, a new structure. It is the head of a large movement with all the characteristics of a small government. A court is established for the administration of justice, possibly laws are promulgated and the work of indoctrination of the peasant masses continues, extended also to workers if there are any near, to draw them to the cause. An enemy action is launched and defeated; the number of rifles increases; with these the number of men fighting with the guerrilla band increases. A moment arrives when its radius of action will not have increased in the same proportion as its personnel; at that moment a force of appropriate size is separated, a column or a platoon, perhaps, and this goes to another place of combat.

The work of this second group will begin with somewhat different characteristics because of the experience that it brings and because of the influence of the troops of liberation on the war zone. The original nucleus also continues to grow; it has now received substantial support in food, sometimes in guns, from various places; men continue to arrive; the administration of government, with the promulgation of laws, continues; schools are established, permitting the indoctrination and training of recruits. The leaders learn steadily as the war develops, and their capacity of command grows under the added responsibilities of the qualitative and quantitative increases in their forces.

If there are distant territories, a group departs for them at a certain moment, in order to confirm the advances that have been made and to continue the cycle.

But there will also exist an enemy territory, unfavorable for guerrilla warfare. There small groups begin to penetrate, assaulting the roads, destroying bridges, planting mines, sowing disquiet. With the ups and downs characteristic of warfare the movement continues to grow; by this time the extensive work among the masses makes easy movement of the forces possible in unfavorable territory and so opens the final stage, which is suburban guerrilla warfare.

Sabotage increases considerably in the whole zone. Life is paralyzed; the zone is conquered. The guerrillas then go into other zones, where they fight with the enemy army along defined fronts; by now heavy arms have been captured, perhaps even some tanks; the fight is more equal. The enemy falls when the process of partial victories becomes transformed into final victories, that is to say, when the enemy is brought to accept battle in conditions imposed by the guerrilla band; there he is annihilated and his surrender compelled.

This is a sketch that describes what occurred in the different stages of the Cuban war of liberation; but it has a content approximating the universal. Nevertheless, it will not always be possible to count on the degree of intimacy with the people, the conditions, and the leadership that existed in our war. It is unnecessary to say that Fidel Castro possesses the high qualities of a fighter and statesman: our path, our struggle, and our triumph we owed to his vision. We cannot say that without him the victory of the people would not have been achieved; but that victory would certainly have cost must more and would have been less complete.

CHAPTER III

ORGANIZATION OF THE

GUERRILLA FRONT

1. SUPPLY

A good supply system is of basic importance to the guerrilla band. A group of men in contact with the soil must live from the products of this soil and at the same time must see that the livelihood continues of those who provide the supplies, the peasants; since in the hard guerrilla struggle it is not possible, above all at the beginning, for the group to dedicate its own energies to producing supplies, not to mention that these supplies would be easily discovered and destroyed by enemy forces in a territory likely to be completely penetrated by the action of repressive columns. Supply in the first stages is always internal.

As the guerrilla struggle develops, it will be necessary to arrange supply from outside the limits or territory of the combat. At the beginning the band lives solely on what the peasants have; it may be possible to reach a store occasionally to buy something, but never possible to have lines of supply, since there is no territory in which to establish them. The line of supply and the store of food are conditioned by the development of the guerrilla struggle.

The first task is to gain the absolute confidence of the inhabitants of the zone; and this confidence is won by a positive attitude toward their problems, by help and a constant program of orientation, by the defense of their interests and the punishment of all who attempt to take advantage of the chaotic moment in which they live in order to use pressure, dispossess the peasants, seize their harvests, etc. The line should be soft and hard at the same time: soft and with a spontaneous cooperation for all those who honestly sympathize with the revolutionary movement; hard upon those who are attacking it outright, fomenting dissensions, or simply communicating important information to the enemy army.

Little by little the territory will be cleared, and there will then be a greater ease of action. The fundamental principle that ought to prevail is that of paying always for all merchandise taken from a friend. This merchandise can consist of crops or of articles from commercial establishments. Many times they will be donated, but at other times the economic conditions of the peasantry prevent such donations. There are cases in which the necessities of warfare force the band to take needed food from stores without paying for it, simply because there is no money. In such cases the merchant ought always to be given a bond, a promissory note, something that certifies to the debt, "the bonds of hope" already described. It is better to use this method only with people who are outside the limits of the liberated territory, and in such cases to pay as soon as possible all or at least a part of the debt. When conditions have improved sufficiently to maintain a territory permanently free from the dominion of the opposing army, it is possible to set up collective plantings, where the peasants work the land for the benefit of the guerrilla army. In this way an adequate food supply of a permanent character is guaranteed.

If the number of volunteers for the guerrilla army is much greater than the number of arms, and political circumstances prevent these men from entering zones dominated by the enemy, the rebel army can put them to work directly on the land, harvesting crops; this guarantees supply and adds something to their record of service looking toward future promotion to the status of combatants. However, it is more advisable that the peasants themselves sow their own crops; this results in work performed more effectively, with more enthusiasm and skill. When conditions have ripened even more, it is possible, depending on the crops involved, to arrange purchases of entire harvests in such a way that they can remain in the field or in warehouses for the use of the army.

When agencies also charged with the duty of supplying the peasant population have been established, all food supplies will be concentrated in these agencies in order to facilitate a system of barter among the peasants, with the guerrilla army serving as intermediary.

If conditions continue to improve, taxes can be established; these should be as light as possible, above all for the small producer. It is important to pay attention to every detail of relations between the peasant class and the guerrilla army, which is an emanation of that class.

Taxes may be collected in money in some cases, or in the form of a part of the harvest, which will serve to increase the food supplies. Meat is one of the articles of primary necessity. Its production and conservation must be assured. Farms should be established under peasants having no apparent connection with the army, if the zone is not secure; they will devote themselves to the production of chickens, eggs, goats, and pigs, starting with stock that has been bought or confiscated from the large landowners. In the zones of big estates there are usually large quantities of cattle. These can be killed and salted and the meat maintained in condition for consumption for a long period of time.

This will also produce hides. A leather industry, more or less primitive, can be developed to provide leather for shoes, one of the fundamental accessories in the struggle. In general, necessary foods are the following (depending on the zone): meat, salt, vegetables, starches, or grains. The basic food is always produced by the peasants; it may be "malanga," as in the mountainous regions of Oriente Province in Cuba; it may be corn, as in the mountainous regions of Mexico, Central America, and Peru; potatoes, also in Peru; in other zones, such as Argentina, cattle; wheat in others; but always it is necessary to assure a supply of the fundamental food for the troop as well as some kinds of fat which permit better food preparation; these may be animal or vegetable fats.

Salt is one of the essential supplies. When the force is near the sea and in contact with it, small dryers should be established immediately; these will assure some production in order always to have a reserve stock and the ability to supply the troops. Remember that in wild places such as these, where only some of the foods are produced, it is easy for the enemy to establish an encirclement that can greatly hurt the flow of supplies to the zone. It is well to provide against such eventualities through peasant organization and civil organizations in general. The inhabitants of the zone should have on hand a minimum food supply that will permit them at least to survive, even though poorly, during the hardest phases of the struggle. An attempt should be made to collect rapidly a good provision of foods that do not decompose—such grains, for example, as corn, wheat, rice, etc., which will last quite a long time; also flour, salt, sugar, and canned goods of all types; further, the necessary seeds should be sown.

A moment will arrive when all the food problems of the troops in the zone are solved, but large quantities of other products will be needed: leather for shoes, if it has not been possible to create an industry for supplying the zone; cloth and all the accessory items necessary for clothing; paper, a press or mimeograph machine for newspapers, ink, and various other implements. In other words, the need for articles from the outside world will increase in the measure that the guerrilla bands become organized and the organization becomes more complex. In order for this need to be met adequately it is necessary that the organized lines of supply function perfectly. These organizations are composed basically of friendly peasants. They should have two poles, one in the guerrilla zone and one in a city. Departing and radiating from the guerrilla zones, lines of supply will penetrate the whole territory, permitting the passage of materials. Little by little the peasants accustom themselves to the danger (in small groups they can work marvels) and come to place the material that is needed in the indicated spot without running extreme risks. These movements can be carried out at night with mules or other similar transport animals or with trucks, depending on the zone. Thus, a very good supply may be achieved. This type of line of supply is for areas near places of operation.

It is also necessary to organize a line of supply from distant areas. These organizations should produce the money needed for making purchases and also the implements that cannot be produced in small towns or provincial cities. The organization will be nourished with direct donations from sectors sympathetic to the struggle, exchanged for secret "bonds," which should be delivered. A strict control over the personnel charged with the management of this operation should always be maintained. Serious consequences should follow any neglect of the indispensable moral requisites involved in this responsibility. Purchases can be made with cash and also with "bonds of hope" when the guerrilla army, having departed from its base of operations, menaces a new zone. In these cases there is no way to avoid taking the merchandise from any merchant; he must rely on the good faith and capabilities of the guerrilla armies to make good on his account.

For all lines of supply that pass through the country, it is necessary to have a series of houses, terminals, or way-stations, where supplies may be hidden during the day while waiting to be moved by night. These houses should be known only to those directly in charge of the food supplies. The least possible number of inhabitants should know about this transport operation, and these should be persons in whom the organization has the greatest confidence.

The mule is one of the most useful animals for these tasks. With an incredible resistance to fatigue and a capacity to walk in the hilliest zones, the mule can carry more than 100 kilograms on its back for many days. The simplicity of its food needs also makes it an ideal means of transport. The mule train should be well supplied with shoes; the muleteers should understand their animals and take the best possible care of them. In this way it is possible to have regular four-footed armies with an unbelievable utility. But frequently, despite the strength of the animal and its capacity to bear up through the hardest days, difficulty of passage will make it necessary to leave the cargo in fixed sites. In order to avoid this necessity, there should be a team charged with making trails for this class of animals. If all these conditions are met, if an adequate organization is created, and if the rebel army maintains excellent relations as needed with the peasants, an effective and lasting supply for the whole troop is guaranteed.

2. CIVIL ORGANIZATION

The civil organization of the insurrectional movement is very important on both fronts, the external and the internal. Naturally, these two have characteristics that are as different as their functions, though they both perform tasks that fall under the same name. The collections that can be carried out on the external front, for example, are not the same as those which can take place on the internal front; neither are the propaganda and the supply. Let us describe first the tasks on the internal front. Here we are dealing with a place dominated, relatively speaking, by the forces of liberation.

Also, it is to be supposed that the zone is adapted to guerrilla warfare, because when these conditions do not exist, when the guerrilla fighting is taking place in poorly adapted terrain, the guerrilla organization increases in extension but not in depth; it embraces new places, but it cannot arrive at an internal organization, since the whole zone is penetrated by the enemy. On the internal front we can have a series of organizations which perform specific functions for more efficiency in administration. In general, propaganda belongs directly to the army, but it also can be separated from the army if kept under its control. (This point is so important that we will treat it separately.) Collections are a function of the civil organization, as are the general tasks of organizing the peasants and workers, if these are present. Both of these classes should be governed by one council.

Raising supplies, as we explained in a previous chapter, can be carried out in various ways: through direct or indirect taxes, through direct or indirect donations, and through confiscations; all this goes to make up the large chapter on supplies for the guerrilla army.

Keep in mind that the zone ought by no means to be impoverished by the direct action of the rebel army, even though the latter will be responsible indirectly for the impoverishment that results from enemy encirclement, a fact that the adversary's propaganda will repeatedly point out. Precisely for this reason conflicts ought not to be created by direct causes. There ought not be, for example, any regulations that prevent the farmers of a zone in liberated territory from selling their products outside that territory, save in extreme and transitory circumstances and with a full explanation of these interruptions to the peasantry. Every act of the guerrilla army ought always to be accompanied by the propaganda necessary to explain the reasons for it. These reasons will generally be well understood by a peasantry that has sons, fathers, brothers, or relations within this army, which is, therefore, something of their own.

In view of the importance of relations with the peasants, it is necessary to create organizations that make regulations for them, organizations that exist not only within the liberated area, but also have connections in the adjacent areas. Precisely through these connections it is possible to penetrate a zone for a future enlargement of the guerrilla front. The peasants will sow the seed with oral and written propaganda, with accounts of life in the other zone, of the laws that have already been issued for the protection of the small peasant, of the spirit of sacrifice of the rebel army; in a word, they are creating the necessary atmosphere for helping the rebel troops.

The peasant organizations should also have connections of some type that will permit the channeling and sale of crops by the rebel army agencies in enemy territory through intermediaries more or less benevolent, more or less friendly to the peasant class. Joined with a devotion to the cause which brings the merchant to defy dangers in such cases, there also exists the devotion to money that leads him to take advantage of the opportunity to gain profits.

We have already spoken, in connection with supply problems, of the importance of the department of road construction. When the guerrilla band has achieved a certain level of development, it no longer wanders about through diverse regions without an encampment; it has centers that are more or less fixed. Routes should be established varying from small paths permitting the passage of a mule to good roads for trucks. In all this, the capacity of the organization of the rebel army must be kept in mind, as well as the offensive capacity of the enemy, who may destroy these constructions and even make use of roads built by his opponent to reach the encampments more easily. The fundamental rule should be that roads are for assisting supply in places where any other solution would be impossible; they should not be constructed except in circumstances where there is a virtual certainty that the position can be maintained against an attack by the adversary. Another exception would be roads built without great risk to facilitate communication between points that are not of vital importance.

Furthermore, other means of communication may be established. One of these that is extremely important is the telephone. This can be strung in the forest with the convenience that arises from using trees for posts. There is the advantage that they are not visible to the enemy from above. The telephone also presupposes a zone that the enemy cannot penetrate.

The council—or central department of justice, revolutionary laws, and administration—is one of the vital features of a guerrilla army fully constituted and with territory of its own. The council should be under the charge of an individual who knows the laws of the country; if he understands the necessities of the zone from a juridical point of view, this is better yet; he can proceed to prepare a series of decrees and regulations that help the peasant to normalize and institutionalize his life within the rebel zone.

For example, during our experience in the Cuban war we issued a penal code, a civil code, rules for supplying the peasantry and rules of the agrarian reform. Subsequently, the laws fixing qualifications of candidates in the elections that were to be held later throughout the country were established; also the Agrarian Reform Law of the Sierra Maestra. The council is likewise in charge of accounting operations for the guerrilla column or columns; it is responsible for handling money problems and at times intervenes directly in supply.

All these recommendations are flexible; they are based upon an experience in a certain place and are conditioned by its geography and history; they will be modified in different geographical, historical, and social situations.

In addition to the council, it is necessary to keep the general health of the zone in mind. This can be done by means of central military hospitals that should give the most complete assistance possible to the whole peasantry. Whether adequate medical treatment can be given will depend upon the stage reached by the revolution. Civil hospitals and civil health administration are united directly with the guerrilla army, and their functions are performed by officers and men of the army, who have the dual function of caring for the people and orienting them toward better health. The big health problems among people in these conditions are rooted in their total ignorance of elementary principles of hygiene. This aggravates their already precarious situation.

The collection of taxes, as I have already said, is also a function of the general council.

Warehouses are very important. As soon as a place is taken that is to serve as a base for the guerrilla band, warehouses should be established in the most orderly fashion possible. These will serve to assure a minimum care of merchandise and, most important, will provide the control needed for equalizing distribution and keeping it equitable at later times.

Functions are different on the external front both in quantity and in quality. For example, propaganda should be of a national, orienting type, explaining the victories obtained by the guerrilla band, calling workers and peasants to effective mass fights, and giving news, if there is any, of victories obtained on this front itself. Solicitation of funds is completely secret; it ought to be carried out with the greatest care possible, isolating small collectors in the chain completely from the treasurer of the organization.

This organization should be distributed in zones that complement each other in order to form a totality, zones that may be provinces, states, cities, villages, depending on the magnitude of the movement. In each of them there must be a finance commission that takes charge of the disposal of funds collected. It is possible to collect money by selling bonds or through direct donations. When the development of the struggle is more advanced, taxes may be collected; when industries come to recognize the great force that the insurrectional army possesses, they will consent to pay. Supply procurement should be fitted to the necessities of the guerrilla bands; it will be organized in the form of a chain of merchandise in such a way that the more common articles are procured in nearby places, and the things that are really scarce or impossible to procure locally, in larger centers. The effort always is to keep the chain as limited as possible, known to the smallest number of men; it can thus perform its mission for a longer time.

Sabotage should be directed by the civil organization in the external sector in coordination with the central command. In special circumstances, after careful analysis, assaults on persons will be used. In general we consider that this is not desirable except for the purpose of eliminating some figure who is notorious for his villainies against the people and the virulence of his repression. Our experience in the Cuban struggle shows that it would have been possible to save the lives of numerous fine comrades who were sacrificed in the performance of missions of small value. Several times these ended with enemy bullets of reprisal on combatants whose loss could not be compared with the results obtained. Assaults and terrorism in indiscriminate form should not be employed. More preferable is effort directed at large concentrations of people in whom the revolutionary idea can be planted and nurtured, so that at a critical moment they can be mobilized and with the help of the armed forces contribute to a favorable balance on the side of the revolution.

For this it is necessary also to make use of popular organizations of workers, professional people, and peasants, who work at sowing the seed of the revolution among their respective masses, explaining, providing revolutionary publications for reading, teaching the truth. One of the characteristics of revolutionary propaganda must be truth. Little by little, in this way, the masses will be won over. Those among them who do the best work may be chosen for incorporation into the rebel army or assignment to other tasks of great responsibility.

This is the outline of civil organization within and outside guerrilla territory at a time of popular struggle. There are possibilities of perfecting all these features to a high degree. I repeat once more, it is our Cuban experience which speaks through me; new experiences can vary and improve these concepts. We offer an outline, not a bible.

3. THE ROLE OF THE WOMAN

The part that the woman can play in the development of a revolutionary process is of extraordinary importance. It is well to emphasize this, since in all our countries, with their colonial mentality, there is a certain underestimation of the woman which becomes a real discrimination against her.

The woman is capable of performing the most difficult tasks, of fighting beside the men; and despite current belief, she does not create conflicts of a sexual type in the troops.

In the rigorous combatant life the woman is a companion who brings the qualities appropriate to her sex, but she can work the same as a man and she can fight; she is weaker, but no less resistant than he. She can perform every class of combat task that a man can at a given moment, and on certain occasions in the Cuban struggle she performed a relief role.

Naturally the combatant women are a minority. When the internal front is being consolidated and it is desirable to remove as many combatants as possible who do not possess indispensable physical characteristics, the women can be assigned a considerable number of specific occupations, of which one of the most important, perhaps the most important, is communication between different combatant forces, above all between those that are in enemy territory. The transport of objects, messages, or money, of small size and great importance, should be confided to women in whom the guerrilla army has absolute confidence; women can transport them using a thousand tricks; it is a fact that however brutal the repression, however thorough the searching, the woman receives a less harsh treatment than the man and can carry her message or other object of an important or confidential character to its destination.

As a simple messenger, either by word of mouth or of writing, the woman can always perform her task with more freedom than the man, attracting less attention and at the same time inspiring less fear of danger in the enemy soldier. He who commits brutalities acts frequently under the impulse of fear or apprehension that he himself will be attacked, since this is one form of action in guerrilla warfare.

Contacts between separated forces, messages to the exterior of the lines, even to the exterior of the country; also objects of considerable size, such as bullets, are transported by women in special belts worn beneath their skirts. But also in this stage a woman can perform her habitual tasks of peacetime; it is very pleasing to a soldier subjected to the extremely hard conditions of this life to be able to look forward to a seasoned meal which tastes like something. (One of the great tortures of the war was eating a cold, sticky, tasteless mess.) The woman as cook can greatly improve the diet and, furthermore, it is easier to keep her in these domestic tasks; one of the problems in guerrilla bands is that all works of a civilian character are scorned by those who perform them; they are constantly trying to get out of these tasks in order to enter into forces that are actively in combat.

A task of great importance for women is to teach beginning reading, including revolutionary theory, primarily to the peasants of the zone, but also to the revolutionary soldiers. The organization of schools, which is a part of the civil organization, should be done principally through women, who arouse more enthusiasm among children and enjoy more affection from the school community. Likewise, when the fronts have been consolidated and a rear exists, the functions of the social worker also fall to women who investigate the various economic and social evils of the zone with a view to changing them as far as pos-sible.

The woman plays an important part in medical matters as nurse, and even as doctor, with a gentle-ness infinitely superior to that of her rude companion in arms, a gentleness that is so much appreciated at moments when a man is helpless, without comforts, perhaps suffering severe pain and exposed to the many dangers of all classes that are a part of this type of war.

Once the stage of creating small war industries has begun, the woman can also contribute here, espe-cially in the manufacture of uniforms, a traditional employment of women in Latin American countries. With a simple sewing machine and a few patterns she can perform marvels. Women can take part in all lines of civil organization. They can replace men perfectly well and ought to do so, even where persons are needed for carrying weapons, though this is a rare ac-cident in guerrilla life.

It is important to give adequate indoctrination to men and women, in order to avoid all kinds of mis-behavior that can operate to hurt the morale of the troops; but persons who are otherwise free and who love each other should be permitted to marry in the Sierra and live as man and wife after complying with the simple requirements of the guerrilla band.

4. MEDICAL PROBLEMS

One of the grave problems that confronts the guer-rilla fighter is exposure to the accidents of his life, es-pecially to wounds and sicknesses, which are very frequent in guerrilla warfare. The doctor performs a function of extraordinary importance in the guerrilla band, not only in saving lives, in which many times his scientific intervention does not count because of the limited resources available to him; but also in the task of reinforcing the patient morally and making him feel that there is a person near him who is dedicated with all his force to minimizing his pains. He gives the wounded or sick the security of knowing that a person will remain at his side until he is cured or has passed danger.

The organization of hospitals depends largely upon the stage of development of the guerrilla band. Three fundamental types of hospital organization corresponding to various stages can be mentioned.

In this development we have a first, nomadic phase. In it the doctor, if there is one, travels constantly with his companions, is just another man; he will probably have to perform all the other functions of the guerrilla fighter, including that of fighting, and will suffer at times the depressing and desperate task of treating cases in which the means of saving life are not available. This is the stage in which the doctor has the most influence over the troops, the greatest importance for their morale. During this period in the development of the guerrilla band the doctor achieves to the full his character of a true priest who seems to carry in his scantily equipped knapsack needed consolation for the men. The value of a simple aspirin to one who is suffering is beyond calculation when it is given by the friendly hand of one who sympathetically makes the suffering his own. Therefore the doctor in the first stage should be a man who is totally identified with the ideals of the revolution, because his words will affect the troops much more deeply than those spoken by any other member.

In the normal course of events in guerrilla warfare another stage is reached that could be called "semi-nomadic." In it there are encampments, more or less frequented by the guerrilla troops; friendly houses of complete confidence where it is possible to store objects and even leave the wounded; and a growing tendency for the troop to become settled. At this stage the task of the doctor is less trying; he may have emergency surgical equipment in his knapsack and another more complete outfit for less urgent operations in a friendly house. It is possible to leave the sick and wounded in the care of peasants who will give their help with great devotion. He can also count on a larger number of medicines kept in convenient places; these should be completely catalogued as well as possible, considering the circumstances in which he lives. In this same semi-nomadic state, if the band operates in places that are absolutely inaccessible, hospitals can be established to which the sick and wounded will go for recovery.

In the third stage, when there are zones invulnerable to the enemy, a true hospital organization is constructed. In its most developed form, it can consist of three centers of different types. In the combat category there ought to be a doctor, the combatant the most loved by the troop, the man of battle, whose knowledge does not have to be too deep. I say this because his task is principally one of giving relief and of preparing the sick or wounded, while the real medical work is performed in hospitals more securely situated. A surgeon of quality ought not to be sacrificed in the line of fire.

When a man falls in the front line, stretcher-bearers, if these are available given the organization of the guerrilla band, will carry him to the first post; if they are not available, his companions themselves will perform this duty. Transport of the wounded in rough zones is one of the most delicate of all tasks and one of the most painful experiences in a soldier's life. Perhaps the transport of a wounded man is harder on all concerned, because of his sufferings and of the spirit of sacrifice in the troop, than the fact itself of being wounded, however grave it may be. The transport can be carried out in different ways according to the characteristics of the ground. In rough and wooded places, which are typical in guerrilla warfare, it is necessary to walk single file. Here the best system is to use a long pole, with the patient carried in a hammock that hangs from it.

The men take turns carrying the weight, one before and one behind. They should yield place to two other companions frequently, since the shoulders suffer severely and the individual gradually wears himself out carrying this delicate and heavy burden.

When the wounded soldier has passed through this first hospital, he then goes with the information as to what has been done for him to a second center, where there are surgeons and specialists depending upon the possibilities of the troop. Here the more serious operations needed for saving life or relieving individuals from danger are performed.

Afterwards, at a third level, hospitals with the greatest comforts possible are established for direct investigation in the zones affected of the causes and effects of illnesses that afflict the inhabitants of the area. These hospitals of the third group, which correspond to a sedentary life, are not only centers of convalescence and of operations of less urgency, but also establishments serving the civil population, where the hygienists perform their orienting function. Dispensaries that will permit an adequate individual surveillance should also be established. The hospitals of this third group can have, if the supply capability of the civil organization permits, a series of facilities that provide diagnosis even with laboratory and x-ray facilities.

Other useful individuals are the assistants to the doctor. They are generally youths with something of a vocation and some knowledge, with fairly strong physiques; they do not bear arms, sometimes because their vocation is medicine, but usually because there are insufficient arms for all who want them. These assistants will be in charge of carrying most of the medicines, an extra stretcher or hammock, if circumstances make this possible. They must take charge of the wounded in any battle that is fought.

The necessary medicines should be obtained through contacts with health organizations that exist in territory of the enemy. Sometimes they can be obtained from such organizations as the International Red Cross, but this possibility should not be counted upon, especially in the first moments of the struggle. It is necessary to organize an apparatus that will permit rapid transport of needed medicines in case of danger and that will gradually supply all the hospitals with the supplies needed for their work, military as well as civil. Also, contacts should be made in the surrounding areas with doctors who will be capable of helping the wounded whose cases are beyond the capacities or the facilities of the guerrilla band.

Doctors needed for this type of warfare are of different characteristics. The combatant doctor, the companion of men, is the type for the first stage; his functions develop as the action of the guerrilla band becomes more complicated and a series of connected organisms are constructed. General surgeons are the best acquisition for an army of this type. If an anesthetist is available, so much the better; though almost all operations are performed, not with gas anesthesia, but using "largactil" and sodium pentothal, which are much easier to administer and easier to procure and conserve. Besides general surgeons, bone specialists are very useful, because fractures occur frequently from accidents in the zone; they are also frequently caused by bullets producing this type of wound in limbs. The clinic serves the peasant mass mainly, since in general, sicknesses in the guerrilla armies are so easy of diagnosis as to be within the reach of anybody. The most difficult task is the cure of those produced by nutritional deficiencies.

In a more advanced stage there may even be laboratory technicians, if there are good hospitals, in order to have a complete outfit. Calls should be made to all sectors of the profession whose services are needed; it is quite likely that many will respond to this call and come to lend their help. Professionals of all classes are needed; surgeons are very useful, dentists as well. Dentists should be advised to come with a simple campaign apparatus and a campaign-type drill; working with this they can do practically everything necessary.

5. SABOTAGE

Sabotage is one of the invaluable arms of a people that fights in guerrilla form. Its organization falls under the civil or clandestine branch, since sabotage should be carried out, of course, only outside the territories dominated by the revolutionary army; but this organization should be directly commanded and oriented by the general staff of the guerrillas, which will be responsible for deciding the industries, communications, or other objectives that are to be attacked.

Sabotage has nothing to do with terrorism; terrorism and personal assaults are entirely different tactics. We sincerely believe that terrorism is of negative value, that it by no means produces the desired effects, that it can turn a people against a revolutionary movement, and that it can bring a loss of lives to its agents out of proportion to what it produces. On the other hand, attempts to take the lives of particular persons are to be made, though only in very special circumstances; this tactic should be used where it will eliminate a leader of the oppression. What ought never to be done is to employ specially trained, heroic, self-sacrificing human beings in eliminating a little assassin whose death can provoke the destruction in reprisal of all the revolutionaries employed and even more.

Sabotage should be of two types: sabotage on a national scale against determined objectives, and local sabotage against lines of combat. Sabotage on a national scale should be aimed principally at destroying communications. Each type of communication can be destroyed in a different way; all of them are vulnerable. For example, telegraph and telephone poles are easily destroyed by sawing them almost all the way through, so that at night they appear to be in normal condition; a sudden kick causes one pole to fall and this drags along with it all those that are weak, producing a blackout of considerable extent.

Bridges can be attacked with dynamite; if there is no dynamite, those made of steel can be made to fall very easily with an oxyacetylene blow torch. A steel truss bridge should be cut in its main beam and in the upper beam from which the bridge hangs. When these two beams have been cut at one end with the torch, they are then cut at the opposite end. The bridge will fall completely on one side and will be twisted and destroyed. This is the most effective way to knock out a steel bridge without dynamite. Railroads should also be destroyed, as should roads and culverts; at times trains should be blown up, if the power of the guerrilla band makes this possible.

The vital industries of each region at certain moments will also be destroyed by utilizing the necessary equipment. In these cases it is necessary to have an overall view of the problem and to be sure that a center of work is not destroyed unless the moment is decisive, since this brings with it as a consequence massive unemployment of workers and hunger. The enterprises belonging to the potentates of the regime should be eliminated (and attempts made to convince the workers of the need for doing so), unless this will bring very grave social consequences.

We reiterate the importance of sabotage against communications. The great strength of the enemy army against the rebels in the flatter zones is rapid communication; we must, then, constantly undermine that strength by knocking out railroad bridges, culverts, electric lights, telephones; also aqueducts and in general everything that is necessary for a normal and modern life.

Around the combat lines sabotage should be performed in the same way but with much more audacity, with much more dedication and frequency. Here it is possible to count on the invaluable aid of the flying patrols of the guerrilla army, which can descend into these zones and help the members of the civil organization perform a given task. Again, sabotage ought to be aimed principally at communications, but with much more persistence. All factories, all centers of production that are capable of giving the enemy something needed to maintain his offensive against the popular forces, ought also to be liquidated.

Emphasis should be placed on seizing merchandise, cutting supplies as much as possible, if necessary frightening the large landowners who want to sell their farm products, burning vehicles that travel along the roads, and using them to blockade the roads. It is expedient in every action of sabotage that frequent contact be made with the enemy army at points not far away, always following the system of hit and run. It is not necessary to put up a serious resistance, but simply to show the adversary that in the area where the sabotage has been carried out there are guerrilla forces disposed to fight. This forces him to take a large number of troops, to go with care, or not to go at all.

Thus, little by little, all the cities in the zone surrounding guerrilla operations will be paralyzed.

6. WAR INDUSTRY

Industries of war within the sector of the guerrilla army must be the product of a rather long evolution; they also depend upon control of territory in a geographic situation favorable for the guerrilla. At a time when there are liberated zones and when strict blockades are established by the enemy over all supplies, different departments will be organized as necessary, in the manner already described. There are two fundamental industries, of which one is the manufacture of shoes and leather goods. It is not possible for a troop to walk without shoes in wooded zones, hilly, with many rocks and thorns. It is very difficult to march without shoes in such conditions; only the natives, and not all of them, can do it. The rest must have shoes. The industry is divided into two parts, one for putting on half-soles and repairing damaged shoes; the other will be devoted to the manufacture of rough shoes. There should be a small but complete apparatus for making shoes; since this is a simple industry practiced by many people in such regions it is very easy to procure. Connected with the shoe repair works there ought always to be a shop making all classes of canvas and leather goods for use by the troop, such as cartridge belts and knapsacks. Although these articles are not vital, they contribute to comfort and give a feeling of autonomy, of adequate supply, and of self-reliance to the troop.

An armory is the other fundamental industry for the small internal organization of the guerrilla band.

This also has different functions: that of simple repair of damaged weapons, of rifles, and other available arms; the function of manufacturing certain types of combat arms that the inventiveness of the people will create; and the preparation of mines with various mechanisms. When conditions permit, equipment for the manufacture of powder may be added. If it is possible to manufacture the explosive as well as the percussion mechanisms in free territory, brilliant achievements can be scored in this category, which is a very important one, because communications by road can be completely paralyzed by the adequate employment of mines.

Another group of industries that has its importance will make iron and tin products. In the iron works will be centered all labor connected with the equipping of the mules, such as making their shoes. In the tin works the fabrication of plates and especially of canteens is important. A foundry can be joined with the tin works. By melting soft metals it is possible to make grenades, which with a special type of charge will contribute in an important way to the armament of the troop. There ought to be a technical team for general repair and construction work of varied types, the "service battery," as it is called in regular armies. With the guerrillas it would operate as such, taking care of all necessities, but without any vestige of the bureaucratic spirit.

Someone must be in charge of communications. He will have as his responsibility not only propaganda communications, such as radio directed toward the outside, but also telephones and roads of all types. He will use the civil organization as necessary in order to perform his duties effectively. Remember that we are in a period of war subject to attack by the enemy and that often many lives depend upon timely communication.

For accommodating the troop it is well to have

cigarette and cigar factories. The leaf can be bought in selected places and carried to free territory where the articles for consumption by the soldiers can be manufactured. An industry for preparing leather from hides is also of great importance. All these are simple enterprises that can operate quite well anywhere and are easy to establish in the guerrilla situation. The industry for making leather requires some small construction with cement; also it uses large amounts of salt; but it will be an enormous advantage to the shoe industry to have its own supply of raw material. Salt should be made in revolutionary territory and accumulated in large quantities. It is made by evaporating water of a high saline concentration. The sea is the best source, though there may be others. It is not necessary to purify it of other ingredients for purposes of consumption, though these give it a flavor that is disagreeable at first.

Meat should be conserved in the form of jerked beef, which is easy to prepare. This can save many lives among the troop in extreme situations. It can be conserved with salt in large barrels for a fairly long time, and it can then be eaten in any circumstances.

7. PROPAGANDA

The revolutionary idea should be diffused by means of appropriate media to the greatest depth possible. This requires complete equipment and an organization. This organization should be of two types which complement each other in covering the whole national area: for propaganda originating outside free territory, that is, from the national civil organization; and propaganda originating within, that is, from the base of the guerrilla army. In order to coordinate these two propagandas, the functions of which are strictly related, there should be a single director for the whole effort.

Propaganda of the national type from civil organizations outside free territory should be distributed in newspapers, bulletins, and proclamations. The most important newspapers will be devoted to general matters in the country and will inform the public exactly of the state of the guerrilla forces, observing always the fundamental principle that truth in the long run is the best policy. Besides these publications of general interest there must be others more specialized for different sectors of the population. A publication for the countryside should bring to the peasant class a message from their companions in all the free zones who have already felt the beneficial effects of the revolution; this strengthens the aspirations of the peasantry. A workers' newspaper will have similar characteristics, with the sole difference that it cannot always offer a message from the combatant part of that class, since it is likely that workers' organizations will not operate within the framework of guerrilla warfare until the last stages.

The great watchwords of the revolutionary movement, the watchword of a general strike at an opportune moment, of help to the rebel forces, of unity, etc., should be explained. Other periodicals can be published; for example, one explaining the tasks of those elements in the whole island which are not combatants but which nevertheless carry out diverse acts of sabotage, of attempts, etc. Within the organization there can be periodicals aimed at the enemy's soldiers; these will explain facts of which they are otherwise kept ignorant. News bulletins and proclamations about the movement are very useful.

The most effective propaganda is that which is prepared within the guerrilla zone. Priority will be given to the diffusion of ideas among natives of the zone, offering explanations of the theoretical significance of the insurrection, already known to them as a fact. In this zone there will also be peasant periodicals, the general organ of all the guerrilla forces, and bulletins and proclamations. There will also be the radio.

All problems should be discussed by radio—for example, the way to defend oneself from air attacks and location of the enemy forces, citing familiar names among them. Propaganda for the whole nation will use newspapers of the same type as those prepared outside free territory, but it can produce fresher and more exact news, reporting facts and battles that are extremely interesting to the reader. Information on international affairs will be confined almost exclusively to commentary on facts that are directly related to the struggle of liberation.

The propaganda that will be the most effective in spite of everything, that which will spread most freely over the whole national area to reach the reason and the sentiments of the people, is words over the radio. The radio is a factor of extraordinary importance. At moments when war fever is more or less palpitating in every one in a region or a country, the inspiring, burning word increases this fever and communicates it to every one of the future combatants. It explains, teaches, fires, and fixes the future positions of both friends and enemies. However, the radio should be ruled by the fundamental principle of popular propaganda, which is truth; it is preferable to tell the truth, small in its dimensions, than a large lie artfully embellished. On the radio news should be given, especially of battles, of encounters of all types, and assassinations committed by the repression; also, doctrinal orientations and practical lessons to the civil population; and, from time to time, speeches by the chiefs of the revolution. We consider it useful that the principal newspaper of the movement bear a name that recalls something great and unifying, perhaps a national hero or something similar. Also, it should explain in articles of depth where the armed movement is going. It ought to create a consciousness of the great national problems, besides offering sections of more lively interest for the reader.

8. INTELLIGENCE

"Know yourself and your adversary and you will be able to fight a hundred battles without a single disaster." This Chinese aphorism is as valuable for guerrilla warfare as a biblical psalm. Nothing gives more help to combatant forces than correct information. This arrives spontaneously from the local inhabitants, who will come to tell its friendly army, its allies, what is happening in various places; but in addition it should be completely systematized. As we saw, there should be a postal organization with necessary contacts both within and outside guerrilla zones for carrying messages and merchandise. An intelligence service also should be in direct contact with enemy fronts. Men and women, especially women, should infiltrate; they should be in permanent contact with soldiers and gradually discover what there is to be discovered. The system must be coordinated in such a way that crossing the enemy lines into the guerrilla camp can be carried out without mishap.

If this is well done with competent agents the insurgent camp will be able to sleep more quietly.

This intelligence will be concerned principally, as I have already said, with the front line of fire or the forward enemy encampments that are in contact with no man's land; but it ought also to develop in the same measure as the guerrilla band develops, increasing its depth of operation and its potential to foresee larger troop movements in the enemy rear. Though all inhabitants are intelligence agents for the guerrilla band in the places where it is dominant or makes incursions, it is wise to have persons especially assigned to this duty. The peasants, not accustomed to precise battle language, have a strong tendency to exaggerate, so their reports must be checked. As the spontaneous forms of popular collaboration are molded and organized, it is possible to use the intelligence apparatus not only as an extremely important auxiliary but also as a weapon of attack by using its personnel, for example, as "sowers of fear." Pretending to be on the side of the enemy soldiers, they sow fear and instability by spreading discouraging information. By knowing exactly the places where the enemy troop is going to attack, it is easy to avoid him or, when the time is ripe, to attack him at places where it is least expected. Mobility, the basic tactic, can be developed to the maximum.

9. TRAINING AND INDOCTRINATION

The fundamental training of the soldier of liberation is the life itself with the guerrilla band, and no one can be a chief who has not learned his difficult office in daily armed exercises. Life with some companions will teach something about the handling of arms, about principles of orientation, about the manner of treating the civil population, about fighting, etc.; but the precious time of the guerrilla band is not to be consumed in methodical teaching. This begins only when there is a large liberated area and a large number of persons are needed for carrying out a combat function. Schools for recruits will then be established.

These schools then perform a very important function. They are to form new soldiers from persons who have not passed through that excellent sieve of for-

midable privations, guerrilla combatant life. Other
privations must be suffered at the outset to convert
them into the truly chosen. After having passed
through very difficult tests, they will arrive at incorporating themselves into the kingdom of an army that
lives from day to day and leaves no traces of its path
anywhere. They ought to perform physical exercises,
mainly of two types: an agile gymnastic with training
for war of a commando type, which demands agility
in attack and withdrawal; and hikes that are hard
and exhausting that will serve to toughen the recruit
for this kind of existence. Above all, they should live
in the open air. They should suffer all the inclemen-
cies of the weather in close contact with nature, as the
guerrilla band does.

The school for recruits must have workers who will
take care of its supply needs. For this there should
be cattle sheds, grain sheds, gardens, dairy, everything necessary, so that the school will not constitute
a charge on the general budget of the guerrilla army.
The students can serve in rotation in the work of supply, either as punishment for bad conduct or simply
as volunteers. This will depend upon characteristics
proper to the zone where the school is being held.
We believe that a good principle is to assign volunteers and to cover the remaining work quotas with
those who have the poorest conduct and show the
poorest disposition for learning warfare.

The school should have its small medical organization with a doctor or nurse, according to the possibilities; this will provide the recruits with the best
possible attention.

Shooting is the basic apprenticeship. The guerrilla
fighter should be carefully trained in this respect, so
that he will try to expend the least possible amount
of ammunition. He begins by practicing what is
called dry shooting. It consists of seating the rifle
firmly on any kind of wooden apparatus as shown in

TARGET PRACTICE.

the picture. Without moving or firing the rifle the recruits direct the movement of a target until they think they have a hole at the center exactly in the line of sight. A mark is made on a backboard that remains stationary. If the mark for three tries gives a single point, this is excellent. When circumstances permit, practice with 22-calibre rifles will begin; this is very useful. If there is an excess of ammunition or a great need for preparing soldiers, opportunity will be given to fire with bullets.

One of the most important courses in the school for recruits, one which we hold to be basic and which can be given in any place in the world, is in meeting attack from the air. Our school had been positively identified from the air and received attacks once or twice daily. The form in which the students resisted the impact of these continuous bombardments on their regular places of instruction virtually showed which of the young men had possibilities for becoming useful soldiers in battle.

The important thing, that which must never be

neglected in a school for recruits, is indoctrination; this is important because the men arrive without a clear conception as to why they come, with nothing more than very diffuse concepts about liberty, freedom of the press, etc., without any clear foundation whatever. Therefore, the indoctrination should be carried out with maximum dedication and for the maximum amount of time possible. These courses should offer elementary notions about the history of the country, explained with a clear sense of the economic facts that motivate each of the historic acts; accounts of the national heroes and their manner of reacting when confronted with certain injustices; and afterwards an analysis of the national situation or of the situation in the zone. A short primer should be well studied by all members of the rebel army, so that it can serve as a skeleton of that which will come later.

There should also be a school for training teachers, where agreement can be reached on the choice of texts to be used, taking as a basis the contribution that each book can make to the educational process.

Reading should be encouraged at all times, with an effort to promote books that are worthwhile and that enlarge the recruit's facility to encounter the world of letters and great national problems. Further reading will follow as a vocation; the surrounding circumstances will awaken new desires for understanding in the soldiers. This result will be produced when, little by little, the recruits observe in their routine tasks the enormous advantages of men who have passed through the school over the remainder of the troop, their capacity for analyzing problems, their superior discipline, which is another of the fundamental things that the school should teach.

This discipline should be internal, not mechanical but justified by reasons and designed to produce formidable benefits in moments of combat.

10. THE ORGANIZATIONAL STRUCTURE OF THE ARMY OF A REVOLUTIONARY MOVEMENT

As we have seen, a revolutionary army of a guerrilla type, whatever its zone of operations, should also have a non-combatant organization for the performance of a series of extremely important auxiliary missions. We shall see later that this whole organization converges to lend the army maximum help, since obviously the armed fight is the crucial factor in the triumph.

The military organization is headed by a commander-in-chief, in the case of the Cuban experience by a comandante, who names the commanders of the different regions or zones; these latter have authority to govern their respective territories of action, to name column commanders, that is to say, the chiefs of each column, and the other lower officers.

Under the commander-in-chief there will be the zone commanders; under them several columns of varying size, each with a column commander; under the column commanders there will be captains and lieutenants, which, in our guerrilla organization, were the lowest grade. In other words, the first rank above the soldiers was the lieutenant.

This is not a model but a description of one reality, of how the organization worked in one country where it proved possible to achieve triumph over an army that was fairly well organized and armed. Even less here than in other respects is our experience a pattern. It simply shows how as events develop it is possible to organize an armed force. The ranks certainly have no importance, but it is important that no rank should be conferred that does not correspond to the effective battle force commanded. Ranks should not be given to persons who have not passed through the sieve of sacrifice and struggle, for that would conflict with morality and justice.

The description given above refers to a well-developed army, already capable of waging a serious combat. In the first stage of the guerrilla band, the chief can take the rank he likes, but he will still command only a small group of men.

One of the most important features of military organization is disciplinary punishment. Discipline must be one of the bases of action of the guerrilla forces (this must be repeated again and again). As we have already said, it should spring from a carefully reasoned internal conviction; this produces an individual with inner discipline. When this discipline is violated, it is necessary always to punish the offender, whatever his rank, and to punish him drastically in a way that hurts.

This is important, because pain is not felt by a guerrilla soldier in the same way as by a soldier of the regular army. The punishment of putting a soldier in jail for ten days constitutes for the guerrilla fighter a magnificent period of rest; ten days with nothing to do but eat, no marching, no work, no standing the customary guards, sleeping at will, resting, reading, etc. From this it can be deduced that deprivation of liberty ought not to be the only punishment available in the guerrilla situation.

When the combat morale of the individual is very high and self-respect strong, deprivation of his right to be armed can constitute a true punishment for the individual and provoke a positive reaction. In such cases, this is an expedient punishment.

The following painful incident is an example. During the battle for one of the cities of Las Villas province in the final days of the war, we found an individual asleep in a chair while others were attacking positions in the middle of the town. When ques-

tioned, the man responded that he was sleeping because he had been deprived of his weapon for firing
accidentally. He was told that this was not the way
to react to punishment and that he should regain his
weapon, not in this way, but in the first line of combat.

A few days passed, and as the final assault on the
city of Santa Clara began, we visited the first-aid hospital. A dying man there extended his hand, recalling
the episode I have narrated, affirmed that he had been
capable of recovering his weapon and had earned
the right to carry it. Shortly afterwards, he died.

This was the grade of revolutionary morale that our
troop achieved through the continual exercise of
armed struggle. It is not possible to achieve it at the
outset, when there are still many who are frightened,
and subjective currents serve to put a brake on the influence of the Revolution; but finally it is reached
through work and through the force of continual example.

Long night watches and forced marches can also
serve as punishments; but the marches are not really
practical, since they consume the individual to no
purpose other than that of punishment, and they require guards who also wear themselves out. The
guards suffer the further inconvenience of having to
keep a watch on the persons being punished, who
are soldiers of scant revolutionary mentality.

In the forces directly under my command I imposed the punishment of arrest with privation of
sweets and cigarettes for light offenses and a total
deprivation of food for worse offenses. The result was
magnificent, even though the punishment was terrible; it is advisable only in very special circumstances.

1. ORGANIZATION IN SECRET OF THE FIRST GUERRILLA BAND

Guerrilla warfare obeys laws, some derived from the general laws of war and others owing to its own special character. If there is a real intention to begin the struggle from some foreign country or from distant and remote regions within the same country, it is obvious that it must begin in small conspiratorial movements of secret members acting without mass support or knowledge. If the guerrilla movement is born spontaneously out of the reaction of a group of individuals to some form of coercion, it is possible that the later organization of this guerrilla nucleus to prevent its annihilation will be sufficient for a beginning. But generally guerrilla warfare starts from a well-considered act of will: some chief with prestige starts an uprising for the salvation of his people, beginning his work in difficult conditions in a foreign country.

Almost all the popular movements undertaken against dictators in recent times have suffered from the same fundamental fault of inadequate preparation. The rules of conspiracy, which demand extreme secrecy and caution, have not generally been observed. The governmental power of the country frequently knows in advance about the intentions of the group or groups, either through its secret service or from imprudent revelations or in some cases from outright declarations, as occurred, for example, in our case, in which the invasion was announced and summed up in the phrase of Fidel Castro: "In the year '56 we will be free or we will be martyrs."

Absolute secrecy, a total absence of information in the enemy's hands, should be the primary base of the movement. Secondly and also very important is selection of the human material. At times this selection can be carried out easily, but at others it will be extremely difficult, since it is necessary to rely on those elements that are available, long-time exiles or persons who present themselves when the call goes out simply because they understand that it is their duty to enroll in the battle to liberate their country, etc. There may not be the necessary facilities for making a complete investigation of these individuals. Nevertheless, even though elements of the enemy regime introduce themselves, it is unpardonable that they should later be able to pass information, because in the period just prior to an action all those who are going to participate should be concentrated in secret places known only to one or two persons; they should be under the strict vigilance of their chiefs and without the slightest contact with the outside world. Whenever there are concentrations, whether as a preparation for departure or in order to carry out preliminary training or simply to hide from the police, it is necessary always to keep all new personnel about whom there is no clear knowledge available away from the key places.

In underground conditions no one, absolutely no one, should know anything more than the strictly indispensable; and there ought not to be talk in front of anyone. When certain types of concentration have been carried out, it is necessary even to control letters that leave and arrive in order to have a total knowledge of the contacts that the individuals maintain; no one should be permitted to live alone, nor to go out alone; personal contacts of the future member of the liberating army, contacts of any type, should be prevented by every means. However positive the role of women in the struggle, it must be emphasized that they can also play a destructive part. The weakness for women that young men have when living apart from their habitual medium of life in special, even psychic conditions, is well known. As dictators are well aware of this weakness, they try to use it for infiltrating their spies. At times the relationship of these women with their superiors is clear and even notorious; at other times, it is extremely difficult to discover even the slightest evidence of contact; therefore, it is necessary also to prohibit relations with women.

The revolutionary in a clandestine situation preparing for war should be a complete ascetic; this also serves to test one of the qualities that later will be the basis of his authority, discipline. If an individual repeatedly disobeys orders of his superiors and makes contacts with women, contracts friendships that are not permitted, etc., he should be separated immediately, not merely because of the potential dangers in the contacts, but simply because of the violation of revolutionary discipline.

Unconditional help should not be expected from a government, whether friendly or simply negligent, that allows its territory to be used as a base of operations; one should regard the situation as if he were in a completely hostile camp. The few exceptions that of course can occur are really confirmations of the general rule.

We shall not speak here of the number of persons that should be readied. This depends upon so many and such varied conditions that it is practically impossible to specify. But the minimum number with which it is possible to initiate a guerrilla war can be mentioned. In my opinion, considering the normal desertions and weaknesses in spite of the rigorous process of selection, there should be a nucleus of 30 to 50 men; this figure is sufficient to initiate an armed fight in any country of the Americas with their conditions of favorable territory for operations, hunger for land, repeated attacks upon justice, etc.

Weapons, as has already been said, should be of the same type as those used by the enemy. Considering always that every government is in principle hostile to a guerrilla action being undertaken from its territory, the bands that prepare themselves should not be greater than approximately 50 to 100 men per unit. In other words, though there is no objection to 500 men initiating a war, all 500 should not be concentrated in one place. They are so numerous as to attract attention and in case of any betrayal of confidence or of any raid, the whole group falls; on the other hand, it is more difficult to raid various places simultaneously.

The central headquarters for meetings can be more or less known, and the exiled persons will go there to hold meetings of all types; but the leaders ought not to be present except very sporadically, and there should be no compromising documents. The leaders should use as many different houses as possible, those least likely to be under surveillance. Arms deposits should be distributed in several places, if possible; these should be an absolute secret, known to only one or two people.

Weapons should be delivered into the hands of those who are going to use them only when the war is about to be initiated. Thus a punitive action against persons who are training, while leading to their imprisonment, will not produce a loss of arms that are very difficult to procure. Popular forces are not in any condition to suffer such a loss.

Another important factor to which due attention must be given is preparation of the forces for the extremely hard fight that is going to follow. These forces should have a strict discipline, a high morale, and a clear comprehension of the task to be performed, without conceit, without illusions, without false hopes of an easy triumph. The struggle will be bitter and long, reverses will be suffered; they can be at the brink of annihilation; only high morale, discipline, faith in final victory, and exceptional leadership can save them. This was our Cuban experience; at one time twelve men were able to form the nucleus of the future army, because all these conditions were met and because the one who led us was named Fidel Castro.

Besides ideological and moral preparations, careful physical training is necessary. The guerrillas will, of course, select a mountainous or very wild zone for their operations. At any rate, in whatever situation they find themselves, the basic tactic of the guerrilla army is the march, and neither slow men nor tired men can be tolerated. Adequate training therefore includes exhausting hikes day and night, day after day, increasing gradually, always continued to the brink of exhaustion, with emulation used to increase speed. Resistance and speed will be fundamental qualities of the first guerrilla nucleus. Also a series of theoretical principles can be taught, for example, direction finding, reading, and forms of sabotage. If possible, there should be training with military rifles, frequent firing, above all at distant targets, and much instruction about the way to economize bullets.

To the guerrilla fighter, economy and utilization of ammunition down to the last bullet should be almost like religious tenets. If all these admonitions are followed, the guerrilla forces may well reach their goal.

2. DEFENSE OF POWER
THAT HAS BEEN WON

Naturally victory cannot be considered as finally won until the army that sustained the former regime has been systematically and totally smashed. Further, all the institutions that sheltered the former regime should be wiped out. But since this is a manual for guerrilla bands we will confine ourselves to analyzing the problem of national defense in case of war or aggression against the new power.

The first development we meet is that world public opinion, "the respectable press," the "truthful" news agencies of the United States and of the other countries belonging to the monopolies will begin an attack on the liberated country, an attack as aggressive and systematic as the laws of popular reform. For this reason not even a skeleton of personnel from the former army can be retained. Militarism, mechanical obedience, traditional concepts of military duty, discipline and morale cannot be eradicated with one blow. Nor can the victors, who are good fighters, decent and kind-hearted, but at the same time generally lacking education, be allowed to remain in contact with the vanquished, who are proud of their specialized military knowledge in some combat arm—in mathematics, fortifications, logistics, etc.—and who hate the uncultured guerrilla fighters with all their might.

There are, of course, individual cases of military men who break with the past and enter into the new organization with a spirit of complete cooperation. These persons are doubly useful, because they unite with their love of the people's cause the knowledge necessary for carrying forward the creation of the new popular army. A second step will be consequent upon the first: as the old army is smashed and dismembered as an institution and its former posts occupied by the new army, it will be necessary to reorganize the new force. Its former guerrilla character, operating under independent chiefs without planning, can be changed; but it is very important to emphasize that operational concepts of the guerrilla band should still serve as the guide to structure. These concepts will determine the organic formation and the equipment of the popular army. Care should be taken to avoid the error that we fell into during the first months of trying to put the new popular army into the old bottles of military discipline and ancient organization. This error can cause serious maladjustments and can lead to a complete lack of organization.

Preparation should begin immediately for the new defensive war that will have to be fought by the people's army, accustomed to independence of command within the common struggle and dynamism in the management of each armed group. This army will have two immediate problems. One will be the incorporation of thousands of last-hour revolutionaries, good and bad, whom it is necessary to train for the rigors of guerrilla life and to give revolutionary indoctrination in accelerated and intensive courses. Revolutionary indoctrination that gives the necessary ideological unity to the army of the people is the basis of national security both in the long and short runs. The other problem is the difficulty of adaptation to the new organizational structure.

A corps to take charge of sowing the new truths of the Revolution among all the units of the army should immediately be created. It should explain to the soldiers, peasants, and workers, who have come out of the mass of the people, the justice and the truth of each revolutionary act, the aspirations of the Revolution, why there is a fight, why so many companions have died without seeing the victory. United to this intensive indoctrination, accelerated courses of primary instruction that will begin to overcome illiteracy should also be given, in order to improve the rebel army gradually until it has become an instrument of high technical qualifications, solid ideological structure, and magnificent combat power.

Time will create these three qualities. The military apparatus can continue to be perfected as time goes on; the former combatants can be given special courses to prepare them to serve as professional military men who will then give annual courses of instruction to the people joining voluntarily or by conscription. This will depend on national characteristics and rules cannot be stated.

From this point forward we are expressing the opinion of the command of the Rebel Army with respect to the policy to be followed in the concrete Cuban situation, given the menace of foreign invasion, the conditions of the modern world at the end of 1959 or the beginning of 1960, with the enemy in sight, analyzed, evaluated, and awaited without fear. In other words, we are no longer theorizing for the instruction of others about what has already been done; rather we theorize about what has been done by others in order to apply it ourselves in our own national defense.

As our problem is to theorize about the Cuban case, to locate and test our hypothesis on the map of American realities, we present as an epilogue the following analysis of the Cuban situation, its present and its future.

ANALYSIS
OF THE CUBAN SITUATION,
ITS PRESENT AND ITS FUTURE

A year has now passed since the flight of the dictator, the culmination of a long armed civil struggle by the Cuban people. The achievements of the government in the social, economic, and political fields are enormous; nevertheless, it is necessary to analyze them, to evaluate each act and to show precisely the dimensions of our Cuban Revolution. This national Revolution, fundamentally agrarian, having the enthusiastic support of workers, of people from the middle class and today even of owners of industry, has acquired a continental and world-wide importance, enhanced by its peculiar characteristics and by the inflexible will of the people.

It will not be possible to present a synthesis, however brief, of all the laws passed, all of them undoubtedly of popular benefit. It will be enough to select a few for special emphasis and to show at the same time the logical chain that carries us forward, step by step, in a progressive and necessary order of concern for the problems of the Cuban people.

The first alarm for the parasitic classes of the country is sounded in the rent law, the reduction of electric rates, and government intervention in the telephone

company followed by a reduction in rates, all decreed in rapid succession. Those who had thought
Fidel Castro and the men who made this Revolution
to be nothing more than politicians of the old style,
manageable simpletons with beards their only dis-
tinction, now began to suspect that something deeper
was emerging from the bosom of the Cuban people
and that their privileges were in danger. The word
"Communism" began to envelop the figures of the
leaders and of the triumphant guerrilla fighters; consequently the word anti-Communism, as the position
dialectically opposed, began to serve as a nucleus for
all those who resented the loss of their unjust privileges.

The law on vacant lots and the law on installment
sales aggravated this sensation of malaise among the
usurious capitalists. But these were minor skirmishes
with the reactionaries; everything was still all right
and possible. "This crazy fellow," Fidel Castro, could
be counseled and guided to good paths, to good
"democratic" paths, by a Dubois or a Porter. It was
necessary to place hope in the future.

The Agrarian Reform law was a tremendous jolt.
Most of those who had been hurt now saw clearly.
One of the first was Gaston Baquero, the voice of reaction; he had accurately interpreted what was going
to happen and had retired to quieter scenes under
the Spanish dictatorship. There were still some who
thought that "the law is the law," that other governments had already promulgated such laws, theoretically designed to help the people. Carrying out these
laws was another thing. That brash and complex
child that had the initials INRA for its familiar name
was treated at the beginning with peevish and touch-
ing paternalism within the ivory towers of learning,
pervaded with social doctrines and respectable theories of public finance, to which the uncultivated and
absurd mentalities of the guerrilla fighters could not

arrive. But INRA advanced like a tractor or a war tank, because it is tractor and tank at the same time, breaking down the walls of the great estates as it passed and creating new social relations in the ownership of land. This Cuban Agrarian Reform appeared with various characteristics important for America. It was anti-feudal in the sense that it eliminated the Cuban-style latifundia, annulled all contracts that called for payment of rent of land in crops, and liquidated the servile relations that existed principally in coffee and tobacco production, two important branches of our agriculture. But it also was an Agrarian Reform in a capitalist medium to destroy the pressure of monopoly on human beings, isolated or joined together, to help them work their land honorably and to produce without fear of the creditor or the master. It had the characteristic from the first moment of assuring to peasants and agricultural workers, those who give themselves to the soil, needed technical help from competent personnel; machinery; financial help provided through credits from INRA or para-state banks; and big help from the "Association of People's Stores" that has developed on a large scale in Oriente and is in process of development in other provinces. The state stores, replacing the old usurers, provide just financing and pay a just price for the harvest.

Compared with the other three great agrarian reforms in America (Mexico, Guatemala, and Bolivia) the most important distinctive characteristic is the decision to carry Cuban reform all the way, without concessions or exceptions of any kind. This total Agrarian Reform respects no rights that are not rights of the people nor singles out any class or nationality for discriminatory treatment: the force of the law falls equally on the United Fruit Company and on the King Ranch, as on the big Cuban landowners.

Under these conditions land is being cleared,

mainly for the production of crops which are very important to the country, rice, oil-producing grains and cotton; these are being intensively developed. But the nation is not satisfied and is going to recover all its stolen resources. Its rich sub-soil, which has been a field of monopolist voracity and struggle, is virtually recovered by the petroleum law. This law, like the Agrarian Reform and all the others promulgated by the Revolution, responds to Cuba's irresistible necessities, to urgent demands of a people that wishes to be free, that wishes to be master of its economy, that wishes to prosper and to reach ever higher goals of social development. But for this very reason it is an example for the continent and feared by the oil monopolies. It is not that Cuba directly hurts the petroleum monopoly substantially. There is no reason to believe the country to be rich in reserves of the prized fuel, even though there are reasonable hopes of obtaining a supply that will satisfy its internal needs. On the other hand, by its law Cuba gives a palpable example to the brother peoples of America, many of them foraged by these monopolies or pushed into intercine wars in order to satisfy the necessities or appetites of competing trusts. At the same time Cuba shows the possibility of acting in America and the exact hour when action ought to be considered. The great monopolies also cast their worried look upon Cuba; not only has someone in the little island of the Caribbean dared to liquidate the interests of the omnipotent United Fruit Company, legacy of Mr. Foster Dulles to his heirs; but also the empires of Mr. Rockefeller and the Deutsch group have suffered under the lash of intervention by the popular Cuban Revolution.

This law, like the mining law, is the response of the people to those who try to check them with threats of force, with aerial incursions, with punishments of whatever type. Some say that the mining law is as important as the Agrarian Reform. We do not consider that it has this importance for the economy of the country in general, but it introduces another new feature: a 25 percent tax on the amount of product exported, to be paid by companies that sell our minerals abroad (leaving now something more than a hole in our territory). This not only contributes to our Cuban welfare; it also increases the relative strength of the Canadian monopolies in their struggle with the present exploiters of our nickel. Thus the Cuban Revolution liquidates the latifundia, limits the profits of the foreign monopolies, limits the profits of the foreign intermediaries that dedicate themselves with parasitic capital to the commerce of importation, launches upon the world a new policy in America, dares to break the monopolist status of the giants of mining, and leaves one of them in difficulty, to say the least. This signifies a powerful new message to the neighbors of the great stronghold of monopoly, and causes repercussions throughout America. The Cuban Revolution breaks all the barriers of the news syndicates and diffuses its truth like a shower of dust among the American masses anxious for a better life. Cuba is the symbol of nationality renewed and Fidel Castro the symbol of liberation.

By a simple law of gravity the little island of one hundred fourteen thousand square kilometers and six and one-half million inhabitants assumes the leadership in the anticolonial struggle in America, in which serious handicaps in other countries permit Cuba to take the heroic, glorious and dangerous advanced post. The economically less weak nations of colonial America, the ones in which national capitalism develops haltingly in a continuous, relentless, and at times violent struggle against the foreign monopolies, now cede their place gradually to this small, new champion of liberty, since their governments do not have sufficient force to carry the fight forward. This is not a simple task, nor is it free from danger and difficulties. The backing of a whole people and an enormous charge of idealism and spirit of sacrifice are needed in the nearly solitary conditions in which we are carrying it out in America. Small countries have tried to maintain this post before Guatemala, the Guatemala of Quetzal, that dies when it is imprisoned in a cage, the Guatamala of the Indian Tecum Umam, fell before the direct aggression of the colonialists. Bolivia, the country of Morillo, the proto-martyr of American independence, yielded to the terrible hardships of the struggle after setting three examples that served as the foundation of the Cuban Revolution: the suppression of the army, agrarian reform, and nationalization of mines—maximum source of riches and at the same time maximum source of tragedy.

Cuba knows about these previous examples, knows the failures and the difficulties, but it knows also that we are at the dawning of a new era in the world. The pillars of colonialism have been swept aside by the power of the national and popular struggle in Asia and Africa. Solidarity among peoples does not now come from religion, customs, tastes, racial affinity or its lack. It arises from a similarity in economic and social conditions and from a similarity in desire for progress and recuperation. Asia and Africa joined hands in Bandung; Asia and Africa come to join hands with colonial and indigenous America through Cuba, in Havana.

On the other hand, the great colonial powers have lost ground before the struggle of the peoples. Belgium and Holland are two caricatures of empires; Germany and Italy lost their colonies. France is bitterly fighting a war that is lost. England, diplomatic and skillful, liquidates political power while maintaining the economic connections.

American capitalism replaced some of the old co-

lonial capitalisms in the countries that began their independent life. But it knows that this is transitory
and that there is no real security for its financial spec-
ulations in these new territories. The octopus cannot
there apply its suckers firmly. The claw of the imperial eagle is trimmed. Colonialism is dead or is dying a natural death in all these places.

America is something else. It has been some time
since the English lion with its voracious appetite departed from our America and the young and charm-
ing Yankee capitalists installed the "democratic" version of the English clubs, imposing their sovereign
domination over every one of the twenty republics.

This is the colonial realm of North American monopoly, its reason for being and last hope, the "back-
yard of its own house." If all the Latin American peoples should raise the flag of dignity, as Cuba has
done, monopoly would tremble; it would have to accommodate to a new political-economic situation and
to substantial prunings of profits. Monopoly does not
like profits to be pruned, and the Cuban example,
this "bad example" of national and international dignity, is gaining strength in the countries of America.
Each time that an impudent people cries out for liberation, Cuba is accused; and it is true in a sense that
Cuba is guilty, because Cuba has shown the way, the
way of the armed popular fight against armies supposed to be invincible, the way of struggle in wild
places to wear down and destroy the enemy far from
his bases, in a word, the way of dignity.

This Cuban example is bad, a very bad example,
and monopoly cannot sleep quietly while this bad
example remains at its feet, defying danger, advancing toward the future. It must be destroyed, voices declare. It is necessary to intervene in this bastion of
"Communism," cry the servants of monopoly dis-
guised as representatives in Congress. "The Cuban sit-

uation is very disturbing," say the artful defenders of the trusts; we all know that their meaning is: "It must be destroyed."

Very well. What are the different possibilities of aggressive action to destroy the bad example? One could be called the purely economic. This begins with a restriction on credit by North American banks and suppliers to all businessmen, national banks, and even the National Bank of Cuba. Credit is thus restricted in North America, and through the medium of associates an attempt is made to have the same policy adopted in all the countries of Western Europe; but this alone is not sufficient.

The denial of credits strikes a first strong blow at the economy, but recovery is rapid and the commercial balance evens out, since the victimized country is accustomed to living as best it can. It is necessary to apply more pressure. The sugar quota is brought into the picture: yes, no, no, yes. Hurriedly the calculating machines of the agents of monopoly total up all sorts of accounts and arrive at the final conclusion: it is very dangerous to reduce the Cuban quota and impossible to cancel it. Why very dangerous? Because besides being bad politics, it would awaken the appetite of ten or fifteen other supplier countries, causing them tremendous discomfort, because they would all consider they had a right to something more. It is impossible to cancel the quota, because Cuba is the largest, most efficient, and cheapest provider of sugar to the United States, and because sixty percent of the interests that profit directly from the production and commerce in sugar are United States interests. Besides, the commercial balance is favorable to the United States; whoever does not sell cannot buy; and it would set a bad example to break a treaty. Further, the supposed North American gift of paying nearly three cents above the market price is only the result of North American incapacity to produce sugar cheaply. The high wages and the low productivity of the soil prevent the Great Power from producing sugar at Cuban prices; and by paying this higher price for a product, they are able to impose burdensome treaties on all beneficiaries, not only Cuba. Impossible to liquidate the Cuban quota.

We do not consider likely the possibility that monopolists are employing a variant of the economic approach in bombarding and burning sugar cane fields, hoping to cause a scarcity of the product. Rather this appears to be a measure calculated to weaken confidence in the power of the revolutionary government. (The corpse of the North American mercenary stains more than a Cuban house with blood; it also stains a policy.[6] And what is to be said of the gigantic explosion of arms destined for the Rebel Army?[7])

Another vulnerable place where the Cuban economy can be squeezed is the supply of raw materials, such as cotton. However, it is well known that there is an over-production of cotton in the world, and any difficulty of this type would be transitory. Fuel? This is worth some attention; it is possible to paralyze a country by depriving it of fuel, and Cuba produces very little petroleum. It has some heavy fuel that can be used to operate its steam-driven machinery and some alcohol that can be used in vehicles; also, there are large amounts of petroleum in the world. Egypt can sell it, the Soviet Union can sell it, perhaps Iraq will be able to sell it shortly. It is not possible to develop a purely economic strategy.

As another possibility of aggression, if to this economic variant were added an intervention by some puppet power, the Dominican Republic, for example,

[6] A plane was damaged by the explosion of its own bomb dropped on Cuban territory. It crashed into a house, killing the pilot, who was an American. He carried charts showing that the plane had taken off from a field in Florida. The United States Government apologized.

[7] On March 4, 1960, a Belgian ship, *La Coubré*, loaded with ammunition for the Cuban armed forces, exploded in Havana harbor, killing approximately 100 persons. The cause of the explosion has never been established.

it would be somewhat more of a nuisance; but the United Nations would doubtless intervene, with nothing concrete having been achieved.

Incidentally, the new course taken by the Organization of American States creates a dangerous precedent of intervention. Behind the shield of the Trujillo pretext, monopoly solaces itself by constructing a means of aggression. It is sad that the Venezuelan democracy has put us in the difficult position of having to oppose an intervention against Trujillo. What a good turn it has done the pirates of the continent!

Among the new possibilities of aggression is physical elimination by means of an assault on the old "crazy fellow," Fidel Castro, who has become by now the focus of the monopolies' wrath. Naturally, measures must be arranged so that the other two dangerous "international agents," Raul Castro and the author, are also eliminated. This solution is appealing; if simultaneous assaults on all three or at least on the directing head succeeded, it would be a boon to the reaction. (But do not forget the people, Messrs. Monopolists and agents, the omnipotent people who in their fury at such a crime would crush and erase all those who had anything to do directly or indirectly with an assault on any of the chiefs of the Revolution; it would be impossible to restrain them.)

Another aspect of the Guatemalan variant is to put pressure on the suppliers of arms, in order to force Cuba to buy in Communist countries and then use this as an occasion to let loose another shower of insults. This could give results. "It may be," someone in our government has said, "that they will attack us as Communists, but they are not going to eliminate us as imbeciles."

Thus it begins to appear as if a direct aggression on the part of the monopolies will be necessary; various possible forms are being shuffled and studied in the IBM machines with all processes calculated. It occurs to us at the moment that the Spanish variant could be used. The Spanish variant would be one in which some initial pretext is seized upon for an attack by exiles with the help of volunteers, volunteers who would be mercenaries of course, or simply the troops of a foreign power, well supported by navy and air, well enough supported, shall we say, to be successful. It could also begin as a direct aggression by some state such as the Dominican Republic, which would send some of its men, our brothers, and many mercenaries to die on these beaches in order to provoke war; this would prompt the pure-intentioned monopolists to say that they do not wish to intervene in this "disastrous" struggle between brothers; they will merely limit and confine and freeze the war within its present limits by maintaining vigilance over the skies and seas of this part of America with cruisers, battleships, destroyers, aircraft carriers, submarines, minesweepers, torpedo boats, and airplanes. And it could happen that while these zealous guardians of continental peace were not allowing a single boat to pass with things for Cuba, some, many, or all of the boats headed for the unhappy country of Trujillo would escape the iron vigilance. Also they might intervene through some "reputable" inter-American organ, to put an end to the "foolish war" that "Communism" had unleashed in our island; or, if this mechanism of the "reputable" American organ did not serve, they might intervene directly, as in Korea, using the name of the international organ in order to restore peace and protect the interests of all nations.

Perhaps the first step in the aggression will not be against us, but against the constitutional government of Venezuela, in order to liquidate our last point of support on the continent. If this happens, it is possible that the center of the struggle against colonialism will move from Cuba to the great country of Bolivar. The people of Venezuela will rise to defend their liberties with all the enthusiasm of those who know that they are fighting a decisive battle, that behind defeat lies the darkest tyranny and behind victory the certain future of America. A stream of popular struggles can disturb the peace of the monopolist cemeteries formed out of our subjugated sister republics.

Many reasons argue against the chance of enemy victory, but there are two fundamental ones. The first is external: this is the year 1960, the year that will finally hear the voices of the millions of beings who do not have the luck to be governed by the possessors of the means of death and payment. Further, and this is an even more powerful reason, an army of six million Cubans will grasp weapons as a single man in order to defend its territory and its Revolution. Cuba will be a battlefield where the army will be nothing other than part of the people in arms. After destruction in a frontal war, hundreds of guerrilla bands under a dynamic command and a single center of orientation, will fight the battle all over the country. In cities the workers will die in their factories or centers of work, and in the country the peasants will deal out death to the invader from behind every palm tree and from every furrow of the new mechanically plowed field that the Revolution has given them.

And around the world international solidarity will create a barrier of hundreds of millions of people protesting against aggression. Monopoly will see how its pillars are undermined and how the spider web curtain of its newspaper lies is swept away by a puff. But let us suppose that they dare to defy the popular indignation of the world; what will happen here within?

The first thing to be noted, given our position as an easily vulnerable island without heavy arms, with a very weak air force and navy, is the necessity of applying the guerrilla concept to the fight for national defense.

Our ground units will fight with the fervor, decision, and enthusiasm of which the sons of the Cuban Revolution are capable in these glorious years of our history. But if the worst occurs, we are prepared to continue fighting even after the destruction of our army organization in a frontal combat. In other words, confronting large concentrations of enemy forces that succeed in destroying ours, we would change immediately into a guerrilla army with a good sense of mobility, with unlimited authority in our column commanders, though with a central command located somewhere in the country giving the necessary direction and fixing the general overall strategy.

The mountains would be the last line of defense of the organized armed vanguard of the people, which is the Rebel Army; but in every house of the people, on every road, in every forest, in every piece of national territory the struggle would be fought by the great army of the rearguard, the entire people trained and armed in the manner now to be described.

Since our infantry units will not have heavy arms, they will concentrate on anti-tank and anti-air defense. Mines in very large numbers, bazookas or anti-tank grenades, anti-aircraft cannon of great mobility and mortar batteries will be the only arms of any great power. The veteran infantry soldier, though equipped with automatic weapons, will know the value of ammunition. He will guard it with loving care. Special installations for reloading shells will accompany each unit of the army, maintaining reserves of ammunition even though precariously.

The air force will probably be badly hurt in the first moments of an invasion of this type. We are basing our calculations upon an invasion by a first-class foreign power or by a mercenary army of some other power, helped either openly or surreptitiously by this great power of first magnitude. The national air force, as I said, will be destroyed, or almost destroyed; only reconnaissance or liaison planes will remain, especially helicopters for minor functions.

The navy will also be organized for this mobile strategy; small launches will give the smallest target to the enemy and maintain maximum mobility. The great desperation of the enemy army in this case as before will be to find something· to receive his blows. Instead he will find a gelatinous mass, in movement, impenetrable, that retreats and never presents a solid front, though it inflicts wounds from every side.

It is not easy to overcome an army of the people that is prepared to continue being an army in spite of its defeat in a frontal battle. Two great masses of the people are united around it: the peasants and the workers. The peasants have already given evidence of their efficiency in detaining the small band that was marauding in Pinar del Rio. These peasants will be trained principally in their own regions; but the platoon commanders and the superior officers will be trained, as is now already being done, in our military bases. From there they will be distributed throughout the thirty zones of agrarian development that form the new geographical division of the country. This will constitute thirty more centers of peasant struggle, charged with defending to the maximum their lands, their social conquests, their new houses, their canals, their dams, their flowering harvests, their independence, in a word, their right to live.

At the beginning they will oppose also a firm resistance to any enemy advance, but if this proves too strong for them, they will disperse, each peasant becoming a peaceful cultivator of his soil during the day and a fearsome guerrilla fighter at night, scourge of the enemy forces. Something similar will take place

among the workers; the best among them will be
trained also to serve thereafter as chiefs of their companions, teaching them principles of defense. Each
social class, however, will have different tasks. The
peasant will fight a battle typical of the guerrilla
fighter; he should learn to be a good shot, to take advantage of all the difficulties of the ground and to
disappear without ever showing his face. The workers,
on the other hand, have the advantage of being within
a modern city, which is a large and efficient fortress;
at the same time their lack of mobility is a drawback.
The worker will learn first to block the streets with
barricades of any available vehicle, furniture, or
utensil; to use every block as a fortress with communications formed by holes made in interior walls; to use
that terrible arm of defense, the "Molotov cocktail";
and to coordinate his fire from the innumerable loop-
holes provided by the houses of a modern city.

From the worker masses assisted by the national
police and those armed forces charged with the defense of the city, a powerful block of the army will
be formed; but it must expect to suffer great losses.
The struggle in the cities in these conditions cannot
achieve the facility and flexibility of the struggle in
the countryside: many will fall, including many leaders, in this popular struggle. The enemy will use tanks
that will be destroyed rapidly as soon as the people
learn their weaknesses and not to fear them; but before that the tanks will leave their balance of victims.

There will also be other organizations related to
those of workers and peasants: first, the student militias, which will contain the flower of the student
youth, directed and coordinated by the Rebel Army;
organizations of youth in general, who will participate
in the same way; and organizations of women, who
will provide an enormous encouragement by their
presence and who will do such auxiliary tasks for their
companions in the struggle as cooking, taking care of

the wounded, giving final comfort to those who are
dying, doing laundry, in a word, showing their com-
panions-in-arms that they will never be absent in the
difficult moments of the Revolution. All this is
achieved by wide-scale organization of the masses
supplemented with patient and careful education, an
education that begins and is confirmed in knowledge
acquired from their own experience; it should concentrate on reasoned and true explanations of the
facts of the Revolution.

The revolutionary laws should be discussed, explained, studied in every meeting, in every assembly,
wherever the leaders of the Revolution are present for
any purpose. Also, the speeches of the leaders, and in
our case particularly of the undisputed leader, should
constantly be read, commented upon, and discussed. People should come together in the country to
listen by radio, and where there are more advanced
facilities, to watch by television these magnificent
popular lessons that our Prime Minister gives.

The participation of the people in politics, that is
to say, in the expression of their own desires made
into laws, decrees, and resolutions, should be constant. Vigilance against any manifestations opposed
to the Revolution should also be constant; and vigilance over morale within the revolutionary masses
should be stricter, if this is possible, than vigilance
against the non-revolutionary or the disaffected. It
can never be permitted, lest the Revolution take the
dangerous path of opportunism, that a revolutionary
of any category should be excused for grave offenses
against decorum or morality simply because he is a
revolutionary. The record of his former services may
provide extenuating circumstances and they can always be considered in deciding upon the punishment, but the act itself must always be punished.

Respect for work, above all for collective work and
work for collective ends, ought to be cultivated. Vol-

unteer brigades to construct roads, bridges, docks or dams, and school cities should receive a strong impulse; these serve to forge a unity among persons showing their love for the Revolution with works.

An army that is linked in such ways with the people, that feels this intimacy with the peasants and the workers from which it emerged, that knows besides all the special techniques of its warfare and is psychologically prepared for the worst contingencies, is invincible; and it will be even more invincible as it makes the just phrase of our immortal Camilo a part of the flesh of the army and the citizenry: "The army is the people in uniform." Therefore, for all these reasons, despite the necessity that monopoly suppress the "bad example" of Cuba, our future is brighter than ever.

GUERRILLA WARFARE: A METHOD

Guerrilla warfare has been employed on innumerable occasions throughout history in different circumstances to obtain different objectives. Lately it has been employed in various popular wars of liberation when the vanguard of the people chose the road of irregular armed struggle against enemies of superior military power. Asia, Africa, and Latin America have been the scene of such actions in attempts to obtain power in the struggle against feudal, neo-colonial, or colonial exploitation. In Europe, guerrilla units were used as a supplement to native or allied regular armies.

In America, guerrilla warfare has been employed on several occasions. As a case in point, we have the experience of César Augusto Sandino fighting against the Yankee expeditionary force on the Segovia of Nicaragua. Recently we had Cuba's revolutionary war. Since then in America the problem of guerrilla war has been raised in discussions of theory by the progressive parties of the continent with the question of whether its utilization is possible or convenient. This has become the topic of very controversial polemics.

This article will express our views on guerrilla warfare and its correct utilization. Above all, we must emphasize at the outset that this form of struggle is a means to an end. That end, essential and inevitable for any revolutionary, is the conquest of political power. Therefore, in the analysis of specific situations in different countries of America, we must use the concept of guerrilla warfare in the limited sense of a method of struggle in order to gain that end.

Almost immediately the question arises: Is guerrilla warfare the only formula for seizing power in all of Latin America? Or, at any rate, will it be the predominant form? Or simply, will it be one formula among many used during the struggle? And ultimately we may ask: Will Cuba's example be applicable to the present situation on the continent? In the course of polemics, those who want to undertake guerrilla warfare are criticized for forgetting mass struggle, implying that guerrilla warfare and mass struggle are opposed to each other. We reject this implication, for guerrilla warfare is a people's war; to attempt to carry out this type of war without the population's support is the prelude to inevitable disaster. The guerrilla is the combat vanguard of the people, situated in a specified place in a certain region, armed and willing to carry out a series of warlike actions for the one possible strategic end—the seizure of power. The guerrilla is supported by the peasant and worker masses of the region and of the whole territory in which it acts. Without these prerequisites, guerrilla warfare is not possible.

We consider that the Cuban Revolution made three fundamental contributions to the laws of the revolutionary movement in the current situation in America. First, people's forces can win a war against the army. Second, one need not always wait for all conditions favorable to revolution to be present; the insurrection itself can create them. Third, in the underdeveloped parts of America, the battleground for armed struggle should in the main be the countryside. (*Guerrilla Warfare*)

Such are the contributions to the development of the revolutionary struggle in America, and they can be applied to any of the countries on our continent where guerrilla warfare may develop.

The Second Declaration of Havana points out,

In our countries two circumstances are joined: underdeveloped industry and an agrarian system of feudal character. That is why no matter how hard the living conditions of the urban workers are, the rural population lives under even more horrible conditions of oppression and exploitation. But, with few exceptions, it also constitutes the absolute majority, sometimes more than 70 percent of the Latin American population.

Not counting the landlords who often live in the cities, this great mass earns its livelihood by working as peons on plantations earning miserable wages. Or they till the soil under conditions of exploitation no different than those of the Middle Ages. These circumstances determine in Latin America that the poor rural population constitutes a tremendous potential revolutionary force.

The armies are set up and equipped for conventional warfare. They are the force whereby the power of the exploiting classes is maintained. When they are confronted with the irregular warfare of peasants based on their home ground, they become absolutely powerless; they lose ten men for every revolutionary fighter who falls. Demoralization among them mounts rapidly when they are beset by an invisible and invincible army which provides them no chance to display their military academy tactics and their military fanfare, of which they boast so much, to repress the city workers and students.

The initial struggle of small fighting units is constantly nurtured by new forces; the mass movement begins to grow bold, the old order bit by bit breaks into a thousand pieces, and that is when the working class and the urban masses decide the battle.

What is it that from the very beginning of the fight makes those units invincible, regardless of the number, strength, and resources of their enemies? It is the people's support, and they can count on an ever-increasing mass support.

But the peasantry is a class which, because of the ignorance in which it has been kept and the isolation in which it lives, requires the revolutionary and political leadership of the working class and the revolutionary intellectuals. Without that, it cannot alone launch the struggle and achieve victory.

In the present historical conditions of Latin America, the national bourgeoisie cannot lead the antifeudal and anti-imperialist struggle. Experience demonstrates that in our nations this class—even when its interests clash with those of Yankee imperialism—has been incapable of confronting imperialism, paralyzed by fear of social revolution and frightened by the clamor of the exploited masses.

Completing the foresight of the preceding statements, which constitute the essence of the revolutionary declaration of Latin America, the Second Declaration of Havana in the following paragraphs states:

The subjective conditions in each country, the factors of revolutionary consciousness, of organization, of leadership, can accelerate or delay revolution, depending on the state of their development. Sooner or later, in each historic epoch, as objective conditions ripen, consciousness is acquired, organization is achieved, leadership arises, and revolution is produced.

Whether this takes place peacefully or comes into the world after painful labor does not depend on the revolutionaries; it depends on the reactionary forces of the old society. Revolution, in history, is like the doctor who assists at the birth of a new life: he does not use forceps unless necessary, but he will unhesitatingly use them every time labor requires them. It is a labor which brings the hope of a better life to the enslaved and exploited masses.

In many Latin American countries revolution is inevitable. This fact is not determined by the will of anyone. It is determined by the horrible conditions of exploitation under which the American people live, the development of a revolutionary consciousness in the masses, the worldwide crisis of imperialism, and the universal liberation movements of the subjugated nations.

We shall begin from this basis to analyze the whole matter of guerrilla warfare in Latin America.

We have already established that it is a means of struggle to attain an end. First, our concern is to analyze the end in order to determine whether the winning of power in Latin America can be achieved in other ways than armed struggle. Peaceful struggle can be carried out through mass movements compelling—in special crisis situations—the governments to yield; thus, eventually the popular forces would take over and establish a dictatorship of the proletariat. Theoretically this is correct. When analyzing this in the Latin American context, we must reach the following conclusions: Generally on this continent there exist objective conditions which propel the masses to violent actions against their bourgeois and landlord governments. In many countries there exist crises of power and also some subjective conditions for revolution. It is clear, of course, that in those countries where all of these conditions are found, it would be criminal not to act to seize power. In other countries where these conditions do not occur, it is right that different alternatives will appear and out of theoretical discussions the tactic proper to each country should emerge. The only thing which history does not admit is that the analysts and executors of proletarian policy be mistaken.

No one can solicit the role of vanguard of the party as if it were a diploma given by a university. To be the vanguard of the party means to be at the forefront of the working class through the struggle for achieving power. It means to know how to guide this fight through shortcuts to victory. This is the mission of our revolutionary parties and thus the analysis must be profound and exhaustive so that there will be no mistakes.

At the present time we can observe in America an unstable balance between oligarchical dictatorship and popular pressure. We mean by "oligarchical" the reactionary alliance between the bourgeoisie and the landowning class of each country which has a greater or lesser preponderance of feudalism.

These dictatorships carry on within a certain "legal" framework which they adjudicated themselves to facilitate their work throughout the unrestricted period of their class domination. Yet we are passing through a stage in which the masses' pressure is very strong and is straining bourgeois legality so that its own authors must violate it in order to halt the impetus of the masses.

Barefaced violation of all legislation or of laws specifically instituted to sanction ruling class deeds only increases the tension of the people's forces. Thus the oligarchical dictatorship attempts to use the old legal order to change constitutionality and further oppress the proletariat without a frontal clash. Nevertheless, at this point, a contradiction arises. The people no longer support the old much less the new coercive measures established by the dictatorship and try to smash them. We should never forget the class character, authoritarian and restrictive, which typifies the bourgeois state. Lenin refers to it in the following manner: "The state is the product and the manifestation of the irreconcilability of class antagonisms. The state arises when, where, and to the extent that class antagonisms objectively cannot be reconciled. And, conversely, the existence of the state proves that class antagonisms are irreconcilable." (*State and Revolution*)

In other words, we should not allow the word "democracy" to be utilized apologetically to represent the dictatorship of the exploiting classes and to lose its deeper meaning and acquire the meaning of granting the people certain liberties, more or less good. To struggle only to restore a certain degree of bourgeois legality without considering the question of revolutionary power is to struggle for the return of a dictatorial order established by the dominant social classes. In other words, it is to struggle for a lighter iron ball to be fixed to the prisoner's chain.

In these conditions of conflict, the oligarchy breaks its own contracts, its own mask of "democracy," and attacks the people, though it will always try to use the superstructure it has formed for oppression. Thus, we are faced once again with a dilemma: What must be done? Our reply is: Violence is not the monopoly of the exploiters and as such the exploited can use it too and, what is more, ought to use it when the moment arrives. Martí said, "He who wages war in a country, when he can avoid it, is a criminal, just as he who fails to promote war which cannot be avoided is a criminal."

Lenin said, "Social democracy has never taken a sentimental view of war. It unreservedly condemns war as a bestial means of settling conflicts in human society. But social democracy knows that as long as society is divided into classes, as long as there is exploitation of man by man, wars are inevitable. In order to end this exploitation we cannot walk away from war, which is always and everywhere begun by the exploiters, by the ruling and oppressing classes." He said this in 1905. Later in the "Military Program of the Proletarian Revolution," a far-reaching analysis of the nature of class struggle, he affirmed: "Whoever recognizes the class struggle cannot fail to recognize civil wars, which in every class society are the natural, and under certain conditions, inevitable continuation, development, and intensification of the class struggle. All the great revolutions prove this. To repudiate civil war, or to forget about it, would mean sinking into extreme opportunism and renouncing the socialist revolution." That is to say, we should not fear violence, the midwife of new societies; but violence should be unleashed at that precise moment in which the leaders have found the most favorable circumstances.

What will these be? Subjectively, they depend on two factors which complement each other and which deepen during the struggle: consciousness of the necessity of change and confidence in the possibility of this revolutionary change. Both of these factors, with the objective conditions (which are favorable in all Latin America for the development of the struggle), with the firm will to achieve it as well as the new correlation of forces in the world, will determine the mode of action.

Regardless of how far away the socialist countries may be, their favorable influence will be felt by the people who struggle, just as their example will give the people further strength. Fidel Castro said on July 26 [1963]: "And the duty of the revolutionaries, especially at this moment, is to know how to recognize and how to take advantage of the changes in the correlation of forces which have taken place in the world and to understand that these changes facilitate the people's struggle. The duty of revolutionaries, of Latin American revolutionaries, is not to wait for the change in the correlation of forces to produce a miracle of social revolutions in Latin America but to take full advantage of everything in it that is favorable to the revolutionary movement—and to make revolution!"

There are some who say, "Let us admit that in certain specific cases revolutionary war is the best means to achieve political power; but where do we find the great leaders, the Fidel Castros, who will lead us to victory?" Fidel Castro, as any human being, is the product of history. The political and military chieftains who will lead the insurrectional uprisings in America, merged if possible in one man, will learn the art of war during the course of war itself. There is neither trade nor profession that can be learned from books alone. In this case, the struggle itself is the great teacher.

Of course, the task will not be easy nor is it exempt from grave dangers throughout. During the development of armed struggle, there are two moments of extreme danger for the future of the revolution. The first of these arises in the preparatory stage and the way with which it is dealt will give the measure of determination to struggle as well as clarity of purpose of the people's forces. When the bourgeois state advances against the people's positions, obviously there must arise a process of defense against the enemy who at this point, being superior, attacks. If the basic subjective and objective conditions are ripe, the defense must be armed so that the popular forces will not merely become recipients of the enemy's blows. Nor should the armed defense camp be allowed to be transformed into the refuge of the pursued.

Guerrilla warfare may adopt a defensive movement at a certain point, yet it carries within itself the capacity to attack the enemy and must develop it constantly. This capacity is what determines, with the passing of time, the catalytic character of the people's forces. That is, guerrilla warfare is not passive self-defense; it is defense with attack. And from the moment we recognize it as such, it has as its final goal the conquest of political power.

This moment is important. In social processes the difference between violence and nonviolence cannot be measured by the number of shots exchanged; rather, it lies in concrete and fluctuating situations. And we must be able to see the right moment in which the people's forces, conscious of their relative weakness and their strategic strength, must take the initiative against the enemy so the situation will not deteriorate. The equilibrium between oligarchic dictatorship and the popular pressure must be changed. The dictatorship tries to function without resorting to force. Thus, we must try to oblige the dictatorship to resort to violence, thereby unmasking its true nature as the dictatorship of the reactionary social classes. This event will deepen the struggle to such an extent that there will be no retreat from it. The performance of the people's forces depends on the task of forcing the dictatorship to a decision—to retreat or unleash the struggle—thus beginning the stage of long-range armed action.

The skillful avoidance of the next dangerous moment depends on the growing power of the people's forces. Marx always recommended that once the revolutionary process has begun the proletariat strike blows again and again without rest. A revolution which does not constantly expand is a revolution which regresses. The fighters, if weary, begin to lose faith; and at this point some of the bourgeois maneuvers may bear fruit—for example, the holding of elections to turn the government to another gentleman with a sweeter voice and more angelic face than the outgoing tyrant or the staging of a coup by reactionaries generally led by the army with the direct or indirect support of the progressive forces. There are others, but it is not our intention to analyze such tactical stratagems.

Let us emphasize the military coup mentioned previously. What can the military contribute to democracy? What kind of loyalty can be asked of them if they are merely an instrument for the domination of the reactionary classes and imperialist monopolies and if, as a caste whose worth rests on the weapon in their hands, they aspire only to maintain their prerogatives?

When, in difficult situations for the oppressors, the military establishment conspires to overthrow a dictator who in fact has been defeated, it can be said that they do so because the dictator is unable to preserve their class prerogatives without extreme violence, a method which generally does not suit the interests of the oligarchies at that point.

This statement does not mean to reject the service of military men as individual fighters who, once separated from the society they served, have in fact now rebelled against it. They should be used in accordance with the revolutionary line they adopt as fighters and not as representatives of a caste.

A long time ago Engels, in the preface to the third edition of *Civil War in France,* wrote,

The workers were armed after every revolution; for this reason the disarming of the workers was the first commandment for the bourgeois at the helm of the state. Hence, after every revolution won by the workers, a new struggle ending with the defeat of the workers. (Quoted by Lenin in *State and Revolution*)

This play of continuous struggle, in which some change is obtained and then strategically withdrawn, has been repeated for many dozens of years in the capitalist world. Moreover, the permanent deception of the proletariat along these lines has been practiced for over a century.

There is danger also that progressive party leaders, wishing to maintain conditions more favorable for revolutionary action through the use of certain aspects of bourgeois legality, will lose sight of their goal (which is common during the action), thus forgetting the primary strategic objective: the seizure of power.

These two difficult moments in the revolution, which we have analyzed briefly, become obvious when the leaders of

Marxist-Leninist parties are capable of perceiving the implications of the moment clearly and of mobilizing the masses to the fullest, leading them on the correct path of resolving fundamental contradictions.

In developing the thesis, we have assumed that eventually the idea of armed struggle as well as the formula of guerrilla warfare as a method of struggle will be accepted. Why do we think that in the present situation of America guerrilla warfare is the best method? There are fundamental arguments which in our opinion determine the necessity of guerrilla action as the central axis of struggle in Latin America.

First, accepting as true that the enemy will fight to maintain itself in power, one must think about destroying the oppressor army. To do this, a people's army is necessary. This army is not born spontaneously; rather it must be armed from the enemy's arsenal and this requires a long and difficult struggle in which the people's forces and their leaders will always be exposed to attack from superior forces and be without adequate conditions of defense and maneuverability.

On the other hand, the guerrilla nucleus, established in terrain favorable for the struggle, ensures the security and continuity of the revolutionary command. The urban forces, led by the general staff of the people's army, can perform actions of the greatest importance. However, the eventual destruction of these groups would not kill the soul of the revolution; its leadership would continue from its rural bastion to spark the revolutionary spirit of the masses and would continue to organize new forces for other battles.

Moreover, in this region begins the construction of the future state apparatus entrusted to lead the class dictatorship efficiently during the transition period. The longer the struggle becomes, the larger and more complex the administrative problems; and in solving them, cadres will be trained for the difficult task of consolidating power and, at a later stage, economic development.

Second, there is the general situation of the Latin American peasantry and the ever more explosive character of the struggle against feudal structures within the framework of an alliance between local and foreign exploiters.

Returning to the Second Declaration of Havana,

At the outset of the past century, the peoples of America freed themselves from Spanish colonialism, but they did not free themselves from exploitation. The feudal landlords assumed the authority of the governing Spaniards, the Indians continued in their painful serfdom, the Latin American man remained a slave one way or another, and the minimum hopes of the peoples died under the power of the oligarchies and the tyranny of foreign capital. This is the truth of America, to one or another degree of variation. Latin America today is under a more ferocious imperialism, more powerful and ruthless, than the Spanish colonial empire.

What is Yankee imperialism's attitude confronting the objective and historically inexorable reality of the Latin American revolution? To prepare to fight a colonial war against the peoples of Latin America; to create an apparatus of force to establish the political pretexts and the pseudo-legal instruments underwritten by the representatives of the reactionary oligarchies in order to curb, by blood and by iron, the struggle of the Latin American peoples.

This objective situation shows the dormant force of our peasants and the need to utilize it for Latin America's liberation.

Third, there is the continental nature of the struggle. Could we imagine this stage of Latin American emancipation as the confrontation of two local forces struggling for power in a specific territory? Hardly. The struggle between the people's forces and the forces of repression will be to the death. This too is predicted by the paragraphs cited previously.

The Yankees will intervene due to solidarity of interest and because the struggle in Latin America is decisive. As a matter of fact, they are intervening already as they prepare the forces of repression and the organization of a continental apparatus of struggle. But, from now on, they will do so with all their energies; they will punish the popular forces with all the destructive weapons at their disposal. They will not allow a revolutionary power to consolidate; and, if it ever happens, they will attack again, will not recognize it, and will try to divide the revolutionary forces. Moreover, they will infiltrate saboteurs, create border problems, will force other reactionary states to oppose it, and will impose economic sanctions attempting, in one word, to annihilate the new state.

This being the panorama in Latin America, it is difficult to achieve and consolidate victory in a country which is isolated. The unity of the repressive forces must be confronted with the unity of the popular forces. In all countries where oppression reaches intolerable proportions, the banner of rebellion must be raised; and this banner of historical necessity will have a continental character.

As Fidel stated, the cordilleras of the Andes will be the Sierra Maestra of Latin America; and the immense territories which this continent encompasses will become the scene of a life or death struggle against imperialism.

We cannot predict when this struggle will reach a continental dimension nor how long it will last. But we can predict its advent and triumph because it is the inevitable result of historical, economic, and political conditions; and its direction cannot change.

The task of the revolutionary forces in each country is to initiate the struggle when the conditions are present there, regardless of the conditions in other countries. The development of the struggle will bring about the general strategy. The prediction of the continental character of the struggle is the outcome of the analysis of the strength of each contender, but this does not exclude independent outbreaks. As the beginning of the struggle in one area of a country is bound to cause its development throughout the region, the beginning of a revolutionary war contributes to the development of new conditions in the neighboring countries.

The development of revolution has normally produced high and low tides in inverse proportion. To the revolution's high tide corresponds the counterrevolutionary low tide and vice versa, as there is a counterrevolutionary ascendancy at moments of revolutionary decline. In those moments, the situation of the people's forces becomes difficult; and they should resort to the best means of defense in order to suffer the least damage. The enemy is extremely powerful, it is of continental scope. For this reason, the relative weakness of the local bourgeoisie cannot be analyzed with a view toward making decisions within restricted boundaries. Still less can one think of an eventual alliance by these oligarchies with a people in arms.

The Cuban Revolution sounded the bell which gave the alarm. The polarization of forces will become complete: exploiters on one side and exploited on the other. And the mass of the petty bourgeoisie will lean to one side or the other according to their interests and the political skill with which they are handled. Thus, neutrality will be an exception. This is how revolutionary war will be.

Let us think how a guerrilla focus can start. Nuclei with relatively few persons choose places favorable for guerrilla warfare, with the intention of unleashing a counterattack or to weather the storm, and there they start taking action. However, what follows must be very clear: At the beginning the relative weakness of the guerrilla is such that they should work only toward becoming acquainted with the terrain and its surroundings while establishing connections with the population and fortifying the places which eventually will be converted into bases.

A guerrilla force which has just begun its development must follow three conditions in order to survive: constant mobility, constant vigilance, constant distrust. Without the adequate use of these three conditions of military tactics, the guerrilla will find it hard to survive. We must remember that the heroism of the guerrilla fighter, at this moment, consists of the scope of the planned goal and the enormous number of sacrifices that he must make in order to achieve it. These sacrifices are not made in daily combat or face-to-face battle with the enemy; rather, they will adopt more subtle and difficult forms for the guerrilla fighter to resist physically and mentally.

Perhaps the guerrillas will be punished heavily by the enemy, divided at times into groups with those who are captured to be tortured. They will be pursued as hunted animals in areas where they have chosen to operate; the constant anxiety of having the enemy on their track will be with them. They must distrust everyone, for the terrorized peasants in some cases will give them away to the repressive troops in order to save themselves. Their only alternatives are life or death, at times when death is a concept a thousand times present and victory only a myth for a revolutionary to dream of.

This is the guerrilla's heroism. This is why it is said that walking is a form of fighting and to avoid combat at a given moment is also another form. Facing the general superiority of the enemy at a given place, one must find a form of tactics with which to gain a relative superiority at that moment either by being capable of concentrating more troops than the enemy or by using fully and well the terrain in order to secure advantages that unbalance the correlation of forces. In these conditions, tactical victory is assured; if relative superiority is not clear, it is better not to act. As long as the guerrilla is in the position of deciding the "how" and the "when," no combat should be fought that will not end in victory.

Within the framework of the great politicomilitary action, of which they are a part, the guerrilla will grow and reach consolidation. Thus, bases will continue to be formed, for they are essential to the success of the guerrilla army. These bases are points which the enemy can enter only at the cost of heavy losses; they are the revolution's bastions, both refuge and starting point for the guerrilla's more daring and distant raids.

One comes to this point if difficulties of a tactical and political nature have been overcome. The guerrillas cannot forget their function as vanguard of the people—their mandate— and as such they must create the necessary political conditions for the establishment of a revolutionary power based on the masses' support. The peasants' aspirations or demands must be satisfied to the degree and form which circumstances permit so as to bring about the decisive support and solidarity of the whole population.

If the military situation will be difficult from the very first moment, the political situation will be just as delicate; if a single military error can liquidate the guerrilla, a political error can hold back its development for long periods. The struggle is politico-military and as such it must be developed and understood.

In the process of the guerrilla growth, the fighting reaches a point where its capacity for action covers a given region for which there are too many men in too great a concentration in the area. There begins the beehive action in which one of the commanders, a distinguished guerrilla, hops to another region and repeats the chain of development of guerrilla warfare. He is, nevertheless, subject to a central command.

It is imperative to point out that one cannot hope for victory without the formation of a popular army. The guerrilla forces can be expanded to a certain magnitude; the people's forces, in the cities and in other areas, can inflict losses; but the military potential of the reactionaries will still remain intact. One must always keep in mind the fact that the final objective is the enemy's annihilation. Therefore, all these new zones which are being created, as well as the zones infiltrated behind enemy lines and the forces operating in the principal cities, should be under one unified command.

Guerrilla war or war of liberation will generally have three stages: First, the strategic defensive when the small force nibbles at the enemy and runs; it is not sheltered to make a passive defense within a small circumference but rather its defense consists of the limited attacks which it can strike successfully. After this comes a state of equilibrium in which the possibilities of action on both sides—the enemy and the guerrillas— are established. Finally, the last stage consists of overrunning the repressive army leading to the capture of the big cities, large-scale decisive encounters, and at last the complete annihilation of the enemy.

After reaching a state of equilibrium when both sides respect each other and as the war's development continues, the guerrilla war acquires new characteristics. The concept of maneuver is introduced: large columns which attack strong points; mobile warfare with the shifting of forces and means of attack of relative potential. But due to the capacity for resistance and counterattack that the enemy still has, this war of maneuver does not replace guerrilla fighting: rather, it is only one form of action taken by the guerrillas until that time when they crystallize into a people's army with an army corps. Even at this moment the guerrilla, marching ahead of the action of the main forces, will play the role of its first stage, destroying communications and sabotaging the whole defensive apparatus of the enemy.

We have predicted that the war will be continental. This means that it will be a protracted war; it will have many fronts; and it will cost much blood and countless lives for a long period of time. But another phenomenon occurring in Latin America is the polarization of forces, that is, the clear division between exploiters and exploited. Thus when the armed vanguard of the people achieves power, both the imperialists and the national exploiting class will be liquidated at one stroke. The first stage of the socialist revolution will have crystallized, and the people will be ready to heal their wounds and initiate the construction of socialism.

Are there possibilities less bloody? Awhile ago the last dividing up of the world took place in which the United States took the lion's share of our continent. Today the imperialists of the Old World are developing again—and the strength of the European Common Market frightens the United States itself. All this might lead to the belief that there exists the possibility for us merely to observe as spectators the struggle among the imperialists trying to make further advances, perhaps in alliance with the stronger national bourgeoisie. Yet a passive policy never brings good results in class struggle and alliances with the bourgeoisie, though they might appear to be revolutionary, have only a transitory character. The time factor will induce us to choose another ally. The sharpening of the most important contradiction in Latin America appears to be so rapid that it disturbs the "normal" development of the imperialist camp's contradiction in its struggle for markets.

The majority of national bourgeoisie have united with North American imperialism; thus their fate shall be the same as that of the latter. Even in the cases where pacts or common contradictions are shared between the national bourgeoisie and other imperialists, this occurs within the framework of a fundamental struggle which will embrace sooner or later *all the exploited and all the exploiters.* The polarization of antagonistic forces among class adversaries is up till now more rapid than the development of the contradiction among exploiters over the splitting of the spoils. There are two camps: the alternative becomes clearer for each individual and for each specific stratum of the population.

The Alliance for Progress attempts to slow that which cannot be stopped. But if the advance of the European Common Market or any other imperialist group on the American market were more rapid than the development of the fundamental contradiction, the forces of the people would only have to penetrate into the open breach, carrying on the struggle and using the new intruders with a clear awareness of what their true intentions are.

Not a single position, weapon, or secret should be given to the class enemy, under penalty of losing all. In fact, the eruption of the Latin American struggle has begun. Will its storm center be in Venezuela, Guatemala, Colombia, Peru, Ecuador? Are today's skirmishes only manifestations of a restlessness that has not come to fruition? The outcome of today's struggles does not matter. It does not matter in the final count that one or two movements were temporarily defeated because what is definite is the decision to struggle which matures every day, the consciousness of the need for revolutionary change, and the certainty that it is possible.

This is a prediction. We make it with the conviction that history will prove us right. The analysis of the objective and subjective conditions of Latin America and the imperialist world indicates to us the certainty of these assertions based on the Second Declaration of Havana.

SOURCE: *Cuba Socialista* (Havana), September 1963, pp. 1–17.

MESSAGE TO THE
TRICONTINENTAL

Now is the time of the furnaces, and
only light should be seen.

José Martí

Twenty-one years have already elapsed since the end of the last
world conflagration; numerous publications, in every possible
language, celebrate this event, symbolized by the defeat of
Japan. There is a climate of apparent optimism in many areas of
the different camps into which the world is divided.

Twenty-one years without a world war, in these times of
maximum confrontations, of violent clashes and sudden
changes, appears to be a very high figure. However, without
analyzing the practical results of this peace (poverty, degrada-
tion, increasingly larger exploitation of enormous sectors of
humanity) for which all of us have stated that we are willing to
fight, we would do well to inquire if this peace is real.

It is not the purpose of these notes to detail the different conflicts of a local character that have been occurring since the
surrender of Japan, neither do we intend to recount the numerous and increasing instances of civilian strife which have
taken place during these years of apparent peace. It will be
enough just to name, as an example against undue optimism,
the wars of Korea and Vietnam.

In the first one, after years of savage warfare, the Northern
part of the country was submerged in the most terrible devasta-

tion known in the annals of modern warfare: riddled with bombs; without factories, schools or hospitals; with absolutely no shelter for housing ten million inhabitants.

Under the discredited flag of the United Nations, dozens of countries under the military leadership of the United States participated in this war with the massive intervention of U.S. soldiers and the use, as cannon fodder, of the South Korean population that was enrolled. On the other side, the army and the people of Korea and the volunteers from the Peoples' Republic of China were furnished with supplies and advice by the Soviet military apparatus. The U.S. tested all sorts of weapons of destruction, excluding the thermonuclear type, but including, on a limited scale, bacteriological and chemical warfare.

In Vietnam, the patriotic forces of that country have carried on an almost uninterrupted war against three imperialist powers: Japan, whose might suffered an almost vertical collapse after the bombs of Hiroshima and Nagasaki; France, who recovered from that defeated country its Indo-China colonies and ignored the promises it had made in harder times; and the United States, in this last phase of the struggle.

There were limited confrontations in every continent although in Our America, for a long time, there were only incipient liberation struggles and military coups d'etat until the Cuban revolution resounded the alert, signaling the importance of this region. This action attracted the wrath of the imperialists and Cuba was finally obliged to defend its coasts, first in Playa Girón, and again during the Missile Crisis.

This last incident could have unleashed a war of incalculable proportions if a U.S.-Soviet clash had occurred over the Cuban question.

But, evidently, the focal point of all contradictions is at present the territory of the peninsula of Indo-China and the adjacent areas. Laos and Vietnam are torn by a civil war which has ceased being such by the entry into the conflict of U.S. imperialism with all its might, thus transforming the whole zone into a dangerous detonator ready at any moment to explode.

In Vietnam the confrontation has assumed extremely acute characteristics. It is not our intention, either, to chronicle this war. We shall simply remember and point out some milestones.

In 1954, after the annihilating defeat of Dien-Bien-Phu, an agreement was signed at Geneva dividing the country into two separate zones; elections were to be held within a term of 18 months to determine who should govern Vietnam and how the country should be reunified. The U.S. did not sign this document and started maneuvering to substitute the emperor, Bao-Dai, who was a French puppet, for a man more amiable to its purposes. This happened to be Ngo-Din-Diem, whose tragic end—that of an orange squeezed dry by imperialism—is well known by all.

During the months following the agreement, optimism reigned supreme in the camp of the popular forces. The last pockets of the anti-French resistance were dismantled in the South of the country—and they awaited the fulfillment of the Geneva agreements. But the patriots soon realized there would be no elections—unless the United States felt itself capable of imposing its will in the polls, which was practically impossible even resorting to all its fraudulent methods. Once again the fighting broke out in the South and gradually acquired full intensity. At present the U.S. army has increased to over half a million invaders while the puppet forces decrease in number and, above all, have totally lost their combativeness.

Almost two years ago the United States started bombing systematically the Democratic Republic of Vietnam, in yet another attempt to overcome the belligerance [sic] of the South and impose, from a position of strength, a meeting at the conference table. At first, the bombardments were more or less isolated occurrences and were adorned with the mask of reprisals for alleged provocations from the North. Later on, as they increased in intensity and regularity, they became one gigantic attack carried out by the air force of the United States, day after day, for the purpose of destroying all vestiges of civilization in the Northern zone of the country. This is an episode of the infamously notorious "escalation."

The material aspirations of the Yankee world have been fulfilled to a great extent, regardless of the unflinching defense of the Vietnamese anti-aircraft artillery, of the numerous planes shot down (over 1,700) and of the socialist countries aid in war supplies.

There is a sad reality: Vietnam—a nation representing the

aspirations, the hopes of a whole world of forgotten peoples—is tragically alone. This nation must endure the furious attacks of U.S. technology, with practically no possibility of reprisals in the South and only some of defense in the North—but always alone.

The solidarity of all progressive forces of the world towards the people of Vietnam today is similar to the bitter irony of the plebeians coaxing on the gladiators in the Roman arena. It is not a matter of wishing success to the victim of aggression, but of sharing his fate; one must accompany him to his death or to victory.

When we analyze the lonely situation of the Vietnamese people, we are overcome by anguish at this illogical moment of humanity.

U.S. imperialism is guilty of aggression—its crimes are enormous and cover the whole world. We already know all that, gentlemen! But this guilt also applies to those who, when the time came for a definition, hesitated to make Vietnam an inviolable part of the socialist world; running, of course, the risks of a war on a global scale—but also forcing a decision upon imperialism. And the guilt also applies to those who maintain a war of abuse and snares—started quite some time ago by the representatives of the two greatest powers of the socialist camp.

We must ask ourselves, seeking an honest answer: Is Vietnam isolated, or is it not? Is it not maintaining a dangerous equilibrium between the two quarrelling powers?

And what great people these are! What stoicism and courage! And what a lesson for the world is contained in this struggle! Not for a long time shall we be able to know if President Johnson ever seriously thought of bringing about some of the reforms needed by his people—to iron out the barbed class contradictions that grow each day with explosive power. The truth is that the improvements announced under the pompous title of the "Great Society" have dropped into the cesspool of Vietnam.

The largest of all imperialist powers feels in its own guts the bleeding inflicted by a poor and underdeveloped country; its fabulous economy feels the strain of the war effort. Murder is ceasing to be the most convenient business for its monopolies.

Defensive weapons, and never in adequate number, is all these extraordinary soldiers have—besides love for their homeland, their society, and unsurpassed courage. But imperialism is bogging down in Vietnam, is unable to find a way out and desperately seeks one that will overcome with dignity this dangerous situation in which it now finds itself. Furthermore, the Four Points put forward by the North and the Five Points of the South now corner imperialism, making the confrontation even more decisive.

Everything indicate [*sic*] that peace, this unstable peace which bears that name for the sole reason that no worldwide conflagration has taken place, is again in danger of being destroyed by some irrevocable and unacceptable step taken by the United States.

What role shall we, the exploited people of the world, play? The peoples of the three continents focus their attention on Vietnam and learn their lesson. Since imperialists blackmail humanity by threatening it with war, the wise reaction is not to fear war. The general tactics of the people should be to launch a constant and a firm attack in all fronts where the confrontation is taking place.

In those places where this meager peace we have has been violated, which is our duty? To liberate ourselves at any price.

The world panorama is of great complexity. The struggle for liberation has not yet been undertaken by some countries of ancient Europe, sufficiently developed to realize the contradictions of capitalism, but weak to such a degree that they are unable either to follow imperialism or even to start on its own road. Their contradictions will reach an explosive stage during the forthcoming years—but their problems and, consequently, their own solutions are different from those of our dependent and economically underdeveloped countries.

The fundamental field of imperialist exploitation comprises the three underdeveloped continents: America, Asia, and Africa. Every country has also its own characteristics, but each continent, as a whole, also presents a certain unity.

Our America is integrated by a group of more or less homogeneous countries and in most parts of its territory U.S. monopolist capitals maintain an absolute supremacy. Puppet governments or, in the best of cases, weak and fearful local rulers, are incapable of contradicting orders from their Yankee master. The United States has nearly reached the climax of its political and economic domination; it could hardly advance much more; any change in the situation could bring about a setback. Their policy is to maintain that which has already been conquered. The line of action, at the present time, is limited to the brutal use of force with the purpose of thwarting the liberation movements, no matter of what type they might happen to be.

The slogan "we will not allow another Cuba" hides the possibility of perpetrating aggressions without fear of reprisal, such as the one carried out against the Dominican Republic or before that the massacre in Panama—and the clear warning stating that Yankee troops are ready to intervene anywhere in America where the ruling regime may be altered, thus endangering their interests. This policy enjoys an almost absolute impunity: the OAS is a suitable mask, in spite of its unpopularity; the inefficiency of the UN is ridiculous as well as tragic; the armies of all American countries are ready to intervene in order to smash their peoples. The International of Crime and Treason [sic] has in fact been organized. On the other hand, the autochthonous bourgeoisies have lost all their capacity to oppose imperialism—if they ever had it—and they have become the last card in the pack. There are no other alternatives; either a socialist revolution or a make-believe revolution.

Asia is a continent with many different characteristics. The struggle for liberation waged against a series of European colonial powers resulted in the establishment of more or less progressive governments, whose ulterior evolution have brought about, in some cases, the deepening of the primary objectives of national liberation and in others, a setback towards the adoption of pro-imperialist positions.

From the economic point of view, the United States had very little to lose and much to gain from Asia. These changes benefited its interests; the struggle for the overthrow of other neocolonial powers and the penetration of new spheres of action in the economic field is carried out sometimes directly, occasionally through Japan.

But there are special political conditions, particularly in Indo-China, which create in Asia certain characteristics of capital importance and play a decisive role in the entire U.S. military strategy.

The imperialists encircle China through South Korea, Japan, Taiwan, South Vietnam and Thailand at least.

This dual situation, a strategic interest as important as the military encirclement of the Peoples' Republic of China and the penetration of these great markets—which they do not dominate yet—turns Asia into one of the most explosive points of the world today, in spite of its apparent stability outside of the Vietnamese war zone.

The Middle East, though it geographically belongs to this continent, has its own contradictions and is actively in ferment; it is impossible to foretell how far this cold war between Israel, backed by the imperialists, and the progressive countries of that zone will go. This is just another one of the volcanoes threatening eruption in the world today.

Africa offers an almost virgin territory to the neocolonial invasion. There have been changes which, to some extent, forced neocolonial powers to give up their former absolute prerogatives. But when these changes are carried out uninterruptedly, colonialism continues in the form of neocolonialism with similar effects as far as the economic situation is concerned.

The United States had no colonies in this region but is now struggling to penetrate its partners' fiefs. It can be said that following the strategic plans of U.S. imperialism, Africa constitutes its long range reservoir; its present investments, though, are only important in the Union of South Africa and its penetration is beginning to be felt in the Congo, Nigeria and other countries where a violent rivalry with other imperialist powers is beginning to take place (in a pacific manner up to the present time).

So far it does not have there great interests to defend except its pretended right to intervene in every spot of the world where its monopolies detect huge profits or the existence of large reserves of raw materials.

All this past history justifies our concern regarding the possibilities of liberating the peoples within a long or a short period of time.

If we stop to analyze Africa we shall observe that in the Portuguese colonies of Guinea, Mozambique and Angola the struggle is waged with relative intensity, with a concrete success in the first one and with variable success in the other two. We still witness in the Congo the dispute between Lumumba's successors and the old accomplices of Tshombe, a dispute which at the present time seems to favor the latter: those who have "pacified" a large area of the country for their own benefit—though the war is still latent.

In Rhodesia we have a different problem: British imperialism used every means within its reach to place power in the hands of the white minority, who, at the present time, unlawfully holds it. The conflict, from the British point of view, is absolutely unofficial; this Western power, with its habitual diplomatic cleverness—also called hypocrisy in the strict sense of the word—presents a facade of displeasure before the measures adopted by the government of Ian Smith. Its crafty attitude is supported by some Commonwealth countries that follow it, but is attacked by a large group of countries belonging to Black Africa, whether they are or not servile economic lackeys of British imperialism.

Should the rebellious efforts of these patriots succeed and this movement receive the effective support of neighboring African nations, the situation in Rhodesia may become extremely explosive. But for the moment all these problems are being discussed in harmless organizations such as the UN, the Commonwealth and the OAU.

The social and political evolution of Africa does not lead us to expect a continental revolution. The liberation struggle against the Portuguese should end victoriously, but Portugal does not mean anything in the imperialist field. The confrontations of revolutionary importance are those which place at bay all the imperialist apparatus; this does not mean, however, that we should stop fighting for the liberation of the three Portuguese colonies and for the deepening of their revolutions.

When the black masses of South Africa or Rhodesia start their authentic revolutionary struggle, a new era will dawn in Africa. Or when the impoverished masses of a nation rise up to rescue their right to a decent life from the hands of the ruling oligarchies.

Up to now, army putsches follow one another; a group of officers succeeds another or substitute a ruler who no longer serves their caste interests or those of the powers who covertly manage him—but there are no great popular upheavals. In the Congo these characteristics appeared briefly, generated by the memory of Lumumba, but they have been losing strength in the last few months.

In Asia, as we have seen, the situation is explosive. The points of friction are not only Vietnam and Laos, where there is fighting; such a point is also Cambodia, where at any time a direct U.S. aggression may start, Thailand, Malaya, and, of course, Indonesia, where we can not assume that the last word has been said, regardless of the annihilation of the Communist Party in that country when the reactionaries took over. And also, naturally, the Middle East.

In Latin America the armed struggle is going on in Guatemala, Colombia, Venezuela and Bolivia; the first uprisings are cropping up in Brazil [*sic*]. There are also some resistance focuses which appear and then are extinguished. But almost all the countries of this continent are ripe for a type of struggle that, in order to achieve victory, cannot be content with anything less than establishing a government of socialist tendencies.

In this continent practically only one tongue is spoken (with the exception of Brazil, with whose people, those who speak Spanish can easily make themselves understood, owing to the great similarity of both languages). There is also such a great similarity between the classes in these countries, that they have attained identification among themselves of an *international americano* type, much more complete than in the other continents. Language, habits, religion, a common foreign master, unite them. The degree and the form of exploitation are similar for both the exploiters and the men they exploit in the majority of the countries of Our America. And rebellion is ripening swiftly in it.

We may ask ourselves: how shall this rebellion flourish? What type will it be? We have maintained for quite some time now that, owing to the similarity of their characteristics, the struggle in Our America will achieve, in due course, continental proportions. It shall be the scene of many great battles fought for the liberation of humanity.

Within the frame of this struggle of continental scale, the battles which are now taking place are only episodes—but they have already furnished their martyrs, they shall figure in the history of Our America as having given their necessary blood in this last stage of the fight for the total freedom of man. These names will include Comandante Turcios Lima, padre Camilo Torres, Comandante Fabricio Ojeda, Comandantes Lobatón and Luis de la Puente Uceda, all outstanding figures in the revolutionary movements of Guatemala, Colombia, Venezuela and Peru.

But the active movement of the people creates its new leaders; César Montes and Yon Sosa raise up their flag in Guatemala; Fabio Vázquez and Marulanda in Colombia; Douglas Bravo in the Western part of the country and Américo Martín in El Bachiller, both directing their respective Venezuelan fronts.

New uprisings shall take place in these and other countries of Our America, as it has already happened in Bolivia, and they shall continue to grow in the midst of all the hardships inherent to this dangerous profession of being modern revolutionaries. Many shall perish, victims of their errors; others shall fall in the touch battle that approaches; new fighters and new leaders shall appear in the warmth of the revolutionary struggle. The people shall create their warriors and leaders in the selective framework of the war itself—and Yankee agents of repression shall increase. Today there are military aids in all the countries where armed struggle is growing; the Peruvian army apparently carried out a successful action against the revolutionaries in that country, an army also trained and advised by the Yankees. But if the focuses of war grow with sufficient political and military insight, they shall become practically invincible and shall force the Yankees to send reinforcements. In Peru itself many new figures, practically unknown, are now reorganizing the guerrilla. Little by little, the obsolete weapons, which are sufficient for the repression of small armed bands, will be exchanged for modern armaments and the U.S. military aids will be substituted by actual fighters until, at a given moment, they are forced to send increasingly greater number of regular troops to ensure the relative stability of a government whose national puppet army is disintegrating before the impetuous attacks of the guerrillas. It is the road of Vietnam; it is the road that should be followed by the people; it is the road that will be followed in Our America, with the advantage that the armed groups could create Coordinating Councils to embarrass the repressive forces of Yankee imperialism and accelerate the revolutionary triumph.

America, a forgotten continent in the last liberation struggles, is now beginning to make itself heard through the Tricontinental and, in the voice of the vanguard of its peoples, the Cuban Revolution, will today have a task of much greater relevance: creating a Second or a Third Vietnam, or the Second *and* Third Vietnam of the world.

We must bear in mind that imperialism is a world system, the last stage of capitalism — and it must be defeated in a world confrontation. The strategic end of this struggle should be the destruction of imperialism. Our share, the responsibility of the exploited and underdeveloped of the world is to eliminate the foundations of imperialism: our oppressed nations, from where they extract capitals, raw materials, technicians and cheap labor, and to which they export new capitals — instruments of domination — arms and all kinds of articles; thus submerging us in an absolute dependance [*sic*].

The fundamental element of this strategic end shall be the real liberation of all people, a liberation that will be brought about through armed struggle in most cases and which shall be, in our America, almost indefectibly, a Socialist Revolution.

While envisaging the destruction of imperialism, it is necessary to identify its head, which is no other than the United States of America.

We must carry out a general task with the tactical purpose of getting the enemy out of its natural environment, forcing him to fight in regions where his own life and habits will clash with the existing reality. We must not underrate our adversary; the U.S. soldier has technical capacity and is backed by weapons and resources of such magnitude that render him frightful. He lacks the essential ideologic motivation which his bitterest enemies of today—the Vietnamese soldiers—have in the highest degree. We will only be able to overcome that army by undermining their morale—and this is accomplished by defeating it and causing it repeated sufferings.

But this brief outline of victories carries within itself the immense sacrifice of the people, sacrifices that should be demanded beginning today, in plain daylight, and which perhaps may be less painful than those we would have to endure if we constantly avoided battle in an attempt to have others pull our chestnuts out of the fire.

It is probable, of course, that the last liberated country shall accomplish this without an armed struggle and the sufferings of a long and cruel war against the imperialists—this they might avoid. But perhaps it will be impossible to avoid this struggle or its effects in a global conflagration; the suffering would be the same, or perhaps even greater. We cannot foresee the future, but we should never give in to the defeatist temptation of being the vanguard of a nation which yearns for freedom, but abhors the struggle it entails and awaits its freedom as a crumb of victory.

It is absolutely just to avoid all useless sacrifices. Therefore, it is so important to clear up the real possibilities that dependent America may have of liberating itself through pacific means. For us, the solution to this question is quite clear: the present moment may or may not be the proper one for starting the struggle, but we cannot harbor any illusions, and we have no right to do so, that freedom can be obtained without fighting. And these battles shall not be mere street fights with stones against tear-gas bombs, or of pacific general strikes; neither shall it be the battle of a furious people destroying in two or three days the repressive scaffolds of the ruling oligarchies; the struggle shall be long, harsh, and its front shall be in the guerrilla's refuge, in the cities, in the homes of the fighters—where the repressive forces shall go seeking easy victims among their families—in the massacred rural population, in the villages or cities destroyed by the bombardments of the enemy.

They are pushing us into this struggle; there is no alternative: we must prepare it and we must decide to undertake it.

The beginnings will not be easy; they shall be extremely difficult. All the oligarchies' powers of repression, all their capacity for brutality and demagoguery will be placed at the service of their cause. Our mission, in the first hour, shall be to survive;

later, we shall follow the perennial example of the guerrilla, carrying out armed propaganda (in the Vietnamese sense, that is, the bullets of propaganda, of the battles won or lost—but fought—against the enemy). The great lesson of the invincibility of the guerrillas taking root in the dispossessed masses. The galvanizing of the national spirit, the preparation for harder tasks, for resisting even more violent repressions. Hatred as an element of the struggle; a relentless hatred of the enemy, impelling us over and beyond the natural limitations that man is heir to and transforming him into an effective, violent, selective and cold killing machine. Our soldiers must be thus; a people without hatred cannot vanquish a brutal enemy.

We must carry the war into every corner the enemy happens to carry it: to his home, to his centers of entertainment; a total war. It is necessary to prevent him from having a moment of peace, a quiet moment outside his barracks or even inside; we must attack him wherever he may be; make him feel like a cornered beast wherever he may move. Then his moral fiber shall begin to decline. He will even become more beastly, but we shall notice how the signs of decadence begin to appear.

And let us develop a true proletarian internationalism; with international proletarian armies; the flag under which we fight would be the sacred cause of redeeming humanity. To die under the flag of Vietnam, of Venezuela, of Guatemala, of Laos, of Guinea, of Colombia, of Bolivia, of Brazil—to name only a few scenes of today's armed struggle—would be equally glorious and desirable for an American, an Asian, an African, even a European.

Each spilt drop of blood, in any country under whose flag one has not been born, is an experience passed on to those who survive, to be added later to the liberation struggle of his own country. And each nation liberated is a phase won in the battle for the liberation of one's own country.

The time has come to settle our discrepancies and place everything at the service of our struggle.

We all know great controversies rend the world now fighting for freedom; no one can hide it. We also know that they have reached such intensity and such bitterness that the possibility of dialogue and reconciliation seems extremely difficult, if not impossible. It is a useless task to search for means and ways to propitiate a dialogue which the hostile parties avoid. However, the enemy is there; it strikes every day, and threatens us with new blows and these blows will unite us, today, tomorrow, or the day after. Whoever understands this first, and prepares for this necessary union, shall have the people's gratitude.

Owing to the virulence and the intransigence with which each cause is defended, we, the dispossessed, cannot take sides for one form or the other of these discrepancies, even though sometimes we coincide with the contentions of one party or the other, or in a greater measure with those of one part more than with those of the other. In time of war, the expression of current differences constitutes a weakness; but at this stage it is an illusion to attempt to settle them by means of words. History shall erode them or shall give them their true meaning.

In our struggling world every discrepancy regarding tactics, the methods of action for the attainment of limited objectives should be analyzed with due respect to another man's opinions. Regarding our great strategic objective, the total destruction of imperialism by armed struggle, we should be uncompromising.

Let us sum up our hopes for victory: total destruction of imperialism by eliminating its firmest bulwark: the oppression exercised by the United States of America. To carry out, as a tactical method, the peoples' gradual liberation, one by one or in groups: driving the enemy into a difficult fight away from its own territory; dismantling all its sustenance bases, that is, its dependent territories.

This means a long war. And, once more we repeat it, a cruel war. Let no one fool himself at the outstart and let no one hesitate to start out for fear of the consequences it may bring to his people. It is almost our sole hope for victory. We cannot elude the call of this hour. Vietnam is pointing it out with its endless lesson of heroism, its tragic and everyday lesson of struggle and death for the attainment of final victory.

There, the imperialist soldiers endure the discomforts [*sic*] of those who, used to enjoying the U.S. standard of living, have to live in a hostile land with the insecurity of being unable to move without being aware of walking on enemy territory:— death to those who dare take a step out of their fortified encampment. The permanent hostility of the entire population. All this has internal repercussion in the United States; propitiates the resurgence of an element which is being minimized in spite of its vigor by all imperialist forces: class struggle even within its own territory.

How close we could look into a bright future should two, three or many Vietnams flourish throughout the world with their share of deaths and their immense tragedies, their everyday heroism and their repeated blows against imperialism, impelled to disperse its forces under the sudden attack and the increasing hatred of all peoples of the world!

And if we were all capable of uniting to make our blows stronger and infallible and so increase the effectiveness of all kinds of support given to the struggling people—how great and close would that future be!

If we, in a small point of the world map, are able to fulfill our duty and place at the disposal of this struggle whatever little of ourselves we are permitted to give: our lives, our sacrifice, and if some day we have to breathe our last breath on any land, already ours, sprinkled with our blood, let it be known that we have measured the scope of our actions and that we only consider ourselves elements in the great army of the proletariat but that we are proud of having learned from the Cuban Revolution, and from its maximum leader, the great lesson emanating from his attitude in this part of the world: "What do the dangers or the sacrifices of a man or of a nation matter, when the destiny of humanity is at stake."

Our every action is a battle cry against imperialism, and a battle hymn for the people's unity against the great enemy of mankind: the United States of America. Wherever death may surprise us, let it be welcome, provided that this, our battle cry, may have reached some receptive ear and another hand may be extended to wield our weapons and other men be ready to intone the funeral dirge with the staccato singing of the machine guns and new battle cries of war and victory.

SOURCE: Pamphlet, published in English by the Executive Secretariat of the Organization of the Solidarity of the Peoples of Africa, Asia, and Latin America, Havana, April 16, 1967.

CASE HISTORIES OF GUERRILLA
MOVEMENTS AND POLITICAL CHANGE

The case histories that follow are intended as brief summaries of the guerrilla movements in seven Latin American nations— Guatemala, Venezuela, Peru, Bolivia, Colombia, Nicaragua, and El Salvador—from 1959 to 1984. These nations were chosen for consideration because they were, or recently have become, or have become again, the scene of revolutionary guerrilla movements that either were rural-based or counted upon a significant rural component.[1] In most of these cases the guerrilla movements failed to achieve their political objectives; in others the struggle continues; and in Nicaragua, after repeated military defeats in the 1960s and early 1970s, the revolutionaries gained military success.

For each of the countries discussed below there exists a significant professional literature, some of which we have cited in the notes to aid those readers who wish to pursue in more detail the experiences of a particular country. Our intent here is to outline for each country (1) the political context of the guerrilla struggle, (2) the origins and leadership of the guerrilla movements, (3) the politico-military evolution of the movements until approximately 1970, and (4) the post-1970 events in each country. In addition to a chronological summary, we have highlighted in each case four basic variables critical to Che Guevara's analyses of the potential for guerrilla movements in Latin America:

1. The national political context, including: (a) existence (or lack thereof) of a Caribbean-type dictatorship; (b) the legiti-

macy of the incumbent government (i.e., whether it came to power through popular elections); (c) the institutional strength (where it existed) of liberal democracy, including continuity and honesty of elections, and strength and diversity of the nation's labor movement, peasant organizations, and other political movements; (d) "objective conditions" and "subjective conditions" for revolution.

2. The suitability of the physical terrain for guerrilla warfare ("zones difficult to reach, either because of dense forests, steep mountains, impassable deserts or marshes").

3. The salience and political relevance of the "agrarian question" ("the guerrilla fighter is above all an agrarian revolutionary").

4. Revolutionary Marxist traditions and/or historical guerrilla movements that contributed to a popular base for new guerrilla *focos* ("The guerrilla fighter needs help from the people of the area. This is an indispensable condition").

Beyond these variables explicit in Che Guevara's *Guerrilla Warfare*, we have also considered for each country the role of the United States counterinsurgency programs, the political response of incumbent governments, the nature of political and ideological fragmentation of the guerrilla movements, and, finally, the current status of revolutionary guerrilla movements.

NOTES

1. For treatment of the most extensive urban guerrilla movements, see James Kohl and John Litt, *Urban Guerrilla Warfare in Latin America* (Cambridge, Mass.: MIT Press, 1974); Abraham Guillén, *Philosophy of the Urban Guerrilla*, trans. and ed. Donald C. Hodges (New York: William Morrow, 1973); Jean Lartéguy, *The Guerrillas*, trans. Stanley Hochman (New York: New American Library, 1970; João Quartim, *Dictatorship and Armed Struggle in Brazil*, trans. David Fernbach (London: New Left Review, 1971); Carlos Marighella, *Escritos de Carlos Marighella* (São Paulo: Editorial Livramento, 1979); João Batista Berado, *Guerrilhas e Guerrilheiros, no drama da América Latina* (São Paulo: Edicoes Populares, 1981); Donald C. Hodges and Abraham Guillén, *Revaloración de la guerrilla urbana* (Mexico, D.F.: El Caballito, 1977).

GUATEMALA

MEXICO

PETÉN

BELIZE

CARIBBEAN
SEA 16°

HUEHUETENANGO

ALTA
VERAPAZ

EL QUICHÉ

Lago de
Izabal

Huehuetenango

Panzos

IZABAL

SAN
MARCOS

TOTONICAPÁN

BAJA
VERAPAZ

ZACAPA

Zacapa

QUEZALTENANGO

SOLOLÁ

EL
PROGRESO

GUATEMALA

CHIMALTENANGO

RETALHULEU

CHIQUIMULA

HONDURAS

SUCHITEPÉQUEZ

Guatemala
City

JALAPA

SACATEPÉQUEZ

Esquintla

SANTA
ROSA

JUTIAPA

ESCUINTLA

EL SALVADOR

14°

PACIFIC
OCEAN

—·—·— International boundary
—————— Department boundary
⊙ National capital
• Other major city

| 0 | 25 | 50 | 75 Mi. |
| 0 | 25 | 50 | 75 | 100 Km. |

GUATEMALA

POLITICAL CHRONOLOGY

sion force to train in Guatemala. Defense Minister Peralta Azurdia heads coup against Ydígoras (March 1963).

1963–66   Administration of Colonel Enrique Peralta Azurdia. Strong anti-Communist rhetoric accompanies new Law for Defense of Democratic Institutions. Increasing confrontation between FAR and military units. Peralta Azurdia announces "operation honesty" to end corruption.

1966–69   Administration of Julio César Méndez Montenegro, the only "civilian" administration from 1958 to 1984. Fierce fighting with guerrillas. Increase in activity of right-wing death squads. Turcios Lima dies in accident (1966). U.S. ambassador assassinated (1968). Guerrillas suffer serious military and political setbacks (1968–70). Colonel Carlos Arana Osorio heads counterinsurgency "Operation Guatemala" in Zacapa.

1970–84   Sequence of "elected" military administrations.

1970–74   Administration of General Carlos Arana Osorio; transition to institutionalized military regime. Focus on modernization and attraction of foreign capital. Beginnings of Guerrilla Army of the Poor (EGP) in Ixcan (1972–75). Fierce repression of Communist party leadership and increase in political murders.

1974–78   Administration of General Kjell Laugerud García. 1976 earthquake devastates part of Guatemala. Upsurge in urban labor movement and protests. Revival of guerrilla movements in rural areas. U.S. State Department designates Guatemala as a "gross and consistent violator of human rights" (1977).

1978–82   Administration of General Romeo Lucas García. Massacre of peasants at Panzós (May 1978); riots over bus fares (October 1978); increasing political unrest. Emergence of ESA death squads, increasing control by military over Guatemalan economy and society. Growth of guerrilla movements. Occupation by guerrillas of Spanish embassy (January 1980); regime responds with military attack. URNG unites FAR, EGP, and ORPA in strategy of "popular revolutionary war" (January 1982).

1982   Elections in March, followed by "internal coup" that installs General José Efraín Ríos Montt as president.

1982–83   General Ríos Montt announces sweeping reforms and war against corruption. Intensification of counterinsurgency programs. Plan Victoria 82 leaves thousands of civilian casualties in growing civil war. Montt's evangelical religion and other disagreements with military and civilian elites provoke coup.

1983   Coup substitutes General Humberto Mejía Victores for Ríos Montt. Elections scheduled for March 1984 amid continued political instability, economic recession, and military efforts against growing insurgency.

BACKGROUND

The political history of Guatemala is the story of personalist dictatorships, supported by military forces and "legitimized" by periodic "elections." In the 105 years before 1944 four dictators occupied the presidency of the country for more than 70 years. Since 1954, military officers and one civilian president have reduced the average tenure of dictators considerably but have done nothing to improve the miserable conditions experienced by the majority of the Guatemalan population.

This generalized misery and poverty serve as a permanent seed of social and political discontent. Nurture of the seed by a variety of revolutionary movements and guerrilla cadres since the early 1960s has made Guatemala a bloody battleground for followers of Che Guevara's example and for the forces of counterrevolution and counterinsurgency. Since 1961 Guatemala has been in a more or less permanent state of internal war as the early *foquistas* have evolved toward the strategy of prolonged popular war.

From 1944 to 1954 a series of political and socioeconomic changes introduced by Presidents Juan José Arévalo (1944– 50) and Jacobo Arbenz (1951–54) initiated agrarian reforms, mobilization of urban and rural labor, democratization of the political process, and a surge of Guatemalan nationalism. Inasmuch as these reforms included expropriation of idle agricultural lands owned by the powerful United Fruit Company and participation by Communists and other leftists in Guatemalan politics, U.S. policy makers determined that the Arbenz government represented a Communist threat to the Western Hemisphere.

Pressured by United Fruit Company's public relations campaign against the Guatemalan government and, perhaps more important, determined to protect American investors throughout Latin America from expropriation of their property, the United States government adopted an increasingly hostile policy toward Guatemala. Of even more importance than the concern for investors, however, was the belief by high-level policy makers that Guatemala represented the first instance of Soviet penetration of the Western Hemisphere. When conspiracies with Nicaraguan dictator Anastasio Somoza and the governments of El Salvador, Costa Rica, and Caribbean nations failed to produce a surrogate invasion force, the United States carried out a "liberationist" coup that installed Colonel Carlos Castillo Armas as the new Guatemalan president and ended what the Eisenhower administration had characterized as "a mortal threat to our own national security."[1]

Just before the U.S. intervention in Guatemala, U.S. policy makers imposed the "Caracas Declaration of Solidarity" upon the majority of the members of the Organization of American States (OAS). This declaration in many respects set the tone for the next twenty years of cold war–oriented U.S. policy toward Latin America. Clearly aimed at Guatemala, the declaration asserted that "the domination or control of the political institutions of any American State by the international communist movement extending to this Hemisphere the political system of an extra continental power, would constitute a threat to the sovereignty and political independence of the American States, endangering the peace of America."[2] The declaration underplayed U.S. concern for American investment in Latin America. Secretary of State John Foster Dulles made clear that even "if the United Fruit matter were settled, if they gave a gold piece for every banana, the problem would remain as it is today as far as the presence of communist infiltration in Guatemala is concerned. That is the problem, not United Fruit."[3]

Thus cold war politics brought U.S. military intervention in Guatemala in the mid-1950s even before the Cuban revolution and Che Guevara threatened the export of Cuban socialism. Che Guevara's personal participation on the losing side of this episode in Guatemala would greatly influence his later revolutionary writing and action. U.S. intervention made clear the need for a revolutionary army to defend any revolutionary regime in Latin America and also prepared the Cubans and Che for the Bay of Pigs invasion by U.S.-supported anti-Castro Cubans in 1961—an intervention planned and executed by many of the same people responsible for the Guatemalan "success" of 1954.

Reversals of the agrarian reforms of the Arévalo and Arbenz governments; the assassination of peasant, union, and political leaders; and an end to even the superficial forms of democratic processes (with the exception of periodic "elections") set a precedent for Guatemalan politics for the next three decades. Personalist political parties allied with different factions within the armed forces, along with weak local versions of reformist parties (for example, the Christian Democrats), barely masked the military domination of national politics. Disputes among military factions and their civilian cohorts produced destructive coups and attempted coups whose major effects were to further alienate the majority of the population from politics and to require the United States to replace equipment lost in internecine combat.

Though it lacked the "strongman" caudillo (like Batista in Cuba, Trujillo in the Dominican Republic, or Somoza in Nicaragua), Guatemala met the basic requisites of a Caribbean dictatorship with little, but perhaps enough, of the democratic mask that Che Guevara suggested would impede the successful development of guerrilla movements.

Notwithstanding its dictatorial politics and rural poverty, Guatemala, like Peru, Bolivia, and Ecuador, posed a difficulty for revolutionary guerrilla movements little considered by Che Guevara in *Guerrilla Warfare* or its elaboration in 1963, "Guerrilla Warfare: A Method." Guatemala's population is predominantly Indian, with as much as 70 percent of the people functionally illiterate in Spanish. Moreover, this Indian population is itself linguistically and ethnically diverse. Centuries-long exploitation of the Indian population by Guatemala's elites and *ladinos* makes it extremely difficult to rally the overwhelmingly rural population to any ideologically based political movement.[4]

However, the mobilization of rural workers and peasants in the early 1950s for agrarian reform and rural unionization programs demonstrated the revolutionary potential in the rural regions. Concrete demands for land, higher wages, and an end to master-servant social relations, rather than ideological consciousness, motivated campesino organization and political participation. During these years more than 200,000 rural workers and peasants affiliated with peasant syndicates supported the reforms initiated by the Arbenz government. By June of 1954, over 600,000 hectares of land were expropriated, with accompanying strikes, rallies, and land occupation by peasant organizations.[5]

Temporary beneficiaries of the reforms, Indian peasants soon paid the price of the U.S.-supported counterrevolution. Many were brutally slaughtered and peasant and union leaders were persecuted and assassinated. The restoration of the *latifundia* once again subordinated the rural population to the approximately 2 percent of landowners who had controlled more than 70 percent of the country's farmland in 1950.

The memory of this repression and of the reforms that might have been is a two-edged sword. Fear of violence intimidates much of the rural population while the legacy of hope of the Arévalo-Arbenz years provides a powerful symbol for revolutionary cadres. Just as agricultural cooperatives became synonymous with "Communism" for the landlords and for reactionary elements in the Church and the military, hope for a new agrarian reform links the peasantry to the guerrilla struggle whenever there is opportunity for effective action. Thus guerrilla leader César Montes noted:

> In all the peasant areas we have visited, we easily explain ourselves by saying that the FAR [Rebel Armed Forces] struggle is merely the prolongation by other means of the 1944 revolution. The CIA won and Guatemala lost because that revolution was led by the national bourgeoisie. Now the peasants and working class know that they must not put more trust in other classes than in themselves, in their own strength. Despite its limitations the 1944–54 revolution is a great source of lessons for us and plays an important role as a historical national example of revolution. It has kept the revolutionary flame burning in Guatemala—a unique feature of our country—because it provides a real and living example of what a revolution is. That's a point of reference that anyone can understand.[6]

The campesinos are not interested in the cold war or

"Communism"; they recognize their allies and enemies by the practical consequences of revolutionary or counterrevolutionary action. Either side may win them over, in the short run, with pragmatic policies offering minimal economic and social gains.

Added to cultural and linguistic barriers, past failures and repression discourage successful recruitment of the Indian population to movements headed by urban political elites— university students, middle-class army officers, intellectuals, and reformist or revolutionary political parties. Even when people are sympathetic to opponents of the regime, commitment to revolutionary struggle requires, as Che Guevara learned, long-term political education, building of trust, and "mass work" by insurgents. Centuries of changes in regime without benefit to the Indian peoples makes their commitment to any political movement a high risk with little expectation of altering the social and economic legacy of the past. No insurgent movement in Guatemala has overcome these obstacles, although leftist Catholic and Marxist efforts in the early 1970s and 1980s seem to have aroused significant levels of opposition to the successive dictatorships and recurrent waves of political assassinations and "disappearances."

Even if the social characteristics of Guatemala made pragmatic deviations from Che Guevara's principles in *Guerrilla Warfare* necessary, certain aspects of Guatemala's political and social reality conformed precisely to Guevara's original formulations:

1. Guatemala, despite periodic "elections," lacked any effective semblance of a formal democracy and any effective commitment of the general population to a supposed legitimate political regime. Unlike Cuba or Nicaragua, however, Guatemala lacked the personal embodiment of dictatorship (like Batista in Cuba or Somoza in Nicaragua) to serve as a focus of revolutionary struggle.

Guatemala has lacked an effective political party system or moderate political movements that offered realistic alternatives for political reform. Unlike Peru, Bolivia, Venezuela, or Colombia, the country has no powerful reformist political organizations with strong ties to urban and rural workers and peasants. And unlike that of El Salvador, the

Guatemalan military created no single official party of its own to substitute for an effective, competitive party system.

2. The physical terrain of certain areas of Guatemala provides considerable opportunity for guerrilla operations and the possibility for creating a "counter-state" in the countryside. Again, however, in the isolated rural regions and the highlands the dominant Indian population proved extremely difficult to incorporate into revolutionary movements in the 1960s, somewhat obviating the suitability of physical terrain for guerrilla operations.

3. Guatemala was and is a predominantly rural society, with power and wealth based upon the traditional and plantation *latifundia.* In the early 1960s over 65 percent of the population was classified as "active in agriculture" and less than 10 percent worked in manufacturing industries. The most important political, social, and economic issues for the population focused on land and agrarian reform.

   The poverty, misery, and exploitation of the rural population conformed closely to Che Guevara's portrayal of the general objective conditions that would provide the basis for revolutionary struggle and political recruitment of the rural population by the guerrilla cadres.

4. Guatemala lacked a strong vanguard party, rural cadres, and linkages between urban and rural opposition movements. This meant that substantial "political work" was required to stimulate the creation of appropriate subjective conditions for successful revolutionary efforts in the countryside. It also meant that a guerrilla *foco* might precipitate insurgency, as in Cuba, but would need to work hard to build the necessary links with political parties and urban groups in order to create a broad-based popular coalition for revolutionary action.

ORIGINS OF THE GUERRILLA MOVEMENTS IN THE 1960s

From the very outset of U.S. counterrevolutionary efforts in the 1960s, Guatemala played a central role. The brother of Guatemala's ambassador to the United States provided one of his large rural estates as a base for the CIA to train anti-Fidelista

Cubans for the Bay of Pigs invasion and Guatemala's government assured a supply of prostitutes for the invasion forces-in-training.[7]

This subordination of Guatemalan territory and sovereignty to U.S. politico-military policy alienated a number of young nationalist military offficers. On November 13, 1960, a group of these military officers led a coup attempt similar in many respects to numerous previous coups throughout Latin America and Guatemala. Protesting against government corruption and violations of the constitution, and proclaiming the need for social, economic, and political reform, the young officers also pointed to the use of Guatemala as a training camp for the CIA in explaining the motivation for their uprising. After taking over two garrisons (Fort Matamoros and the military air base at Zacapa) the would-be coup was defeated with support from Cuban exile pilots and U.S. naval units.[8]

Although the insurrectionists included young officers trained by the United States—Marco Antonio Yon Sosa, Luis Trejos, Luis Turcios Lima—President Miguel Ydígoras (himself later a victim of a U.S.-supported coup) blamed Cuba, former presidents Arévalo and Arbenz, and local Communists for the uprising.[9] After a brief exile in Honduras and El Salvador, Turcios Lima, Yon Sosa, and other insurgents determined to oust Ydígoras found refuge and a small amount of support among the peasantry in the countryside. Thus, dissident military officers seeking political and economic reform provided the initiative and leadership elements for the Guatemalan guerrillas of the early 1960s.

After contacts with Guatemala's fragmented political parties and labor movements produced little practical support for the insurgency against the Ydígoras government, the young officers and their supporters decided upon guerrilla warfare in the tradition of Sandino in Nicaragua (see the section on Nicaragua below) and Fidel Castro in Cuba. Based in the mountains of Izabal, in the Sierra de Las Minas, the eclectic guerrilla cadre of nationalists, Communists, reformists, and peasant soldiers called upon the Guatemalan people to join their struggle to overthrow the Ydígoras regime: "Democracy vanished from our country long ago. No people can live in a country where there is no democracy. That is why the demand for changes is mounting in our country. We can no longer carry on in this way. We must overthrow the Ydígoras government and set up a government which respects human rights, seeks ways and means to save our country from its hardships, and pursues a serious self-respecting foreign policy."[10]

Seemingly intent on a typical ouster of the incumbent government, the rebels attacked military installations, murdered key government officials, and "expropriated" money from the United Fruit Company and from other symbols of the government's alliance with foreigners. Lacking any clear ideological underpinnings or direction from revolutionary political cadres, the insurgents sought to win over dissident military officers (their former professional colleagues), students, and middle-class professionals. Though much less politically sophisticated, this strategy foreshadowed the popular revolutionary war doctrine of the late 1970s and early 1980s in its effort to bring together a disparate ideological and multiclass coalition.

Ydígoras's notorious subordination to U.S. foreign policy and the demands of the United Fruit Company (despite his earlier anti-U.S. rhetoric), combined with the ambitions of Guatemala's opposition politicians (Christian Democrats, National Liberation Movement, Revolutionary Party), produced a joint manifesto calling for Ydígoras's resignation.[11] Student protests and riots in Guatemala City brought the only response that could permit Ydígoras's political survival: militarization of the regime and intensified repression. On March 16, 1962, Ydígoras turned control of Guatemala City over to the army; a month later a government reorganization left the foreign minister as the only civilian in the cabinet.

The guerrillas melted back into the countryside under military pressure from the Guatemalan army. Efforts to recruit new supporters and renew the military struggle met disastrous results. An attempt made on November 13, 1962, in commemoration of the 1960 uprising, to establish a guerrilla front in the western part of the country failed for lack of peasant support, and the leaders were captured and shot.[12] From the military debacle, Turcios Lima and other guerrilla leaders sought new alliances and political direction. Cadres from the weak, outlawed, but determined Partido Guatemalteco de Trabajo (PGT,

Guatemalan Communist Party), still recovering from the persecution after the "liberationist" *golpe* of 1954, joined forces with Turcios Lima and student activists (the "12 of April Movement") to form the Rebel Armed Forces (FAR).[13]

POLITICO-MILITARY EVOLUTION OF THE GUERRILLA STRUGGLE

Never a homogeneous movement, the FAR suffered from the outset from disputes over the tactical and moral desirability of supporting candidates in upcoming mayoral and presidential elections, over its relationship to the PGT, over its basic program, and over military operations. When President Ydígoras's defense minister, Colonel Enrique Peralta Azurdia, carried out a coup on March 30, 1963, because Guatemala was "on the brink of an internal conflict as a result of subversion promoted by pro-Communist sectors, and because of the infiltration of Communists that had become more alarming each day," this at least eliminated the electoral option as a matter of contention within FAR. Peralta Azurdia intended to achieve a military resolution of the political crisis; his administration began a reign of terror, while U.S.-supported counterinsurgency forces targeted guerrillas, "Communists," and opposition political movements of various political persuasions.[14]

Colonel Peralta justified his coup as an effort to avoid an imminent civil war and the establishment of a Communist regime. His government shortly proclaimed a Law for the Defense of Democratic Institutions and decreed prison terms for persons distributing "Communist" literature (two years), membership in the Communist party (ten years), and "terrorism" (fifteen years). Frustrated by its inability to destroy the guerrilla cadres in Esquintla, Zacapa, and Izabal, the government intensified persecution of labor leaders, while incidents of intimidation, torture, and "disappearances" of peasants increased.

In turn, the FAR provoked government repression with attacks on military units, kidnapings of government officials, and sabotage. Never a real military threat to the regime, the guerrillas did challenge the political stability of the country by eroding Peralta Azurdia's control of his own coalition and providing ammunition for the nonrevolutionary opposition political forces.

Peralta's nationalist sentiments precluded total acquiescence to the United States, which wished to increase its participation in the counterinsurgency program. Peralta also prided himself on his pledge to clean up Guatemalan politics through "operation honesty" and promised to return the country to formal democracy. When election results in March 1966 seemed to reject Peralta's handpicked candidate (and the string of military governments since 1954), Peralta faced a difficult dilemma. The candidate with a plurality of votes, Julio César Méndez Montenegro (Partido Revolucionario, PR) campaigned on a platform of renewing the 1944–54 reforms and a vague commitment to social justice. Méndez Montenegro's brother, Mario, the leader of the remnants of the Arbenz coalition, had been assassinated (or committed suicide, depending upon whose version is accepted). His death added to the mystique of the Partido Revolucionario's 1944–54 legacy and the desire for a civilian president. Ironically, many of Méndez Montenegro's supporters criticized the outgoing government for its poor relations with the U.S. and failure to end the guerrilla insurgency.

Since Méndez Montenegro had won only a plurality of the votes, Congress would determine the next president in a "secondary election." After a period of Byzantine negotiations and intrigue, including challenges to PR congressmen under the terms of the Law of Defense of Democratic Institutions and the passage of an amnesty covering all military and police personnel for acts committed in repressing subversion, Julio César Méndez Montenegro was confirmed as Guatemala's new president—the first civilian in sixteen years.

Méndez Montenegro accepted the presidency having already promised the military and U.S. policy makers to deal harshly with the guerrillas. Less than two weeks after taking office he began a tour of the country's important military installations. At each base he reassured the military of his esteem and respect for the military institutions. In practice he served at the pleasure of the military, and his vice-president, Marroquín Rojas, had close ties to the military and civilian forces that pushed for harsh, systematic repression of the "Communists." Efforts by the new government to distribute land to small numbers of peasants and to initiate tax reforms incurred the wrath of the ever present extreme right. "Private" death squads, linked to the minister of defense, Colonel Arriaga Bosque, published a death list of supposed Communists and kidnaped, tortured, and executed supposed subversives. The New Anti-Communist Organization (NOA), with the slogan "See a Communist, kill a Communist"; the National Organized Anti-Communist Movement (MANO); and the Anti-Communist Council of Guatemala (CADEG) intensified their terrorist attacks even as the defense minister proclaimed that "all the subversion in Guatemala in recent times has come from Havana."

Colonel Arana Osorio, commander of military operations in Zacapa, and civilian right-wing terrorists cooperated closely in the anti-Communist campaign. In December 1966 new legislation authorized landowners to serve as surrogate security personnel; from three thousand to five thousand casualties followed in the Zacapa-Izabal sector. Even members of the president's own Partido Revolucionario suffered attacks by the security forces and their civilian allies. Méndez Montenegro, unable to control the government terrorist apparatus over which he theoretically presided, turned to the United States for more assistance in the antiguerrilla campaign.

The guerrillas responded in kind; a number of U.S. military personnel died in battle while others were assassinated by leftist militants in the years 1965–70. In 1968 the FAR killed U.S. Ambassador John Gordon Mein as he attempted to escape from his would-be kidnapers. Eduardo Galeano, a noted Uruguayan intellectual and author of a study on Guatemala, described the situation in 1967 in the following grim terms:

> The Army is the master of the situation in Guatemala. The military brass do not stop to knock on the door of Méndez Montenegro, who is constitutionally—but only constitutionally—their commander-in-chief. The upcoming budget must be slashed because the oligarchy won't pay taxes. The only untouchable appropriations are those of the Defense Ministry. The President is a virtual prisoner, but the military don't trust him and never did. . . .

The armed forces' "civic action" plans consist not only of distributing powdered milk, medicines, and promises to villagers in areas subject to guerrilla influence, but also include intelligence operations often of a "dirty" type. All this is part of the "encircle and annihilate" campaign that the army has carried on against the guerrillas. Murder is blended with demagogy: while one hand kills people, the other distributes goodies. "You have to have a guerrilla unit nearby to get drinking water," said an Izabal peasant with a sense of humor.[15]

Gradually the guerrilla movements lost ground to the counterinsurgency programs. Defectors, informers, and increased participation by U.S. personnel imposed serious military setbacks on the guerrilla forces. The death of guerrilla leader Turcios Lima in a car accident in October 1966 and penetration of the Sierra de Las Minas by the Guatemalan army led to attempts to reunify the fragmented guerrilla politico-military alliance—and also to César Montes's bitter reaffirmation of the need for armed struggle and his condemnation of the PGT: "Let us see what the results are, after four years of struggle: 300 revolutionaries fallen in battle and 3000 common people murdered by the regime of Julio César Méndez Montenegro. The PGT (its ruling clique) contributed the ideas and the FAR the dead."[16]

More dead were added when Mexican soldiers killed Yon Sosa in exile (1970). Ultimately even the MR-13 dissolved as a military force of significance. Without strong political support networks, beset by ideological and personalist disputes, lacking sufficient military training and provisions, and unable to create the subjective conditions for a broad popular uprising against the military regimes, the guerrilla *focos* failed in their immediate revolutionary tasks.

1970–PRESENT

By 1970 the Guatemalan military and its American allies had won a temporary military victory over the fragmented guerrilla movements and the political left. Perhaps more significant in the long term, however, the increased militarization of the Guatemalan government and the erosion of the weak parties and movements of the reformist center pointed toward the next decade of fraudulently elected military dictators who maintained themselves in power through coercion and the spoils of public investment in economic modernization. This modernization brought a 200 percent expansion in lands cultivated in export crops between 1950 and 1978 and a 10 percent decline in acreage in corn, the basic staple of the Guatemalan people. Income distribution became more concentrated and malnutrition more widespread, and the percentage of government budgets allocated to health and education declined. In early February 1976, a devastating earthquake struck Guatemala, increasing the misery suffered by the growing number of urban shanty town dwellers as well as villagers throughout the country. When selected urban unions, including workers at Guatemala City's Coca-Cola franchise, responded to the deterioration of living conditions and mass dismissals with strikes, the government accused the workers of "political delinquency" and called them "enemies of national reconstruction." Assassinations of labor leaders throughout the country followed.[17] For Guatemala the Alliance for Progress and the modernization of the 1960s and the 1970s brought the very antithesis of "constructive democratic change." The process that defeated the guerrilla insurgents had also destroyed the limited hope for political pluralism and social reform in Guatemala.

From 1970 to 1975 sporadic guerrilla operations by remnants of the FAR and by other fighters in the countryside and urban areas met harsh repression by successive military regimes. In 1972, the PGT lost much of its central committee to government security forces. With intensified repression, the Guatemalan political rhetoric and emphasis on economic modernization more and more resembled that of the military regimes in the Southern Cone of South America. It even seemed at times that Guatemalan military antipolitics and anti-Communism exceeded in virulence the military regimes in Chile and Argentina.[18] In 1977 the Ejército Secreto Anticommunista (ESA, Secret Anticommunist Army) gained notoriety as a leading right-wing assassination organization, following the bloody path blazed by MANO, NOA, and OJO ("Eye for an eye") earlier in the 1970s.

The Guatemalan regime's systematic barbarism conflicted with U.S. President Jimmy Carter's new human rights focus in foreign policy. When a U.S. State Department report in the spring of 1977 severely criticized the military government, the Guatemalans announced in advance of any U.S. formal action that they would reject military assistance conditioned by U.S. intervention in Guatemala's internal affairs. Relations between the Carter administration and Guatemala deteriorated to the point that the U.S. ambassador lost much of the customary influence enjoyed by his predecessors. To fill the gap left by the cutoff of U.S. military assistance, Guatemala turned to Israel, Argentina, and other anti-Communist allies.

Progressive clergy who worked among the rural and urban poor increasingly became subject to persecution. With agricultural labor unions still illegal, peasants attempted to use agricultural cooperatives and clergy-sponsored "base communities" to improve their living conditions and to defend land tenure claims against the encroachment of large landowners. The identification of Indian and campesino organizations with progressive Catholic leaders made the clergy targets of violence. Several years of government repression culminated in a May 1978 military attack and massacre of protesting peasants, joined arm in arm with nuns and priests, at Panzos in El Quiché.

Meanwhile, fragments of the FAR and other guerrilla forces reorganized to form the core of the Organization of the People in Arms (ORPA, survivors of the Edgar Ibarra Guerrilla Front), isolated in Ixam along with the Guerrilla Army of the Poor (EGP). From 1975 to 1980 the EGP gradually expanded its military and political activities, operating primarily in El Quiché and Zacapa, and reemphasized César Montes's earlier focus on incorporating the Indian population into the revolutionary struggle. In late January 1980 a group of Indians and guerrillas occupied the Spanish embassy in Guatemala City to draw attention to their demands for the restoration of their lands. Guatemalan security forces stormed the embassy, and numerous casualties resulted from a fire caused by the attack. The EGP also carried out urban guerrilla operations and selective assassinations of military and civilian leaders.[19] By 1981 the climate of uncertainty, state terrorism, and guerrilla terrorism practically returned Guatemala to the bloodiest situations of the mid-1960s.

The victory of the Sandinistas in Nicaragua in 1979 renewed the hopes of the revolutionary forces and reinforced the determination of the military regime and its civilian allies to repress the resurgence of the guerrilla struggle. Economic recession from 1979 to 1981, combined with rising prices (11 percent per year in 1980 and 1981) and widespread unemployment and underemployment (34 percent of the labor force at the end of 1980), fueled antigovernment sentiments.[20] An agreement by ORPA and the EGP to form a united front in 1980 and to seek alliances with democratic opposition groups further threatened the incumbent government.

With the election of President Reagan in 1980, the shift of the United States back to a hard-line anti-Communist foreign policy greatly encouraged the Guatemalan military. To meet the resurgent guerrilla challenge and to end the personalism and corruption of General Lucas García's administration, junior officers and their sympathizers carried out a coup in 1982. The new government, headed by General Ríos Montt—a member of a non-Catholic charismatic Christian sect, pledged to end the guerrilla menace and to carry out socioeconomic reforms. Like several of his predecessors in the 1960s, Ríos Montt achieved some early military successes against the EGP guerrillas. The regime declared victory in 1983.[21]

After more than two decades of protracted, if uneven, struggle and numerous military defeats, some survivors of the first guerrilla outbreaks—for example, César Montes—continued in their revolutionary efforts. Changes in ideological and tactical emphasis and modifications in military tactics and terrain all reflected the pragmatic adaptation of Che Guevara's basic doctrines from *foquismo* to prolonged popular war. In 1983, as in the early 1960s, the United States gave military and economic assistance to the most recent military leaders, though some congressional critics attempted to prevent the formal resumption of military assistance and the certification of improvement in Guatemala's human rights record. U.S. policy confirmed Che Guevara's essential analysis of the revolutionary tasks in Central America and the Caribbean, even if the simplistic *foquista* formulation of the early 1960s had long since been negated by the bloody reality of Guatemalan history from 1960 to 1983.

In the early 1980s the most prominent replacement for the *foco* thesis consisted of prolonged popular war—a politico-military alliance of "workers, peasants, Indians, Catholics, Protestants, men and women old enough to think and fight, and all patriotic and democratic sectors." In early 1982, the EGP, FAR, ORPA, and sectors of the PGT formed a united front called the Guatemalan National Revolutionary Unity (URNG) in an effort to coordinate military activity (similar fronts had been formed in Nicaragua and El Salvador). Though unable to overcome the complex ideological and personal differences that fragmented the revolutionary movement in Guatemala, this initiative toward military coordination reflected the lessons of the Sandinista victory in Nicaragua in 1979 and the growing political sophistication of Guatemala's revolutionary forces. By April 1982 the URNG pushed for a broader revolutionary coalition of the sort that allowed the 1979 Sandinista victory in Nicaragua. In March 1983 the North American Congress on Latin America (NACLA) graphically summarized the array of antiregime politico-military organizations in Guatemala as follows:

Guerrilla Army of the Poor (EGP)
Biggest of the four groups, with massive organized support in the Indian highlands of El Quiché, Alta and Baja Verapaz, Huehuetenango and Chimaltenango. Operates on seven fronts, including the east of Guatemala. The only guerrilla organization with a truly national structure, it works closely with the farmworkers' CUC. Believes in uniting military and political aspects of the war. Commander-in-Chief: Rolando Morán.

Rebel Armed Forces (FAR)
Descendant of the FAR of the 1960s. Had strong influence in the labor movement of the 1970s. Concentrating on this sector, it only resumed military action in 1978, and has now organized fronts in Guatemala City, Chimaltenango and three areas of the remote, underpopulated Petén. Commander-in-Chief: Pablo Monsanto.

Organization of the People in Arms (ORPA)
Broke from the FAR in 1971 over its neglect of the indigenous question. Launched publicly in 1979. Unlike the EGP, it has no mass organization, but wide peasant support, and works largely as a military entity. ORPA draws its strength from the Indian departments of San

Marcos, Quezaltenango, Sololá, Totonicapán and Huehuetenango. Commander-in-Chief: Gaspar Ilom.

Guatemalan Labor Party (PGT)

The traditional Communist party, now split into three wings, divided mainly on the role of armed struggle. The main body, or camarilla, is criticized by dissidents for neglecting the military work agreed at the 1969 Party Congress. In the 1960s the FAR—then a military commission of the PGT—went independent. More recently, the "Leadership Nucleus" (PGT Núcleo de Dirección Nacional) and the PGT Military Commission have also broken away. All three factions are active militarily, but none is strong. In the labor unions, the PGT camarilla has regained considerable strength.

In January 1982, the EGP, FAR, ORPA and the PGT–Núcleo de Dirección Nacional joined forces in the Guatemalan National Revolutionary Unity (URNG). Discussion is underway to incorporate the remaining PGT factions into the unity.

A fifth politico-military organization, the Revolutionary Movement of the People (MRP-Ixim), rejects membership in the URNG. Originally formed by ORPA dissidents under the name of Nuestro Movemiento (Our Movement), but later joined by militants expelled from the FAR and EGP, and members of the PGT Military Commission. Began actions as the MRP-Ixim in July 1982.[22]

Despite the renewed repression and apparent military victories of the Ríos Montt regime, the Guerrilla Army of the Poor called for an "agrarian, anti-imperialist, and anti-capitalist revolution." It was clear, in light of the last quarter century of struggle, that General Ríos Montt's victory could be no more permanent than the "victories" of Peralta Azurdia, Méndez Montenegro, Arana Osorio, and the military governments in the decade 1970–80. Indeed, Ríos Montt himself was overthrown in mid-1983 by more traditional officers who disliked his evangelical religious affiliation and cronyism. The legacy of Che Guevara and the recent victories of the Sandinistas continued to threaten the old order through 1983 even as the military regime, like its many predecessors, declared victory over the guerrillas. Without a real political and economic transformation, there was less likelihood of "constructive democratic change" in Guatemala in 1984 than in 1961.

In many ways the tragedy of Guatemala epitomized the consequences of U.S. policies that insisted on interpreting political change in Latin America in the framework of a cold war confrontation of super powers and their surrogates. The 1954 CIA-directed ouster of the Arbenz government in the name of hemispheric security established the precedent for future U.S. actions in Cuba, the Dominican Republic, Brazil, Bolivia, Chile, and Central America. In Guatemala itself U.S. cold war policies buttressed a succession of military regimes which, when juxtaposed to Cuban-supported revolutionary insurgencies, transformed the liberal vision of the Alliance for Progress in Guatemala into the reality of a military terrorist state.

During 1983 and 1984 thousands of Guatemalan refugees from the continuing guerrilla war became a matter of more serious international concern as the makeshift refugee camps in southern Mexico served also as bases of support for the guerrilla fighters. Occasional encroachments by Guatemalan troops into Mexican territory intensified pressures for the relocation of the camps farther north and for better Mexican control of its territory against both Guatemalan insurgents and Guatemalan government forces. Meanwhile, political uncertainty and economic hardship persisted within Guatemala. Pawns of cold war confrontations between superpowers and their surrogates, the impoverished people of Guatemala faced an apparently permanent state of internal war.

NOTES

1. Richard H. Immerman, *The CIA in Guatemala: The Foreign Policy of Intervention* (Austin: University of Texas Press, 1982), p. 82. Debate still continues whether the U.S. intervention in Guatemala in 1954 was motivated primarily by concern for the perceived Communist threat in Latin America or by concern for economic interests, including those of the United Fruit Company. See Stephen Kinzer and Stephen Schlesinger, *Bitter Fruit: The Untold Story of the America Coup in Guatemala* (New York: Doubleday, 1982); Cole Blasier, *The Hovering Giant: U.S. Responses to Revolutionary Change in Latin America* (Pittsburgh: University of Pittsburgh Press, 1976; Suzanne Jonas and David Tobis, eds., *Guatemala* (Berkeley: NACLA, 1974); Thomas and Marjorie Melville, *Guatemala: The Politics of Land Ownership* (New York:

Free Press, 1971); Miguel Ydígoras Fuentes, *My War with Communism* (Englewood Cliffs, N.J.: Prentice-Hall, 1963); Ronald M. Schneider, *Communism in Guatemala, 1944–1954* (New York: Praeger, 1958); U.S. Department of State, *Intervention of International Communism in the Americas*, Department of State Publication no. 5556 (Washington, D.C., 1954).

2. "Caracas Declaration of Solidarity, 1954," in *Interamerican Relations*, 92d Cong., 2d sess., printed for the use of the Committee on Foreign Affairs, October 10, 1972, pp. 153–54.

3. Immerman, *The CIA*, p. 82.

4. For background on Guatemalan ethnic and social structure, see Neale V. Pearson, "Guatemala: The Peasant Union Movement, 1944–1954," in Henry A. Landsberger, ed., *Latin American Peasant Movements* (Ithaca, N.Y.: Cornell University Press, 1969) pp. 323–73; Comité InterAmericano de Desarrollo Agrícola (CIDA), *Tenencia de la Tierra y Desarrollo Socio-Economico del Sector Agrícola: Guatemala* (Washington, D.C.: Pan American Union, 1965); Humberto Flores Alvarado, *La Estructura Social Guatemalteca* (Guatemala: Editorial Rumbos Nuevos, 1968); Nathan Whetten, *Guatemala: The Land and the People* (New Haven, Conn.: Yale University Press, 1961); Eric Wolf, *Sons of the Shaking Earth* (Chicago: University of Chicago Press, 1959); George McBride and Merle A. McBride, "Highland Guatemala and Its Maya Communities," *Geographical Review* 32 (1942): 252–68; Richard N. Adams, *Encuesta sobre la cultura de los ladinos en Guatemala* (Guatemala City: Editorial del Ministerio de Educacion, 1955); Richard N. Adams, *Crucifixion by Power: Essays on Guatemalan National Social Structure, 1944–1966* (Austin: University of Texas Press, 1970); Robert Carmack, *The Quiché Mayas of Utatlan* (Norman: University of Oklahoma Press, 1981); Kay Warren, *The Symbolism of Subordination: Indian Identity in a Guatemalan Town* (Austin: University of Texas Press, 1978).

5. CIDA, *Guatemala*; Gerrit Huizer, The *Revolutionary Potential of Peasants in Latin America* (Lexington, Mass.: Lexington Books, 1972), pp. 136–40.

6. Eduardo Galeano, *Guatemala, Occupied Country*, trans. Cedric Belfrage (New York: Monthly Review Press, 1969), p. 17.

7. Kinzer and Schlesinger, *Bitter Fruit*.

8. Richard Gott, *Guerrilla Movements in Latin America* (Garden City, N.Y.: Doubleday, 1971), p. 46.

9. Ydígoras, *My War*, p. 160.

10. Cited in Gott, *Guerrilla Movements*, pp. 52–53, after report from Hsinhua News Agency, 20 February 1962.

11. See Ydígoras's *My War*, pp. 159–60, where he justifies his having allowed the establishment of the anti-Cuban bases in Guatemala and sees a Communist conspiracy to corrupt the Guatemalan military with subversive propaganda.

12. Cited by Gott, *Guerrilla Movements*, p. 56, after *Le Monde*, 7 February 1966.

13. According to the official history, FAR was organized in December 1962 as a coalition of the MR-13 of November Revolutionary Movement, the PGT, and the MR-12 de Abril. Thereafter the MR-12 dissolved, and the MR-13, after coming under Trotzkyist influence, left the FAR. The Edgar Ibarra Guerrilla Front included a coalition of Communists (PGT), MR-13, and Communist Youth (Juventud Patriótica del Trabajo, JPT). While affiliated with FAR, this Guerrilla Front became "virtually autonomous." In March of 1965 the FAR was resurrected by the PGT and Edgar Ibarra Front leadership. This alliance lasted until Turcios's death in 1966.

Emilio Román, a revolutionary–evangelical pastor, with experience going back to the 1954 slaughter in the countryside, helped incorporate Indian (Cakchiquel) fighters into the Guerrilla Front. See Turcios Lima, *Biografía y documentos* (Montevideo: Ediciones de la Banda Oriental, 1969), pp. 32–33. See also Pablo Monsanto, "The Foco Experience: The Guerrillas' First Years," in J. L. Fried et al., eds., *Guatemala in Rebellion: Unfinished Revolution* (New York: Grove Press, 1982), pp. 261–64.

14. In a letter dated 4 May 1963, Che Guevara commented: "In Guatemala the guerrillas are fighting. The people have to some extent taken up arms. There is only one possibility of slowing the development of a struggle that shows all signs of developing toward a Cuba or Algerian-type revolution. Imperialism has that possibility, although I am not sure if they will bother to use it: 'free elections' with Arévalo." In Ernesto Che Guevara, *Reminiscences of the Cuban Revolutionary War* (New York: Grove Press, 1968), p. 265; cited in Gott, *Guerrilla Movements*, p. 58.

15. Galeano, *Guatemala*, pp. 77–78.

16. Cited in *Granma*, February 25, 1968, after Luis Mercier Vega, Guerrillas in Latin America, trans. Daniel Weissbert (New York: Praeger, 1969).

17. See World Bank, *Guatemala: Economic and Social Positions and Prospects* (Washington, D.C., 1978); James F. Petras and Morris H. Morley, "Economic Expansion, Political Crisis and U.S. Policy in Central America," *Contemporary Marxism* no. 3 (Summer 1981): 69–88; Union of Food and Allied Workers Association, *The Coca-Cola Guatemala Campaign, 1979–1981* (Geneva, 1981); NACLA, "Guatemala—The War Is Not Over," *Report on the Americas* 17,

no. 2 (March–April 1983), pp. 4–6; articles from *Compañero* (San Francisco: Solidarity Publications, 1982), pp. 10–11.

18. For a discussion of antipolitics, see Brian Loveman and Thomas M. Davies, Jr., *The Politics of Antipolitics* (Lincoln: University of Nebraska Press, 1978).

19. Guatemala's third-ranking army chief and the head of the IV Corps of the national police was assassinated in 1980; the interior minister and chief of the national police survived assassination attempts. See Daniel L. Premo, "Guatemala," in Robert Wesson, ed., *Communism in Central America and the Caribbean* (Stanford, Calif.: Hoover Institution Press, 1982), p. 91. For a collection of articles on the guerrillas in the late 1970s and early 1980s, see Fried et al., *Guatemala*. The Institute for Policy Studies' "Background Information on Guatemala, the Armed Forces and U.S. Military Assistance," June 1981, reviews the organization and activity of the military, police, and security apparatus in Guatemala during this period, as well as U.S. military assistance and sales to Guatemala from 1950 to 1982.

20. InterAmerican Development Bank, *Economic and Social Progress in Latin America, The External Sector,* 1982 Report (Washington, D.C., 1982).

21. According to NACLA's *Report on the Americas* ("Guatemala — The War Is Not Over"), the Ríos Montt offensive accomplished the following: "It massacred anywhere from 5,000 to 10,000 unarmed campesinos, and uprooted more than a million from their homes. One hundred thousand more languish in Mexican refuge, and all available testimony shows they blame the Army for their trauma. Large stretches of the highlands are devastated; the local economy is in turmoil.

". . . Yet the Ríos Montt offensive failed to deal the Left a strategic defeat — using the best-trained counterinsurgency army in Central America operating at full strength. The brutality of Plan Victoria 82 was explicitly aimed at breaking the EGP, strongest of the four guerrilla groups, but it has failed to do so. In the new year, aerial bombing, village raids and kidnapping expanded to San Marcos in the west, with ORPA the new target. In El Petén in the north, FAR areas too have been hit by Army sweeps, though with less publicity."

22. Ibid., p. 9.

CARIBBEAN   SEA

72°
68°
64°
60°
12°

ZULIA
FALCÓN
DISTRITO FEDERAL
NUEVA ESPARTA
TRINIDAD AND TOBAGO

Maracaibo
Puerto Cabello
La Guaira
Carúpano
ATLANTIC OCEAN

Lago de Maracaibo
LARA
YARACUY
Caracas
Maracay
MIRANDA
SUCRE

TRUJILLO
COJEDES
CARABOBO
ARAGUA
MONAGAS

MÉRIDA
PORTUGUESA
GUÁRICO
ANZOÁTEGUI
DELTA AMACURO

TÁCHIRA
BARINAS
8°

APURE

COLOMBIA
BOLÍVAR
GUYANA

4°

VENEZUELA

AMAZONAS
BRAZIL

- – - – - International boundary
———— Department boundary
○ National capital
• Other major city

| 0 | 100 | 200 | 300 Mi. |
| 0 | 100 | 200 | 300 | 400 Km. |

VENEZUELA

POLITICAL CHRONOLOGY

1945–48 Trienio administration. Acción Democrática (AD) and Junta Revolucionaria de Gobierno implement reformist program, including agrarian reform, mobilization of peasantry, and modification of oil industry leases.

1948–52 Military junta. Repression of AD and reformist movements. Labor and peasant movements demobilized and AD leaders go underground or into exile.

1952–58 Dictatorship of Marcos Pérez Jiménez, a brutal and corrupt authoritarian administration supported by the United States.

1958–59 Junta de gobierno after an uprising and coup against Pérez Jiménez; opposition parties and movements attempt to create basis for coalition and transition to democratic regime.

1959–64 Administration of Rómulo Betancourt (AD). Fidel Castro visits Caracas; antigovernment demonstrations, divisions within AD over domestic and foreign policy (1959). MIR leaves AD. Insurrection in Caracas (October 1960). In late 1961–early 1962 first guerrilla *focos* begin operation. Military uprisings at Carupano and Puerto Cabello, May–June 1962. FALN formally established early 1963. Cuban arms shipment captured (November 1963); relations with Cuba deteriorate. General elections won by AD candidate Raúl Leoni.

1964–69   Administration of Raúl Leoni (AD). Amnesty offered to guerrillas and Communists (PCV). Douglas Bravo expelled from PCV and becomes most visible guerrilla leader. PCV rejects "armed struggle" through *focos* and wages ideological conflict with Cuban-supported guerrillas. Guerrillas suffer numerous casualties without significant military or political successes.

1969–74   Administration of Rafael Caldera (COPEI), first administration of Christian Democrats in Venezuela. Caldera announces pacification program. Communist party regains legal status; amnesty offered to prominent guerrilla leaders; renewal of diplomatic relations with Soviet Union and improved relations with Cuba. Sporadic guerrilla operations under Douglas Bravo based in Falcon-Lara region at very low levels.

1974–79   Administration of Carlos Andrés Pérez (AD). Return of most prominent surviving guerrilla leaders to conventional politics; many ex-guerrillas serve in congress. Nationalization of oil industry undercuts leftist appeals; guerrilla movements practically disappear. Pérez supports Sandinistas against Somoza in Nicaragua.

1979–84   Administration of Luis Herrera Campins (COPEI). In April 1979, Douglas Bravo accepts new amnesty offer. Termination of last important rural *focos.* Venezuelan economy faces economic crisis from world recession. Venezuela plays active role in seeking peaceful solution to guerrilla struggles in Central America.

1984–   Administration of Jaime Lucinschi (AD).

BACKGROUND

In 1959 Venezuela took a dramatic turn toward liberal democracy after a century and a half of dictatorship, brutality, civil wars, and *caudillismo.* Between 1834 and 1888 no civilian presided over Venezuela; from 1892 to 1908, the military rulers returned, followed by the lengthy (1908–35) corrupt and repressive dictatorship of Juan Vicente Gómez. Subsequent military presidents (1935–45) softened the repressive character of the Gómez regime, but a brief reformist interlude from 1945 to 1948, the so-called *trienio,* was followed by ten more years of personalist military rule by Marcos Pérez Jiménez.[1]

Like his Dominican counterpart, Rafael Trujillo, dictator Pérez Jiménez would have been an ideal target for Guevarist-inspired guerrillas. Lacking legitimacy, ruthless and venal, brutal in its treatment of political opposition, the Pérez Jiménez regime, despite efforts to mask its illegitimacy with fraudulent elections and a new constitution (1953), ideally fit Guevara's model of a Caribbean dictatorship. But Pérez Jiménez fled into exile to the Dominican Republic a year before the victory of Fidel Castro's forces in Cuba. After an interim government under Admiral Wolfgang Larrazábal, national elections, regarded by all concerned as honest, brought Rómulo Betancourt to the nation's presidency—the first president in Venezuelan history to come to office through popular elections and to turn over power to a popularly elected successor.

Still, in 1959 Venezuela seemed an unlikely candidate for the establishment, let alone institutionalization, of liberal democracy. There was no historical basis for believing that the coup which had ousted Pérez Jiménez and the subsequent elections would lead to a functioning democracy.

In Venezuela, however, unlike Guatemala, there had gradually evolved a system of modern political parties with pragmatic and relatively effective leadership. The principal leaders of these parties, men like Betancourt, Rafael Caldera, and Jóvito Villalba, emerged from the youthful "generation of 1928" which had first challenged the Gómez dictatorship. These men had headed the *trienio* experiment from 1945 to 1948 and then led the opposition to Pérez Jiménez both within Venezuela and from exile. The political parties that developed from these experiences, Acción Democrática (AD, a social democratic party), Comité Pro Elecciones Independiente (COPEI, a social Christian movement), and the Unión Republicana Democrática (URD, an urban populist party), along with a moderate Communist party (PCV), established linkages or helped to create urban and rural worker-peasant movements. In time, these movements and parties, though far from consolidated in their position in 1959, came to offer viable alternatives to Caribbean dictatorship.

In 1958 the three major non-Marxist parties named above had concluded an agreement—the Pact of Punto Fijo—that guaranteed participation of all parties in a coalition government no matter which candidate won the presidential elections of that year. After Betancourt's victory the pact was honored; and despite later disagreements and defections from the coalition, this initial cooperation of the centrist parties provided a basis for pluralism in national politics and hope for a future for constitutional government.

In the next two decades, Venezuelan liberal democracy (what Che Guevara called "oligarchic dictatorship") survived both rightist coup attempts and leftist guerrilla movements in urban and rural areas without the institutionalization of military terror on the Guatemalan, Brazilian, or Argentine models. To a very great extent Venezuela's successful avoidance of rightist dictatorship and the defeat of leftist guerrilla movements was the result of increasing oil revenues for use in domestic programs and effective political leadership by members of the two major political parties, AD and COPEI. Under pressure from both rightist and leftist opposition, the early AD governments sometimes resorted to firm repression, suspension of constitutional guarantees, extensive use of the secret police and informers, and harsh interrogation of political prisoners. Nonetheless, the Venezuelan regime never adopted on a wide scale the extreme measures of the Guatemalans or, later, the Brazilians, Argentines, or Chileans. Right-wing death squads were not allowed to operate with impunity nor were they encouraged by the government. Indeed, the greatest strength of the government consisted of the broad support it counted upon from the campesinos in the rural areas and from some of the urban working-class organizations. Unlike those of Guatemala, the Venezuelan guerrilla movements never gained the sympathy of the peasantry.

The reason the guerrilla organizations lacked support lay in the recent history of Venezuela. Post–World War II developments in Venezuela began with a premonition of reform and the threat of revolution. Somewhat as in Guatemala from 1945 to 1953, the Venezuelan *trienio* government under Betancourt initiated dramatic social, economic, and agrarian reforms; created a Ministry of Labor; recognized the legitimacy of URD, AD, COPEI, and the Communist party. Electoral reforms, support for unionization of peasants and urban workers, and challenges to foreign domination of the oil industry all represented progressive changes in Venezuelan politics. This reformist climate permitted Rómulo Gallegos of AD to become in 1948 the first president of the counry to be chosen directly by the Venezuelan people under the new provisions for universal suffrage.

Labeled subversive and Communist by the Venezuelan oligarchy and its foreign allies, the *trienio*-AD government fell to a military coup in 1948. The persecution, torture, and murder of opposition forces that followed proved less systematic and more selective, however, than the Guatemalan massacres after 1954.[2] Betancourt himself reinforced the charismatic image he had gained in his earlier years of clandestine political activity (1935–45) at the same time that increased persecution by the regime decimated the AD's strength after 1954. When Seguridad Nacional chief Pedro Estrada emerged as a power in his own right, the infamous Guasina concentration camp became home for numerous opposition political leaders. Unfortunately, the Eisenhower administration paid special homage to Pérez Jiménez's strong "anti-Communism" and the favorable treatment of U.S. investors by awarding the dictator the Legion of Merit and even inviting Pedro Estrada to Washington to meet with Secretary of State John Foster Dulles.

Despite exile and the brutality of the U.S.-supported dictatorship, internal political opposition to Pérez Jiménez never disappeared. After 1954 the exiled leaders of the various political parties maintained contact with their clandestine party organizations and with the urban and rural labor movements. Unhindered by significant linguistic or ethnic cleavages like those in Guatemala, Peru, and Bolivia, the working-class movements and organizations, allied with AD, COPEI, URD, and the Communists, as well as students, businessmen, and progressive military officers survived the ten-year dictatorship with strengthened roots to participate in the general strike that ousted Pérez Jiménez in 1958.[3]

The return of Betancourt in 1959 therefore represented in many ways the culmination of a quarter-century struggle as well as reaffirmation of the hopes and aspirations of the *trienio*. Even as the guerrillas in Guatemala had proclaimed themselves the standard bearers of the ousted Arévalo and Arbenz regimes in that country, Betancourt and AD were elected to renew the struggle for progress in Venezuela.

Just as Fidel Castro overthrew Batista in Cuba in early 1959, the popularly elected administration of Betancourt, drawing upon the legacy of the *trienio,* initiated five years of nationalistic and reformist policies. A new Ministry of Mines and Hydrocarbons was established to increase Venezuela's participation in the profits of the oil industry. Agrarian reform; unionization of the peasantry; industrial projects in steel and petrochemicals; public works, housing, and public service projects were instituted; and for the first time, the national budget contained a larger allocation for education than for the Ministry of Defense.

Too moderate for Venezuela's revolutionaries and too revolutionary for the old guard, the Betancourt government nevertheless represented a real reformist departure for Venezuela. As such it was attacked by international and domestic foes at both ends of the ideological spectrum. Dominican dictator Trujillo sent assassination teams to murder Betancourt and supported efforts at military coups within Venezuela.[4] Military nationalists attempted several *golpes,* and Cuban-inspired (and sometimes -supported) urban and rural guerrillas proclaimed war against the Betancourt administration, rallying splinter movements from Betancourt's own party to the guerrilla cause.[5]

The specific political and social conditions in Venezuela in 1959, however, measured by Che Guevara's criteria in *Guerrilla Warfare,* seemed less favorable to revolutionaries than did conditions in Guatemala—notwithstanding Guevara's own strong support for the Venezuelan guerrillas:

1. The Carribbean-type dictatorship in Venezuela had been ousted in 1958 and replaced late that year by a popularly elected president. Many Venezuelans remembered Betancourt's role in the 1945–48 reform movement, and the new government was perceived as legitimate, perhaps more so than any previous government in Venezuelan history. As Che Guevara pointed out in *Guerrilla Warfare,* this sort of regime made a poor target for guerrilla movements.

Moreover, the party system in Venezuela was on the upswing in 1959. Several centrist parties, along with the Communists, competed openly for political office and even participated in the government coalition. These parties all had important linkages to labor, peasant organizations, and student movements. At the least, even when some groups broke with AD and the coalition, political opposition remained possible, if not always assured. As Che Guevara noted, the guerrilla is likely to be most successful where popular belief holds that there is no realistic alternative to revolutionary violence.

2. The physical terrain of Venezuela offered considerable opportunity for the establishment of guerrilla *focos*. The lack of political roots in the countryside, however, made the rural regions dangerous to guerrilla cadres—particularly the young, urban-bred students, intellectuals, politicos, or nationalist military officers who led the first *focos*.

3. Although rural poverty and the *latifundia* system in Venezuela conformed in some respects to the Latin American image portrayed by Che Guevara, the incumbent regime was sponsoring an agrarian reform program, including support of rural labor organizations. Moreover, the economic, social, and political focus had shifted to urban areas and petroleum in Venezuela, unlike much of Latin America where agriculture played a predominant role. The "agrarian question" had significant salience in Venezuela but less than, for example, in Guatemala. With an urban population of almost 70 percent in 1960 and an ongoing agrarian reform program— including close ties between the major organization and AD—the Venezuelan countryside seemed much less promising for guerrillas than the mountains and coasts of Guatemala, El Salvador, Nicaragua, Peru, or Ecuador. In any case, the Venezuelan guerrillas proved unable to develop an effective "counterstate" in the countryside.

The poverty and exploitation of the Venezuelan campesinos and urban poor conformed to a great extent to Che Guevara's portrayal of the general conditions that would provide the basis for revolutionary struggle in Latin America. However, these groups in the period 1959–63 did not perceive armed struggle as the only means to improve their condition. In this sense Che's emphasis on subjective conditions was correct—but would work against the guerrilla movements in Venezuela during these years.

4. Venezuela's revolutionary Marxist tradition was quite recent and relatively weak. The Communist party and the Movement of the Revolutionary Left—MIR–Armed Forces of National Liberation (FALN) militants who broke away from AD, COPEI, or URD—faced overwhelming obstacles in creating the appropriate subjective conditions for successful revolutionary movements in the countryside. They therefore combined urban terror and random attacks on government and private property with rural guerrilla operations.

ORIGINS OF THE GUERRILLA MOVEMENTS IN THE 1960s

The Venezuelan guerrillas of the early 1960s came from the universities of Caracas, from dissident elements of AD, URD, and COPEI, and, after 1962, from unsuccessful military uprisings headed by nationalist officers. In addition, before the Venezuelan Communist party's mid-1960s decision to withdraw temporarily from the military struggle, guerrilla leaders emerged from the PCV and from some Communist-dominated labor organizations. Similar in social class, education, and even political experience to the officials of the incumbent government, the guerrillas lacked well-developed ties to urban or rural working-class organizations. They also lacked, with the exception of defectors from the Venezuelan armed forces, military training or experience. In this respect the Venezuelan guerrillas initially proved even less prepared for armed struggle than the first guerrilla leaders in Guatemala.

The immediate events preceding overt urban terror and the establishment of rural *focos* involved splinter political movements within AD and URD. Influenced by developments in Cuba and a rising nationalist, anti-American sentiment in the country, students, political dissidents, and nationalist military officers, along with the PCV, pressured the Betancourt administration to enact sweeping social, economic, and political reforms. By May 1960, Domingo Alberto Rangel, Moisés Moleiro, and Américo Martín led the formation of a splinter party called Acción Democrática Izquierdista. (This develop-ment parallels similar events with APRA and Apra Rebelde in Peru and the traditional parties of Colombia during the same period.) Soon thereafter this group changed its name to Movi-miento de Izquierda Revolucionaria (MIR) and proclaimed it-self a Marxist movement.[6] MIR included most of the AD youth movement and a number of the party's deputies in the con-gress. Demonstrations against the Betancourt government in the universities and high schools were met with police repres-sion and closure of the schools by order of the president him-self. National guardsmen even violated university autonomy by invading the campuses and confronting student centers of rebellion.[7] Violence spread to working-class neighborhoods and the government faced an imminent insurrection in Cara-cas—where, counter to his overall victory, Betancourt had lost badly in the presidential elections. Continued government suppression of the student uprisings contributed to URD's withdrawal from the government coalition.

President Betancourt placed blame for the insurrection on MIR and the Communist party. After suspending constitution-al guarantees and appealing to the military to restore order, he declared his enmity toward Cuban-inspired "Castro-Communism" and the local Communists. Subsequently the AD government suffered another setback as Raul Ramos Jiménez led another split from the party in late 1961, taking an additional twenty-six deputies from the AD congressional del-egation and increasing the government's dependence upon the AD-COPEI alliance.

Beset by reactionary obstructionism and leftist student demonstrations and urban violence, the Betancourt govern-ment now faced the first declared rural guerrilla *focos* orga-nized by Communists, Miristas, and a small number of URD dissidents. Weakly organized, ideologically heterogeneous, and militarily inept, the guerrilla bands nevertheless operated in the states of Lara, Falcón, Portuguesa, Mérida, Miranda, Carabobo, Yaracuy, Trujillo, and Zulia. Most of these small, uncoordinated *focos* met immediate defeat at the hands of the Venezuelan military assisted by the United States counterin-surgency programs and even anti-Fidelista Cubans cooperat-ing with the security forces. Lacking any unified political or military command, poorly trained—indeed, little more than frustrated urban political cadres and intellectuals—the initial *focos* achieved even less military success than had their Guatemalan counterparts.

The guerrilla forces received reinforcement from discontented military officers after unsuccessful coup attempts in 1962. In May of that year a naval captain led an uprising at the naval base of Carúpano (250 miles east of Caracas). In words reminiscent of Turcios Lima's proclamation in Guatemala, Captain Jesus Teodoro Molina Villegas explained the motivation of this rebellion:

We can no longer ignore the numberless abuses, arbitrary actions, murders and tortures to which the people are subjected, which have led to the destruction of peace and harmony among Venezuelans. The country is reliving, under Betancourt's reign of terror, the old division of Venezuelans into two groups: those who have every guarantee and those who have none, the persecuted and the persecutors, prisoners and jailers. . . . One of the main aims of our movement is to restore the democratic system where the constitution really holds sway, where the rights of all Venezuelans and the decisions of the National Congress are respected, so that within this framework of real democratic liberties the country can reconstruct its economy, give work to the hundreds of thousands of unemployed, raise the income of the Venezuelans, carry out a genuine Agrarian Reform and develop the economy on the basis of the higher national interest.[8]

Though supported by opposition politicians, including the PCV, the Carúpano uprising was quickly defeated by loyal air force and army units. In response the AD government further restricted MIR and PCV political activities. A second rebellion on June 3, 1962, at Puerto Cabello (seventy miles west of Caracas) required bloody counterattacks and hundreds of casualties before forces loyal to the government achieved victory. Many of the defeated officers and soldiers, having no other place to turn, found refuge and purpose with the guerrilla *focos* in Falcón and Lara states.[9] Thus while they did not form the original cadres of the Venezuelan guerrillas, some military officers appealed to their former comrades-in-arms to join the new armed forces of national liberation.

By the end of 1962, the AD government, supported by a

majority of the rural population and the provincial urban centers, had inflicted military defeat on the rural *focos,* the urban resistance of Caracas (the so-called tactical combat units), and the two principal military uprisings. In addition, the Betancourt administration pushed forward with its reform program in anticipation of the upcoming presidential elections of 1963, thereby undercutting the political appeal of armed struggle.

Military support also proved critical to Betancourt's success. Like the only Guatemalan civilian president of the 1960s, President Betancourt visited the most important military installations of the country and tried to improve living conditions in the barracks and to impress upon the armed forces the government's concern with military professionalization and welfare. The administration expanded loan programs for noncoms and officers for the purchase of private housing and provided other concrete, visible benefits to military personnel. Perhaps most important, President Betancourt maintained relatively good channels of communication with the officer corps, informed them of the government's intentions and programs, and attempted to insulate the military from "politics."

These efforts yielded excellent results, undermining both leftist and rightist insurrections. In none of the rightist uprisings from 1959 to 1961 did the major garrisons (Caracas and Maracay) participate; in the face of both the leftist-supported coup attempts in 1962 and the FALN (see below, next paragraph), the bulk of the officer corps clearly preferred the reforms of Betancourt to the Fidelista alternative. Military suppression of the guerrilla fighters and participation in limited civic action programs sustained the Betancourt government against the revolutionary challenge.

Faced with four years of bitter conflict and few positive results to show for it, the remnants of the disparate opposition (the PCV, MIR, and URD militants, Carúpano and Puerto Cabello survivors, and other anti-regime forces) formally created in 1963 a "unified" revolutionary movement, the Armed Forces of National Liberation (FALN). The official leader of the FALN, Captain Manuel Ponte Rodríguez, had led the Puerto Cabello uprising, and initial FALN documents reflected the military education and values of the disaffected officers: FALN combatants were to respect the lines and property of civilians and of police and military personnel not engaged in operations against FALN units, were to use weapons only in self-defense or under official FALN orders, and to treat prisoners with respect and protect their lives.[10]

Like their Guatemalan counterparts, the FALN claimed to welcome military defectors into the revolutionary fold. In fact the FALN seemed to express a sincere hope that patriotic military officers could substantially assist in the revolutionary task: "The creation of the FALN provides a way out for every honest, patriotic, nationalist, democratic or revolutionary officer. We are building popular institutions in which we can really put into practice our sublime ideals of patriotism and heroism in service of the Fatherland and the people."[11]

Communist participation in the FALN was predicated on the formation of a parallel united political leadership group, the Frente de Liberación Nacional (FLN, National Liberation Front), which could offer a political alternative to the AD-COPEI coalition. Just as they sought to dominate the equivalent political front in Guatemala, the Communists dominated the FLN in Venezuela. Communist political strategy was reflected in the effort to create a program appealing to a multiclass popular-front coalition: "The construction of a united front for national liberation is Venezuela's most urgent task today. Workers, farmers, students, white-collar workers, professionals, artists, writers and poets, businessmen with progressive ideas, sincere clergymen; men and women of all ideologies, religious creeds and political party backgrounds; all who desire a Venezuela master of her own destiny and her own riches, belong to this broad united front of liberation."[12]

POLITICO-MILITARY EVOLUTION OF THE GUERRILLA STRUGGLE

The struggle against the Betancourt government began in the streets of Caracas and was led by urban political cadres, students, and intellectuals. By the fall of 1960 the MIR, through its official publication, *Izquierda,* demanded the overthrow of the government: "The country continues being drowned in the ineptitude of its rulers. There can be no other way out than a change of government, the substitution of the present regime by another which responds to the interests of the people. . . . But it is necessary now to be categorical. We do not advocate the change of government through a barracks revolt or a palace coup. Nor do we impose on the masses an insurrection which they are not capable of carrying out at this moment."[13]

President Betancourt had been in office less than two years, but the MIR already asserted that the scheduled 1963 presidential elections would offer no possibility of change and that only a mass uprising could institute the needed revolutionary changes. Urban street demonstrations, assaults, kidnapings, and "expropriations" (bank robberies to finance revolutionary activity), intended to undermine the government, instead inspired the resentment and anger of most of the urban population. Bombings, assassinations, sabotage (especially of U.S.-owned installations), and disruption of urban transportation systems further alienated many urban residents, including the poor and unemployed of the *barrios*. (Che Guevara had admonished in *Guerrilla Warfare* that "it is necessary to distinguish clearly between sabotage, a revolutionary and highly effective method of warfare, and terrorism, a measure that is generally ineffective and indiscriminate in its results, since it often makes victims of innocent people.")

The Betancourt administration rallied its supporters with pleas to maintain order, and Rafael Caldera, the leader of COPEI, the country's second most important political party and the AD's coalition partner, firmly supported the government.[14]

Unsuccessful in urban revolt, the MIR, PCV, and their allies in the FALN turned the rural *foco*—without ever entirely abandoning urban action. The Betancourt administration responded with vigorous military repression and with socioeconomic progress that dealt political defeat to the guerrilla movements.

U.S. military training, supplies, and participation in the counterinsurgency efforts greatly assisted the Venezuelan forces' violent suppression of the revolutionary cadres.[15] Political defeat of the guerrillas occurred long before the revolutionary leaders acknowledged the futility of further armed struggle. As the Betancourt administration moved toward its close, the FALN called for a general strike in November 1963 to emphasize its campaign against the upcoming presidential elections. Not only did the strike fail, but over 90 percent of the Venezuelan electorate participated in the elections and chose AD candidate Raul Leoni as the country's next president. Despite FALN threats to execute people waiting in line to vote, those elections provided AD with a majority in both houses of Congress. COPEI's Rafael Caldera, a strong supporter of the anti-guerrilla campaign and of the AD-COPEI cooperation, finished second. The Venezuelan populace simply did not share the FALN's rejection of elections and the possibility of democratic reform. Much more than the military defeats, the guerrillas' inability to create the subjective conditions for revolution (what Che Guevara defined as the essential revolutionary task) ensured their failure.

The open support provided by Fidel Castro to the Venezuelan guerrillas and the Cuban leader's vitriolic attacks on President Betancourt seemed to arouse Venezuelan nationalism against both foreign involvement and the supra-national loyalties of the guerrilla forces. In any case, the elections of 1963 illustrated emphatically that guerrilla insurgency without lengthy political work at all levels would fail in Venezuela.

In 1964 the new president, Raul Leoni, offered a general amnesty to the guerrillas of the PCV, MIR, and FALN who would abandon the armed struggle and return to democratic political competition. This offer divided the FALN even as the government intensified its efforts against the rebels. Political debate within the PCV and MIR (many of whose leaders had been imprisoned or killed or were in exile) led gradually to a decision by the PCV to abandon the armed struggle.[16] Whereas the Venezuelan Communists initially espoused armed struggle much more stridently than had their Guatemalan compatriots, they also withdrew relatively quickly from the guerrilla struggle in response to government efforts at repression and then reconciliation.

In the period 1965–67 Douglas Bravo, FALN guerrilla leader, and other Communists in the FALN found themselves expelled from the PCV for rejecting the party's tactical change and discipline. Meanwhile, PCV leaders engaged in bitter rhetorical exchanges with Fidel Castro and the Cuban leadership.[17] Military defeat, defections, betrayals, and ideological fragmentation of the guerrillas pushed Douglas Bravo further toward a strategy of protracted popular warfare as the short-term prospects of the *foco* tactics looked grimmer.

In March 1966 the AD government released Jesus Farias (secretary general of the PCV) and Domingo Alberto Rangel (well-known intellectual and former leader of the MIR) from prison, where they had been incarcerated since 1963. The government also liberated long-term PCV leaders Eduardo and Gustavo Machado. Acceding to the amnesty program, these former guerrillas and urban revolutionaries moved decisively against Bravo and the FALN, seeking to wrest control of the FLN (the political front) from the proponents of the armed struggle. When Fabricio Ojeda, another eminent FALN guerrilla leader who had earlier participated in the interim government that replaced Pérez Jiménez (1958–59) went to La Guaira to mediate with the PCV, military intelligence units captured him. According to the government, Ojeda subsequently hanged himself in his cell. Whether or not Ojeda's death resulted from betrayal by the PCV, it meant the loss of a key person in any effort to reforge the revolutionary unity and created another martyr in the ranks of the guerrillas of the 1960s.

By 1968, FALN's situation appeared pathetic. Che Guevara's death in Bolivia the previous year further disheartened the remnants of the guerrilla *focos.* Nevertheless, MIR proclaimed its determination to carry on the revolutionary struggle "despite the torture, the desertions, the assassinations, and the vicious propaganda of the enemy."[18] Its revolutionary proclamations did nothing, however, to overcome reality.

The year 1969 saw a first in Venezuela: the election of an opposition candidate who peacefully assumed the presidency. In his inaugural address, COPEI's Rafael Caldera offered amnesty to all insurgents in exchange for respect of democratic processes. Moreover, he offered to legalize the PCV (an offer extended to MIR in 1973); to free well-known Communists and guerrilla leaders such as Pompeyo Marquez and Teodoro Petkoff; and to negotiate with Douglas Bravo and the FALN. Although Bravo ultimately rejected the amnesty offer, one authority asserts that Caldera's new pacification initiative "broke the back of the guerrilla movement" and quotes testimony that

Orestes Guerra Matos, a member of the Central Committee of the Cuban Communist party, . . . said that the guerrillas were tired and dispirited due to their lack of victories since the moment when Caldera became president.

The pacification program succeeded partly because of external developments. Under President Caldera, Venezuela established or reestablished diplomatic relations with various communist countries, including the Soviet Union. The official Soviet position of peaceful coexistence, which generally opposed the export of the revolution through violence, coincided with the pacification program's aims. The Cuban government's decision—made in response to strong Soviet pressure—to curtail the support of insurgent groups clearly hurt the Douglas Bravo–led FALN, and made it easier for the guerrillas to consider the promises of pacification.[19]

After a month of negotiations Douglas Bravo decided to continue the guerrilla struggle, unlike many former guerrillas who soon occupied a place in the Venezuelan congress as they returned to civilian life and national politics. At the same time, President Caldera made the pacification program even more palatable to some on the political left by exchanging ambassadors with the Soviet Union and seeking to improve relations with Cuba. Of course, the military defeats inflicted upon the guerrillas by the two AD administrations made the Christian Democratic "pacification" program attractive to many of the leftist politicians and intellectuals tired of clandestinity and discouraged by the Venezuelan people's rejection of revolutionary violence. Although some guerrilla activity continued, especially in the Falcón-Lara region, where Douglas Bravo persisted, the Venezuelan government reported fewer than ten guerrilla fighters killed by government forces from 1969 to 1974.[20]

The Venezuelan government provided genuine political options, changes in public policy, and improvements in the living conditions of some of the rural and urban poor. Made possible to great extent by revenue from the oil industry, this effort on the part of Venezuela's two major parties confirmed

Che Guevara's prediction that liberal democracy—the appearance of alternatives to armed struggle—would work to the disadvantage of guerrilla *focos* in Latin America. The Venezuelan political system failed to meet the basic social and economic needs of millions of the country's inhabitants, but the belief that democratic change might still improve their situation—and the clear evidence that changes in regime could occur through elections—undermined both the appeal of revolutionary politics and the support by the vast majority of the population for armed struggle.

1970 TO THE PRESENT

Although lacking substantial political support, some guerrilla fighters nevertheless continued military operations in the rural and urban areas into the 1970s. After presidential elections in 1973 and the return of AD to the presidency with the victory of President Carlos Andrés Pérez, a number of former guerrillas opposed the new administration from the relative safety of the congress. Included in their numbers was Américo Martín, whom Che Guevara had hailed in the 1960s, in his call for "one, two, many Viet Nams," as leader of one of the Venezuelan *focos.*

Nationalization of the oil industry in 1976 further undercut both leftist and rightist critics of Venezuelan democracy. Lacking both an effective agrarian platform, in part because of government agrarian reform policies from the early 1960s, and now losing the nationalist initiative, the Venezuelan left returned almost entirely to conventional opposition party politics. In 1978 Américo Martín presented himself as MIR's presidential candidate. Defeated handily by the Christian Democrat, Luis Herrera Campins (and also by the AD candidate, as well as by the candidates of other small parties), Martín and his leftist compatriots received less than 15 percent of the vote for congressional seats. Even if this participation in electoral politics is viewed as a temporary tactic, it contributed to the perceived legitimacy of liberal democracy and to belief in the possibility of social reform without insurgency.

The return of the majority of the surviving guerrilla leaders to conventional political activity culminated in 1979 when the COPEI administration of Herrera Campins announced an amnesty for more than one hundred political prisoners and remaining guerrillas, including Douglas Bravo. Whereas Bravo had rejected the amnesty offered in 1969 and continued the struggle against the government of Carlos Andrés Pérez, he now agreed to end almost two decades of armed struggle.[21] In April 1979, Bravo returned to legal public life with a speech in Coro, capital of Falcón state, where he had long led the guerrillas. Acting as a member of a political party, the Partido Revolucionario de Venezuela (PRV, Revolutionary Party of Venezuela), Bravo asked for a minute of silence to honor guerrilla comrades killed in armed struggle—Camilo Torres in Colombia, Carlos Fonseca in Nicaragua, Fabricio Ojeda and Chema Saher in Venezuela, and *comandante* Che Guevara.

There is, of course, no guarantee that significant armed struggle will not return to Venezuela. Poverty, misery, and even the "agrarian question"—the objective conditions Che Guevara postulated for the initiation of guerrilla warfare—continue to exist on a wide scale. International recession, a debt crisis shared with other Latin American nations, and rising unemployment in the early 1980s put new pressure on the Venezuelan political system. Since the early 1960s, however, the political response of the Venezuelan national administrations, along with the apparent consolidation of constitutional liberal democracy, make Venezuela a less likely arena for successful armed struggle than many other Latin American nations. As Che Guevara accurately stated, guerrilla warfare is an essentially political struggle. In Venezuela effective statecraft and political leadership, combined with reformist policies financed with oil revenues, have so far proved an effective barrier to the success of guerrilla-based revolutionary warfare.

Along with the strong domestic political leadership and economic advantages that helped to defeat the Venezuelan guerrilla movements, U.S. support for Venezuela's reformist political parties and U.S. restraint in dealing with Venezuela's nationalization of the petroleum industry contributed to the survival of constitutional government in Venezuela. The Venezuelan leadership's explicit rejection of Marxist ideology and of Cuban influence in politics provided no pretext for U.S. intervention even when U.S. economic interests were threatened or adversely affected by new Venezuelan legislation. Unlike the Guatemalan or, later, the Cuban (1959–62) and Nicaraguan (1979–84) governments, Venezuelan governments exercised a moderate nationalism without identifying Venezuelan reforms or foreign policy with international socialist movements or revolution.

Thus Venezuelan political leaders of both major parties successfully maneuvered in the cold war of the 1960s and 1970s without allowing Cuban-supported Venezuelan insurgents or U.S.-sponsored counterinsurgency to transform the nation's government into a military dictatorship.

NOTES

1. For overviews of Venezuelan politics during the period 1959–84, see Rómulo Betancourt, *La Revolución democrática en Venezuela*, 4 vols. (Caracas: Imprenta Nacional, 1968); Robert J. Alexander, *The Venezuelan Democratic Revolution* (New Brunswick, N.J.: Rutgers University Press, 1964); idem, *The Communist Party of Venezuela* (Stanford, Calif., Hoover Institution Press, 1969); idem, *Rómulo Betancourt and the Transformation of Venezuela* (New Brunswick, N.J.: Transaction Books, 1982); Loring Allen, *Venezuelan Economic Development: A Politico-Economic Analysis* (Greenwich, Conn.: JAI Press, 1977); David Blank, *Politics in Venezuela* (Boston: Little, Brown & Co., 1973); Glen L. Kolb, *Democracy and Dictatorship in Venezuela (New London: Connecticut College, 1974); Daniel H. Levine, Conflict and Political Change in Venezuela* (Princeton: Princeton University Press, 1973); Edwin Lieuwen, *Venezuela* (London: Oxford University Press, 1961); John D. Martz, *Acción Democrática: Evolution of a Modern Political Party in Venezuela* (Princeton: Princeton University Press, 1968); Talton Ray, *The Politics of the Barrios of Venezuela* (Berkeley: University of California Press, 1969).
2. By 1958–59 some leaders of the Venezuelan Catholic hierarchy also spoke out against the dictatorship; in 1958 the Archbishop of Caracas strongly condemned the Pérez Jiménez regime. This presaged the role of progressive Catholics in revolutionary movements in much of Latin America during the decades 1960–80.

3. For a description of some of the dictator's tactics against AD and other opposition groups, see Alexander, *Rómulo Betancourt*, pp. 326–27. Alexander says of the atrocities that "the toll of AD leaders who died in the underground as well as those who perished in exile was very heavy in those years, and many of those who died were long-time friends and associates of Rómulo. Numerous others suffered severely at the hands of Pedro Estrada's secret police."

4. Alexander, *The Venezuelan Democratic Revolution*, p. 112.

5. Richard Gott, *Guerrilla Movements in Latin America* (Garden City, N.Y.: Doubleday, 1971), pp. 121–214. According to Robert Alexander (*Rómulo Betancourt*, pp. 543–44), "one of the early leaders of MIR . . . told Betancourt later that he estimated MIR had received as much as $600,000 from Cuba for the purchase of arms during the first year of its existence. . . . In addition to money the Cubans were providing training." See also Sheldon B. Liss, *Diplomacy and Dependency: Venezuela, the United States and the Americas* (Salisbury, N.C.: Documentary Publications, 1978), pp. 217–25.

6. For a sympathetic treatment of MIR's origins, evolution, and objectives, see James Petras, "Revolution and Guerrilla Movements in Latin America: Venezuela, Colombia, Guatemala and Peru," in James Petras and Maurice Zeitlin, eds., *Latin America: Reform or Revolution?* (Greenwich, Conn.: Fawcett, 1968), pp. 337–43.

7. In Latin America "university autonomy" theoretically means, among other things, freedom from police or military jurisdiction on the campus. In this case, the government responded to student use of the university as a center for revolutionary activity with military intervention, thereby violating the "sanctity" of academia. See Philip B. Taylor, "Venezuela," in D. M. Condit et al., *Challenge and Response in Internal Conflict*, vol. 3 (Washington, D.C.: American University, 1968), pp. 474–75.

8. Gott, *Guerrilla Movements*, pp. 151–52.

9. Taylor, "Venezuela," p. 476; Alexander, *Rómulo Betancourt*, pp. 490–92; Petras, "Revolution," p. 341.

10. See Gott, *Guerrilla Movements*, pp. 160–61. The FALN departed radically from this original code in a program to "kill a cop a day" and disrupt urban transport.

11. Ibid., p. 165.

12. Ibid., pp. 166–67.

13. See quotation from *Izquierda* in Alexander, *Rómulo Betancourt*, p. 485.

14. "In the face of those insurrectional outbursts, the perfect schematic elaboration of which we have proof in documents captured by the police, the government adopted an attitude which was called mild. For three or four days hundreds of adolescents were burning vehicles, attacked people and property. The government did not break them up for fear that a boy or girl of fourteen might be hit by a bullet; but there came the moment in which there was established a solid and compact united front among men of the ultra-Left, the remains of the dictatorship, and gangsters. One morning the populous neighborhood '23 de Enero,' where more than one hundred thousand persons live, saw the spectacle of commercial establishments ransacked and destroyed, homes assaulted, the *Banco Obrero* dismantled. At that moment I assumed before my country and before history the responsibility of calling upon the armed forces to reestablish public tranquility." See Alexander, *Rómulo Betancourt,* pp. 487 – 88.

15. By 1969 the United States spent almost eight million dollars on military assistance to Venezuela and, even with diminution of the guerrilla threat, continued to provide over one million dollars a year. See U.S. Department of State, "Republic of Venezuela Background Notes," Washington, D.C., 1969, p. 7.

16. Document dated 7 November 1965 and quoted in Fidel Castro's speech at the University of Havana, 13 March 1967. Cited by Gott, *Guerrilla Movements,* p. 189.

17. Examples of these exchanges are cited above in the Introduction.

18. João Batista Bernardo, *Guerrilhas, e Guerrilheiros* (São Paulo: Impressão Dag-Dagostino Artes Gráficas, 1981), p. 133.

19. Donald L. Herman, *Christian Democracy in Venezuela* (Chapel Hill: University of North Carolina Press, 1980), p. 132.

20. Ibid., p. 133.

21. Ironically, Pérez's strong support for the Sandinista guerrillas in Nicaragua greatly assisted the overthrow of dictator Anastasio Somoza in 1979. See Somoza's own bitter denunciation of President Pérez in Anastasio Somoza, as told to Jack Cox, *Nicaragua Betrayed* (Boston: Western Islands, 1980).

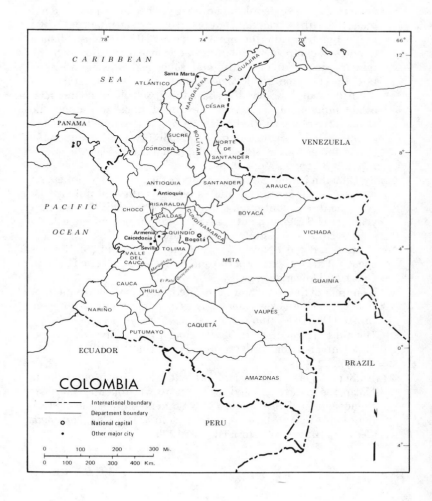

COLOMBIA

- - - International boundary
——— Department boundary
○ National capital
• Other major city

| 0 | 100 | 200 | 300 Mi. |

| 0 | 100 | 200 | 300 | 400 Km. |

COLOMBIA

POLITICAL CHRONOLOGY

1930–36 Administrations headed by presidents from the Liberal party.

1930–34 Administration of Enrique Olaya Herrera (Liberal).

1934–38 Administration of Alfonso López Pumarejo (Liberal). Reformist program called "Revolución en Marcha"; populist reforms, expansion of suffrage, tax reforms, liberalization of laws on unions and collective bargaining; resistance by Conservatives and moderate Liberals.

1938–42 Administration of Eduardo Santos (Liberal) — a moderate Liberal administration. Some retrenchment on reforms of past government.

1942–45 Second administration of Alfonso López Pumarejo; marred by scandal and obstructionism of opposition. Attempted military coup in 1944. President resigns in 1945, replaced by interim coalition headed by Alberto Lleras Camargo. Divisions in Liberal party over populist program and charismatic appeal of Jorge Eliécer Gaitán allow Conservative victory in presidential elections.

1946–50 Administration of Mariano Ospina Pérez (Conservative party). Intensified sectarian conflict; *Bogotazo* (1948) initiates era of *la violencia* (1948–ca. 1958).

1950–53 Administration of Laureano Gómez and Roberto Urdaneta. President Gómez suffers heart attack in 1951;

violencia spreads. Country immersed in civil war with marauding guerrilla bands.

June 1953   Military coup headed by General Gustavo Rojas Pinilla. Amnesty for guerrillas; depoliticization of national police; political prisoners released; women given suffrage.

1954–57   Administration of General Gustavo Rojas Pinilla. National Constituent Assembly gives Rojas Pinilla 1954–58 term in office. Efforts to quell *violencia* and establish a populist administration that replaces Liberal-Conservative basis of politics. Economic recession and political difficulties prove too much for Rojas Pinilla's populism; Rojas attempts to have himself chosen for another four-year term (1957).

May 1957   Military coup ousts Rojas Pinilla after student protests, civic strike, and middle-class opposition grows. New civilian-military coalition.

1957–58   Fifteen months of interim junta as traditional political parties seek new formula for national politics. Pact of Sitges initiates National Front as Conservatives and Liberals agree to "alternate" the presidency.

1958–62   Administration of Alberto Lleras Camargo (Liberal). MOEC founded as first Fidelista movement in Colombia; guerrilla *focos* go into action in 1962. Regime responds with counterinsurgency plans.

1962–66   Administration of Guillermo León Valencia (Conservative). Rise of Colombian *focos* and guerrilla movements. Plan Lazo counterinsurgency program initiated. ELN created (1964). Simacota manifesto (1965). Camilo Torres issues call for "popular unity," joins guerrillas, and dies in combat. FARC created (1966). Guerrilla organizations and "independent republics" suffer defeat at hands of counterinsurgency forces.

1966–70   Administration of Carlos Lleras Restrepo (Liberal). Continued but less significant guerrilla activity. EPL joins in guerrilla struggle (1968). Colombian army almost triples in size (1964–68).

1970–74   Administration of Misael Pastrana Borrero (Conservative). Last official National Front administration; decline of guerrilla movements. Challenge of political reform and other political movements and parties. Two leaders of ELN killed (October 1973); "final eradication" of FARC announced.

1974–78   Administration of Alfonso López Michelsen (Liberal). Resurgence of ELN, FARC. M-19 emerges as leading urban revolutionary organization. Dissatisfaction within Colombian military over failure to destroy guerrillas.

1978–82   Administration of Julio César Turbay Ayala. M-19 continues activities in urban areas. Occupation of Dominican embassy (February 1980); Fidel Castro participates in negotiations to resolve impasse. Scandals involving drugs and corruption within military. ELN and FARC renew sporadic rural operations. Government passes new antisubversive legislation; rightist death squads attack "subversives." Colombia breaks relations with Cuba.

1982–   Administration of Belisario Betancur. Conservative "populist" administration offers amnesties to M-19 and other guerrillas; no definitive "pacification" obtained. Betancur participates in efforts to achieve negotiated settlement of insurgencies in Central America.

BACKGROUND

In 1958 Colombia celebrated the ouster of the populist military dictator Gustavo Rojas Pinilla and the restoration of civilian government. Unlike their Venezuelan neighbors, however, Colombians had experienced little previous military intervention in national governance in the twentieth century. Before the coup that brought Rojas Pinilla to power in 1953, Colombian elites prided themselves on the continuity of civilian rule. Yet in 1953 they welcomed a military coup that promised to end years of civilian-inspired civil war and bloodshed. Unfortunately, in Colombia civilian rule did not mean internal peace. Indeed, as a popular saying had it, "En Colombia que es la tierra de las cosas singulares, dan la paz los militares y los civiles dan la guerra" (Colombia is an unusual place; the military brings peace and the civilians bring war).

Political violence has been endemic to Colombia throughout its national history. Unlike many other Latin American nations, Colombia never overcame the nineteenth-century political divisions between Conservatives (clericals) and Liberals (anticlericals); never resolved the nineteenth-century issues of centralism versus federalism; never established a national government that truly forged and administered a nation; never replaced personalism, factionalism, and the quest for partisan hegemony with a modern political agenda. Unable to accommodate new political groups and movements during the socioeconomic change of the late nineteenth and early twentieth centuries, the Colombian political system did not even enjoy the benefits of social peace bestowed by "Liberal" dictators like Porfirio Díaz in Mexico or Guzmán Blanco in Venezuela.

Recurrent civil war, regional insurrections, "revolutions," "disturbances," blood feuds, and vendettas throughout the nineteenth century culminated in the "war of a thousand days" (1899–1902). This war left over 100,000 dead, thousands more maimed, the economy prostrate, and ended in a draw. Conservatives retained the presidency but concluded separate peace treaties with several Liberal generals in different parts of the country. These treaties presaged the next half century of intraparty and interparty competition and feuds—with no final reconciliation.

The years 1902–46 are treated in conventional Colombian historiography as years of "social peace" and evolution of constitutional government.[1] In some ways they were. Colombians were spared widespread civil wars; the country was governed by elected civilian presidents; the congress functioned more or less as one would expect from an oligarchic legislature; coup attempts by the military were infrequent and military dictators nonexistent. Despite the corruption and fraud typical of elections, Colombian citizens of all classes tended to identify with one of the two major parties. Given the economic crisis of the 1930s and the more typical authoritarian response in the Caribbean and Central America, Colombia seemed to represent a "democratic" departure from the Latin American norm.

During these years Colombian governments included factions of both national parties. Usually the clerical-anticlerical issues and the conflicts over the extent of national administration in the hinterland could be temporarily resolved with appropriate distribution of patronage, government contracts, and gentlemanly accords among the members of the political class, the *gente decente,* who ruled the nation.

However, Conservative party dominance in the first decades of the twentieth century was accompanied by mounting social tension. Workers' movements upset the old order, and peasant demands for land reform, better wages, and improved working conditions led to considerable violence.[2] Brutal suppression of a strike by the United Fruit Company's banana workers in 1928, street demonstrations in Bogotá in June 1929, and unsuccessful but widespread insurrections in July 1929 divided the Conservative party before the 1930 presidential elections. This division permitted the election of a Liberal candidate (backed by dissident Conservatives) to begin sixteen years of Liberal party control of the presidency (1930–46).

The first Liberal administration (Olaya Herrera, 1930–34) took some halting steps toward social and economic reform without menacing the Colombian oligarchy; the following administration of Alfonso López Pumarejo (1934–38) proved too serious in its reformist policies for the Conservatives and many of the president's Liberal compatriots. Anticipating to some extent the Guatemalan reforms of 1944–54 and the Venezuelan *trienio* (1945–48), López Pumarejo called his program "Revolucion en Marcha" (Revolution on the March). Borrowing from the Mexican constitution, the New Deal in the United States, the Cárdenas administration in Mexico, and the Peruvian Apristas, President López Pumarejo's program focused upon democratization of Colombian politics, at the very time that the depression moved many Latin American nations back toward authoritarian personalist dictatorships.

Obstructionism within his party and fierce Conservative resistance frustrated López's initiatives. The president threatened to resign in 1937 but finished his term without great success in implementing his most essential programs. Having ignited sparks of hope among the working classes and the peasantry, López Pumarejo was reelected in 1942 after the more moderate administration of Eduardo Santos (1938–42). This time, however, even López's exaggerated moderation could not overcome both Liberal and Conservative antipathy; the president could not complete his terms of office because of scandals involving his family, congressional obstructionism, and an attempted coup in 1944. López resigned in 1945 and was replaced by an interim coalition government headed by

Alberto Lleras Camargo. The leadership of the left wing of the Liberal party now passed to Jorge Eliécer Gaitán, a student leader of modest social origins and great popular appeal. The division of the Liberal party allowed the Conservatives to regain the presidency for the first time since 1930 just as Conservative factionalism had allowed a Liberal victory in 1930.

Unfortunately for Colombia, the spirit of the Conservative party had grown more and more reactionary, with its principal ideologues committed to restoration of the Hispanic-Catholic tradition. There were frontal attacks on even the moderate reforms achieved during the 1930s and early 1940s, along with religious intolerance. In turn the Liberal leadership now devolved on the charismatic personage of Gaitán, a long-time supporter of agrarian reform, peasant organization, and workers' movements. The combination of traditional Conservative-Liberal conflict and the added burden of intensified class conflict made for an irreconcilable confrontation.

Jorge Gaitán was no latecomer to Colombian politics. In 1929 he had served as a Liberal congressman and harshly criticized government repression of the banana workers' strike at Santa Marta.[3] Since the workers' movement confronted a large American firm, Gaitán became a nationalist hero as well as a political patron to the peasantry. Rejected by his Liberal compatriots, Gaitán founded the Unión Nacional Izquierdista Revolucionaria (UNIR) and agitated without great success for social and agrarian reform. After returning to the Liberal party, Gaitán served in congress, the senate, as minister of education, and as mayor of Bogotá. Immensely popular among the working classes and the peasantry, Gaitán represented the progressive hope within the Liberal party.

When López Pumarejo resigned from the presidency in 1945, Gaitán's oratorical skill, charisma, and over two decades of reformist struggle made him a leading Liberal candidate for the presidency in 1946. However, many members of the Liberal party majority feared Gaitán's reformist bent, his populist rhetoric, and his personalist appeal. These elements of the party presented Gabriel Turbay, a much more moderate candidate. Gaitán ran his own separate campaign, supported by socialists, Communists, and leftist Liberals. This split in the

Liberal ranks permitted Conservative candidate Mariano Ospina Pérez to win the presidency.[4]

Though willing to compromise with the moderate Liberals, Ospina Pérez found himself the leader of a party moving even further toward reaction. Spiritually motivated by the Hispanist ideology of Laureano Gómez, the Conservative administration essentially rejected liberal democracy and the political participation of labor and peasant organizations won in the 1930s.[5]

From 1946 on, direct confrontations between organized labor and the new administration resulted from the government's efforts to break the influence of organized labor.[6] Sponsoring the formation of parallel unions, the Conservatives, with the support of moderate Liberals, used all the resources of the government to destroy the emergent popular movements. Threatened by the *trienio* experiment of the Acción Democrática–military junta regime in neighboring Venezuela, the Colombian oligarchy blamed Communists and Venezuela's Rómulo Betancourt for the surge of protest in rural and urban Colombia.

Government violence provoked a violent response. Liberal partisans and guerrillas resisted the Conservative onslaught and Colombia entered the era of "*La Violencia*" (the Violence). Between 1946 and 1953, thousands of Colombians died as Liberal and Conservative militias, guerrillas, and bandits killed, maimed, and butchered their adversaries.[7]

Polarization intensified in June of 1947 when the National Liberal party directorate named Gaitán its leader. This represented a victory for the leftist factions within the party and a clear danger to the moderate Liberals and the Ospina Pérez government. Sporadic partisan violence in the countryside and provincial towns was met with increased government coercion and abuse. The Conservative government seemed determined to achieve hegemony and to turn back the clock fifty years—or, as some argued, several centuries.[8]

In this atmosphere Colombia hosted the Ninth Pan American Conference in Bogotá in April of 1948. Attended by distinguished dignitaries from throughout the hemisphere, the conference provided every opportunity for the opposition to embarrass the Conservative government. Yet no one in attendance anticipated the disaster to follow. April 9 an assassin killed Jorge Gaitán. News of the death spread quickly. Years of frustration exploded into urban insurrection. John Martz, an expert on Colombian politics, suggests that "the death of Gaitán was, for Colombia, comparable to the assassination of Austrian Archduke Franz Ferdinand at Sarajevo."[9]

What followed was more like the urban riots of the 1960s in the United States—but with partisan political overtones.[10] Rioters destroyed much of downtown Bogotá. Conservative newspapers, churches, and the homes of government leaders were put to the torch as the movement degenerated into looting and pillage. Many Liberal police joined the mobs, while army troops defended the presidential palace and indiscriminately killed people on the streets. Violence spread to other urban centers quickly; in some places Liberals ousted Conservative officials and carried out undeclared regional coups. Colombia rapidly fell into chaos.

Thus, just as the 1954 counterrevolution is the starting point for understanding modern Guatemalan politics, so this urban insurrection (called the *Bogotazo*) and the ensuing nationwide violence is the benchmark for recent Colombian history. For the next twenty years Colombians tortured, maimed, and slaughtered one another with a viciousness and barbarity that made them unique in twentieth-century Latin America. Liberal and Conservative partisans alike engaged in widescale brutality, massacre, and inhumanity.[11]

Barbarism did not entirely end "normal" partisan politics. After congressional elections in 1949, the Liberals retained control of the legislature.[12] Sectarian violence remained so intense that in September of 1949, a gunfight in the congress left one Liberal congressman dead and several others wounded. In anticipation of the upcoming presidential elections and the inevitable Conservative victory through fraud and intimidation, the Liberals decided on a strategy of abstentionism. At the same time they moved to impeach President Ospina Pérez. The president responded by closing down congress, imposing press censorship, and declaring a state of siege. Two days after a Liberal-sponsored nationwide strike and an abortive coup attempt, the unopposed Conservative candidate, Laureano Gómez, won the presidential election on November 27, 1950.

For the next three years, even after Gómez's heart attack in 1951 and his semireplacement with the minister of war, Urdaneta Arbalaez, the Gómez administration sought to impose a Hispanist version of dictatorship on Colombia. Downplaying his previous love affair with Franco's Spain and his support for the Axis powers during World War II, Gómez nevertheless explicitly rejected liberal democracy and made clear the reactionary character of his medieval dream for Colombia.

Repression of Liberalism also entailed persecution of Protestant sects (often equated with Communism), the labor movement, peasant organizations, and all forms of political opposition. Purges of Liberal army officers and police added military expertise to the guerrilla partisans while politicizing the armed forces.[13] Sponsoring constitutional change to institutionalize this Colombian version of Franco's Spain, Gómez finally went too far when he attempted to remove General Gustavo Rojas Pinilla from his military command for fear that Rojas Pinilla was becoming too popular or that he offered an alternative to *continuismo*. Although Rojos Pinilla was essentially loyal to Gómez and to the conservative cause, his ambition and his desire to end the violence forced him to assume national direction. For the first time since the nineteenth century, the Colombian military took power, to the great pleasure and relief of the majority of the Colombian people.[14]

Despite Rojas Pinilla's initial popularity and his attempts to create a "third force" in Colombian politics, however, his imitative populism ultimately failed to halt the violence in the countryside or to duplicate the mystique of his role model, Juan Perón in Argentina.[15]

Like Perón, Rojas Pinilla sought to create a clientelistic labor movement, gain support from the armed forces, and erode the power of the traditional parties. As in the Argentine case, economic difficulties, the eventual rejection of the "third force" by the Church (even though Rojas Pinilla continued the persecution of Protestants), loss of military support, the recuperation of the political parties, and Rojas Pinilla's personal indiscretions (including his effort to revise the constitution and extend his term of office to 1962) finally provoked a military coup.[16] In late 1958, the provisional military junta returned political authority to an elected coalition government under the new "National Front" format that assured rotating presidencies of Liberals and Conservatives from 1958 to 1974.

To seal the National Front bargain negotiated in the so-called Pact of Sitges (July 20, 1957) in Spain, Laureano Gómez administered the oath of office to Liberal president Alberto Lleras Camargo. Lleras Camargo declared in his inaugural address that a primary objective of his administration would be to put an end to *la violencia* through an "intense campaign of pacification." By May of 1959 the minister of government, Amaya Rodríguez, announced that the average number of deaths per day from *violencia* had been reduced from 15.2 to 4; two days later, however, renewed violence in Tolima, Caldas, and Valle left over 200 dead.

As the message of Che Guevara swept across Latin America in the early 1960s, Colombia had already experienced several decades of rural violence, guerrilla warfare, and urban disorder. It was a nation whose central government still did not control parts of the countryside, the mountains, and the hinterland. It was also a country in which a new National Front coalition had determined to reassert government control over the national territory. This determination would include redefinition of the political responsibilities of the national police and armed forces as the defenders of the Frente Nacional against internal insurgency.

Given this recent political history of Colombia and the socioeconomic contradictions of the moment (1958–60), Colombians influenced by Che Guevara and the Cuban revolution faced a confusing situation in assessing the possibilities for revolutionary guerrilla warfare:

1. Colombia experienced no Caribbean-type dictatorship in all of the twentieth century. The only military populist leader of the century (Rojas Pinilla, 1953–57) was overthrown almost two years before Fidel Castro's victory in Cuba. The new government installed in 1958 represented a historic effort by the country's two traditional parties to restore internal peace and "democracy" to Colombia.

The major Colombian political parties, Conservative and Liberal, traced their lineage to the nineteenth century and claimed intense, even fanatical loyalties from their multi-class devotees. Indeed, party identification seemed almost "genetic," passed from generation to generation. Peasant and worker identification with the traditional parties served as a significant barrier to recruitment to leftist and revolutionary movements.

Notwithstanding the apparent strength of the party system, the recent conflicts of the two major parties had contributed to two decades of partisan guerrilla violence, banditry, and savagery involving practically genocidal confrontation among families and entire villages. Rather than serving as institutional supports for peaceful democratic processes, electoral competition between the parties had been used to "justify" the *violencia*.

2. The physical terrain of many parts of Colombia, even more so than Guatemala and Venezuela, offered numerous opportunities for guerrilla *focos*. In fact, politically inspired guerrilla bands and "independent republics" of peasantry operated for decades outside the control of the national government before the Cuban revolution. Jungles, mountains, and isolated *llanos* separated from urban centers by difficult terrain and poor transportation systems were ideal centers of guerrilla operations.

3. In 1959 the agrarian question remained a powerful political, economic, and social issue. Peasant grievances of long standing, labor disputes with landlords, the attempted reoccupation of lands abandoned during the *violencia,* the concentration of large amounts of the best agricultural land in some 5,000 *latifundios*, and the desire to participate in traditional export agriculture—coffee and, later, marijuana—all provided the objective conditions for guerrilla leaders to assume the role of agrarian revolutionaries according to Che Guevara's prescription.

Whereas recent massive migrations to urban areas in response to the *violencia* or in quest of better opportunities had reduced pressure on land resources in some regions, more than half of Colombia's population lived in rural areas in 1960. Many resided on tiny smallholds (*minifundio*) too small to support the subsistence needs of a peasant family. Colombia's agriculture in 1960–62 still contributed 30 percent of the value of gross domestic product (about the same as in Guatemala). This compared with only 3.5 percent in Venezuela. Similarly, agricultural exports accounted, by value, for 70–80 percent of total exports. This meant that any real agrarian reform could have significant economic as well as political implications for public policy.

Colombian political elites emphasized the extent of virgin lands and sponsored "colonization" projects to defuse the agrarian issue. While not successful in practical terms, the existence of new lands did reduce to a limited extent the pressure for land redistribution. It also created the perception by some peasants of a government effort to respond to demands for farmland and economic opportunity. In this sense the frontier could erode support for agrarian revolutionaries.

4. Colombia's revolutionary Marxist tradition was, like Venezuela's, quite recent and very weak. Nevertheless, some isolated rural zones with substantial Communist party influence existed as liberated zones or "independent republics." These areas were for decades outside the effective authority of any national government; they might have served as ideal bases for Guevarist-inspired revolutionary movements. For all practical purposes these zones, and others controlled by Liberal guerrillas, bandits, or simply peasant partisans, already maintained a "counter-state" apparatus that provided for "law and order," collected taxes, and performed some functions of regional adminstration. Nowhere else in Latin America did such extensive counter-state institutions exist in the early 1960s; that they antedated the guerrilla revolutionaries of the post-Cuban era provided both opportunities and dilemmas.

ORIGINS OF THE GUERRILLA MOVEMENTS IN THE 1960s

The National Front government came to office promising to restore order and pacify the rural regions subject for years to the *violencia.* U.S. policy makers and Colombian elites firmly believed that the remnants of Liberal guerrillas, bandits, peasant partisans, and the existing "independent republics" potentially offered recruits and base areas for revolutionary guerrilla movements on the Cuban model. This fear was not unfounded, for as a Communist party member, Alberto Gómez, reminded readers in the 1960s, "the first major center of guerrilla struggle in Latin America" had been established with the assistance of the Communist party many years before the Cuban revolution.[17]

The initial rural pacification programs of the Lleras Camargo government failed to prevent urban intellectuals, students, and Liberal party dissidents from taking up the call of Che Guevara and the Cuban revolution. Early in 1960, students in Bogotá founded the Movimiento de Obreros, Estudiantes, Campesinos (MOEC, Workers', Students' and Peasants' Movement), the first self-declared Fidelista organization in the country. This movement sprang originally from a strike protesting an increase in bus fares in the capital (a typical student protest in Latin America). Antonio Larotta and Federico Arango, the movement's early leaders, both were killed by 1962. A guerrilla *foco* initiated by MOEC in Uraba failed disastrously. Though maintaining its existence into the late 1960s, MOEC's major contribution would be to provide the basis for one of Colombia's most important rural guerrilla movements; the National Liberation Army (ELN).[18]

Also founded in the early 1960s, the Frente Unido de Acción Revolucionaria (FUAR, United Front for Revolutionary Action) consisted largely of intellectuals attempting to link the memory and program of Jorge Gaitán to the Cuban revolution (a tactic the Sandinistas in Nicaragua used with greater success; see the section on Nicaragua below). An offshoot of the National Popular Gaitanista Movement (MNPG), organized by Gaitán's daughter and her husband (a former socialist) after a trip to Cuba in 1960, the FUAR allied leftist Liberals, socialists, and revolutionary youth. FUAR received financial support from Cuba and for a brief time seemed to be the leading Fidelista movement in Colombia.[19] Soon, however, Gaitán's daughter and her husband left the movement, asserting it had been penetrated by police spies and that it had failed to reach the masses. Despite the revolutionary proclamations, FUAR never created

a viable revolutionary threat or guerrilla movement that challenged the incumbent government (with the exception of the
pathetic *foco* of several hundred followers of Tulio Bayer in the
department of Vichada).[20] In addition to their inability to emulate the Cuban *foco,* neither FUAR nor MOEC exhibited any
talent for urban guerrilla warfare equal to that of their early
Venezuelan counterparts.

Not until the mid-1960s—after the Colombian military
with vast U.S. military assistance carried out massive counterinsurgency programs against the previously existing guerrilla
movements and "independent republics"—did new revolutionary guerrilla *focos* emerge in Colombia. In January of 1965,
former militants of MOEC, students, professionals, and
peasants led by Fabio Vázquez Castaño occupied the town of
Simacota in Santander. This action of "armed propaganda"
resulted in a political declaration, the Simacota Manifesto,
which defined the role of the ELN in the revolutionary struggle
ahead: "The wealth belonging to the whole Colombian people
is looted by American imperialists. But our people, who have
felt the lash of exploitation, poverty, and reactionary violence,
is rising up and is ready for war. Revolutionary struggle is the
only way for the whole people to overthrow the present rule of
deceit and violence. We, who form part of the National Liberation Army, are in the fight for the national liberation of Colombia. Whether Liberals or Conservatives, the people will
join together to overthrow the oligarchy of both parties."[21]

Supposedly the ELN had originated in the hut of a peasant
named Parmenio in July 1964; since that time it had prepared
itself ideologically, logistically, and militarily for its emergence from secrecy.[22] The ELN program called for the people to
seize power and set up a popular and democratic government,
which would institute genuine agrarian reform; economic and
industrial development, including housing and urban reform;
the organization of a people's credit system; and the organization of a national public health plan to bring medical services
to all sectors of the population. The program sought educational reform, state organization of transportation and upgrading of
the country's road system, incorporation of the small Indian
population into national life, freedom of thought and worship,
an independent foreign policy in opposition to imperialism,

and the formation of a permanent people's army to guarantee the victories of the popular sectors. In effect, the ELN called for a national popular revolution in the spirit of the Cuban experience.

In March 1965, Camilo Torres, a progressive priest and intellectual from an elite Colombian family, issued a call for a movement of "popular unity." Attacking the reactionary role of the Colombian Church, U.S. imperialism, and the Colombian oligarchy, Camilo Torres soon headed an urban political movement sympathetic to the Colombian guerrillas. After bitter confrontation with the Colombian Church hierarchy, Camilo Torres left his priestly duties to dedicate himself to organizing and mobilizing a Frente Unido of "unaligned" forces to challenge the incumbent Frente Nacional.[23]

Calling upon Catholics, Communists, dissident Liberals, workers, peasants, students, and patriotic military officers to oppose the farcical, oppressive Frente Nacional, Camilo Torres became the symbol of the new progressive Church in Latin America. Unfortunately, he proved a poor politician. Unable to accomplish his political task, frustrated by Communist and Liberal sectarianism, Camilo Torres joined the ELN in the mountains, becoming the most celebrated guerrilla priest in Latin America in the 1960s.

In early 1966, Camilo Torres died in combat against the Colombian military's counterinsurgency forces. As Richard Gott, an expert on Latin America guerrilla movements, notes, like Che Guevara, "Camilo Torres in death was a more potent symbol than he had been when alive, especially outside his own country."[24] Though the ELN would achieve few military successes of any consequence in the 1960s, it gave to Marxist revolutionaries throughout Latin America the hope of a new alliance between the guerrillas and Catholic revolutionaries in the anti-imperialist struggle—a hope more and more realized in the 1970s and 1980s with the spread of liberation theology and the recruitment of clerics to the revolutionary cause.[25]

Concerned with the political direction of the revolutionary guerrilla movement in Colombia and the challenge of the ELN, the Colombian Communist party (PCC) decided in early 1966 to assert more formal control over the guerrillas of the southern regions and the remnants of the forces from "independent republics." In 1964 the Communist party had encouraged a "First Southern Guerrilla Conference" which brought together peasants, bandits, and guerrilla leaders from the "independent republics," along with two urban groups, "to coordinate the groups' activities under a single command."[26] This Communist initiative coincided with a massive campaign (Plan Lazo; see below) by the Colombian military to extend national authority to the autonomous zones. With the peasant guerrillas on the defensive (or, using the Communist euphemism, "having adopted the tactic of mobile guerrilla operations"), the tenth congress of the Colombian Communist party in January 1966 recognized the need for full-scale guerrilla struggle even if the conditions were not right for rural insurgency:

> The armed struggle has been going on in Colombia, in its peasant guerrilla form, since even before there could be said to be a revolutionary situation in the country. It would be negative and fatal for the Colombian revolutionary movement to stand by and watch the destruction of this force while waiting for a revolutionary situation to mature before beginning the armed struggle. The armed aggression of the enemy must be met by guerrilla resistance and armed struggle in the countryside. When conditions permit, this should be spread to the cities and working-class areas.[27]

In April 1966 leaders of the "Guerrilla Bloc of the South" established the Fuerzas Armadas Revolucionarias de Colombia (FARC, Revolutionary Armed Forces of Colombia). In a very real sense the organization of the FARC amounted to a defensive reaction to the Colombian- and U.S.-sponsored attack on the "independent republics." Even so, Communist support for FARC proved less than total; like other guerrilla movements in Latin America, the FARC experienced contradictions between the Communists' desire to direct and control the guerrilla organizations and the party's vacillating policies in regard to the relative importance of the electoral struggle versus the armed struggle.

Like their FALN counterparts in Venezuela, some FARC leaders resigned from the Communist party in the period 1967–70, when the party entered into legal (electoral) struggle and deemphasized the guerrilla tactic. Inasmuch as this redefinition of priorities coincided with the Liberal administration's establishment of diplomatic relations with the Soviet Union, many Colombian guerrillas reacted bitterly. By the end of the 1960s, FARC's existence as an important latent force in Colombian politics was overshadowed by the temporary lull on the military front.

Joining the ELN and the FARC in resistance to the Frente Nacional in 1968, the Ejército Popular de Liberación (EPL, Peoples' Liberation Army) added a pro-Peking, Maoist line to the Colombian guerrilla struggle. Some EPL militants had left the Communist party over ideological difference, others came from the old band of the experienced guerrilla leader Manuel Marulanda, former Liberal guerrilla forces, or even Conservative guerrilla cadres. Denouncing the revisionism of the Communists and the FARC, the EPL began military operations in Cordoba province in 1968 after two years of political preparation and organization of the peasantry.[28] The EPL made clear its ideological differences with the Guevara-inspired *foquistas* and the Communists, but also emphasized the lack of alternatives to armed struggle in order to make a revolution in Colombia.

Along with its FARC and ELN compatriots, the EPL remained a very isolated military and political force to the end of the 1960s. Unlike their Venezuelan counterparts, however, the major revolutionary guerrilla movements of Colombia continued in operation into the 1970s despite intense counterinsurgency and civic action programs dedicated ostensibly to their extermination. The legacy of the *violencia,* the political bankruptcy of the Colombian elites, and the inspiration of the Cuban revolution contributed to the guerrillas' survival—if it did not assure their victory.

POLITICO-MILITARY EVOLUTION OF THE STRUGGLE

The basic premise of the Frente Nacional consisted of the return to political power by the traditional political parties, while eliminating the basic source of violent confrontation between them: control of the state apparatus. The coalition agreement provided for even distribution of ministries, governorships, local government positions, and administrative posts between the two parties and among the factions within each party. The presidency would rotate between the two parties (this was the principle of alternation, hotly contested by dissidents within each party). The political truce was to last for sixteen years and to exclude other political forces. In theory this arrangement would allow for the pacification of Colombia, economic stabilization, and an equitable participation of the Liberals and Conservatives in policy making and the fruits thereof. Through popular referendum the two major parties incorporated this political truce into the national constitution. Gradually, however, the exclusion of other political groups became a legal fiction; by 1970 former dictator Rojas Pinilla almost won the presidency by registering his National Popular Alliance (ANAPO) as a dissident faction of both the Liberal and Conservative parties.

The National Front achieved transfers of government that were peaceful, by Colombian standards, during its tenure (1958–74), but it did not secure a growing attachment to or respect for liberal democracy by the Colombian people because it was an obvious farce. Whereas the democratization of Venezuelan politics from 1959 into the 1970s discouraged revolutionary guerrilla movements, Colombian politicians and political parties inspired disdain, despair, and apathy. In the 1960 congressional elections, less than one-third of the eligible voters bothered to cast a ballot; presidential elections in 1962 brought only 100,000 more voters to the polls, although registration had increased by over 1,000,000 since 1960. Almost 70 percent of Colombia's eligible voters abstained from the 1978 presidential elections.[29]

Also unlike Venezuela, Colombia gained from the National Front's vocal acceptance of the Alliance for Progress very little real agrarian reform, little or no income redistribution, and no effective incorporation of the urban workers and peasants into viable organizations connected to the political system.[30] Neither of the two major parties, nor even the leftist wing of the Liberals, achieved anything like the linkages that Venezuela's Acción Democratica or COPEI had established with peasant organizations and the urban labor movement.

More serious still, the commitment by the first two National

Front governments to economic stabilization, diversification, and regional development did almost nothing to ameliorate the miserable working conditions and wages of the majority of the Colombian people. Strikes by workers in a large number of industrial sectors—textile, banking, soft drinks, transport, petroleum—as well as student protest added urban unrest to the continuing (if somewhat diminished) challenge of rural violence. Personalist factions within each party routinely called into question the legitimacy of the principle of alternation and of the political truce itself. Criticism by the elites of the pact reinforced popular cynicism and undermined the pretense that liberal democracy prevailed in Colombia.

With the transition to Conservative president Guillermo León Valencia in August of 1962, the mockery of the popular will became more obvious. Conservatives clearly lacked majority support, yet the majority of Liberal party leaders supported a patrician Conservative for the presidency. Political alienation increased as even the moderate reforms of the Lleras Camargo years proceeded at a slower pace or were reversed. First priority was given to definitive pacification of the countryside. At the insistence of the United States, this concept extended to the "independent republics" where little overt threat to the government existed, but where government authority failed to reach.

Under Lleras Camargo, pacification of the countryside had incorporated the basic doctrines of U.S. counterinsurgency and civic action along with the periodic amnesties offered previously and cooptation or extermination of *antisociales* (antisocial elements). As described by Communist militant Alberto Gómez, these policies reduced the level of violence to some extent but far from ended it: "Rehabilitation was selective and aimed at winning the political support of sections of the peasantry, especially the ex-guerrillas and their leaders, or at least neutralizing them. On the other hand, districts whose population continued to regard the government with distrust were denied economic aid. The local organization in these areas were [*sic*] persecuted as before and many of their leaders, especially ex-guerrillas, were murdered."[31]

Even after these pacification programs, political violence—

that is, between Liberal and Conservative partisans as well as "bandit violence"—remained in 1961–62 two-thirds of what it was in 1958. Government estimates suggested that in 1962, more than 160 guerrilla bands operated with about 3,000 fighters.[32]

The Plan Lazo, a massive, U.S.-funded counterinsurgency operation, was initiated in July of 1962, at the end of the Liberal administration, but unfolded after August 1962 under the direction of General Alberto Ruíz Novoa. Ruíz Novoa had been an active proponent of an expanded role for the armed forces in national development and pacification. His views had been made known in the country's most important military journals—views highly consistent with the counterinsurgency–civic action programs developed by the United States to defeat Guevarista-inspired insurgency.[33] Having served as commander of Colombia's military contingent in Korea, and having absorbed American, French, and Israeli conceptions of civic action and counterinsurgency, Ruíz Novoa combined an intense anti-Communism with a pragmatic vision of a "new army," a politically committed, modernizing armed force.

The Plan Lazo committed the Colombian armed forces to eradicating the guerrilla bands remaining from the *violencia* and to destroying the "independent republics" whose existence defied national sovereignty. The plan marshaled all forces of public order—the military, the national police, national detective forces, internal revenue agents, later even civilian self-defense units—in a unified effort to restore public order. "Perhaps the most notable military aspect" of the program, according to one authority, "was the adoption of counterguerrilla warfare techniques that were highly dependent on sophisticated intelligence-gathering and analysis. . . . Army tactical units acquired a '*comando localizador*,' or unconventional warfare shock group, which clandestinely killed or captured guerrilla and bandit leaders. In addition, Mobile Intelligence Groups (*grupos moviles de inteligencia*) were attached to all major operating units. Their activities seem to have included counterguerrilla work similar to the *comando localizador*, as well as information-gathering."[34]

The Plan Lazo's success in destroying the "independent republics" and many of the old guerrilla bands contained the seeds of an important failure both for the operation's director and for Colombia's dominant political elites. In addition to the harshness of the military campaign itself and the brutal interrogation methods used, Ruíz Novoa's ever more vocal insistence on a political role for the military in integrating Colombian development led to his forced resignation in 1965. Colombian politicians feared a "Brazilian model" coup, perhaps accurately foreseeing the eventual turn of events in Argentina, Peru, and later Chile and Uruguay. More specifically, the Plan Lazo forced the Communist party and other revolutionaries in Colombia to adopt a mobile guerrilla strategy since their long-held base zones no longer offered security.[35]

Under the pressures of revolutionary guerrilla movements and the impetus of the Plan Lazo, the Colombian armed forces nearly trebled in size, increasing from 22,800 in 1964 to 64,000 in 1968. This expansion of the military corresponded to the additional support personnel required for the counterinsurgency programs, including helicopter maintenance and communications equipment.[36] The destruction of the old guerrilla groups and the "independent republics" resulted in dramatically increased military expenditures and operations rather than a diversion of funds to domestic development.

In the subsequent Liberal administration of Carlos Lleras Restrepo (1966–70), the continued, if relatively minor, activities of the FARC, ELN, and EPL, along with urban support networks, required ongoing counterinsurgency operations. Deemphasizing civic action by the military (transferring these programs to civilian agencies), the Lleras Restrepo administration nevertheless carried out Plan Lazo–type counterinsurgency sweeps from 1966 to 1970 in the southern regions and in Cordoba, with a primary emphasis on physical suppression of the guerrillas.[37] During this entire period the major achievement of the guerrilla groups consisted of survival.

With all the special circumstances influencing the development of the guerrilla struggle in Colombia, the immediate military outcome seemed little different than that experienced in Guatemala and Venezuela in the 1960s. With few exceptions the guerrillas operating in isolated rural regions or through urban movements achieved little or no military success. However, the long-term political effect of the Colombian guerrillas and their urban supporters was not yet clear. Into the 1970s the Colombian political system failed to cultivate popular support or to attain legitimacy, but mass popular support for the guerrillas also failed to develop. Leftist factions within the Liberal party, particularly elements of the Movimiento Liberal Revolucionario (MRL, Revolutionary Liberal Movement), student activists, some labor organizations, and many campesinos still looked to the revolutionary, nationalist, anti-imperialist program of Camilo Torres and the guerrilla cadres as Colombia's only realistic alternative to the existing misery and political putrefaction. The legacy of Camilo Torres, the guerrilla priest, drew other Catholics into the revolutionary struggle; other men of the cloth joined several of the guerrilla fronts.

Whereas the Venezuelan guerrillas lost the political battle for revolutionary change even before their military defeat, the military limitations of the Colombian guerrillas contrasted markedly with the failure of the Colombian oligarchy to consolidate a political, social, and economic bulwark against aspirations for revolutionary change. These aspirations, the legacy of Che Guevara, Camilo Torres, and the still-operative ELN and other guerrilla forces critically challenged Colombian elites and their U.S. allies as the country moved into the 1970s. With the majority of Colombia's population politically disaffected but committed neither to the government nor to revolutionary change, the political-military struggle remained undecided.

1970 TO THE PRESENT

The National Front pact officially ended with the conservative administration of Misael Pastrana Borrero (1970–74), notwithstanding the Liberal and Conservative agreement to maintain the coalition arrangement without presidential alternation. Having accomplished the not insignificant feat of reducing the level of rural violence, the National Front partners had nevertheless failed to implement any fundamental structural reforms or to gain wider respect for the principles of liberal democracy.

Reducing the level of rural violence had not entirely eliminated the legacy of *violencia*; explicitly ideological guerrilla movements continued to plague the civilian regime. Adding to the existing problems of chronic rural violence, guerrilla activity, and partisan conflict, Colombia now became the principal supplier of marijuana and cocaine to the United States. Colombian processing plants and smugglers served as conduits for the coca leaf production of Peru and Bolivia. Thousands of Colombian campesinos increased their incomes from cultivation of the drug crop. Reaching to all levels of Colombian society, the drug economy, in practice much larger than the economy based on the official major export crop, coffee, further corrupted the political process, the criminal justice system, the military, and the highest levels of government administration.[38]

Moving toward the end of the original National Front pact, the Pastrana Borrero administration faced the dilemma of implementing proportional representation (rather than "parity") for political parties in departmental assemblies and municipal councils (as provided in a constitutional amendment of 1968). Former dictator Rojas Pinilla's populist ANAPO party represented an important third force in the congress and at the local level; traditional Conservatives and Liberals retained only 46.5 percent of the congressional seats.[39] With two-thirds of the congressional votes necessary on many important issues, the legislative system became stalemated even more than before. Although ANAPO's strength practically disappeared by 1974, a very large increase in voter turnout to support ANAPO in the 1970 elections indicated widespread discontent with the National Front's performance.[40]

When the Pastrana administration took power, the revolutionary guerrilla movements of Colombia remained active but very limited in operational capabilities and influence. In 1973 the government and military command made the decision to eradicate the ELN and the FARC "once and for all." By October 1973, the military had killed two of the three Vásquez Castaño brothers, leaders of the ELN, and captured the organization's principal ideologue, Lara Parada. For the moment the ELN cadres dispersed in northeastern Antioquía and the region of Medio Magdalena. The military then turned its power against the FARC in southern Tolima and Huila; newspapers periodically announced the "final" eradication of the guerrillas.[41]

Just as rural violence and partisan conflict became endemic in Colombia, however, so the guerrilla movements seemed always to resurge. Under Liberal president Alfonso López Michelsen (1974–78), the ELN, supposedly destroyed, celebrated ten years of struggle with several major attacks on government targets; the FARC also renewed its operations. In addition, a new revolutionary movement, the M-19, moved into prominence. At first claiming to be the armed branch of ANAPO, the M-19 invaded the Quinta de Bolívar "to defend the honor of the nation." Evolving slowly, the eclectic M-19 became a more serious urban guerrilla threat to the regime in February 1976. Commemorating the death of Camilo Torres, it initiated a series of urban operations, including "expropriation" of food and consumer goods for distribution to the poor in the city's shantytowns.[42]

The resurgence of guerrilla activity renewed the debate within the military establishment over counterinsurgency and civic action and the political role of the armed forces. General Álvaro Valencia Tovar took up the mantle of Ruíz Novoa from the 1960s; like Ruíz Novoa in the mid-1960s, Valencia Tovar was dismissed (forced into retirement) amid widespread rumors of a coup. Within the military the general's ouster meant victory for the hard-line tendency of Defense Minister Varon Valencia ("increased military action against the guerrillas and a firmer line against the labor and student protest movements").[43] Further unrest in the military followed the involuntary retirement of five more generals in December 1977; the high command called on the government "to implement effective emergency measures and guarantee the armed forces structures and its members the respect they deserve."[44]

The inability of the López Michelsen government and its successor, that of Liberal president Julio César Turbay Ayala (1978–82) to destroy the revolutionary forces pushed Colombia further in the direction of the military regimes in the Southern Cone. Though civilians continued their formal dominance (witness the dismissal of the "political" officers), de facto and de jure military administration over much of the country followed the adoption of "security statutes" that criminalized "subversive propaganda" and "public disorder" (labor or student protests). Military administration—including brutal interrogation, torture, and murder of suspected subversives—belied any pretense of real constitutional government. A massive roundup of "subversives" in the 1979 campaign against the M-19 brought widely protested violations of human rights but still failed to halt M-19's urban operations.[45] M-19 activities included a well-publicized raid on the principal military installation in Bogotá and the capture of a large amount of armaments and the February 1980 occupation of the embassy of the Dominican Republic in Bogotá (which obtained the freedom, through exchange of hostages, of numerous political prisoners and M-19 militants). In this latter episode Fidel Castro participated in the negotiations that facilitated a resolution.

Right-wing and military response came quickly. Military intellectuals resuscitated the Ruíz Novoa–Valencia Tovar line in the *Revista Militar del Ejercito:* "Subversion survives, with greater strength than before, and with the souls of patriotic and loyal soldiers, we have the vague premonition of worse days to come. We are convinced that the army can militarily destroy the guerrillas, but we are also convinced that even with this, subversion will continue as long as the objective and subjective conditions in the economic, social and political fields, which daily impair and disrupt stability, are not modified.[46]

This emphasis on the military's role in eliminating the objective and subjective conditions leading to subversion was a backhanded acknowledgment of Che Guevara's legacy; it also made many Colombians review the recent history of Brazil, Peru, Uruguay, and Chile. President Turbay's own reaffirmation of democratic institutions rang hollow to anyone who lived the Uruguayan or Chilean experiences of 1970–73: "Those who believe in such a possibility [a coup] are mistaken because the armed forces are democratic and loyal to the constitution.''[47] An academic observer commented, perhaps more realistically: "If the armed forces are drawn to oust the civilian elite because of a threat of social revolution, they will be almost certain to play a conservative role in defense of class and institution. . . . Once confronted with the unlikely prospect of another breakdown in civil order, as in 1953, or with a durable, threatening coalition such as Allende headed in Chile, the armed forces would undoubtedly take control of the government.''[48]

Up to 1982 the further militarization of political administration and the lack of any significant reforms by the government reduced the need for an overt military coup. Military participation in the anti-drug programs of the Turbay administration provided additional economic opportunities or, as one writer suggests, "front-line exposure to corruption."[49] By the end of the Turbay government, the defense minister, General Camacho Leyva, renewed the propaganda war against the Colombian Communists and Cuba— alleged supporters of the M-19, ELN, and FARC. In March 1982 the government broke diplomatic relations with Cuba. Two months later the armed forces again declared victory over the guerrillas.

As in Guatemala, however, the military won no real victory over the revolutionary forces despite its immediate tactical successes. Urban violence and sporadic rural guerrilla warfare continued into the adminstration of the newly elected populist-Conservative president, Belisario Betancur (1982–), and was met by counterinsurgency operations. U.S. President Reagan's fiscal year 1982 budget proposal made Colombia the second largest recipient of military assistance after El Salvador, even as President Betancur attempted to move Colombia toward a more independent foreign policy.

Meanwhile, the M-19 and other guerrilla groups, after some initially favorable reactions, rejected the new administration's latest amnesty proposals, declaring that "the question was not about guns, but about social transformation."[50] In the beginning of 1983, Alfonso Yaqui, member of the M-19 political command, asserted that his organization's actions represented a new revolutionary option for Colombia: "For us, political-military action became a form of political participation. Contrary to what happened to earlier movements which only confronted the state's military apparatus, the Army, our actions always had a clear political objective—to force the government to face the problems of the country and seek popular support."[51]

In late 1983 and early 1984, M-19 and the FARC continued military and political activity despite Betancur's amnesty offer. In the meantime, rightist death squads and military counterterrorist operations, which seemed to operate outside the scope of presidential control, assassinated leftists and former guerrillas who had accepted the amnesty. President Betancur sought nevertheless to implement the amnesty on an individual basis and to reincorporate elements of the revolutionary left into the legal political process. The president's efforts, however, could not overcome generations of conflict. In mid-March 1984, a spectacular M-19 military operation forced Betancur to declare a state of siege in several regions of endemic violence as the guerrilla leadership declared the futility of peaceful reform in Colombia. For Colombia, as for Guatemala, the guerrilla struggle continued in the 1980s.

By the end of May 1984, however, President Betancur's crackdown on drug operations, which, some analysts argued, helped to finance the guerrilla organizations, and a renewed offer of an "armed amnesty" seemed to produce a breakthrough: the major guerrilla movements agreed to a truce with the government. Certain key military leaders vehemently opposed the agreement, causing serious dissension within the military establishment. Nevertheless, the president's policies, reminiscent of similar efforts in Venezuela in the late 1960s and the 1970s, gained acceptance, and a tenuous peace prevailed by mid-June 1984. This glimmer of hope notwithstanding, Colombia had still not overcome its legacy of violence or established a real basis for liberal democratic government. Fundamental ideological and policy differences separated the major revolutionary politico-military organizations from President Betancur's populism. It remained unlikely that these conflicts could be reconciled.

Despite two decades of palliative reformist legislation (land reforms, educational reforms, tax reforms), "most of the empirical evidence suggests that the distribution [of income] deteriorated during the 1970s."[52] The military sustained the regime and administered much of the countryside under states of siege or security statutes—a situation not likely to change until a populist administration bent on real socioeconomic reform and political participation by the rural and urban poor makes it imperative to move toward a "solution" modeled on the Chilean or Uruguayan military dictatorship.

NOTES

1. For overviews of Colombian politics, see Robert H. Dix, *Colombia: The Political Dimensions of Change* (New Haven: Yale University Press, 1967); Orlando Fals Borda, *Subversion and Social Change in Colombia* (New York: Columbia University Press, 1969); Vernon Lee Fluharty, *Dance of the Millions: Military Rule and Social Revolution in Colombia, 1930–1956* (Pittsburgh: University of Pittsburgh Press, 1957); Germán Guzmán et al., *La Violencia en Colombia*, 2 vols. (Bogotá: Tercer Mundo, 1963, 1964); John D. Martz, *Colombia: A Contemporary Political Study* (Chapel Hill: University of North Carolina Press, 1962, 1964); Robert Maullin, *Soldiers, Guerrillas, and Politics in Colombia* (Lexington, Mass.: Lexington Books, 1973); Paul Ocquist, *Violence, Conflict and Politics in Colombia* (New York: Academic Press, 1980); James L. Payne, *Patterns of Conflict in Colombia* (New Haven: Yale University Press, 1968); Richard S. Weinert, "Violence in Premodern Societies: Rural Colombia," *American Political Science Review* 60 (June 1966): 340–47.
2. Ocquist, *Violence*, pp. 80–89, details numerous case studies of rural conflicts during the period 1920–40 in Quindio, Sumapaz, southern Tolima, northern Huila, Cundimarca, and other regions of Colombia.
3. At the request of the United Fruit Company for restoration of order, the Colombian government violently suppressed the strike, then massacred, banana workers at Santa Marta in 1928. Partly in response to these events, dissident Liberals, socialists, and Communists, along with worker and student organizations, initiated an abortive armed insurrection in July 1929.
4. Martz, *Colombia*, p. 46, reports the following results: Ospina Pérez, 565,894; Turbay, 437,089; Gaitán, 363,849. Despite the

Liberals' majority position, the split in the party allowed the Conservative candidate to win the election.

5. Explaining his political philosophy in 1953, Gómez declared: "Universal suffrage contradicts the nature of society. The management of the State is by definition a product of the intelligence. An elemental observation shows that intelligence is not equally distributed among the members of the human species. In that aspect society resembles a pyramid whose vertex is occupied by . . . an individual of very outstanding position by his intellectual condition. Below are found those with lesser capacities, who are more numerous. Thus continues a kind of stratification of social capabilities . . . abundant in inverse proportion to the shine of intelligence, until arriving at the base . . . which supports the entire pyramid and is composed of the obscure and inept multitude, where rationality scarcely appears to differentiate between human beings and brutes." cited in Martz, *Colombia*, pp. 149–50.

6. For descriptions of repression of labor organizations from 1945 to 1947, see Ocquist, *Violence*, pp. 112–13; Miguel Urrutia, *Historia del sindicalismo en Colombia* (Bogotá: Ediciones Universidad de los Andes, 1969); Daniel Pecaut, *Política y sindicalismo en Colombia* (Bogotá: La Carreta, 1973); Robert Alexander, *Communism in Latin America* (New Brunswick, N.J.: Rutgers University Press, 1957), pp. 243–52.

7. See Eric Nordlinger, "Conflict Regulation in Divided Societies," Cambridge: Harvard University Center for International Affairs, *Occasional Papers in International Affairs* no. 29, p. 76.

8. See Martz, *Colombia*, pp. 148–69; Antonia Garcia, *Gaitán y el problema de la revolución Colombiana* (Bogotá: Cooperativa de Artes Gráficas, 1955), p. 299. Church spokesmen managed to incorporate the whole gamut of religious, partisan, and cold war issues into their calls for "holy war." Thus Ocquist, *Violence*, p. 173, cites a pastoral delivered by the bishop of Santa Rosa de Osos which reads in part: "Yes, the battle in these moments in the entire world, and especially in Colombia, is against the powers of Hell, which seek to destroy it. It is the battle of Christ against Belial, of good against evil, of the truth against error, of light against darkness, of Rome against Moscow."

9. Eric Hobsbawm suggests that this insurrection represented an incipient social revolution which, for want of leadership, "subsided into a state of disorganization, civil wars, and local anarchy." "The Revolutionary Situation in Colombia," *World Today* 19 (June 1963): 248–58.

10. Just as Che Guevara participated in the 1954 events in Guatemala,

Fidel Castro, as a radical young student, experienced the *Bogotazo* in Colombia in 1948.

11. See Norman A. Bailey, "La Violencia en Colombia," *Journal of InterAmerican Studies,* October 1967, cited in Richard Gott, *Guerrilla Movements in Latin America* (Gardan City, N.Y.: Doubleday, 1971), p. 225: "Certain techniques of death and torture became so common and widespread that they were given names, such as 'qpicar para tamal,' which consisted of cutting up the body of the living victim into small pieces, bit by bit. Or *'bocachiquiar,'* a process which involved making hundreds of small body punctures from which the victim slowly bled to death. Ingenious forms of quartering and beheading were invented and given such names as the *'corte de mica,' 'corte de franela,' 'corte de corbata,'* and so on. Crucifixions and hangings were commonplace, political prisoners were thrown from airplanes in flight, infants were bayoneted, school children, some as young as eight years old, were raped en masse, unborn infants were removed by crude Caesarian section and replaced by roosters, ears were cut off, scalps removed, and so on.".

12. This, despite the vehement opposition of much of the Colombian Church hierarchy. Throughout the country local priests and their religious superiors preached against the evils of Liberalism, Marxism, and Protestantism.

13. See Daniel L. Premo, "The Colombian Armed Forces in Search of a Mission," in Robert Wesson, ed., *New Military Politics in Latin America* (Stanford: Hoover Institution Press, 1982), pp. 153–55. Numerous studies have attempted to explain the causes of the *violencia* in Colombia. Paul Ocquist, *Violence,* pp. 129–53, summarizes the great range of explanations, from partisan conflict to family vendettas, local disputes over land and water rights, or fights over the local coffee crop. Ocquist's list of types of causes—political, socioeconomic, institutional, psychological, cultural, racial—covers a great number of social science theories as well as the particulars of the Colombian case in a highly useful synthesis of the literature.

14. See Rojas Pinilla's call for a return to "Peace, Law, Liberty, Justice for all, without differentiations or preference for the classes more or less favored," cited in Martz, *Colombia,* p. 168.

15. Despite his ultimate ouster in 1957, Rojas Pinilla retained much of his popularity among the urban poor and lower middle class, who remembered his populist policies. This nostalgia almost elected him president of Colombia in 1970. See Dix, *Colombia,* pp. 117–19, for a summary of Rojas Pinilla's programs.

16. For an analysis of the downfall of Rojas Pinilla, see Martz, *Colombia*, pp. 213–27.

17. Alberto Gómez, "The Revolutionary Armed Forces of Colombia and Their Perspectives," *World Marxist Review*, April 1967, cited in Gott, *Guerrilla Movements*, p. 234.

18. German Guzmán Campos, *La Violencia en Colombia, parte descriptiva* (Cali, Colombia: Ediciones Progreso, 1968), pp. 459–60, offers a critical evaluation of MOEC's activities in the early 1960s.

19. Dix, *Colombia*, p. 279.

20. See Gott, *Guerrilla Movements*, pp. 244–46, for descriptions of the Bayer "*foco*."

21. Cited in Gott, *Guerrilla Movements*, pp. 259–60.

22. Ibid., p. 258.

23. See John Gerassi, ed., *Revolutionary Priest: The Complete Writings and Messages of Camilo Torres* (New York: Random House, 1972). In his introduction, "Camilo Torres and the Revolutionary Church," Gerassi analyzes the revolutionary influence and inspiration of Camilo within the Latin American Church.

24. Gott, *Guerrilla Movements*, p. 300.

25. See Penny Lernoux, *Cry of the People: The Struggle for Human Rights in Latin America—The Catholic Church in Conflict with U.S. Policy* (New York: Penguin, 1980, 1982); Gustavo Gutiérrez, *A Theology of Liberation: History, Politics and Salvation* (Maryknoll, N.Y.: Orbis Books, 1973).

26. Maullin, *Soldiers*, p. 30.

27. Cited in Gott, *Guerrilla Movements*, pp. 518–19.

28. Ibid., p. 304.

29. Russell H. Fitzgibbon and Julio A. Fernández, *Latin America: Political Culture and Development*, 2d ed. (Englewood Cliffs, N.J.: Prentice-Hall, 1981), p. 175.

30. See R. Albert Berry and Ronald Soligo, eds., *Economic Policy and Income Distribution in Colombia* (Boulder, Colo.: Westview Press, 1980). Peter Dorner and Herman Felstehausen, "Agrarian Reform and Employment: The Colombian Case," *International Labor Review* 102, no. 3 (September 1970): 221–40, report: "The 196 programmes, while widely hailed as agrarian reform, have done little to expand income or employment opportunities for peasants or to reorder the overall distribution of land" (pp. 222–23).

31. Gómez, "The Revolutionary Armed Forces," p. 248.

32. Maullin, *Soldiers*, p. 28.

33. For discussion of Ruíz Novoa, civic action, and the "new mission" of the Colombian military from 1961 to 1965, see Anthony

P. Maingot, "Colombia," in Lyle N. McAlister et al., *The Military in Latin American Sociopolitical Evolution: Four Case Studies* (Washington, D.C.: American Institute for Research, 1970), pp. 174–78. Jean Larteguy, *The Guerrillas*, trans. Stanley Hochman (New York: World Publishing Co., 1970), p. 161, cites Ruíz Novoa as follows: "The war of the future will be guerrilla warfare. . . . Sometimes it will be Communism that will attempt to seize power by means of subversion. At other times Communism will have to face guerrillas who are trying to recuperate land for the West. At the moment, it is the West that has to recuperate Colombian lands which have fallen into the hands of the Communists."

34. Maullin, *Soldiers*, p. 75. For the romanticized memoirs of "an undercover agent of the Colombian Army," see Evelio Buitrago Salazar, *Zarpazo the Bandit*, trans. M. Murray Lasley (Birmingham: University of Alabama Press, 1977).
35. For the official Communist party version of the Plan Lazo and formation of the FARC, see *Colombia en pie de lucha* (Prague: Editorial Paz y Socialismo, 1967).
36. Premo, "The Colombian Armed Forces," p. 161.
37. See Maullin, *Soldiers,* pp. 45–49, 79.
38. For a discussion of the diplomatic conflict between the U.S. and Colombia over the drug traffic, see Daniel L. Premo, "Colombia: Cool Friendship," in Robert Wesson, ed., *U.S. Influence in Latin America in the 1980s* (Stanford: Hoover Institution Press, 1982), pp. 104–7.
39. ANAPO's populist character is brought home clearly by Robert Dix, "Political Oppositions under the National Front," in R. Albert Berry et al., eds., *Politics of Compromise: Coalition Government in Colombia* (New Brunswick, N.J.: Transaction Books, 1980), pp. 131–79.
40. By 1974 Rojas Pinilla's daughter clearly led ANAPO; Rojas Pinilla, old and ill, died in 1975. ANAPO was essentially a populist and personalist movement that could not survive its leader—unlike *Peronismo* in Argentina. For analysis of the 1970 elections, see Reza Rezazadeh and Joseph McKenzie, *Political Parties in Colombia* (Ann Arbor: University Microfilms, 1978).
41. J. Mark Ruhl, "The Military," in Berry et al., *Politics of Compromise,* pp. 196–97.
42. João Batista Bernardo, *Guerrilhas e Guerrilheiros* (São Paulo: Impressão Dag-Dagostino Artes Gráficas, 1981), p. 148; Premo, "The Colombian Armed Forces," pp. 162–63. Later M-19 initiated rural operations in isolated Caquetá. See NACLA, "Colombia:

Whose Country Is This, Anyway?" *Report on the Americas* 18, no. 3 (May–June 1983).

43. Premo, "The Colombian Armed Forces," p. 163.

44. *El Espectador,* December 20, 1977, pp. 1, 8, cited in Premo, "The Colombian Armed Forces," p. 164. For a sophisticated military analysis of the role of Latin America in the cold war and the Colombian situation, see Brigadier General Fernando Landazabal Reyes, *Factores de Violencia* (Bogotá: Ediciones Tercer Mundo, 1975).

45. Batista, *Guerrilhas,* pp. 148–49.

46. *Revista Militar del Ejercito,* April 1, 1981, as cited in the FBIS, *Daily Report: Latin America,* April 3, 1981, p. vi. Quoted in Premo, "The Colombian Armed Forces," p. 166.

47. Cited in Premo, "The Colombian Armed Forces," p. 166.

48. Ruhl, "The Military," p. 201.

49. Premo, "The Colombian Armed Forces," p. 167.

50. "Colombia, Turbay and M-19 View Betancur," NACLA, *Report on the Americas* 17, no. 1 (January–February 1983): 36. See also "Colombia—Another Threat in the Caribbean," NACLA, *Report on the Americas* 16, no. 5 (September–October 1982).

51. NACLA, "Colombia, Turbay," pp. 38–39.

52. Berry and Soligo, *Economic Policy,* p. 1.

PERU

- – - – International boundary
- ——— Department boundary
- ○ National Capital
- • Other major city

PERU

POLITICAL CHRONOLOGY

1919–30   Administration of Augusto B. Leguía. Attempts at controlled modernization cause dislocations in Peru's traditional sociopolitical system. APRA founded in 1924 in Mexico by Víctor Raúl Haya de la Torre.

1931–33   Administration of Luis Sánchez Cerro, who is assassinated in 1933. Period of repression of APRA and near civil war.

1933–39   Administration of Oscar R. Benavides, selected by congress to complete term of Sánchez Cerro. Continued repression of the APRA and other leftist parties; little reform undertaken.

1939–45   First administration of Manuel Prado. APRA remains underground and therefore able to promise all things to all groups.

1945–48   Administration of José Luis Bustamante y Rivero. APRA becomes legal and adopts a much more conservative political stance. Prominent Aprista leftists leave the party.

1948–56   General Manuel A. Odría takes power in military coup following an abortive APRA coup attempt. APRA outlawed; Haya de la Torre held captive in the Colombian embassy, where he can again be all things to all groups (1948–54). Odría "elected" to six-year term in 1950 and rules dictatorially but in a military populist style. CAEM founded in 1950.

1956–62   Manuel Prado elected to second term after strong challenge from newcomer Fernando Belaúnde Terry. APRA again legalized and supports Prado's conservative policies, thereby alienating its leftist supporters. APRA Rebelde founded in 1960. Haya de la Torre wins 1962 elections but military annuls them and assumes power. Frente de Izquierda Revolucionaria formed in Cuzco to aid Hugo Blanco.

1962–63   Military junta adopts some reform measures, including land reform, in La Convención Valley. APRA Rebelde changes name to Movimiento de Izquierda Revolucionaria. Ejército de Liberación Nacional (ELN) founded by Héctor Béjar.

1963–68   Fernando Belaúnde Terry elected president but coalition of APRA and party of Manuel Odriá block reforms in congress. Hugo Blanco organizes in La Convención Valley (1959–63) and is captured in 1963. Elements of the ELN move into action in 1963. Guillermo Lobatón and the Túpac Amaru *foco* move into action in 1965 and are defeated in 1966. Luis de la Puente Uceda and the Pachacutec *foco* go into action in 1965 and are destroyed. Héctor Béjar and the ELN move into action in 1965 and are defeated; Béjar is captured.

1968–80   Belaúnde Terry overthrown in 1968 by Peruvian military, which embarks upon a far-reaching program of structural change. The "First Phase" of General Juan Velasco Alvarado (1968–75) characterized by extensive land reform and politicization of the countryside and urban centers. The "Second Phase" of General Francisco Morales Bermúdez (1975–80) characterized by sudden slowdown in reform programs, increasing economic decline, and growing popular discontent. The Partido Communista Sendero Luminoso founded (1970) by Abimael Guzmán.

1980–84   Military allows elections. Fernando Belaúnde Terry elected to second term. Sendero Luminoso launches guerrilla offensive (1980), attacks prisons, *guardia civil* outposts, power lines, bridges, and public buildings; state of siege imposed in the department of Ayacucho.

BACKGROUND

Peru shares with Bolivia and Guatemala a political and social history of marginal existence for a large indigenous population outside the modern façade of urban areas and enclave industries. It shares with Colombia, and to a lesser extent Venezuela, a symbolic commitment to liberal democracy despite the resistance of elites to political change and social reform inherent in the liberal democratic state.[1] The result, in twentieth-century Peru, has been a plethora of laws, superficial reforms, and mountains of rhetoric that little altered the misery and poverty of the country's indigenous population and the largely mestizo urban working classes.[2]

The inauguration of Augusto B. Leguía in 1919 constituted a major turning point in Peruvian history. Throughout his eleven-year rule, Leguía sought to restructure Peruvian society, modernize the economy, and reorder the nation's priorities to favor the urban-industrial sector. Like his successors, however, Leguía eschewed revolution. On the contrary, he sought to implement certain reforms and structural modifications in order to preserve basically intact the essential features of the old socioeconomic hierarchy.

As is usually the result in traditional society, however, those palliative reforms caused severe dislocations in the Peruvian policy and unleashed new forces that were to challenge elite control of the nation for the next sixty years. The new economic and political groups favored by Leguía, upon which he had based his regime, never united into a cohesive political party. Instead, they remained divided and often mutually antagonistic.

Moreover, the 1920s had witnessed an increase in Indian peasant violence and uprisings in the sierra,[3] and this, coupled with increasing demands and pressure from urban labor and middle-sector groups, produced a potentially volatile climate. Out of this milieu emerged one of the most important Marxist leaders and theoreticians in Latin American history—José Carlos Mariátegui.[4] Antedating Che Guevara's emphasis on the agrarian question as the key to social change in Latin America, Mariátegui sought to formulate an indigenous brand of socialism based on the ancient pre-Colombian Indian communal land tenure system, the *ayllu*. He argued forcibly that the alleviation of Indian oppression depended solely on land reform: "The agrarian problem presents itself above all as the problem of liquidating feudalism in Peru."[5] Peruvian leftists and radicals since, including the guerrillas of the 1960s, have been tremendously influenced by Mariátegui's analysis, and thus the twin problems of agrarian reform and alleviation of Indian oppression have been viewed as the sine qua non of any revolutionary movement in Peru.

The Indian and mestizo peasants of the sierra, however, were almost totally isolated from the mainstream of Peruvian politics and economics. Those who counted most lived on the coast, and most of the moderate reformers and radicals of the 1930s joined Peru's most important mass-based political party, the Alianza Popular Revolucionaria Americana (APRA), founded in 1924 by Víctor Raúl Haya de la Torre. Like AD in Venezuela and the MNR in Bolivia, APRA was vertical in organization and cut across class lines through its populist appeals.[6] The party has been pictured by its admirers as a grassroots lower- and middle-class reform movement designed to end foreign and oligarchical domination of the economy, to raise the standard of living of all Peruvians, to incorporate the Indian mass into national life, and to democratize the sociopolitical structure of the country. In contrast, opponents of the party and its leader point to their propensity for violence and usually characterize their program as being designed to obliterate all that was good in Peruvian society and replace it with a godless form of communistic dictatorship that would reduce everyone to the level of pack animals.

Both views are highly simplistic and tend to distort the APRA movement and its role in Peruvian society. Though admittedly extremist in many of his earlier statements and writings, particularly in his more radical student days (1918–23), Haya de la Torre never really called for, nor favored, a leveling social revolution. On the contrary, careful scrutiny of the party's political platform in the 1930s reveals that the party focused on the better-off elements (usually unionized) of the laboring class of urban centers and the large coastal haciendas, on white-collar workers in rural and urban centers, on small landowners, and on the middle class in general.

Pleasing both lower-class radicals and middle-class reformers would have been an impossibility if Haya and the Apristas had been allowed to function openly. The fact is that Haya and the Apristas were forced underground in the period 1934–44 and again in the years 1948–56. This clandestine status allowed Haya to be all things to all people of all political persuasions. To his middle-sector supporters, he preached modernization and guaranteed that the masses would not get out of control. To his radical and lower-class followers, he promised revolution and violent change.[7]

The result was that APRA retained many of those who might have been expected to join the Communist party of Peru (PCP) or other more radical political groups. Thus, the revolutionary tradition in Peru in the period 1930–60 is really the tradition of APRA, which helps to explain the fragmentation of the left and the emergence of guerrilla movements in the 1960s.

Even without APRA, it would have been almost impossible for other leftist parties or movements to develop in Peru after 1931. Elected president in that year, Colonel Luis Sánchez Cerro immediately adopted the politics of repression, directed primarily at APRA, but at other leftist groups as well. Following Sánchez Cerro's assassination by an Aprista fanatic in 1933, General Oscar R. Benavides assumed control and ruled until 1939. This was a period of economic crisis and civil disorder bordering on civil war, and Benavides ruled with an iron hand, effectively silencing all opposition, both rightist and leftist.

Manuel Prado was elected president in 1939, but the elected government that replaced the dictatorship continued to deny the APRA legal participation in the political process and the party remained underground until Prado left office in 1945. As might be expected from the scion of one of Peru's most powerful oligarchic families, Prado tolerated neither dissent nor movements to restructure the Peruvian land tenure system, either by outsiders or by the peasants themselves.

With the election in 1945 of José Luis Bustamante y Rivero as president, the pattern of authoritarianism was interrupted in Peru, as it was in other parts of Latin America after World War II. The APRA, allowed to campaign openly for the first time since 1931, nearly captured control of the congress, and now their more radical followers expected them to fulfill their long-standing commitments to land reform, Indian integration, and removal of foreign capitalists from the economy. Instead, the Apristas adopted a rather conservative position on all these issues and refused to entertain even a moderate land reform program. Moreover, Haya had substantially moderated his position on foreign investment and United States imperialism, thereby alienating important leftist elements of the party, just as he would do again in the period 1956–62.[8]

The experiment with liberal democracy, 1945–48, was a failure. The Apristas, believing that they alone were responsible for Bustamante's election, moved quickly to control both the congress and the executive. When Bustamante refused to yield, the Apristas went on the offensive, harassing the administration at every opportunity. In addition, radical elements within the party grew increasingly restless and prone to use violent means. Finally, in October 1948, Aprista radicals joined some disaffected junior officers and staged a coup attempt. Bustamante responded by outlawing the APRA, but senior military officers had had enough; they overthrew Bustamante and installed General Manuel A. Odría, who immediately jailed hundreds of Apristas and forced Haya to remain a prisoner in the Colombian embassy until 1954.

The eight-year rule of Odría (the *ochenio*, 1948–56), in some ways resembled the military populism practiced by Juan Perón in Argentina and Gustavo Rojas Pinilla in Colombia. Although he tolerated no political dissent, Odría made a concerted effort to win urban labor support through the granting of seven wage increases and additional fringe benefits. Moreover, he used moneys generated from Peru's postwar export boom to finance expanded social security coverage, state subsidies of food prices, and the construction of hundreds of new schools. His wife, María Delgado de Odría, sought to emulate Evita Perón by founding a national charitable association, the María Delgado de Odría Center of Social Assistance, which distributed food and clothing to the poor of Lima's growing shantytowns (*barriadas*).[9]

In the rural sector, Odría supported the land oligarchy and moved forcefully against Indian peasant efforts to improve their socioeconomic condition. Indeed, in an effort to stem the flight of peasants to the urban centers of the nation, Odría even instituted a type of internal passport for Indians.

The net result of Odría's programs was to blunt lower- and middle-class opposition on the coast and suppress all dissent in the sierra. The Communist party was tolerated as long as it operated within very strict parameters. Since Haya and the APRA were forced into hiding, they could again adopt the mantle of radicalism, and many young leftists joined the party in the period 1948–56, just as they had done from 1934 to 1945.

The elections of 1956 signified a return to multiparty, liberal-state politics in Peru. Odría, recuperating slowly from a severely fractured leg, supported Hernando de Lavalle. Manuel Prado returned from Europe to run a second time. The most interesting candidate, however, was Fernando Belaúnde Terry, a young architect who entered the contest just a few weeks before the election. Belaúnde drew enthusiastic support from middle-sector groups, young reformers, and even some radicals in both the urban and rural regions and might very likely have won had not the Apristas thrown their considerable strength behind Prado.

The election of Prado signified a continuation of oligarchic control of the nation, particularly in the rural sector. While not overtly oppressive like his predecessor, Prado was forced to adopt austerity measures in order to stave off economic collapse—measures which fell particularly hard on the urban working classes while contributing to a 50 percent rise in income among entrepreneurial and managerial groups. Moreover, almost no resources were invested in the agrarian sector, and this, coupled with an explosion in rural population, resulted in increasing the number of landless peasants and decreasing peasant income.[10] Finally, although Prado publicly supported land colonization projects and appointed a commission to make recommendations for a national land reform law, nothing was done to alleviate the plight of the peasantry.[11]

By 1961, Peru had one of the most inequitable land distribution patterns in Latin America. The large estates (*latifundia*), which comprised a mere 1.2 percent of the total land holdings, controlled 75.2 percent of the arable land, while the tiny estates (*minifundia*) comprised 84.4 percent of the total land holdings yet controlled only 6 percent of the arable land.[12]

Politically, the most important result of Prado's second term was the further tarnishing of APRA's reform-radical image. Haya and the Apristas wholeheartedly supported Prado and his fiscal policies under an agreement known as the *convivencia* (literally, "living together"), thereby earning the enmity of leftists and middle-class reformers all over the nation. This most recent disaffection culminated in another splintering of the party and the formation of APRA Rebelde in 1960 (see below). These Aprista dissidents were, in many ways, ideologically akin to those groups that broke away from the AD in Venezuela and the Liberal party in Colombia.

Thus, the years following the Cuban revolution found Peru in serious economic trouble, with increasing unrest evident in both the urban and rural sectors. In 1962, seven candidates vied for the presidency, but only four evidenced any real popular support: Belaúnde Terry, running for the new reformist party, Acción Popular; Haya de la Torre for APRA; Héctor Cornejo Chávez for the recently formed Christian Democrats; and Manuel Odría, on a political comeback, for the Unión Nacional Odriísta (UNO). Haya won with 557,000 votes, Belaúnde Terry garnered 544,000, while Odría picked up 520,000, but Haya did not have the required one-third of the votes cast, so the election was thrown into the congress. There Haya struck a deal with his implacable enemy, Odría, whereby Odría would assume the presidency and APRA would control the Congress. This was too much for the military, and ten days before Prado's term expired, the army took power, annulled the elections, and ruled until new elections could be held in 1963.

Those expecting a return to the traditional military politics of the 1930s and 1940s, however, were soon surprised. Part of the difference lay in the fact that the new military rulers were products of the Center for High Military Studies (CAEM). Founded as a military school in 1950, CAEM was patterned after both the Escola Superior de Guerra in Brazil and the War College in the United States.[13] Simply stated, CAEM military doctrine expanded the concept of national security to encompass all those political, economic, and social conditions that affect the power of a nation. Moreover, the doctrine held that economic development was synonymous with national defense and security. Thus, if they were to fulfill their constitutional *and* institutional charge of guarding the fatherland and maintaining internal order, Peru's generals would have to involve themselves directly in the modernization process. In Peru, this meant a frontal attack on the traditional land tenure system, recognized as the source of a serious economic bottleneck and burgeoning social discontent.

While its programs did not approach in scope those of the 1968–80 period, the military junta did move to help low-income families obtain housing in Lima and actually initiated several pilot land reform and colonization projects, including one in La Convención Valley (see below). Clearly the military had come to realize the necessity of socioeconomic reform in Peru.

In 1963, new elections were held, and although the candidates remained basically the same, the outcome was different. With the support of the Christian Democrats, Belaúnde Terry won more than the required third of the votes (708,000), while Haya (623,000) and Odría (463,000) trailed behind.

Belaúnde was inaugurated amid a popular outpouring of hope and enthusiasm for the future. He was relatively young and extremely charismatic, and had spoken eloquently of his dreams and plans for the betterment of conditions for all Peruvians.[14] He had campaigned all over the country and appeared to possess, more than any previous president, an understanding of the complex diversity that is Peru. From the outset, he sought to construct a reform program which would meet the needs of the proletariat and middle-sector elements of the coast, on the one hand, and the Indian and mestizo peasants of the sierra on the other.

The new administration pledged to decentralize and streamline the government and urged the creation of self-help projects in the sierra. A program of "Popular Cooperation" promised local groups that the government would provide the tools and materials necessary to construct schools, roads, and small public works projects if the people would offer their cooperative labor. Idealistic young Peruvian urbanites also joined Popular Cooperation, a type of domestic Peace Corps, and went off to work in isolated regions.

President Belaúnde dreamed of opening Peru's vast jungle region to settlement by constructing a north-south Marginal Highway, hoping thereby to relieve population pressure on sierran lands. In addition, he promised to implement a true land reform coupled with irrigation projects and the technical advice and credit support that the new landowners would require.

In all of these aspirations, Belaúnde enjoyed widespread support, not only from a significant percentage of the population, but also from the Catholic Church and the military, two corporate groups that had historically served as bastions of traditionalism. Moreover, his calls for reform coincided nicely with the goals of John F. Kennedy's Alliance for Progress, and the country came alive with energetic priests, young bureaucrats and students, and U.S. Peace Corps volunteers.

Dreams of a new Peru collapsed, however, when confronted with the realities of party politics in the congress. APRA and the supporters of Odría, with a clear majority in both houses of congress between them, formalized the pact they had made in 1962 and moved to obstruct the president's program, particularly Cooperación Popular and Belaúnde's proposed land reform law.[15] The law that finally passed in 1964 represented a compromise between the two most conservative proposals (those of APRA and UNO) and as such constituted almost no threat to the large landholders. The huge coastal plantations were explicitly excluded from the law, while other exclusions and impossibly long and complicated litigation procedures protected haciendas in the sierra.[16]

Belaúnde's acceptance of this law cost him what little leftist support he still retained (he had formally denounced the Communist party and other far left groups in December 1963) as well as many moderate reform elements. Finally, United States Alliance for Progress funds, which were absolutely crucial to Belaúnde's development plans, were suspended over Belaúnde's refusal to guarantee the International Petroleum Company's near monopoly of Peruvian petroleum resources.

Given these many political difficulties, a casual observer might have concluded in 1960 or 1965 that Peru was ripe for a Guevara-type revolution. Several aspects of Peruvian reality did indeed conform to Guevara's formulations; others, however, as in the cases of Guatemala, Colombia, and Venezuela, would prove obstacles to revolutionary guerrilla movements:

1. Peru is not and never has been a Caribbean-type dictatorship. Despite periodic military coups and dictatorships, the nation has a long tradition of at least paying lip service to the tenets of the liberal democratic state, and the elections held since 1930 have been relatively honest. As a result, the Peruvian electorate has long viewed the elected officials as legitimate. In the early 1960s, both APRA and Acción Popular represented vocal reformist alternatives to violent revolution. No hated dictator (like Batista, Trujillo, or Somoza) served as a symbolic target of revolutionary movements.

   Moreover, as the oldest, largest, and most powerful of the middle-sector reform parties, APRA has maintained strong ties to coastal plantation workers, urban labor and middle sector elements along the coast. Despite APRA's conservative drift over a thirty-year period, it could still marshal at least 30 percent of the electorate in the 1960s.

2. The physical terrain of Peru is formidable. Sixty percent of the nation lies east of the Andes mountain chains, with a third of that in the 4,000–11,000 feet range (the *Ceja de la Montaña,* "the Eyebrow of the Jungle") and the rest of the nearly impregnable and largely unpopulated Amazon Basin. A sparseness of population would serve more than anything to isolate any guerrillas there. The sierran region, with 30 percent of Peru's area, is characterized by extreme altitudes (12,000–16,000 feet) and little vegetation. Coastal dwellers (most of the guerrilla leaders) usually fall prey to *soroche* (mountain sickness caused by oxygen deprivation) and even if they can function, there is little cover on the treeless, windswept plateaus. The coast contains almost 50 percent of the population but only 10 percent of the area. It is narrow, flat, and dry and does not meet Guevara's criteria for acceptably difficult terrain.

3. Peru was a traditional, rural nation until very recently. In 1940, 35 percent of the population was considered urban, a figure which rose to 47 percent in 1961 and 60 percent by 1972. In 1940, 25 percent of the population resided on the coast while 62 percent lived in the sierra. By 1972, 45 percent lived on the coast and only 44 percent in the sierra.[17] Moreover, as the percentage of rural, sierran dwellers decreased, so did the area's economic and political strength; in 1960, 55 percent of Peru's gross national product was produced by the coast, while only 40 percent came from the sierra. The extreme poverty and wretched social conditions of the rural peasants conform nicely to Guevara's theories of the necessary

objective conditions of rural poverty, but as in Guatemala, recruitment to revolutionary movements faced extreme difficulty because
of cultural and linguistic barriers (many Indian peasants spoke
only Quechua or Aymara) and the historic fear and hatred of the
Indians for urban "*mistis*," or whites. Indeed, few Indians joined
the guerrilla movements of the 1960s.
4. Peru, like Guatemala, Venezuela, Colombia, and Bolivia, lacked a
strong vanguard party. Indeed, the left in Peru, while relatively
large in numbers, was among the most fragmented in Latin America. Moreover, no leftist parties or movements had developed rural
cadres; linkages between urban and rural movements were extremely poor. Thus guerrilla leaders found it almost impossible to
create the subjective conditions necessary for successful rural insurgency. *Focos* could be and were established, but the fragmentation of leftist parties, combined with historical antipathy between
rural peoples and urbanites (particularly Indians and whites), precluded the creation of a broad-based popular movement.

ORIGINS OF THE GUERRILLA MOVEMENTS IN THE 1960s

Almost all analysts of the guerrilla movements in Peru begin by
labeling them unmitigated disasters, and so they were. But
there were three very distinct movements during this period
and it would be historically inaccurate to lump them together
except in a very general way.[18] The first movement, which never developed into a guerrilla *foco*, was led by Hugo Blanco in La
Convención and Lares valleys during the period 1959–63. The
second and third took place in the Cuzco and Ayacucho regions and included the actual establishment of *focos* by Luis de
la Puente Uceda and Héctor Béjar.

Hugo Blanco was born and raised in the southern Peruvian
city of Cuzco, the former Inca capital and long a stronghold of
both the Communist party of Peru (PCP) and the Peruvian
Socialist party (PSP). After graduating from high school, he
went to Argentina and enrolled at the University of La Plata,
where he fell under the influence of Hugo Bressano, a professor
and leader of a Trotskyist political faction, Palabra Obrera. In
1956 he went to Lima and joined the Peruvian Trotskyist Partido Obrero Revolucionario (POR). Returning to Cuzco in 1958,
Blanco soon moved into the Convención Valley, which lies

some ninety miles north of Cuzco along the Urubamba River. What happened over the next five years is clear, but Blanco's role has been distorted. As one writer notes, "The reputation of Blanco was magnified to such legendary proportions as to obscure the important processes which contributed to the emergence of a peasant labor organization in La Convención years before the advent of Blanco."[20]

Indeed, the entire socioeconomic development and structure of the valley made it unique in Peru.[21] The sixty-mile-long valley is narrow and contains several distinct agricultural eco-zones. The upper end is 5,100 feet above sea level, dropping to 2,790 feet at the southern end. The valley floor had long been used for the cultivation of such tropical crops as sugar cane, cacao, coca, and some tea and coffee. The steep slopes of the valley, particularly at the higher elevations, were ideally suited to coffee production, but the lack of a cheap, effective transportation system precluded its development.

The valley was carved up into large estates with a labor force composed primarily of sierran Indians who worked a fixed number of days (*condiciones*) for the *hacendados* in return for the use of a plot of land (the plots were always situated on the less desirable slopes). Then an economic revolution occurred. In 1928 a railroad was built from Cuzco to the fabulous Inca ruins of Machu Picchu and later extended to Huadquiña at the entrance to La Convención. In 1933 a road was built from Machu Picchu to the provincial capital of Quillabamba.

These new transportation lines, together with the arrival of middlemen merchants from Cuzco who bypassed the *hacendados* and offered the peasants direct marketing of their crops enabled the peasants to grow coffee profitably for the first time. In order to care properly for their coffee trees, the peasants had to reduce the number of work days they owed the *hacendados*. The first arrivals (*arrendires*) therefore subcontracted with another peasant (*allegado*) to work for them in return for part of the *arrendire*'s land. The system became even more complicated when many *allegados* also subcontracted with newer arrivals (*sub-allegados*).

In order to maximize their personal income, each of these groups shared the need to reduce the work *condiciones*. The result was the growth of a sophisticated peasant union movement complete with organized protests and petitions to the federal government and close ties with the Federación de Trabajadores de Cuzco (FTC), which supplied the peasant unions with lawyers and labor organizers. When Blanco arrived to work as an *allegado,* therefore, the peasants already had a fairly well developed organizational structure in place. It is true that Blanco, aided by his fluency in Quechua, vastly expanded, redirected, and intensified it, but he did not create it. Finally, it must be remembered that Blanco was primarily a peasant organizer, not a guerrilla fighter. Nevertheless, Blanco's Marxist ideology clearly threatened the old order of Peru, and in this sense the La Convención movements became part of the broader confrontation between the incumbent regime and Peruvian revolutionaries.

Unlike Blanco, Luis de la Puente Uceda and Héctor Béjar were legitimate guerrilla leaders who sought to emulate the successes of Che Guevara and the Cuban revolution. Both were committed to guerrilla warfare as a revolutionary tactic, both established *focos* in Peru, and both failed miserably. Moreover, their defeat spelled the end to guerrilla movements in Peru until the rise of the Sendero Luminoso in the 1980s.

De la Puente was born on the strongly Aprista north coast known as the Sólido Norte. He was a distant relative of Haya de la Torre and, in his youth, was a fervent supporter of APRA.[22] Following the 1948 military coup, de la Puente was jailed and then exiled to Mexico. In 1954 he returned to Peru clandestinely to participate in a revolt against the Odría government. Arrested again, he spent the next two years in prison.

He returned to the University of Trujillo to study law, specializing in agrarian law. He was critical of the *convivencia* between Manuel Prado and Haya de la Torre, but he remained within Aprista ranks. The real turning point in his political evolution came in 1959 when he traveled to Cuba to attend the International Agrarian Reform Forum. There he engaged in a debate with Cuban president Oswaldo Dórticos regarding the political nature of the Cuban agrarian reform.[23]

In October 1959, at the Fourth National Convention of APRA, de la Puente and other young dissidents presented a motion condemning the policies of the Prado administration and APRA's public support of them. The signers of the petition were suspended from the party, whereupon they formed a group called the Comité Aprista de Defensa de los Principios y de la Democracia Interna (Aprista Committee for the Defense of Principles and Internal Democracy). Finally, despairing of any hope for change in Haya de la Torre's position, the group broke away from APRA, much as had the young leftists in 1948, and formed APRA Rebelde. The political efforts of APRA Rebelde were directed almost exclusively toward effecting agrarian reform, and to that end they presented a draft law to the congress in 1961.[24]

De la Puente himself, on the other hand, continued his radical political development. In 1960 and 1961 he made several trips to Cuba to study at first hand its revolutionary experience. In 1961 he was convicted of the manslaughter of an Aprista thug who had attacked him and was sentenced to a year in jail. While in prison, he continued to direct APRA Rebelde and in April 1962 changed its name to Movimiento de Izquierda Revolucionaria (MIR, Revolutionary Left Movement).

After completing his prison term, de la Puente traveled to La Convención Valley, where in October 1962 he met with Hugo Blanco. By this time, de la Puente was committed to guerrilla warfare, but the two men failed to reach an agreement. Historian Víctor Villaneuva concludes that "their political and methodological differences precluded them from uniting for the benefit of the revolution."[25]

During 1963 de la Puente traveled to China, North Vietnam, and North Korea, where he met Mao Tse Tung, Ho Chi Minh, and Kim Il Sung. Returning to Peru, he continued to redefine his ideas. Then in a lengthy speech on February 7, 1964, he vehemently attacked APRA, President Belaúnde and the corrupt policies of the government, the Peruvian bourgeoisie, landowners, the International Petroleum Company, elections, and political agreements. He praised Fidel Castro and the Cuban revolution, proclaiming that "revolution is the only way left open to our people."[26] Shortly after this declaration, de la Puente and other MIR leaders went underground and prepared to initiate their guerrilla struggle.

Like de la Puente and the MIR, Héctor Béjar and others

formed the Ejército de Liberación Nacional (ELN, National Liberation Army), as a splinter movement from a traditional Peruvian political party which they deemed too conservative—the Peruvian Communist party.[27] As Béjar later wrote: "The impact of the Cuban Revolution was very great and it was soon reflected in the political organizations. A group of young people broke off from the APRA . . ." but "the repercussions were even greater in the Communist Party and they were reinforced by the impact of the Twentieth Congress of the Communist party of the Soviet Union and the polemic with the Communist party of China. In Peru, the party's whole ideological, theoretical, and practical structure automatically came under discussion."[28]

Béjar goes on: "From its very beginning the ELN . . . was composed of a small group of young people. Among them were high school and college students, workers, and a few peasants. Many came from the Communist Youth and the Communist Party but, for a variety of reasons, they had ceased to observe party discipline or to work actively in its organizations. . . . The ELN wanted the party to grow but [from] the peasant masses and the dense proletarian agricultural, manufacturing, and mining centers."[29]

Elements of the ELN first went into action on May 2, 1963, when a group of thirty-five to forty men, some of whom had been trained in Cuba, crossed into Peru from Bolivia near the Peruvian town of Puerto Maldonado. Their goal was to link up with Hugo Blanco and supply his peasant organization with guerrilla cadres. From the outset, the venture was a fiasco. Some of the group was captured on May 14, and the next day there was an armed clash in which several died, including the poet Javier Heraud, for whom the ELN's 1965 guerrilla front was named.[30]

Some did escape and went underground to organize. By 1964, the ELN had elaborated a program of action that was to be implemented through guerrilla warfare. It called for

(1) People's government.
(2) Expulsion of all foreign monopolies.
(3) Agrarian revolution.

(4) Friendship with all the peoples of the world.

(5) National sovereignty.

... Two methods were held to be fundamental to our success: armed struggle and popular unity. They complemented each other dialectically since in Peru one is not possible without the other.[31]

POLITICO-MILITARY EVOLUTION OF THE GUERRILLA STRUGGLE

The Peruvian guerrilla movements of the mid-1960s suffered from the same ideological, organizational, and personalist fragmentation as their counterparts in Central America, Venezuela, and Colombia. Likewise, the Peruvian guerrilla leadership emerged from urban political movements and parties without good ties in the countryside. Students, intellectuals, party cadres, and idealists, these emulators of Fidel Castro and Che Guevara lacked the experience, training, and political preparation to succeed against the Peruvian government's counterinsurgency efforts. Bitter conflicts among the revolutionaries exacerbated these difficulties. One of the most charismatic of these revolutionary leaders was Hugo Blanco, whose success as a peasant organizer is well documented. When he arrived in La Convención Valley in 1958, there were six peasant unions, a number that increased to over one hundred by 1962. Moreover, Blanco was an effective strike organizer, particularly among the *allegados* and *sub-allegados*; but his tactics and his deep commitment to Trotskyist ideology soon brought him into conflict with the *arrendires,* the FTC in Cuzco, and the orthodox Communist party of Peru, which labeled him "a provocateur and agent of Yankee imperialism."[32] These divisions were exacerbated by the involvement of the Peruvian Trotskyist party (POR) and the Latin American branch of the Fourth International, the Secretariado Latinoamericano de Trotskyismo Ortodoxo (SLATO, the Latin American Secretariat of Orthodox Trotskyism), based in Buenos Aires.

In 1960 the POR met in Arequipa and formulated a revolutionary plan which was to include the use of guerrilla warfare, a step that Villanueva has criticized as being over optimistic and poorly conceived.[33] Once committed, however, the POR moved quickly to implement the plan and requested assistance from SLATO in Buenos Aires. SLATO did send three of its best organizers to Lima to help with the movement.[34]

In 1961, the Frente de Izquierda Revolucionaria (FIR, Revolutionary Left Front) was formed to serve as the vanguard party, but from the outset there were deep divisions between the Lima-based POR and Blanco and his followers in Cuzco. As Ricardo Letts Colmenares later wrote: "The whole political apparatus was oddly and mistakenly mixed up with the relatively strong military apparatus. Yet neither of them was at all strongly connected with the other end of this revolutionary axis, the peasant end, the Cuzco and Convención leaders."[35]

Disagreements over goals, tactics, and which group was to wield ultimate power in the national directorate of the FIR worsened over the next few months. This was nowhere more evident than in the disastrous efforts to secure funds for the movement. In December 1961 a robbery netted only $2,000 in usable bills, but a second robbery in April 1962 secured approximately $120,000. The problem was how to get the money to Cuzco, and the plan adopted proved extraordinarily ill-advised, ending in the capture by the police of all the money and the men transporting it.

Meanwhile, Blanco was encountering difficulties from every direction. Already condemned by the Communist party and in serious conflict with the FTC, which wanted to use elections to strengthen leftist political representation instead of resorting to violence, Blanco ran afoul of even the Trotskyists. In March 1962, Blanco and the Cuzco-based branch of FIR issued an ultimatum that either a national congress of FIR would be held in Cuzco in April or the Cuzco leadership would simply assume overall command of the movement. Bressano responded by removing Blanco and others from their leadership positions.

Buffeted from all sides, Blanco returned to La Convención to resume his organizing but quickly encountered opposition there, too. In 1962, he ran for secretary-general of the Federación Provincial de Campesinos de La Convención y Lares (Provincial Federation of the Peasants of La Convención and Lares). Supported almost exclusively by the *allegados* and *sub-*

allegados, his election resulted in the withdrawal of the *arren-dires* from the Federation.

Despite these defections, Blanco moved ahead by issuing an agrarian reform decree for the valley which called for the distribution of uncultivated land to the poorest peasants and the granting of plots to the *arrendires* and *allegados*.[36] The decree and the violent peasant land invasions which ensued provoked a strong reaction from the Peruvian national police (the Guardia Civil), and in a small skirmish at one Guardia outpost, Blanco shot and killed a policeman. Isolated politically and relentlessly hunted by the police, Blanco was finally captured in May 1963 and later sentenced to twenty years in jail.

So ended Peru's first revolutionary movement of the 1960s. It never took the form of a *foco* and Blanco quite obviously did not view himself as either a guerrilla or a disciple of Che. Still, the Blanco episode is important in the evolution of the guerrilla struggle: first, because of the myth that grew about Blanco the guerrilla leader, and second, because of the reaction of the Peruvian government.

In April 1962, in an effort to ameliorate the situation in La Convención, Manuel Prado issued a presidential decree abolishing the *condiciones* in the valley, but held that the peasants must pay rent on their individual parcels. Then in March 1963 the military junta which had replaced Prado granted the peasants de facto ownership of their parcels on the condition that the peasants would pay the government for the land and the government would, in turn, reimburse the *hacendados*.[37]

Thus, the primary goals of the peasants — ownership of their plots and abolition of the *condiciones*—had been achieved. There was nothing left to be offered by future guerrilla leaders, as Luis de la Puente would discover. Blanco and de la Puente both operated in much the same region, but as Richard Gott has stated: "They failed to overlap in time. For Hugo Blanco's movement essentially consisted of organized peasants in desperate need of guerrilla support, while de la Puente's guerrilla movement failed largely through lack of support from the organized peasantry. Hugo Blanco's peasants seized the land, but had no guns to defend their gains. De la Puente's well-armed guerrillas had no peasants to defend."[38]

Without doubt, de la Puente was the premier guerrilla

theoretician in Peru. Regarding the salient questions of the creation of the vanguard party and of objective and subjective conditions, he wrote:

We believe that the party of the Peruvian revolution will shape itself within the insurrectional process, and that its cadres and leaders will emerge from the struggle itself. We do not use a party label; we call ourselves what we really are, a movement which aspires to be a promoter of the party of the Peruvian revolution.

... It is unnecessary to speak about the objective conditions because they are not only ripe now but have always been. I think there is not a country in America where infra- and super-structural conditions are so unjust, so rotten, so archaic as in ours.

As to the subjective conditions, we start from the idea that they are not fully ripe, but that the beginning of the insurrectional process will be the triggering factor leading to their development in ways which no one can foresee.[39]

De la Puente also insisted, along with Che Guevara, that "the Peruvian revolution is part of the continental and world process, which demands progressive forms of integration in every aspect and stage, in order to defeat the oligarchic and imperialist forces which are working together all over the continent."[40]

De la Puente and others succeeded in establishing several *focos,* but they were quickly destroyed by the Peruvian army owing to a number of errors, including divisions within the Peruvian left and the guerrillas themselves, poor site selection, and a misreading of the political proclivities of the peasants. Moreover, both the Peruvian Communist party and the pro-Chinese Communists condemned the guerrillas for failing to create a vanguard party, and most of all, for failing to create first the necessary subjective conditions in the countryside. Neither group offered any support whatsoever.[41]

The MIR maintained that the revolution should be led by a party: The MIR. The ELN believed that the leadership should be able to assimilate the other revolutionary forces that were operating in the country in 1962. Moreover, the ELN advocated the broad concept of a revolutionary army that we have already described, a plan designed to keep the army from being restricted to the members of one party.

... The ELN favored immediate action to be initiated by an armed group that would, in the course of combat, build its own social base. The MIR believed that it was first necessary to build a social base among the peasantry by means of clandestine work in the countryside, using the method of "secret armed propaganda."

But it would be superficial to point only to disagreement over tactics as the reason for the separation of the MIR and the ELN. One must examine the history of the Peruvian Left to understand why that division was possible.

The cause lay in the fact that almost all the members of the MIR and the ELN, or at least those cadres whose opinions carried decisive weight in the two organizations, were people who had been educated in opposing political camps. The MIR was produced by a split in the APRA, while the ELN was led by former Communist Party cadres. There was an invisible wall between these groups, made up of the prejudices that still tied them to their past, for the struggle between the APRA and the Communist Party had covered several decades of Peruvian political history and still influenced them, even though they wouldn't admit it. It was difficult for the two groups to find a common language.[42]

The guerrilla groups never resolved their differences and were crushed individually by the Peruvian armed forces. The MIR established three *focos*: The "Túpac Amaru" group, headed by Guillermo Lobatón, was situated in the jungle area of Satipo, northeast of the central Andean city of Huancayo; a group in northern Peru inside the Ecuadorian border, headed by Fernando Gasco, never did go into action; and the "Pachacutec" *foco* situated on Mesa Pelado above La Convención Valley and headed by Luis de la Puente and Rubén Tupayachi. Finally, there was the ELN *foco*, "Javier Heraud," led by Héctor Béjar, in the department of Ayacucho.

Guillermo Lobatón and the Túpac Amaru group were the first to go into action in June 1965.[43] They attacked several haciendas and police outposts, blew up several bridges, and ambushed a Guardia Civil patrol. At that point, the army moved in several units with support helicopters and air force planes and drove the guerrillas out of their base camp. About the same time, United States Green Berets arrived to participate in a CIA-backed effort to aid the Peruvian army.[44] By November the army had the guerrillas on the run and on January 7, 1966, Lobatón and the remnants of his band were killed.

Despite his ultimate failure, Lobatón had at least lasted seven months. Luis de la Puente and the Pachacutec group were destroyed almost before they could go into action. Even so, one wonders what success they could have hoped to achieve with the peasants in La Convención Valley, given the defeat of Hugo Blanco and the government's land reform in the area. Moreover, de la Puente's selection of the Mesa Pelado (literally, a bare plateau) for guerrilla activity was questionable at best. Although the area at the lowest levels was covered with thick jungle growth, the plateau itself has an average altitude of 12,000 feet and is covered with thick clumps of Andean grass, *ichu,* which provides no cover. In addition, the plateau receives heavy rainfall throughout the year and temperatures at the top are near freezing.[45]

In any event, it took the Peruvian army and air force, aided by United States counterinsurgency troops, less than two months to obliterate the guerrillas. The barren terrain also allowed for the use of heavy artillery and extensive bombing runs, including the use of napalm. On October 23, 1965, de la Puente and his followers were killed.

When Lobatón went into action in June, Béjar and the ELN *foco* had been in the Ayacucho region only since April. Though unprepared to launch a full-scale guerrilla war, the ELN chose to move in support of the MIR *focos.* On September 25, they attacked the Hacienda Chapi and executed the owners.[46] Since the Peruvian army was already fighting a two-front operation against Lobatón and de la Puente, military units were not dispatched against Béjar until the end of November. Once contact was made, however, the guerrillas were quickly defeated on December 17, 1965. Béjar himself escaped but was later captured and imprisoned. With the military overthrow of Belaúnde in 1968, he was released and went to work for the military government in the mistaken belief that they would carry out a true revolution.[47]

With the defeat of Béjar and the ELN, guerrilla activity in Peru came to an end and would not break out again for fifteen years. The tactics of Guevara had failed miserably in Peru, but they would be attempted again. The reasons for failure were many; some have been noted above. Since only one of the *fo-*

quista leaders, Béjar, lived to reflect on the failure, his analysis is important for those who would follow:

The roots of the failure must be sought in the guerrilla unit itself and in its leadership.

In this case as in others, a group of men, most of them from the city, tried to operate militarily in an unknown environment.

. . . [The guerrillas] left a trail of information behind which many peasants were not able to keep secret when they were tortured and murdered. The guerrilla band did not foresee, in practice, the severity of the repression to come.

. . . Despite friendship, language was always a barrier that separated the rebels from the natives. Peasants identify Spanish with the boss, especially in those places like Ayacucho which have a very large Quechua population. For the guerrillas to gain the trust of the peasantry they must be able to speak Quechua, and not just any Quechua, but the dialect spoken in the zone where they are operating (there are significant variations in the language from region to region in Peru).

. . . In spite of the good will that they earned, the guerrillas lacked a deep understanding of local customs. That would have allowed them to distinguish the traitors from their friends with greater precision and to obtain better and more pertinent information concerning the enemy's movements.

Guerrilla tactics, when applied strictly—with their characteristics of mobility, evasion and secrecy, rapid attack and withdrawal—demand a high degree of physical fitness on the part of the combatants and a leadership with great military ability. The entire group must operate with iron discipline and perfect coordination. The ELN's guerrilla unit, like all the others operating that year, did not possess these qualities to the degree required to overcome the inevitable problems and face a large, well-trained enemy force.[48]

POST-1968 EVENTS

Barely three years after the death of Luis de la Puente, the Peruvian armed forces overthrew the Belaúnde administration and established the Revolutionary Government of the Armed Forces (1968–80). Led by General Juan Velasco Alvarado, the new government broke with tradition and embarked upon a far-reaching socioeconomic reform program designed to end internal strife, economic stagnation, and the potential for guerrilla movements by removing the objective conditions and "harmonizing" Peruvian society.[49]

The showpiece of the regime, and the most important achievement in terms of future Guevara-like guerrilla movements, was the 1969 agrarian reform law, second in scope only to that of the Cuban revolution.[50] The stated goals of the reform were to give land to the landless peasant and to increase food production. The real goal was to remove the source of peasant discontent, thereby ending the threat of future outbreaks of guerrilla activity in the rural sector. Moreover, the new agrarian structure sought to guarantee control over the peasants by integrating them into a tight, vertical structure controlled and operated by the military, a classic example of "military antipolitics."[51]

Despite the near-dictatorial control structure and the fact that the peasants in many ways traded one master (the *hacendado*) for another (a military officer), thousands of acres of land were expropriated and distributed to the various Indian and peasant cooperatives established by the law. Simultaneously, the government mounted an initially effective propaganda and politicization campaign in the countryside to convince the peasants that, in Velasco's words, "the patrón will no longer feed on your poverty."[52] The result was that although the rural sector was in ferment in the period 1969–80, it was basically a populist ferment that precluded the mounting of a successful peasant-supported guerrilla movement; and indeed, no one tried.

By the late 1970s, however, the military "experiment" had clearly failed to achieve most of its goals. Internal shifts in the military regime brought more conservative officers into dominant policy positions by 1975. Runaway inflation, combined with high unemployment rates, a decline in agricultural production, and natural disasters, racked the Peruvian economy. Under these circumstances, the generals turned to the United States, and particularly to the International Monetary Fund (IMF), for assistance. Though that assistance was forthcoming, it was accompanied by the Draconian economic measures which the IMF often imposes: currency devaluation, reduction in government budgets and payrolls, and reduction or abolition of government subsidies of staple food prices.

Finally, in 1980, the generals were forced to step down, hold elections, and allow the man they had deposed some twelve years earlier, Fernando Belaúnde Terry, to assume the presidency again. Simply stated, Belaúnde inherited a socioeconomic and political nightmare that worsened in the early 1980s as Peru was racked by severe floods and droughts.

Out of these circumstances emerged the first guerrilla group in fifteen years—the Partido Communista Sendero Luminoso (the Communist Party of the Shining Path.)[53] It originated in the 1964 split of the Peruvian Communist party into the Moscow-oriented Partido Comunista and the Chinese-oriented Partido Comunista-Bandera Roja. Fragmentation continued until 1970, when the pro-Chinese faction divided into three separate groups, one of which was Sendero Luminoso.

Based at the National University of Huamanga in the south-central department of Ayacucho (one of the most heavily Indian areas of Peru), Sendero Luminoso is led by former professor Abimael Guzmán. One writer has described Sendero as "a strange mix of Gang of Four Maoism and deeply rooted Incan nationalism,"[54] and in fact, as early as 1970, Sendero was sending cadres into the surrounding countryside to learn Quechua and to politicize Indian peasants.

In 1980, Sendero launched its armed offensive. This "armed struggle" will, according to the Senderistas, move through five distinct stages: (1) the gathering of support in the countryside; (2) the assault on the symbols of the bourgeois state; (3) the start of guerrilla warfare; (4) the expansion of popular support; and (5) the collapse of the cities and victory.[55]

Rejecting orthodox Maoism and early Guevarism, the Sendero opted to operate in the rural and urban areas simultaneously. Apparently deciding to move into stage two, attacks on the symbols of the bourgeois state, the Senderistas began blowing up electrical power line pylons, public buildings, and tourist hotels and followed with attacks on Guardia Civil outposts and mining operations to secure weapons and dynamite. Sendero singled out and threatened wealthy landowners, merchants, and public officials in the Ayacucho region. Many of those threatened fled and their property was subsequently distributed to the peasants. Debts owed them were declared null and void. Those who refused to leave were harassed and many were assassinated. Sendero also began the gruesome practice of hanging dead dogs from poles, a practice which has been interpreted both as a repudiation of Chinese leader Deng Xiaoping (Mao's betrayer) and as a historic Indian warning of imminent attack.[56]

In 1982 the Sendero began a series of kidnapings of "enemies of the people," followed by "popular trials" and summary execution. One of the more spectacular attacks came in March 1982, when the Senderistas stormed the Ayacucho prison and freed over 250 prisoners, a tactic reminiscent of the Tupamaros of Uruguay. The government responded by increasing the number of Guardia Civil personnel and by dispatching the specially trained counterinsurgency units of the Guardia known as the *Sinchis*.

Rather than acting as a stabilizing force, however, the ill-trained Guardia and the all-too-often brutal and thuglike *Sinchis* terrorized the small villages and countryside and, in so doing, increased support for the Sendero. Thus, by the end of 1982 most observers concluded that the Sendero not only controlled an area of some 25,000 square miles, but also enjoyed widespread popular support.[57]

Faced with a fast deteriorating situation, the administration of Fernando Belaúnde Terry was forced to declare a state of siege in Ayacucho and to send in over 2,000 regular army soldiers and paratroopers. Using light planes and helicopter gunships, the army began massive counter-guerrilla operations that seriously damaged Sendero but also resulted in hundreds of casualties among the peasants caught in the conflict. Since journalists were barred from the area, reliable data on the number of killings are impossible to obtain, but there appears little doubt that most of the deaths resulted from government search and destroy operations.

That the government's military offensive took a heavy toll of the Senderistas is clear, but two other factors also contributed to Sendero's decline after December 1982. First, instead of consolidating their base of support among the peasants in the area they controlled, the Senderistas instituted rigid economic and political control. Planting quotas were imposed on the small communities in order to reestablish subsistence farming and deny food to the cities. Moreover, the local weekly markets that had flourished since before the Inca Empire were shut down, condemned as bastions of capitalism. Politically, the Senderistas were no more flexible. Once in control in a given area, they vastly increased their efforts to root out "traitors" and "informants," a campaign which reportedly resulted in the assassination or "execution" of untold numbers of peasants.

Finally, the Senderistas abandoned their peasant allies at the first sign of Peruvian troops, thereby exposing them to the government's merciless retaliation.[58] One Senderista was quoted in September 1983 as follows: "These peasants stand in the way of our success. Many are government informers. Others oppose us actively, do not cooperate with us, and even refuse us food and sustenance."[59] The Senderistas may have spoken Quechua, but they were hardly peasants and the Indians knew it.

In its extremism, Sendero seems to have violated Che Guevara's prescription for political victory. From the outset, Sendero not only rejected all cooperation with other leftists; it assailed other Marxists in Peru as "cretins." Sendero also rejected all foreign support, asserting that there is no difference between the United States, the Soviet Union, Cuba, and even China under the current regime—all are fascist. The Peruvian left responded in kind, condemning Sendero and its tactics.

Seemingly unable to learn from the failures of the Venezuelan guerrillas in the early 1960s, Sendero threatened to assassinate anyone who participated in the municipal elections of November 1983. The fact that the elections were held and the left scored impressive victories in Lima (electing a Marxist mayor for the first time in history) and even in Ayacucho attests to Sendero's increasing isolation and decline.

In 1984, the Belaúnde government faced mounting political and economic difficulties, but was hardly the Caribbean-type dictatorship Che describes in *Guerrilla Warfare.* The relatively unrestricted participation of the left in national politics—indeed, its increasing electoral strength—appeared to offer a viable electoral alternative for the nation's disaffected.

Despite its early successes, the Sendero Luminoso no longer constituted a serious threat to the Peruvian polity. Sporadic military attacks will undoubtedly continue to occur, both in

Lima, where many Senderistas seem to have fled, and in the rural areas. But Sendero Luminoso appears destined to repeat the political and military defeats of the Peruvian and other Latin American guerrillas of the 1960s rather than the victory of the Sandinistas in Nicaragua.

Even if Sendero Luminoso should be eradicated by counter-insurgency efforts, however, the deteriorating social and economic conditions of the majority of the Peruvian people provide fertile ground for the cultivation of future insurgencies. The fragility of the Belaúnde administration in 1984, the renewed participation of the military and the Guardia Civil in securing internal order, and the expansion of leftist political forces make Peru a likely scene for recurrent political violence. Whether Peruvian political leaders can achieve the success of the Venezuelans in partially insulating internal politics from confrontations between superpowers, or whether Peru becomes another El Salvador, remains to be seen.

NOTES

1. For a brilliant synthesis of Peru's struggle with modernization and "democracy," see Fredrick B. Pike, *The United States and the Andean Republics: Peru, Bolivia, and Ecuador* (Cambridge, Mass.: Harvard University Press, 1977), particularly chaps. 6–12; see also his *The Modern History of Peru* (New York: Praeger, 1967). Other important studies include David Scott Palmer, *Peru: The Authoritarian Tradition* (New York: Praeger, 1980); Henry F. Dobyns and Paul L. Doughty, *Peru: A Cultural History* (New York: Cambridge University Press, 1977); Carlos A. Astiz, *Pressure Groups and Power Elites in Peruvian Politics* (Ithaca: Cornell University Press, 1969); and Francois Bourricaud, *Power and Society in Contemporary Peru* (New York: Praeger, 1970).

2. The best analysis of the development of the Peruvian export economy is Rosemary Thorp and Geoffrey Bertram, *Peru, 1890–1977: Growth and Policy in an Open Economy* (New York: Columbia University Press, 1978). For an extensive discussion of Indian labor conditions and standards of living in the republican period, see Thomas M. Davies, Jr., *Indian Integration in Peru: A Half Century of Experience, 1900–1948* (Lincoln: University of Nebraska Press, 1974), particularly chaps. 1 and 2. The remainder of

Davies's book is an analysis of the Indian legislation in the twentieth century, concluding that it was, at best, superficial and almost never implemented.

3. For an overview of peasant uprisings, see Wilfredo Kapsoli, *Los movimientos campesinos en el Perú, 1875–1965* (Lima: Delva Editores, 1977); Jean Piel, "A propos d'un soulèvement rural péruvien au début du vingtième siècle: Tocroyoc (1921)," *Révue d'histoire moderne et contemporaine* 14 (1967): 375–405; and Davies, *Indian Integration*, chap. 4.

4. Detailed analysis of his life and work falls outside the scope of this essay, but one must begin with his collected works, *Obras completas de José Carlos Mariátegui*, 10 vols. (Lima: Biblioteca Amauta, 1959–70), particularly his classic *Siete ensayos de interpretación de la realidad peruana*, translated into English by Marjorie Urquidi as *Seven Interpretive Essays on Peruvian Reality* (Austin: University of Texas Press, 1971). There are literally hundreds of articles and books on Mariátegui, but the best and most complete study is Jesús Chavarría, *José Carlos Mariátigui and the Rise of Modern Peru* (Albuquerque: University of New Mexico Press, 1979).

5. *Siete ensayos de interpretación de la realidad peruana*, 10th ed. (Lima: Biblioteca Amauta, 1965), pp. 41–42.

6. Steve J. Stein, *Populism in Peru: The Emergence of the Masses and the Politics of Social Control* (Madison: University of Wisconsin Press, 1980), chap. 1. The analysis of APRA which follows is based on Thomas M. Davies, Jr., "Peru," in Mark Falcoff and Fredrick B. Pike, eds., *The Spanish Civil War: American Hemispheric Perspectives* (Lincoln: University of Nebraska Press, 1982), pp. 203–43. See also Davies, "The Indigenismo of the Peruvian Aprista Party: A Reinterpretation," *Hispanic American Historical Review* 51 (1971): 626–45; and Davies and Víctor Villanueva, eds., *300 documentos para la historia del APRA: Conspiraciones apristas de 1935 a 1939* (Lima: Editorial Horizonte, 1978).

7. For abortive Aprista revolutions in the 1930s, see Davies and Villanueva, *300 documentos*.

8. For charges that Haya betrayed the party principles, see Luis Eduardo Enríquez, *Haya de la Torre: La estafa política más grande de América* (Lima: Ediciones del Pacífico, 1951); Magda Portal, *Quiénes traicionaron al pueblo?* (Lima: Empresa Editora "Salas é Hijos," 1950); and Víctor Villanueva, *La tragedia de un pueblo y un partido (páginas para la historia del Apra)*, 2d ed. (Lima: Talleres Gráficos "Victory," 1956).

9. For a succinct analysis of Odría's populist style, see Pike, *The United States and the Andean Republics*, pp. 295–97.

10. For a measured account of economic conditions and crises during Prado's presidency, see Pike, *Modern History of Peru*, pp. 296–99.

11. Comisión para la Reforma Agraria y la Vivienda, *La reforma agraria en el Perú: Exposición de motivos y proyecto de ley* (Lima: Talleres Gráficos P. L. Villanueva, S.A., 1960).

12. The best analysis of the Peruvian land tenure structure is Comité Interamericano de Desarrollo Agrícola, *Tenencia de la tierra y desarrollo socio-económico del sector agrícola—Perú* (Washington, D.C.: Unión Panamericana, 1966). For an excellent table of land tenure and income in Peru in 1961, see Dobyns and Doughty, *Peru*, p. 309.

13. The best study of CAEM is Víctor Villanueva, *El CAEM y la revolución de la fuerza armada* (Lima: Instituto de Estudios Peruanos, 1972). See also Brian Loveman and Thomas M. Davies, Jr., eds., *The Politics of Antipolitics: The Military in Latin America* (Lincoln: University of Nebraska Press, 1978), particularly chap. 1, 5, and 6.

14. See, for example, Fernando Belaúnde Terry, *Peru's Own Conquest* (Lima: American Studies Press, 1965).

15. All the major parties introduced their own land reform laws, the texts of which are reprinted in *Reforma agraria peruana: 5 proyectos de ley* (Lima: Editorial Thesis, 1963).

16. One of the best descriptions of 1960s land reform laws in Latin America is Ernest Feder, *The Rape of the Peasantry: Latin America's Landholding System* (Garden City, N.Y.: Doubleday, 1971), particularly pt. 3.

17. For this and other population data by departments, see Dobyns and Doughty, *Peru*, pp. 300–301.

18. For an excellent survey of the early literature on guerrilla movements in Peru through 1971, see Leon G. Campbell, "The Historiography of the Peruvian Guerrilla Movement," *Latin American Research Review* 8, no. 1 (Spring 1973): 45–70.

19. The literature on Hugo Blanco and his movement is quite extensive, but one must begin with Blanco's own account, *Land or Death: The Peasant Struggle in Peru* (New York: Pathfinder Press, 1972). Other important sources include Víctor Villanueva, *Hugo Blanco y la rebelión campesina* (Lima: Editorial Juan Mejía Baca, 1967); Hugo Neira, *Cuzco: Tierra y muerte* (Lima: Populibros, 1964), later revised, expanded, and published as *Los Andes: Tierra o muerte* (Santiago de Chile: Editorial ZYX, 1968); Gonzalo Añi Castillo, *Historia secreta de las guerrillas* (Lima: Ediciones "Más Allá," 1967); Wesley W. Craig, Jr., "Peru: The Peasant Movement

of La Convención," in Henry A. Landsberger, ed., *Latin American Peasant Movements* (Ithaca: Cornell University Press, 1969), pp. 274–96; Richard Gott, *Guerrilla Movements in Latin America* (Garden City, N.Y.: Doubleday, 1971), pp. 314–29; Eric J. E. Hobsbawm, "A Case of Neo-feudalism: La Convención, Peru," *Journal of Latin American Studies* 1, pt. 1 (May 1969): 31–50; and Mario Antonio Malpica, *Biografía de la revolución* (Lima: Ediciones Ensayos Sociales, 1967), pp. 442–79.

20. Craig, "Peru," p. 275.

21. For a superb analysis of this development, see ibid., pp. 274–88. See also Hobsbawm, "A Case of Neo-feudalism."

22. The early biographical data are taken from Movimiento de Izquierda Revolucionaria (MIR), *Obras de Luis de la Puente Uceda* (Lima: Voz Rebelde Ediciones, 1980), pp. xxix–xxx; and from Gott, *Guerrilla Movements*, pp. 336–50. Other important sources for the study of de la Puente's ideology and guerrilla activity are Luis de la Puente Uceda, *Manual de capacitación ideológica* (Lima: Ediciones Illarek-Chaska, 1980); Roger Mercado, *Las guerrillas del Perú: El MIR: de la prédica ideológica a la acción armada* (Lima: Fondo de Cultura Popular, 1967); Malpica, *Biografía de la revolución*, pp. 479–522; and Añi Castillo, *Historia secreta de las guerrillas*.

23. For a partial text of this debate, see Malpica, *Biografía de la revolución*, pp. 501–5; some of it has been translated into English and reprinted in Gott, *Guerrilla Movements*, pp. 338–39.

24. The draft law is reprinted in Carlos Malpica, *Guerra a muerte al latifundia: Proyecto de ley de reforma agraria del M.I.R.* (Lima: Ediciones "Voz Rebelde," 1963), pp. 19–155.

25. Villanueva, *Hugo Blanco*, p. 132.

26. The speech was originally printed in Mercado, *Las guerrillas del Perú*, pp. 66–90. It is also in MIR, *Obras de Luis de la Puente*, pp. 3–20, and in English translation in Gott, *Guerrilla Movements*, pp. 534–50, and Luis E. Aguilar, ed., *Marxism in Latin America*, rev. ed. (Philadelphia: Temple University Press, 1978), pp. 243–51.

27. Although less has been written about Béjar and the ELN than about de la Puente and the MIR, Béjar himself has published *Peru 1965: Notes on a Guerrilla Experience* (New York: Monthly Review Press, 1970). The most important ELN documents are to be found in Mercado, *Las guerrillas del Perú*, pp. 181–93, much of which has been translated into English and reprinted in Gott, *Guerrilla Movements*, pp. 373–78.

28. Béjar, *Peru 1965*, p. 47.

29. Ibid., pp. 60, 66.
30. For sharply differing accounts of this incident, see Perú, Ministerio de Guerra, *Las guerrillas en el Perú y su represión* (Lima: Ministerio de Guerra, 1966), pp. 28–29; Ricardo Letts Colmenares, "Perú: Revolución, insurrección, guerrillas," in Malpica, *Biografía de la revolución*, pp. 476–78; Mercado, *Las guerrillas del Perú*, pp. 55–60; and Gott, *Guerrilla Movements*, pp. 330–35.
31. Béjar, *Peru 1965*, pp. 61–62.
32. Villanueva, *Hugo Blanco*, p. 77.
33. Ibid., pp. 79–80.
34. The best account of the Trotskyist activities and the political evolution of the movement is ibid. The major highlights are paraphrased in Gott, *Guerrilla Movements*, pp. 320–29.
35. Quoted in Malpica, *Biografía de la revolución*, p. 477, and reprinted in Gott, *Guerrilla Movements*, p. 322.
36. For the complete text of the decree, see Villanueva, *Hugo Blanco*, pp. 127–28.
37. Perú, *Decreto-Ley No. 14444. Se declara zona inicial de applicación de la reforma agraria en el Departamento del Cuzco los valles de Lares y el de La Convención* (Lima: Litografía Huascarán, 1963).
38. Gott, *Guerrilla Movements*, p. 313.
39. Luis de la Puente Uceda, "The Peruvian Revolution: Concepts and Perspectives," *Monthly Review* 17, no. 6 (November 1965): 21, 25, 27.
40. Ibid., pp. 24–25.
41. For a good analysis of the Russian and Chinese Communist parties' positions, including extensive quotations from relevant documents, see Gott, *Guerrilla Movements*, pp. 381–89.
42. Béjar, *Peru 1965*, pp. 70, 72–73.
43. The best military account of the Peruvian army's defeat of the guerrillas, albeit biased in the extreme, is Perú, *Las guerrillas en el Perú*. See also Mercado, *Las guerrillas del Perú*, and Gott, *Guerrilla Movements*, pp. 351–80.
44. See Victor Marchetti and John D. Marks, *The CIA and the Cult of Intelligence* (New York: Alfred A. Knopf, 1974), pp. 124–25.
45. For a good description of the area, together with maps and pictures, see Perú, *Las guerrillas en el Peru*, p. 31.
46. For accounts of this and subsequent actions, see Béjar, *Peru 1965*, pp. 88–111; Mercado, *Las guerrillas del Perú*; Perú, *Las guerrillas en el Perú*; and Gott, *Guerrilla Movements*, pp. 372–80. There is also a semifictional film version entitled *The Principal Enemy*.
47. See Héctor Béjar, *La revolución en la trampa* (Lima: Ediciones Socialismo y Participación, 1976).

48. Béjar, *Peru 1965*, pp. 110–11.
49. The literature on the Peruvian "revolution" is voluminous and covers all aspects of the regime. Space limitations preclude even a representative listing of works, but the reader is directed particularly to Abraham F. Lowenthal, ed., *The Peruvian Experiment: Continuity and Change under Military Rule* (Princeton: Princeton University Press, 1975); Cynthia McClintock and Abraham F. Lowenthal, eds., *The Peruvian Experiment Reconsidered* (Princeton: Princeton University Press, 1983); Alfred Stepan, *The State and Society: Peru in Comparative Perspective* (Princeton: Princeton University Press, 1978); Palmer, *Peru;* Loveman and Davies, *The Politics of Antipolitics;* Villanueva, *El CAEM;* and Víctor Villanueva, *El ejército peruano: Del caudillismo anárquico al militarismo reformista* (Lima: Librería-Editorial Juan Mejía Baca, 1973).
50. Perú, *Reforma agraria. Decreto-Ley No. 17716* (Lima, 1969).
51. Loveman and Davies, *The Politics of Antipolitics.*
52. Perú, *Velasco la voz de la revolución: Discursos del Presidente de la República General de División Juan Velasco Alvarado,* 2 vols. (Lima: Ediciones Participación, 1972), 1:55.
53. The discussion that follows draws heavily from Roger Mercado, *El Partido Comunista del Perú: Sendero Luminoso* (Lima: Ediciones de Cultura Popular, 1982); Cynthia McClintock, "Democracies and Guerrillas: The Peruvian Experience," *International Policy Report,* September 1983; idem, "Sendero Luminoso: Peru's Maoist Guerrillas," *Problems of Communism,* September–October 1983, pp. 19–34; and idem, "Government Policy, Rural Poverty, and Peasant Protest in Peru: The Origins of the Sendero Luminoso Rebellion," paper delivered at the September 1983 meeting of the American Political Science Association. See also Sandra L. Woy Hazleton, "Political Opposition in Peru: Parliamentary and Revolutionary Challenges," paper delivered at the September 1983 meeting of the Latin American Studies Association; Sandra L. Woy Hazleton with Stephen M. Gorman, "The Peruvian Left since 1977: Ideology, Programs, and Behavior," paper delivered at the September 1982 meeting of the American Political Science Association; and Carol Barton, "Peru: 'Dirty War' in Ayacucho," *NACLA Report on the Americas* 18, no. 3 (May–June 1983): 36–39. Also, before tight press censorship was imposed in 1982, there were numerous articles of varying quality in Peruvian newspapers and magazines. See particularly *Caretas, Oiga,* and *Equis.*
54. Barton, "Peru," p. 38. For a superb monograph on the colonial roots of Indian culture in the region, see Steve J. Stern, *Peru's Indi-*

an Peoples and the Challenge of Spanish Conquest: Huamanga to 1640 (Madison: University of Wisconsin Press, 1982).

55. McClintock, "Sendero Luminoso," p. 21.
56. Ibid., and Hazleton, "Political Opposition in Peru," p. 13.
57. Barton, "Peru," pp. 37 – 38; Kenneth Freed, "Pocket of Terrorism Stirs Fears among Peruvian Peasants," *Los Angeles Times,* February 20, 1983; McClintock, "Sendero Luminoso," p. 30.
58. See Barton, "Peru," p. 38, and McClintock, "Sendero Luminoso," p. 32.
59. Quoted in McClintock, "Sendero Luminoso," p. 32.

BOLIVIA

POLITICAL CHRONOLOGY

1932–35   Chaco War with Paraguay disrupts traditional Bolivian society. Partido Obrero Revolucionario founded (1934).

1936–43   Reform-minded military officers David Toro and Germán Busch take power in 1936 on a program of "military socialism"; first "social" constitution written (1938). Partido de la Izquierda Revolucionario founded (1940); Movimiento Nacionalista Revolucionario (MNR) founded by Víctor Paz Estenssoro (1942).

1943–52   Military rule in Bolivia, including the neofascist administration of Gualberto Villarroel (1943–46).

1952–64   Bolivian national revolution led by Víctor Paz Estenssoro (president 1952–56, 1960–64) and Hernán Siles Zuazo (president 1956–60) of the MNR. Mining companies nationalized and extensive land reform undertaken, particularly in 1956–64. Massive U.S. aid and poor economic planning leads to inflation and discontent, especially among the tin miners.

1964–67   Paz Estenssoro overthrown by military led by General René Barrientos. Che Guevara arrives in La Paz (1966) to lead continent-wide revolution, moves into action in March 1967, is captured and executed in October 1967.

1967–84   Military rule in Bolivia. René Barrientos killed (1969), replaced by Alfredo Ovando Candía (1969–70), military

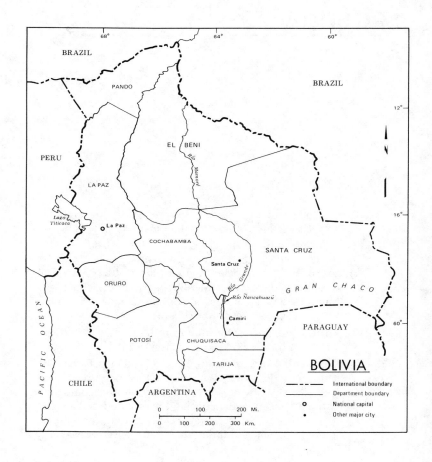

populist Juan José Torres (1970–71), authoritarian military regime of Hugo Banzer (1971–78), and others. Hernán Siles Zuazo elected president in 1982; faces serious economic crisis.

BACKGROUND

With the tragic exception of Haiti, no other American republic matches Bolivia's incredible history of political, economic, and social chaos. One of the two or three poorest nations in the hemisphere, Bolivia has had dozens of presidents and illegal changes of regime since independence (1825), twenty-nine between 1880 and 1952 alone.[1] In the early 1950s the fragile Bolivian political system rested on an archaic, manorial social system in which the majority Indian population suffered extreme exploitation and deprivation in the large *latifundias* that dominated the rural sector.

A country whose population was overwhelmingly rural (78 percent in 1952), Bolivia had experienced little of the modernization and urbanization typical of its southern neighbors or even Peru. Dependent upon tin mined by Indian workers for its major source of foreign exchange, the Bolivian monoproduct economy generally fared even less well than other Latin American mono-product exporters of agricultural or mineral commodities. In the agricultural sector a mere 9.4 percent of landowners controlled 92 percent of the arable land in holdings of more than 1,000 hectares, yet they cultivated less than 2 percent of it. In contrast, 61 percent of farm units controlled .28 percent total area and 8.1 percent of cultivated land in parcels of less than 5 hectares.[2]

Sharp class divisions and unequal distribution of wealth and income combined in Bolivia with stark racial, linguistic, and cultural barriers. A small white and mestizo elite ruled a vast population of Quechua-, Aymara-, and Guaraní-speaking Indian peasants. Forced to work on the large estates, the Indians did not participate in the economic, social, and political affairs of their nation, except insofar as their labor produced wealth for a tiny minority.

Had this system endured largely unchanged until 1966

when Che Guevara arrived in La Paz to initiate a guerrilla *foco* in Bolivia, the conditions confronting Che Guevara's forces would certainly have been different. In practice, however, Bolivia experienced fundamental changes between 1952 and 1966; the Bolivian national revolution, one of the three social revolutions experienced in Latin America before 1979, dramatically transformed the mining region and the countryside.[3]

The revolution had its origins in the Chaco War (1932–35) between Bolivia and Paraguay. Fought over the nearly worthless Gran Chaco, a largely unpopulated swampy region, this senseless conflict cost Bolivia more than 65,000 lives and thousands of square miles of national territory; it also disrupted the nation to such an extent that the traditional order collapsed. The military, led by Colonels David Toro and Germán Busch, disparaged the ineptitude of civilian politicians and the corrupting influence of politics in Bolivian national life. Promising to save Bolivia from the civilian politicians— who had impeded the war effort—the military assumed power in 1936 with a program of "military socialism."[4]

Although marred by coups and political and social violence, the next decade saw the writing in 1938 of a new "social" constitution, patterned after the 1917 Mexican and 1933 Peruvian documents. Three new political parties also emerged: the Partido Obrero Revolutionario (POR, Revolutionary Workers Party), Partido de la Izquierda Revolucionaria (PIR, Party of the Revolutionary Left), and the Movimiento Nacionalista Revolucionario (MNR, Nationalist Revolutionary Movement). Founded in 1934, the POR grew to become the most powerful and important Trotskyist party in Latin America, even controlling the Bolivian labor movement for a time in the 1950s. The PIR, founded in 1940, adopted a Marxist stance and called for the socialization of the means of production and the full integration of the Indian population into national life. The third and most important, the MNR, formed in the early 1940s and led by Víctor Paz Estenssoro and Hernán Siles Zuazo, was composed largely of young intellectuals and middle-sector groups who sought profound structural changes in Bolivia and looked initially to fascism as their political model.

All of these parties favored the nationalization of the tin mines and foreign-owned enterprises, supported the rights of the miners, and called for the destruction of the *latifundio* land tenure system and alleviation of the "Indian problem." Although they were unable to gain power immediately (the MNR did play a major role in the regime of Gualberto Villarroel, 1943–46), these parties continued to grow in membership and strength. Finally in April 1952, the MNR, backed by miner and civilian militias as well as some national police units, defeated the army and installed Víctor Paz Estenssoro as president and Hernán Siles Zuazo as vice-president of Bolivia.

By 1952, the MNR had dropped its pro-fascist stance and had become the party of miners, urban labor, and leftist middle-sector civilians. In this it resembled, at least in terms of rhetoric, the APRA in Peru and AD in Venezuela. In terms of actual political action, the MNR vastly outdistanced its Peruvian and Venezuelan counterparts and could legitimately claim to represent many of the radical and reformist elements in the society.

The new government moved swiftly to consolidate its power and carry out the stated goals of the revolution. It created a new labor confederation, Central Obrero Boliviano (COB, Bolivian Workers Central), in which the more radical POR and PIR were allowed substantial representation. It drastically reduced the size of the military and allowed the urban and rural militias to retain their arms. It created a national monopoly over the export and sale of all minerals and nationalized the three largest Bolivian tin companies.

It was in the areas of land reform and Indian rights, however, that the MNR made its most lasting impact. Responding to Indian pressure for reform and land takeovers, the MNR sought to legitimize peasant unions and gain control of rural organizations. The first major step was to enfranchise the Indian peasants by abolishing literacy requirements, thereby quadrupling the number of eligible voters. Concomitantly, the Indians, with the aid of urban radicals, began to organize, form militias, and take over the large estates upon which they had been forced to work. With the army all but destroyed, and guns in the hands of peasants for the first time in Bolivian history, the way was clear for a wholesale assault on the land tenure system.

Owing to its urban, middle-sector origins, the MNR leadership was extremely reluctant to "unleash" the peasantry and implement a thoroughgoing agrarian reform. Nevertheless, peasant violence in 1952 and early 1953, together with the need to placate their more radical supporters inside and outside the party, forced the MNR leadership to enact a radical agrarian reform law. Although the law provided for compensation through twenty-five-year bonds and ordered the Indians to make restitution for the lands they had already seized, neither of these provisions was ever enforced.

The result was massive destruction of the Bolivian *latifundia* system and the immediate distribution of lands to individual Indians and Indian *comunidades.* The import of this for future proponents of revolutionary guerrilla warfare in Bolivia cannot be overestimated. One authority, Herbert Klein, has written that "with the elimination of the hated hacendados and many of their *cholo* middlemen, and the granting of land titles, the Indians became a relatively conservative political force in the nation and actually grew indifferent if not hostile to their former urban worker colleagues. The appeasement of their land hunger turned the Indians inward so that for the next two generations the primary concern of the communities and their *sindicatos* was the delivery of modern facilities of health and education and the guaranteeing of their land titles. Otherwise they were receptive to reformist and even conservative policies in the urban centers."[5]

Paz Estenssoro and his successors recognized fully the political advantages of retaining this bloc of peasant support, particularly as the nation's economy began to deteriorate in the late 1950s and early 1960s and the miners, urban labor, and the middle sectors grew dangerously restless. Ongoing land reform represented a cheap but effective means of ensuring that support, so the government greatly accelerated its land distribution program in the years after 1956.[6]

In marked contrast to its policies in Guatemala in 1954, the United States supported the Bolivian national revolution, both financially and politically, and then co-opted it. Although the United States had been opposed to the MNR since 1943, it was because of the party's early fascist leanings, not its later reformist policies. Thus, in 1953, Milton Eisenhower, special ambassador to Latin America, convinced his brother, President

Dwight D. Eisenhower, that despite such "politically undesirable" programs as land reform and expropriation, United States interests would be best served by supporting the "fascist" MNR rather than risking a Communist takeover.[7]

United States aid and control became most evident during the regime of Hernán Siles Zuazo (1956–60). Runaway inflation, costly featherbedding in the mining industry, high unemployment, and general economic decline made the government highly dependent upon U.S. economic assistance. When the United States insisted that Bolivia repay some $56 million worth of loans defaulted on in the 1920s, the Bolivian government was forced to accede to the Draconian measures demanded by the United States and the International Monetary Fund (IMF), including a balanced budget, an end to subsidies of food prices, cuts in social services, devaluation of the currency, and massive cutbacks in public sector employment. In return, the United States Agency for International Development (AID) embarked upon one of the most massive aid programs in U.S. history. In 1957, 32 percent of Bolivian treasury revenues came from AID, with an average of 25.9 percent over the next four years.[8] The United States also assisted greatly in the rebuilding and "professionalization" of the Bolivian military in the late 1950s and early 1960s.

Despite U.S. aid, however, the negative impact of the IMF demands, together with a continued decline in mining exports, caused severe dislocations in the society and cost the MNR most of its miner and leftist urban support. During his second term (1960–64), Paz Estenssoro was forced increasingly to rely on military and peasant support to remain in power. Though he tried to placate the left by naming a long-time radical labor leader, Juan Lechín, as his vice-president, the ploy ultimately failed when Lechín and Siles Zuazo formally broke with the MNR over Paz's decision (supported by the U.S.) to seek a third term in 1964.

Isolated from his own party and facing serious opposition from labor, miner, and leftist intellectuals, Paz chose General René Barrientos as his running mate to assuage the army and then won the election with peasant support. Despite his relatively easy victory, however, it quickly became apparent to the army that Paz could not maintain internal order, so he was ousted in November 1964, and General Barrientos assumed the presidency.

Thus, by 1964, despite the poverty of rural Bolivians and the history of political instability, the Bolivian revolution had created very special circumstances that challenged any literal application of Che Guevara's analysis in *Guerrilla Warfare.*

1. Despite Bolivia's chaotic political history, it was definitely not a Caribbean-type dictatorship in the early 1960s. Since 1952, elections had been held on a regular basis and there was a genuine popular commitment to the goals of the revolution. Although General Barrientos replaced Paz Estenssoro in 1964, his fluency in Quechua and support from the Indian population in key regions made him an unlikely surrogate for Batista (Cuba) or Somoza (Nicaragua).

   Moreover, there was an institutionalized political party system that included both rightist and leftist parties. A centrist political movement, the MNR, seemed to offer a realistic reformist alternative to violent revolution and had indeed carried out some meaningful reforms, particularly in the rural sector.

2. The physical terrain of Bolivia is even more extreme than that of Peru, but the vast majority of the population has always lived on the high altiplano, which offers almost no cover for guerrillas. The heavily forested and jungle regions to the east are relatively unpopulated, offering spatial opportunities to potential guerrilla *focos,* but little opportunity to do political work because of the sparsity of the population.

3. Bolivia was a predominantly rural society in which the Indian peasants had traditionally lived and worked under conditions of extreme poverty and oppression. The agrarian reform program of the 1952 revolution altered parts of that picture drastically. Thousands of peasants were given land; and although land redistribution was not accompanied by technical assistance, credit, or marketing agreements, it all but guaranteed that the Indians would move toward a conservative political position and support the government. Although rural poverty remained the common lot of the population, agrarian reform ceased to be a viable rallying point for revolutionary or guerrilla leaders.

4. Bolivia most definitely lacked a vanguard party, rural

cadres, and linkages between urban and rural opposition movements. The POR, PIR, and the Bolivian Communist Party (PCB) were ineffective in comparison with the MNR, particularly in terms of peasant support. The fact that the majority of peasants remained fiercely loyal to the government meant that it would be almost impossible in much of Bolivia to create the subjective conditions for a successful guerrilla operation. In some ways the MNR ties to the peasantry, like those of AD in Venezuela, APRA in Peru, and Conservatives and Liberals in Colombia, meant that rural guerrilla movements faced not just apathy or distrust, but active hostility.

ORIGINS OF THE GUERRILLA MOVEMENT OF THE 1960s

Bolivia's only guerrilla movement in the 1960s was, from the outset, foreign in origin. Unlike the *focos* of other nations treated in this volume, the Bolivian *foco*, headed by Che Guevara himself, was created to take advantage of the country's geographic location to initiate a continent-wide revolution. As a base for such revolution, Bolivia seemed ideal because it shares borders with five of the other nine republics in South America (Peru, Chile, Argentina, Paraguay, and Brazil). There is no doubt that continental revolution was Che Guevara's goal, and only very secondarily was he interested in Bolivia per se. In this sense, the Bolivian *foco* lacked entirely the domestic political roots of the other movements discussed in this book.

Following his disastrous term as Cuban minister of industries, Che Guevara left Cuba in 1965. Although his whereabouts for the next year are still largely unknown, there are sound reasons to believe that he spent several months in Africa, particularly the Congo, and perhaps even visited Vietnam. By the time he returned to Cuba in 1966, Che was firmly committed to leading a Latin American revolution, a notion which, at least then, had the support of Fidel Castro. According to Richard Gott, an authority on the subject, the original plan called for Che to return to Argentina, resurrect the guerrilla movement of Jorge Masetti, work closely with the guerrilla leader Leonel Brizola in Brazil, and rekindle guerrilla activities in Peru. Bolivia was to be used "as a refuge and a training ground."[9]

During the summer of 1966, however, the plan was altered and Bolivia, rather than Argentina, was designated as the continental headquarters. From the outset, the operation was planned and directed from Cuba and could count on neither Bolivian Communist party support nor Bolivian cadres. Of the fifty guerrillas in Che's *foco,* seventeen were Cuban, twenty-nine Bolivian, three Peruvian, and one East German. All of the officers, however, were Cuban; no Bolivians were among the leaders.[10] Moreover, although Che and the Cubans did make some effort to recruit Bolivians, including Indian miners and peasants, they were hampered by the fact that they could not rely on any Bolivian political party or movement. Che himself noted in late December 1966 that "the Bolivians are good, although there are few of them." A month later he wrote, "Of all the things foreseen, the one that is going slowest is the recruitment of Bolivian combatants."[11]

POLITICO-MILITARY EVOLUTION OF THE GUERRILLA STRUGGLE

From the very beginning, Che and his Cuban comrades faced a number of almost insurmountable problems as they sought to create a successful guerrilla *foco* in Bolivia: (1) the hostility of the Bolivian Communist party (PCB); (2) a woeful lack of knowledge of Bolivian geography which resulted in the selection of a questionable site for a *foco* base; (3) the popularity of President Barrientos, particularly among the peasants; (4) the Sino-Soviet split and Soviet policies of peaceful coexistence with the United States; and (5) the rapid and effective response of the United States counterinsurgency forces.[12]

In the earliest planning stages in Cuba, Mario Monje Molina, the secretary general of the PCB, had been induced to support the operation by a Cuban gift of $25,000 to the PCB and by promises from Fidel Castro that the revolution would be planned and controlled by Bolivians. The money was delivered, but it was perfectly clear throughout that the Cubans had absolutely no intention of relinquishing control to the PCB.

Less than two months after his clandestine arrival in La Paz in November 1966, Che met with Monje Molina. Che's account of that meeting is revealing indeed:

> The meeting was cordial but strained. In the background was the question: What are we here for? . . .
>
> The conversation with Monje began with generalities but he quickly came down to his fundamental premise, stated in three basic conditions:
>
> 1) He would resign as party leader but would obtain its neutrality, and cadres would be brought for the struggle.
>
> 2) He would be the political and military leader of the struggle as long as the revolution was taking place in Bolivia.
>
> 3) He would handle relations with other South American parties, trying to persuade them to support liberation movements (he mentioned Douglas Bravo as an example).
>
> I answered that the first point was a matter for his own judgment as Party Secretary, although I considered his position to be a great mistake. It was vacillating, accommodating, and would protect the good name in history of those who should be condemned for their crookedness. Time would prove me right.
>
> On the third point, I told him I had no objection to his trying but that he would fail. To ask Codovilla to support Douglas Bravo was equivalent to asking him to support an insurrection within his own Party. Time will tell again. [Douglas Bravo was at the time the leader of the Castro-oriented guerrillas of the Venezuelan Armed Forces of National Liberation, Vittorio Codovilla the perennial chief of the Moscow-leaning Argentine Communist Party. Hence Che's sarcastic remark.]
>
> As for the second point, I could not accept it under any conditions. I was to be the military chief and I would not accept any ambiguities on this matter. Here the discussion stalled into a vicious circle.
>
> We agreed I would think it over and talk to the Bolivian comrades. We went over to the new camp. There he spoke to everybody, laying down the alternative of remaining with us or supporting the party. Everyone stayed, and this seemed to be a blow to him.[13]

By the end of January 1967, Che made it clear that the break with the PCB was irrevocable: "As was to be expected, Monje's attitude was evasive since the first moment and treacherous after. Now the party is up in arms against us and I don't know how far they will go, but this does not scare us, and maybe, it will benefit us in the long run. (I'm almost certain of that.) The finest and most combative people will be on our side; they always go through crisis of conscience more or less serious."[14] That the split worsened is obvious in a bitter entry, dated September 24, 1967, in the diary of Pombo, a Cuban whose real name was Harry Villegas Tamayo. Of the PCB he wrote: "1. They have shown no confidence in guerrilla warfare; 2. They have made no efforts to organize themselves, rather, they view it all as not solving anything. They added that they had been concentrating all their efforts toward a general uprising and considered guerrilla warfare as secondary. We asked them what they had done to date; they replied, 'Nothing.' We told them we could not sit around 20 years waiting for them."[15]

Isolated from the PCB and lacking any meaningful contacts with other Bolivian parties or even with the volatile miners, Che was forced to rely upon whatever resources he could muster. The selection of a site for the guerrilla base became, therefore, even more crucial. After several months of searching, Che's Cuban advance men, led by Pombo, found and bought a farm on the Ñancahuazu River. Pombo described the property as being situated "in the southwest region of Santa Cruz province, in a mountainous area of exuberant vegetation but scant water in the general area. The property itself has plenty of water. Ñancahuazu is in a canyon between the Serranias de las Pirirendas to the east and the Serranias Incahuasi to the west; their highest peaks are its eastern and western borders. These ranges join up farther south and continue into the Salta range in Argentina. . . . the farm has the specifications for this sort of work, but not on a large scale as yet, although we shall establish the proper conditions by building a house farther in so that it cannot be seen, as the present one is right where the road ends. The problem, however, lies in the transfer of the people, because we have to fool Algaranaz [an inquisitive neighbor]."

Other descriptions of the site are less positive. Daniel James, editor of Che's *Bolivian Diaries,* writes, "The guerrilla base at Ñancahuazu was perched on the edge of a rocky canyon nearly twelve miles long and more than 309 feet deep. Below was a river 30 feet wide which hugged the canyon walls, leaving no path for man or animal to tread. The forest above was so thick that nothing was visible from the air but treetops."[16] Richard Gott adds that "the area around Ñancahuazu is characterized by hundreds of knife-edge hills bunched together and separated by deep, impenetrable ravines filled with thick tropical vegetation."[17] The difficult terrain may have helped the guerrillas early on, but it also contributed to their downfall in that it led to the permanent division of the guerrilla forces.

Toward the beginning of *Guerrilla Warfare* Che notes, "Wherever a government has come to power through some form of popular consent, fraudulent or not, and maintains at least an appearance of constitutional legality, it is impossible to produce a guerrilla outbreak because all the possibilities of civil struggle have not been exhausted." The fact is that President Barrientos enjoyed widespread popular support, particularly among the middle class, the army, and, most important, the Indian peasants. He not only spoke fluent Quechua; he traveled extensively by helicopter to remote rural regions to enlist peasant backing. Moreover he had continued the agrarian reform program of Paz Estenssoro and the MNR. Ironically, in the very area selected by Che, the government land reform program had delivered plots of ten hectares (about twenty-five acres) to many of the 16,000 families in the region.[18] Thus there is little wonder that the peasants not only refused to support Che, but actually reported his activities to the police. There was no hope of creating the necessary subjective conditions among the peasantry.

Another devastating element for Che was the state of international relations in 1967. Any hope for uniting the left in the world or in Latin America had been shattered by the Sino-Soviet split after 1964. Even if Che had been able to enlist the aid of Monje Molina and the PCB, the Bolivian left would have remained badly divided, as it was elsewhere. Moreover, as noted in the Introduction, Russian Latin American policy after the missile crisis of 1962 changed from support of guerrilla movements to discouragement in order to strengthen the new policy of peaceful coexistence with the United States. Although Fidel Castro obviously favored the export of revolution and the creation of many Vietnams in Latin America, his almost total reliance on Soviet economic and military assistance forced him to be more circumspect. The result was that

Che found he could count on neither the Russians nor the Cubans for extensive material support, a fact which contributed to his demise.[19]

The situation was bad enough, but Che compounded his problems by moving prematurely into action. On March 23, 1967, the guerrillas attacked an advance column of Bolivian soldiers, killing seven and capturing another seven. Then on April 10, the guerrillas again clashed with an army unit, killing ten and capturing thirty. Now out in the open but unable to rely upon support from any group inside or outside Bolivia, it was just a matter of time before the United States–trained Bolivian army would isolate and annihilate Che's forces. Indeed, the United States, acting with great rapidity, moved into Santa Cruz with some twenty special forces troops and began immediately to train a Bolivian ranger unit in counter-guerrilla tactics.[20]

Meanwhile, Che committed a fatal error: he divided his forces on April 15 and was never able to reunite them. The first unit, composed of twenty-seven men, was led by Che, while the second group contained seventeen men and one woman—Tania—and was led by Cuban-born Juan Vitalio Acuña Nuñez (Joaquín). Throughout May, Che searched unsuccessfully for Joaquín and then moved north across the Río Grande, where for the next two months he and his men clashed periodically with Bolivian troops.

Contrary to what Che believed, however, Joaquín had not moved north but had remained in the Ñancahuazu area. Finally, after two deserters led the army to the guerrillas' base camp and supply depots in various caves, Joaquín also moved north, but as his unit was crossing the Río Grande on August 31, it was surprised by the army and destroyed.

The loss of Joaquín's group and the seizure of all their supplies of food, medicine, and munitions by the army marked the end of the guerrilla *foco.* Moreover, in mid-September, the U.S. special forces completed their training of over six hundred Bolivian rangers, who immediately moved into action. Two weeks later, on October 8, 1967, the army surrounded the remaining guerrillas. Che was captured and later executed; the guerrilla *foco* was eliminated.[21]

1967 TO THE PRESENT

The death of Che Guevara in 1967 ended significant guerrilla activity in Bolivia. General Barrientos died in a helicopter crash in 1969 and for the next ten years six generals and several interim civilian administrations succeeded to the presidency of the republic. One of the military presidents, Juan José Torres (1970–71) espoused a populist program that included the abolition of the Bolivian congress and creation of a people's assembly. In other instances civilian politicians temporarily cooperated with the military in sustaining fragile coalitions. From August 1971 until 1978, Colonel (later General) Hugo Banzer, who had commanded the ranger forces, instituted a hard-line anti-Communist administration that banned political party activity and sent many of Bolivia's leading politicians into exile.

At the end of his term of office, General Banzer attempted to "democratize" the political system through elections and to impose his hand-picked successor, General Juan Pereda Asbún. However, the inability of the political system to produce "acceptable" results led to three general elections in 1978 and 1979, several different "presidents," and then a new round of coups. In describing this period, one study concluded: "In less than one hundred days, two new administrations were ushered into the [presidential palace] increasing the number of coups to 201 in Bolivia's 175 year history."[22] The political confusion was resolved temporarily when the Bolivian congress selected Lidia Gueiler Tejada to serve as president for one year until August 6, 1980. Gueiler Tejada also failed to serve out her entire term; another coup in July 1980, headed by General Luis García Meza, returned the country to military rule.

Meanwhile, like the rest of Latin America's people, Bolivia's population became more urban (over 50 percent by 1980) and the economy more diversified. New opportunities for middle-class entrepreneurs and the declining importance of tin gave a greater complexity to the socioeconomic system. The proliferation of political movements and parties presented a confusing array of reformist alternatives whose proponents maintained important worker, peasant, and middle-class support. Of course, the military retained a dominant role in policy making and administration.

As in Colombia, the production of and commerce in drugs in the 1970s became a major "off the books" component of the Bolivian economy and a principal source of wealth for leading military officers. Corruption at the highest levels of government and a growing economic and political crisis, including student protests and strikes by organized labor, forced the military regime to speed up the return to civilian government. In early 1982 the military incumbent, General Celso Torrelio, proposed the gradual "democratization" of the political process, an end to the ban on political party activity, and a loosening of restrictions on organized labor. By June 1982, an amnesty for political exiles initiated the return to Bolivia of the old cast of characters for the upcoming elections: Siles Zuazo, Paz Estenssoro, Juan Lechín, and others. Though elections were scheduled initially for June 1983, the worsening crisis pushed the military government in mid-1980 to reconstitute the previously disbanded congress. Ultimately, in early October 1982, the congress selected former president (1956–60), Hernán Siles Zuazo, who now headed a left-center coalition, as president of Bolivia.

The new president, one of the old-guard MNR leaders who retained widespread popular support among the peasantry, pledged to end corruption, crack down on the drug trade, and inaugurate a "new period of national revolution"—that is, to reactivate the revolution of 1952. Seeking legitimacy in the present from the social revolution of the 1950s, Siles Zuazo reemphasized the agrarian reform issue and his minister of agriculture and peasant affairs called for the rapid transfer of all arable land into the hands of the peasantry.

Facing a serious debt crisis, low prices for tin and other primary exports, and pressure from both the political right and the revolutionary left, the Siles Zuazo administration trod a rocky path in mid-1984. Nevertheless, the continuing marginal existence of the country's Indian population and the renewed operations of the agrarian reform program undercut the efforts of the tiny, fragmented revolutionary left to mount rural-based insurrections. The renewal of party politics, the return, however temporary, to civilian government, and the seeming commitment to socioeconomic reform made the likelihood of successful revolutionary movements in Bolivia extremely remote in the near future. Moreover, the Bolivian military remained willing to employ the force required to put down serious civilian uprisings, and the mass of the peasantry remained unwilling to participate in revolutionary guerrilla warfare. Thus, while many Bolivians were just as poor in 1984 as in 1967, there have been no signs of significant revolutionary guerrilla movements in the country since Che Guevara's death in 1967.

NOTES

1. Herbert S. Klein, *Parties and Political Change in Bolivia, 1880– 1952* (Cambridge: Cambridge University Press, 1969), p. 411. See also Klein's *Bolivia: The Evolution of a Multi-ethnic Society* (New York: Oxford University Press, 1982).

2. Klein, *Bolivia,* pp. 227–28, and Ronald J. Clark, "Agrarian Reform: Bolivia," in Peter Dorner, ed., *Land Reform in Latin America* (Madison: Wisconsin Land Tenure Center, Land Economics, 1971), p. 129.

3. The literature on the revolution is voluminous, but the reader is directed particularly to Robert T. Alexander, *The Bolivian National Revolution* (New Brunswick, N.J.: Rutgers University Press, 1958); Jonathan Kelly and Herbert S. Klein, *Revolution and the Rebirth of Inequality: A Theory Applied to the National Revolution in Bolivia* (Berkeley and Los Angeles: University of California Press, 1981); James M. Malloy, *Bolivia: The Uncompleted Revolution* (Pittsburgh: University of Pittsburgh Press, 1970); James M. Malloy and Richard S. Thorn, *Beyond the Revolution: Bolivia since 1952* (Pittsburgh: University of Pittsburgh Press, 1971); and James W. Wilkie, *The Bolivian Revolution and U.S. Aid since 1952* (Los Angeles: Latin American Center, University of California at Los Angeles, 1969).

4. By far the best and most complete account of the period 1932–52 is Klein, *Parties and Political Change in Bolivia,* pp. 228–402. See also his *Bolivia,* particularly chap. 7.

5. Klein, *Bolivia,* pp. 235–36. There is an extensive literature on the Bolivian land reform program. The reader is directed particularly to William E. Carter, *Aymara Communities and the Bolivian Agrarian Reform* (Gainesville: University of Florida Press, 1965);

Dwight B. Heath, Charles J. Erasmus, and Hans C. Buechler, *Land Reform and Social Revolution in Bolivia* (New York: Praeger, 1969); and the essays by William E. Carter, Melvin Burke, and Madeline Barbara Leons and William Leons in Malloy and Thorn, *Beyond the Revolution*, pp. 233–39.

6. See Melvin Burke, "Land Reform in the Lake Titicaca Region," in Malloy and Thorn, *Beyond the Revolution*, p. 303. For a fascinating analysis of how Paz Estenssoro and the MNR viewed Indian peasants and land reform, the new Indianism, see Fredrick B. Pike, *The United States and the Andean Republics: Peru, Bolivia, and Ecuador* (Cambridge, Mass.: Harvard University Press, 1977), pp. 275–87.

7. See Milton S. Eisenhower, *The Wine Is Bitter: The United States and Latin America* (Garden City, N.Y.: Doubleday, 1963). See also Cole Blasier, *The Hovering Giant: U.S. Response to Revolutionary Change in Latin America* (Pittsburgh: University of Pittsburgh Press, 1976), particularly chaps. 5 and 7.

8. Wilkie, *The Bolivian Revolution*, p. 13.

9. Richard Gott, *Guerrilla Movements in Latin America* (Garden City, N.Y.: Doubleday, 1971), pp. 409–10.

10. See a list of the guerrillas by name, alias, national origin, military rank, and fate in Daniel James, ed., *The Complete Bolivian Diaries of Che Guevara and Other Captured Documents* (New York: Stein and Day, 1969), pp. 324–27.

11. James, *The Complete Bolivian Diaries*, pp. 96, 108.

12. There are many accounts of Che Guevara's Bolivian campaign, but one must begin with Che's own diary, which was published in two different editions: James, *The Complete Bolivian Diaries*, and *The Diary of Che Guevara, Bolivia: November 7, 1966 – October 7, 1967* (New York: Bantam Books, 1968). The James volume is more complete in that it also contains the diaries of Rolando, Pombo, and Braulio, whereas the latter contains a valuable introduction by Fidel Castro. Also important are Rodolfo Bellani, *La tumba del "Che"* (Buenos Aires: Imprenta López, 1965); Regis Debray, *Che's Guerrilla War* (London: Penguin Books, 1975); Luis J. González and Gustavo A. Sánchez Salazar, *The Great Rebel: Che Guevara in Bolivia* (New York: Grove Press, 1969); Gott, *Guerrilla Movements*, pp. 395–481; Marta Rojas and Mirta Rodríguez Calderón, eds., *Tania, the Unforgettable Guerrilla* (New York: Random House, 1971); Jesús Lara, *Guerrilla Inti Paredo* (México, D.F.: Editorial Diógenes, S.A., 1972); I. Lavretski, *Ernesto Che Guevara* (Moscow: Editorial Progreso, 1975); Guido "Inti" Paredo, *Mi campaña junto al "Che"* (La Paz, Bolivia: Oscar Crespo V., Editor,

1970); and Rubén Vásquez Díaz, *Bolivia a la hora del Che* (México, D.F.: Siglo Veintiuno Editores, S.A., 1968).

13. James, *The Complete Bolivian Diaries*, pp. 95–96. Most of Monje Molina's lengthy rebuttal to Che, which was published later, is translated and reprinted in Gott, *Guerrilla Movements*, pp. 430–38.

14. James, *The Complete Bolivian Diaries*, p. 108.

15. Ibid., p. 274.

16. Ibid., p. 32.

17. Gott, *Guerrilla Movements*, p. 421.

18. See Pombo's diary in James, *The Complete Bolivian Diaries*, p. 275.

19. Herbert S. Dinerstein, "Soviet Policy in Latin America," *American Political Science Review* 61, no. 1 (March 1967): 80–90; James, *The Complete Bolivian Diaries*, p. 275.

20. Gott, *Guerrilla Movements*, pp. 446–51.

21. For a good summary of the military campaign, see ibid., pp. 466–81.

22. "Bolivia: The Politics of a Frustrated Revolution," in Russell H. Fitzgibbon and Julio A. Fernandez, *Latin America: Political Culture and Development*, 2d ed. (Englewood Cliffs, N.J.: Prentice-Hall, 1981), p. 226.

HONDURAS

Raití

Puerto Cabezas

NUEVA
SEGOVIA

Ocotal

JINOTEGA

Bocay

MADRIZ

Zinica

ESTELÍ

Pancasán

CHINANDEGA

Matagalpa

Chinandega

LEÓN

MATAGALPA

León

*Lago de
Managua*

BOACO

PACIFIC
OCEAN

Managua

MANAGUA

Masaya

MASAYA

Granada

Diriamba

GRANADA

Jinotepe

CARAZO

RIVAS

CHONTALES

*Lago de
Nicaragua*

RÍO
SAN JUAN

San Carlos

ZELAYA

CARIBBEAN SEA

86°

84°

14°

12°

NICARAGUA

- – · – · – International boundary
- ——— District boundary
- ○ National capital
- • Other major city

0   25   50   75   100 Mi.

0   25   50   75   100   125   150 Km.

COSTA RICA

NICARAGUA

POLITICAL CHRONOLOGY

1927–33 U.S. marines support Nicaraguan government's unsuccessful efforts against guerrilla movement of Augusto César Sandino. 1932 elections bring Liberal Juan Sacasa to the presidency.

1934 Sandino assassinated.

1936–56 Anastasio (Tacho) Somoza García dominates Nicaraguan politics through National Guard, U.S. support, and puppet presidents. "Somoza dynasty" established as family and related economic cliques control Nicaraguan economy.

1956 Somoza García assassinated; Luis Somoza Debayle selected by congress to complete his father's term. Anastasio II (Tachito) Debayle heads National Guard; repression of opposition and incarceration and torture of those suspected to be involved in the assassination.

1957–63 Administration of Luis Somoza Debayle. Initial "liberalization" of political system, followed by several invasions of Nicaragua by internal opposition from bordering countries (1959–61). First *focos* established in emulation of Cubans (1960–62). FSLN founded in Honduras (1961). Bay of Pigs invasion launched from Nicaragua. Somoza declares support for anti-Communist policies of U.S.

1963–66 Administration of René Schick, a part of Somoza's apparatus, who dies in 1966 and is replaced by Interior Minister Lorenzo Guerrero. Country participates in Alliance for Progress programs, Central American Common Market, and CONDECA.

1967   Luis Somoza Debayle dies of heart attack.

1967–71   Administration of Anastasio Somoza Debayle. FSLN attacks Somoza family's "La Perfecta" dairy (August 1967). Defeat of FSLN Pancasán *foco*. FSLN attempts urban guerrilla operations, 1969–70. FSLN Zinica *foco* defeated, 1970–71. Growing political opposition to Somozas by non-Marxist political elites. Somoza agrees to political reforms and need for new election law with interim junta.

1971–72   Triumvirate junta ("Junta of the Three Little Pigs").

1972   Earthquake destroys Managua. Somoza assumes control.

1972–74   Somoza rules by decree. Family and cronies profit from reconstruction and graft.

1970–74   Retrenchment of guerrilla movement and FSLN operations.

1974–79   Administration of Anastasio Somoza Debayle. Tachito (now Tacho II) serves as "elected" president, increasing the levels and sources of political opposition, which includes Christian Democrats, progressive clergy, independents, and labor movement. UDEL formed in 1974 as democratic alliance of opposition. FSLN commandos "crash" Christmas party at home of "Chema" Castillo and almost capture U.S. ambassador. Sporadic guerrilla activity 1975–76. Somoza's counterinsurgency operations, Aguila VI, defeat FSLN. FSLN founder Carlos Fonseca Amador killed in November 1976. Carter administration in U.S. puts pressure on Somoza to respect human rights and democratize Nicaraguan politics (1977–79). Somoza suffers heart attack in July 1977. Assassination of Pedro Joaquín Chamorro in January 1978 unites opposition; riots and general strike follow. Monimbó uprising in February 1978. FSLN commandos capture national congress in August 1978. Businessmen's strike and "September uprising"; final offensive in June 1979. Somoza flees July 17, 1979. FSLN enters Managua.

1979–84   Sandinista regime initiates revolutionary changes in Nicaragua. U.S. supports counterrevolutionary guerrilla movements in Honduras and Costa Rica against revolu-

tionary regime. Some ex-Sandinista commanders join the
guerrilla struggle against new government.

BACKGROUND

In 1979, decades of struggle against the dictatorial dynasty of
the Somoza family culminated in victory for revolutionary
forces in Nicaragua. For the first time since the Fidelista victory in Cuba in 1959, the combination of rural and urban guerrilla operations, student political movements, and multi-class,
pluralist political insurrection brought down a "Caribbean
dictatorship." After twenty years of frustration for revolutionaries throughout the hemisphere and in Nicaragua itself, it
seemed that Che Guevara's inspiration and prescriptions had
resulted in military and political victory for revolutionary
militants in a Latin American country.

In many ways, Nicaragua's twentieth-century political history resembles that of Cuba, the Dominican Republic, and
Panama, with periodic U.S. military occupation punctuating
episodes of violence and civil war.[1] With an economy based on
a small number of agricultural exports dependent on fluctua-
tions in international market prices, Nicaragua had been a
"banana republic," a "coffee republic," and a "banana, coffee,
sugar, and cotton republic." As in many of its Latin American
neighbors, nineteenth- and twentieth-century politics in
Nicaragua revolved around personalist conflicts and archaic
ideological debates between Liberals and Conservatives. Diversification of agriculture and incipient industrialization had
fragmented somewhat the dominant Conservative and Liberal
oligarchy by the mid-twentieth century, but in most respects
the terms of political debate in the ruling classes did nothing to
challenge the fundamental structure of Nicaraguan society:
domination and repression of the vast majority of the population by a small group of landowners, financiers, and foreign
investors under the direct administration of the Somoza family
and the National Guard.

The uniqueness of the Nicaraguan situation resided in the
almost permanent presence of U.S. troops in the country from

1912 to 1933 and the unusually close association between U.S. government officials and U.S. policy in the establishment and maintenance of the Somoza dynasty. Nowhere else in Latin America had U.S. policy been so consistent, so uncompromisingly committed to a personalist, then dynastic dictatorship. Likewise, nowhere else in Latin America did there exist the legacy of a nationalist hero who had successfully resisted, through *guerrilla* warfare, the first large-scale counterinsurgency adventures of the United States in the hemisphere.[2]

From 1912 to 1925, U.S. policy toward Nicaragua centered on maintaining in power the minority governments of a number of Conservative politicians against the threat of Liberal insurrection and civil war. At times as many as 3,000 U.S. marines were required to protect Conservative dictators against Liberal armies; at other times, as few as a hundred U.S. troops served as a reminder that the incumbent regime enjoyed American support. In 1925 intra-party conflict and personalist political strife brought Carlos Solórzano to the presidency, supported by a coalition of Conservatives and dissident Liberals. The new president requested that the United States postpone its plans to withdraw the small contingent of marines which remained in the country and the United States agreed, provided that the new government cooperate in the creation of a national constabulary of the sort that the United States had promoted in Haiti, the Philippines, Cuba, and the Dominican Republic.[3] Opposition forces protested the U.S. plan, but it was eventually adopted with certain modifications that defined the constabulary as "an urban, rural, and judicial police force" rather than as a substitute for the regular army. Shortly thereafter the political situation degenerated once again into civil war, with the small constabulary playing a minor role as a supporter of the Conservative cause. In part on the pretext that Mexican and Communist support for the Liberals endangered American interests, Under Secretary of State Robert Olds justified renewed U.S. military intervention in Nicaragua as follows:

The Central American area down to and including the Isthmus of Panama constitutes a legitimate sphere of influence for the United

States, if we are to have due regard for our own safety and protection. . . . Our ministers accredited to the five little republics stretching from the Mexican border to Panama . . . have been advisors whose advice has been accepted virtually as law . . . we do control the destinies of Central America and we do so for the simple reason that the national interest absolutely dictates such a course.

There is no room for any outside influence other than ours in this region. We could not tolerate such a thing without incurring grave risks.[4]

By March 1927, U.S. forces supporting the Conservative administration again numbered over 2,000. In the hope of preventing full-scale American involvement in the civil war, President Calvin Coolidge sent former secretary of war Henry Stimson to Nicaragua to arrange a settlement between the warring parties and factions. Stimson imposed an agreement on the Conservative president, Adolfo Díaz, and most of the Liberal opposition, including Liberal general Anastasio Somoza García. This agreement provided for: (1) immediate peace; (2) a general amnesty; (3) Liberal participation in the cabinet; (4) American supervision of the disarmament of the adversaries; (5) retention of the marines in the country until a new nonpartisan National Guard, under American officers, could replace them; and (6) U.S. supervision of the 1928 elections. The new Guardia Nacional created in accord with this agreement incorporated some of the remaining members of the old constabulary but essentially represented a new departure for Nicaraguan politics. For the next half century the Guardia would be the most important political institution in the country.

The American intervention produced still another novelty in Nicaraguan politics: a relatively fraud-free election that actually resulted in the opposition (Liberal) candidate winning the presidency. However, the new Liberal president and his immediate successor were unable to persuade dissident Liberal Augusto César Sandino to lay down his arms and join the new coalition of political forces that now dominated Nicaraguan society. During the next five and one-half years, Sandino's guerrillas successfully eluded the American and Nicaraguan military forces and inflicted considerable damage and casualties on them. Adopting a nationalist, and eventually anti-American, posture, Sandino earned the everlasting enmity of the new Guardia, its leader, Anastasio Somoza, and the American military and diplomatic representatives in Nicaragua. Sandino fought against the U.S. marines and the Guardia Nacional from bases in the northern mountains of Nicaragua, taking sanctuary in Honduras when pursuit threatened his forces. Gradually Sandino's guerrilla war put pressure on some of the more southerly urban centers of the country, including, in the early 1930s, Managua. Meanwhile, faced with a seemingly unwinnable war, U.S. public opinion turned against this intervention. By 1932 the U.S. government was withdrawing the major part of the marine contingent and "Nicaraguanizing" the war through expansion of the Guardia Nacional. After supervising the 1932 elections, won by the Liberal candidate, Juan Sacasa, the last marines were withdrawn from Nicaragua. Sandino had survived the counterinsurgency campaign and provided Nicaraguans a legacy of victorious, anti-American nationalism.

In 1934 the new president and the Guardia commander, themselves contesting for effective control of the country, concluded a pact with Sandino that acknowledged the guerrillas' control over the northern sections of the country. General Somoza entered into this pact with great reluctance. Not only did he view it as an insult to the Guardia; he bitterly opposed official recognition of a de facto political and military power apart from the government and the Guardia. Somoza's solution was simple and brutal: he invited Sandino and his generals to a state dinner and then had them murdered. Thus, treachery achieved in a day what years of counterinsurgency had failed to produce—the elimination of Sandino.

Although some of Sandino's lieutenants and followers remained in the mountains as isolated guerrilla forces for some time, the Sandinista movement languished after its leader's assassination and the defeat and death of the Sandinista military leader Pedro Altamirano. By 1936, Anastasio Somoza García had maneuvered himself into the presidency, and from that point until his own assassination in 1956 he controlled Nicaragua as president, as commander of the Guardia, or as both. He did so by manipulating and even altering the constitution, electoral laws, and internal Guardia regulations in order to "legalize" his personal, then dynastic, rule. Occasionally, puppet presidents served the family's interests; at other times Somoza ruled directly. He repressed genuine Conservative party opposition, though he sometimes extended patronage and political position to compliant "opponents" of the regime.

Early in his administration Somoza established the pattern that would prevail throughout the family's domination, imposing special "taxes" on cattle exports, extracting "contributions" from mining and textile firms and kickbacks from government personnel salaries for the Liberal party coffers, acquiring real estate at bargain prices through forced sales and then reselling it to the government for highways or other public projects at considerable profit. Somoza quickly became the wealthiest man in the country; loyal subordinates and Guardia officers also participated in black market commerce and took advantage of opportunities to amass fortunes through corruption.

Thus the United States' occupation of Nicaragua in the early twentieth century and the creation of the Guardia Nacional established the basis for the next four decades of personalistic dictatorial government. General Somoza turned Nicaragua into a political satrapy in which he, his family, and his associates dominated national commerce and agriculture, looted the public treasury, enriched themselves from public contracts, and stole millions of dollars of American foreign assistance funds from the people of Nicaragua.

Always, however, Somoza (Tacho) courted U.S. support and prided himself on the services he provided U.S. governments with his anti-Communism and his willingness to serve as a tool of American intelligence and defense agencies. Throughout the early 1950s he cooperated in U.S.-sponsored intrigues in Central America and the Caribbean, and in 1954 he even boasted of his role in assisting the counterrevolutionary forces that invaded Guatemala under CIA direction. Even when American diplomats sometimes found the Somoza link embarrassing or wished to loosen a bit the ties of "friendship," the Somoza regime continued to play its submissive role to the United States in inter-American relations.

In September 1956, Rigoberto López Pérez, poet and nationalist, assassinated Tacho Somoza in the city of León as the dictator prepared for his next "reelection" campaign. Somoza's eldest son, Luis Somoza Debayle, assumed the interim presidency and his younger legitimate son, Anastasio II (Tachito), assumed command of the Guardia Nacional. Vicious and widespread retribution against suspected participants in the assassination plot resulted in the jailing of numerous opponents and the torture of hundreds of others. The victims included General Emiliano Chamorro; Pedro Joaquín Chamorro, the editor of *La Prensa*; and Tomás Borge Martínez, who would later play an important role as rebel leaders.

Soon after Somoza's assassination the compliant congress elected Luis to fill the remainder of his father's term. The Conservative party decided to boycott the forthcoming 1957 "elections," whereupon, to provide the pretense of an electoral opponent for the presidency, the Somozas revived the Conservative Nationalist party (called the Zancudo, or Mosquito, party by the opposition).

During the next two years various political opponents conspired against the Somoza regime. Meanwhile, political and economic unrest throughout Nicaragua challenged the dynasty. The Nicaraguan Communist party (Partido Socialista Nicaragüense, PSN), founded in 1944, intensified its clandestine activities at the universities, and student protests led to public demonstrations against the regime. Peasant and worker conflicts with landlords and factory owners put strains on the "social stability" that the Somozas so cherished. The formation of the Nicaraguan Social Christian party (PSCN) and the Popular Christian Democratic Movement led eventually to a series of political and military movements against the regime. And even before Fidel Castro triumphed in Cuba, one of the last veterans of Sandino's campaigns of the 1930s, Ramón Raudales, opened a guerrilla front in the mountains of the north, but Tachito Somoza transported anti-guerrilla troops to Nueva Segovia by air and easily defeated the forty-odd guerrillas led by the former Sandino compatriot.[5]

These initiatives by opponents of the regime produced little in the short term beyond the death, imprisonment, and torture of both Conservative and revolutionary rebels. However, the victory of the Cuban guerrilla movement and the defeat of dictator Batista inspired new hope in the Marxist and reformist opposition political leaders in Nicaragua, as well as in a new generation of radicalized students. It was a hope that tied Nicaragua's guerrilla hero of the past to the conflict of the present. As Tomás Borge later wrote, Ramón Raudales was "a kind of bridge between the fight directed by Sandino and the struggle of the new generations of Sandinistas."[6]

In many ways the formulations of Che Guevara in *Guerrilla Warfare* evoked fear on the part of the Somoza dynasty and stimulated hope for its adversaries. Guevara's analysis seemed obviously applicable to the Nicaraguan dictatorship, and the legacy of Sandino allowed the Cuban example to be linked to the heroic, nationalist guerrilla resistance of Sandino.[7]

More specifically, in regard to the socioeconomic and political conditions discussed by Guevara in *Guerrilla Warfare*, Nicaragua, in 1980, seemed to conform more closely to Guevara's analyses than Guatemala, Venezuela, Colombia, Peru, or Bolivia.

1. For years Anastasio Somoza García epitomized the Caribbean-type dictatorship described by Che Guevara as the ideal target of the guerrilla *foco*, and his son's decision to impose a dynastic dictatorship, if anything, increased the regime's vulnerability to *foco*-inspired insurgency. Moreover, Nicaragua had an even less effective system of political parties than Guatemala. The Somoza dynasty used the Liberal Nationalist party (PLN) as an instrument of the family's political control, while tolerating token opposition from the Conservative Nationalist party and the Conservative party so as to preserve the façade of democracy. Though a splinter from the Liberal party, the Independent Liberals (PLI), strenuously opposed the dictatorship from the mid-1940s on (one of their leaders was Tomás Borge), and a weak Social Christian (later Christian Democratic) movement emerged in the late 1940s, no realistic electoral alternative existed while the Somozas controlled the Guardia and manipulated the electoral apparatus. No matter who

might win the elections, the Somozas or their temporary puppets won the vote count. In this sense it became clear to middle-class, elite, and revolutionary opposition movements that no alternative to violence existed if they were to rid Nicaragua of the dynasty. This recognition would, as Che Guevara indicated, provide legitimacy for the revolutionary politico-military movements that arose in the 1960s and 1970s.

2. In addition to considerable rugged and isolated terrain within Nicaragua suitable for guerrilla operations, sparsely populated areas in neighboring Honduras and Costa Rica offered potential bases for guerrilla movements opposed to the Somoza dynasty. Moreover, the tradition of Sandino offered a psychological climate of great utility to guerrilla *focos* on the model offered by Che Guevara in *Guerrilla Warfare.*

As in Guatemala, Venezuela, and Colombia, however, the lack of political ties between the rural sector and urban intellectuals, students, and political cadres made the countryside initially quite dangerous for the opponents of the Somoza dictatorship. In addition, the secret police apparatus of the Somozas covered most of the country, thereby greatly increasing the risk for political opponents of the regime.

In contrast to the Guatemalan, Peruvian, and Bolivian cases, however, no serious cultural or linguistic barriers separated the Nicaraguan revolutionaries from the majority of the peasantry. (Exceptions to this included Indian groups in the sparsely populated northeast.) And, in contrast to the Venezuelan and Colombian cases, the government lacked any effective political linkages with the rural and urban working classes. The Somoza regime had never gained peasant and worker allegiance as had the AD party in Venezuela, APRA in Peru, the MNR in Bolivia, or the traditional parties in Colombia. Thus potential guerrillas had both isolated rural zones in which to train and base an insurrectional *foco* and the political space in which to organize the sort of liberated zones that Guevara believed necessary for the successful evolution of a guerrilla *foco.*

3. Also consistent with Guevara's formulations, Nicaragua re-

mained an essentially rural society in which the concentration of agricultural resources in the hands of a few gave the "agrarian question" great political significance. In 1960 the country had approximately 1,500,000 residents; over 60 percent were classified as "active in agriculture" and only one-third urban, using generous definitions of "urban." Other than Managua with approximately 350,000 people, none of the other major cities—León, Granada, Masaya, and Chinadega—had 50,000 residents. In short, Nicaragua had one major city, several large urbanizing villages, and a population predominantly rural in employment and orientation.

The Nicaraguan economy relied almost exclusively on agriculture for its survival, and as late as 1978 agricultural products (cotton, sugar, coffee, bananas, and livestock) accounted for 94 percent of the value of its exports.[8] Moreover, the growing emphasis on export-oriented agriculture worsened an already bad land tenure structure (in the early 1960s five percent of the agricultural holdings accounted for 60 percent of the farmland) and accelerated the process that pushed thousands of peasants off the land in the 1960s and 1970s.

4. In contrast to the situations in Cuba, where rural labor was organized long before 1959, and in Venezuela, Colombia, and Peru, the Nicaraguan peasantry lacked any long standing relationship with revolutionary or reformist political parties to serve as the basis for an insurrectionary *foco*. Indeed, the repressiveness of the Somoza dynasty prevented the evolution of any strong Marxist revolutionary or reformist political institutions in Nicaragua. This political isolation of most of the peasantry would make very difficult and costly in lives the initial efforts by Guevara-inspired Nicaraguans to create guerrilla *focos* in the 1960s. As Che Guevara insisted in *Guerrilla Warfare,* the essential task of would-be revolutionaries would consist of utilizing the objective conditions of rural misery to create the subjective conditions for victory.

In this task the nationalist, anti-American, anti-Somoza legacy of Sandino would give both a name and a symbol of victorious struggle to the group leading the military movement that toppled the dynasty in the late 1970s — the Sandinista Front For National Liberation (FSLN).

ORIGINS OF THE GUERRILLA MOVEMENTS IN THE 1960s

Like their counterparts in Venezuela, Guatemala, Colombia, and Peru, the Nicaraguan guerrillas in the 1960s came from student movements, dissident elements of the traditional political parties and the new social Christian movements, former Communists (PSN) who adopted Guevarist principles, and a small number of former military (Guardia) personnel. With the exception of the ex-Guardias and a few veterans of the Sandino campaigns of the 1930s, the rebels of the 1960s lacked military skills, political experience, and practical knowledge of rural life, let alone good contacts with the peasant population. For these reasons, and because the shock troops of the Guardia Nacional proved effective counterinsurgency fighters who could count on informants and paramilitary support in isolated regions, the Nicarguan *focos* of the 1960s led invariably to heavy casualties among the guerrilla fighters.

Armed resistance to the Somoza dictatorship after the Cuban victory included both traditional Conservative party and social Christian "invasions" as well as a number of Guevarista-Marxist-inspired military movements. In June of 1959, a military force led by Pedro Joaquín Chamorro, editor of *La Prensa,* and Enrique Lacayo Farfán of the Independent Liberal party invaded Nicaragua from Costa Rica by land and air.[9] Poor planning, lack of familiarity with the invasion zone, and the failure of a rebel-sponsored general strike proved fatal to the movement, which became known as the Movimiento de Olama y Mollejones. The Guardia easily defeated and captured almost all of the approximately one hundred rebels, many of whom were beaten and imprisoned.[10] Inexplicable vacillation on the part of Luis Somoza, however, saved the leaders from execution, and by 1960 most of them were out of prison and participating anew in antigovernment movements. Years later the Somozas' failure to eliminate Pedro Joaquín Chamorro and the young revolutionaries who repeatedly initiated *focos* in the 1960s would spell the end of the dynasty.

Shortly after the failure of the Olama y Mollejones invasion, another invasion force—this one clearly supported by Cuba—entered Nicaragua from Honduras. This force, assisted in Cuba by Che Guevara and launched with the blessing of the anti-Somoza president of Honduras from that country's territory, consisted of radicalized students from Nicaragua, Mexico, and Guatemala and even some Cuban veterans of the Sierra Maestra. Calling themselves the Movimiento 21 de Septiembre in honor of the date of Tacho Somoza's assassination, the fifty-five guerrillas were commanded by a former officer of the Guardia Nacional, Rafael Somarriba, and supplied with weapons by Cuba at their Honduran frontier camp, El Chaparral.

U.S. intelligence and the Honduran military, not in sympathy with the Honduran president, Ramón Villeda Morales, located the guerrilla base camp despite Villeda Morales's efforts to warn the rebels of the danger. On June 23, 1959, Honduran troops surprised the revolutionaries at their base camp, killed or wounded almost half the force, and took the majority prisoner. Among the wounded guerrillas was Carlos Fonseca Amador, a young revolutionary who would later die in the struggle that he unremittingly waged against the Somoza dynasty.

The Somozas' response to these military incidents, beyond harsh and effective suppression of the incipient *focos,* was to remind the United States of the Communist threat to the hemisphere posed by Fidel Castro's and Che Guevara's efforts to duplicate the Cuban victory in Central and South America. For his part, President Eisenhower ordered the U.S. Navy to prevent any "Communist-led" interventions into Central America.[11] Nonetheless, some twenty "armed attacks" or would-be guerrilla movements by a variety of anti-Somoza forces provided bothersome, if ineffective, challenges to the Somozas' regime during the next two years.

The wave of anti-Somoza military activity coincided with renewed anti-regime activity by student groups, the small leftist labor movement, and dissident political parties, both within the country and among Nicaraguans in exile. One of the most important of these groups was the Nicaraguan Revolutionary Youth (JRN) founded by Carlos Fonseca, Tomás Borge, and Silvio Mayorga. Both Fonseca and Borge had experience with the Nicaraguan Communist party (PSN). Fonseca had participated in Communist student movements in the 1950s and had traveled to the Soviet Union, Eastern Europe, and Cuba. Like many of his contemporaries in the rest of Latin America, however, Fonseca left the PSN in 1960 to follow the *foquista* line of Che Guevara. Thus, these three revolutionaries, along with others they would recruit along the way, formed the intellectual foundations for the Frente Sandinista de Liberación Nacional (FSLN), the movement that eventually led the politico-military insurrection which toppled the Somoza dynasty. In this sense, in Nicaragua as in Guatemala, Venezuela, Colombia, and Peru, former militants of the Communist party provided an essential spark for the guerrilla movements of the 1960s.

At about the same time the JRN was founded in Costa Rica, a more broadly based student movement appeared in Managua, calling itself the Patriotic Youth of Nicaragua (JPN). Many eventual leaders and combatants of the FSLN, which was organized later, studied revolutionary theory and learned the politics of opposition to the dictatorship in the JPN. Such FSLN heroes as Doris Tijerino and Julio Buitrago were extremely active in the early days of this student movement. Though ideologically quite diverse, the JPN took the lead in opposing the Somoza regime and served as an important transitional organization for a revolutionary movement that "was in diapers, . . . taking its first steps."[12]

In July 1960, students from the National University of León, participating in the annual student parade, grossly insulted Guardia personnel and hurled rocks at them. The Guardia opened fire, killing some thirty students and wounding many others. Sympathy protests in Managua brought further violence, prompting the government to declare a state of siege, suspend constitutional liberties, and move to restore order. Adding to the political threat, a former Guardia lieutenant led a small contingent of rebels from Honduras against the regime, only to be defeated easily. Subsequent attempts to organize a general strike on the Cuban model failed. Then, in November, another group of rebels waiting to invade Nicaragua from Costa Rica confronted a Costa Rican civil guard unit and shot Commander Alfonso Monge. This action infuriated the Costa Ricans, whose president claimed that the rebels included Cubans.[13] The Somoza government, with the cooperation of the governments in Honduras and Costa Rica, suppressed the new rebel threat as well as the student movement in the country's major centers.

From the general upsurge of anti-Somoza activity—the more than twenty "invasions," the student protests and demonstrations, the renewed activity of opposition political parties, and labor unrest—emerged the first revolutionary politico-military organization of the 1960s in Nicaragua, the FSLN. Founded in Honduras in July 1961 by a small number of dedicated revolutionaries (Carlos Fonseca, Tomás Borge, and Silvio Mayorga being the principal leaders), the FSLN initially had no political base in Nicaragua. Like other such movements in the early 1960s, the FSLN received ideological inspiration from the Communist PSN, from the leaders' participation in student movements opposing the Somoza regime, and from direct contacts with the Cuban revolutionary leadership.

This small, isolated group of very young idealists without military training or lengthy political formation—but with experience in the Somozas' prisons—explicitly modeled their actions during the next decade on the Cuban example and on the theories of Che Guevara. Mayorga and Fonseca both spent time in Cuba in 1960 before organizing the FSLN, and the inspiration and support for the first of several *focos* they attempted to create in the 1960s came immediately from Cuban tutelage. Fonseca headed the JRN, a small group of exiles, while Mayorga and another comrade, Marcos Altamirano, gained leadership roles in the more diverse JPN, based among secondary and university students in Managua and the country's major provincial towns.

Fonseca insisted on the symbolic importance of including Sandino's name in the title of the new movements, but all agreed on basic principles: (1) the struggle in Nicaragua would necessarily be also an anti-imperialist movement; (2) only armed struggle could overthrow the Somoza regime; (3) a guerrilla *foco* would spark the eventual revolutionary victory.[14]

Clearly inspired by Che Guevara and the success of the Cuban revolution, the FSLN cadres undertook several "expropriations" or "recuperations" (bank robberies) to finance their activities and then went underground in Honduras. In the early 1960s a small FSLN guerrilla column composed of Nicaraguan students in exile, survivors of the "El Chaparral" movement, and a number of veterans of previous unsuccessful "invasions" and "uprisings" against the Somozas prepared themselves on the Nicaraguan-Honduran frontier for the launching of a guerrilla *foco*. Armed by Cuba and led by veteran Sandinista colonel Santos López, the youthful revolutionaries sought to topple the Somoza dynasty. As Fidel Castro had drawn strength from the symbolic attachment to the Cuban patriot José Martí, so the young revolutionaries of the FSLN dressed their program in the nationalist garb of Sandinism: "The FSLN leadership had learnt from the Chinese, Vietnamese, and Cuban experiences that a socialist revolution can triumph in the Third World only if it mobilizes the nationalist sentiments of the masses, as well as their ideals of liberty and equality. In declaring itself the inheritor and continuator of Sandino's epic struggle, the FSLN rooted itself in a living Nicaraguan tradition, emerging as the unswerving champion of national independence and identifying against U.S. domination and its local agents."[15]

POLITICO-MILITARY EVOLUTION OF THE STRUGGLE

The initial military operations of the FSLN resulted in unequivocal defeat. After more than a year of preparations in an isolated Honduran frontier region some thirty miles from the Nicaraguan border, the guerrillas attacked and temporarily occupied the villages of Raití and Walquistán. "Expropriating" merchandise from local stores, they acquired supplies for themselves and distributed food and clothing to village inhabitants. A second column, commanded by Colonel Santos López, moved toward the town of Bocay. There they encountered a reinforced Guardia unit and decided to divide their forces into three groups: one, under Modesto Duarte, suffered several casualties and dispersed; a second, led by Tomás

Borge, initially remained downriver near Walquistán; the third decided to attack San Carlos, but became lost in the mountains while trying to take a shortcut.[16] With the help of some local residents the guerrillas finally reached the small village of SanSán, only to encounter forty Guardias. After a firefight in which several guerrillas were killed or wounded, the Sandinistas abandoned the fight.[17]

In retrospect, Tomás Borge, the only member of the original FSLN cadres still alive in the early 1980s, commented: "We made the mistake of attacking Raití, without knowledge of the land or doing any proselytizing and without securing our supply lines. This was a backward area, not only politically, but culturally. Many of the inhabitants didn't know Spanish, so we had communication problems."[18] In short, the FSLN had attempted an invasion of Nicaragua without any popular support, previous political organization, or effective military preparation. In the interim a new military government in Honduras made the older border bases hazardous; the first *foco* ended with a number of casualties and most of the guerrillas captured by Honduran troops and then deported to Mexico.

The year 1963 also brought elections. Anxious to obtain increased Alliance for Progress funding and to refurbish the façade of democracy in Nicaragua, Luis Somoza made René Schick the Liberal party candidate. The Conservative candidate, Fernando Agüero-Rocha, requested supervision of the election by the Organization of American States, but Somoza denied the request. When the Conservative candidate led a march to protest this decision, the Somozas placed him under arrest until after the election. In response, the Conservatives announced a boycott, forcing the dynasty to resurrect again their puppet opposition, the Conservative Nationalist party.

As expected, the Somozas' candidate won a massive electoral victory. From 1963 to 1966 President Schick administered the Somozas' domain, assisted by increasing levels of U.S. military and economic aid. Rewarded for their prompt support of the U.S. intervention in the Dominican Republic in 1965, the Somozas took advantage of the counterinsurgency emphasis in U.S. inter-American policy to strengthen the Guardia and to prepare for the assumption of the presidency in 1967 by

Guardia commander Anastasio Somoza II (Tachito). To further buttress the family's hold on the country, Colonel José Somoza, Luis and Anastasio II's illegitimate half-brother, assumed command of the Guardia's most combat-ready unit, the Somoza Battalion. In 1966 this unit participated in two counterinsurgency exercises with other Central American forces as the United States built up the Central American Defense Council (CONDECA) as a regional response to the export of the Cuban revolution.

President Schick died in August 1966 and was replaced by Minister of Interior Lorenzo Guerrero. In order to challenge Tachito Somoza's candidacy in the upcoming 1967 elections, a united opposition front of Conservatives, Independent Liberals, Christian Democrats, and some leftists joined in a National Opposition Union. Frustrated by the obvious control of elections by the dynasty, opposition leaders, including Fernando Agüero and Pedro Joaquín Chamorro, attempted in January 1967 to incite a popular insurrection in Managua. Thousands of demonstrators called upon the Guardia to overthrow Somoza. Instead, the soldiers turned their guns on the crowds, killing many people and injuring hundreds more. The opposition seized the Gran Hotel, taking 117 hostages. Finally the Papal Nuncio and representatives of the Nicaraguan Church and the U.S. embassy negotiated a truce.

In the meantime, the FSLN continued political work in the urban areas, especially among its student supporters in the Revolutionary Student Front. From 1965 on, this group published sporadically *The Student* and served as a legal front for clandestine activities, propaganda, and political opposition. At the same time, the FSLN protested against the farce of the upcoming elections. It also carried out a number of military operations such as bank robberies and, in August 1967, an attack on the "La Perfecta" dairy controlled by the Somozas, in which security forces surprised the FSLN fighters, killing, wounding, or capturing them. Notwithstanding opposition protests, the "elections" confirmed the dynasty in power. Two months after Tachito's "election" as president in February 1967, his somewhat less militaristic brother, Luis Somoza, died of a heart attack.

Later in the year the Sandinistas attempted to establish a

new rural guerrilla *foco* in a region reconnoitered since the early 1960s by Rigoberto Cruz (Pablo Ubeda). Ammunition and weapons were stored in hidden caches throughout the Pancasán area, situated in the Darien Cordillera fifty kilometers east of Matagalpa. Meanwhile, FSLN guerrilla leaders worked to incorporate local peasants and workers into a network of sympathizers and intelligence gatherers. For approximately three months the thirty-five guerrillas operated without detection. An accidental encounter and exchange of gunfire with local constables confirmed for the Somoza government that a guerrilla column existed in the region and brought a quick response. With the guerrillas divided into three columns, one commanded by Tomás Borge near Matagalpa, one led by Carlos Fonseca at the base camp, and a third led by Silvio Mayorga and Rigoberto Cruz near Quirragua, the Somoza government sent four hundred Guardias of the Somoza Battalion into the area to carry out search and destroy missions. Using local constables and informants to locate the guerrillas, the Guardia troops eventually killed all but fifteen of the original Pancasán cadres, including some FSLN founders. The mission lasted another three months as the Guardias interrogated, threatened, and killed hundreds of suspected FSLN sympathizers.

Analyzing the Pancasán *foco* in retrospect, the FSLN concluded that the terrain had been unfavorable, that the *foco* was poorly equipped and lacked military training, and that insufficient attention had been paid to incorporating local peasants into the movement.[19] Tomás Borge later observed, "We set up a good communication and intelligence network. We gained political control of the area; we had a lot of support. But we had a lot of firefights [with the Guardia] and our military capability was limited."[20]

With the defeat of the guerrillas, Somoza traveled to the village of Jinotza, north of Pancasán, and proclaimed to the nation, "The guerrillas no longer exist. I want to announce that the National Guard exterminated them. I want to announce to the people of Nicaragua and the world that our country is at peace."[21] Somoza was so sure of final victory over the FSLN that the elite counterinsurgency troops returned to Managua and the dictator offered to send a Guardia contingent to Vietnam to support the U.S. war effort. The apparent victory coincided with similar military defeats of guerrilla movements in Guatemala (the death of Turcios Lima) and Bolivia (the death of Che Guevara).

The government followed up the Pancasán victory with urban counterinsurgency actions from 1969 to 1970, partly in response to sporadic FSLN operations against banks and government officials and partly as a systematic effort to destroy, once and for all, the leftist threat. Future leaders of revolutionary Nicaragua, such as Daniel Ortega, were imprisoned and other FSLN militants died in the intensified urban warfare against the Guardia.[22]

Military defeat, imprisonment, torture, and the lack of political success failed to deter the FSLN. By 1970 the Sandinistas were initiating new rural organizational efforts in the Zinica– El Bijao region, some one hundred kilometers north of Pancasán. Despite heavy casualties inflicted by Guardia patrols, the Zinica *foco* continued to recruit local support among the peasantry. More favorable topography and better relations with the peasantry allowed many guerrillas to escape the net of the Guardia's search and destroy missions. Although the Zinica *foco* resulted eventually in another military defeat for the FSLN, it added to the cumulative experience that was gradually creating a heroic, even mythic, image of the valiant "muchachos" who, against impossible odds, continued to fight the Somoza dictatorship.

Such heroics, however, could not alter the stark political realities of failure: Most FSLN leaders of the 1960s were dead, in prison, or in exile. The Nicaraguan guerrillas had, overall, experienced even less military success and generated even less broad-based political support than had the unsuccessful guerrilla *focos* in Guatemala, Venezuela, Colombia, and Peru.

POST-1970 DEVELOPMENTS: SANDINISTA VICTORY

The Guevarista-inspired guerrilla movements of the 1960s had failed dismally in their efforts to spark a politico-military movement that would overthrow Somoza and take control of the Nicaraguan economy from the dynasty. In 1970 the Somoza family owned more than half the agricultural production of the country, large amounts of an expanding industrial sector, a steamship line, a share of the national airline, a half interest in the Intercontinental Hotel, and numerous other enterprises.[23] In addition, the nepotism at high levels of government made Nicaragua an extended patrimonial dictatorship: a cousin headed the National Development Bank, a brother-in-law served as ambassador to the United States, an uncle directed the national electric company, Somoza's American wife served as director for the social security system, and José Somoza remained a key figure in the Guardia.

Economic expansion in the 1960s had provided opportunities for others besides the Somoza clique. From 1960 to 1970 the value of exports rose at an annual rate of 11.5 percent, tripling in total value. Agribusiness, light industry, finance, construction, and real estate speculation fueled by Nicaragua's integration into the Central American Common Market stimulated two large capitalist networks not controlled by the Somozas—the Banco Nicaraguense (BANIC) and the Banco de América (BANAMERICA). Foreign investors, encouraged by Somoza or in partnership with the dynasty, contributed to the boom. The proliferation of business groups and interest associations, while initially serving as props for the Somoza regime, would eventually contribute leadership to the anti-Somoza movements of the mid-1970s as Somoza's greed and primitive patrimonialism excluded even the most powerful independent interests from a share of political power and participation in the new economic opportunities.

In 1970 Somoza received a new American ambassador, Turner B. Shelton, who became a close friend of and apologist for the dictator. Shelton arranged a meeting between President Richard Nixon and Somoza, who donated a million dollars to Nixon's 1972 election campaign.[24] With the approval of the U.S. State Department and Ambassador Shelton, Somoza initiated a series of maneuvers that would allow the revision of Nicaragua's constitution (which prohibited a president from succeeding himself immediately) so as to ensure his continued reign beyond his current term, 1967–72.

To achieve this purpose, Somoza hammered out a pact with the compliant Conservative opposition leader, Fernando Agüero, whereby a three-person junta—two Liberals and one

Conservative—would replace Somoza while a constituent assembly studied electoral reforms. In practice, Somoza retained control through the Liberal majority and the Guardia. An agreement on the reforms reached in March 1971 provided for governance shared by the country's two major parties until the newly scheduled presidential elections of 1974 could be held. In August 1971 congress duly dissolved itself and Somoza assumed all government functions until a new congress could be seated after the February 1972 legislative elections. After those "elections," which Somoza's liberal party won handily, the Conservatives were given 40 percent of the seats in the legislative assembly, as per the Somoza-Agüero pact, and Agüero occupied the Conservative minority position on the three-person junta that would officially administer the country until Somoza resumed command in 1974.

Heralded by Somoza and Ambassador Shelton as the beginning of a new era of democracy in Nicaragua, this arrangement irreparably split the Conservative party, for Pedro Joaquín Chamorro and the opposition Conservative elite could not ally themselves with their hated adversary. Under Chamorro's leadership, the Conservative National Action (ANC) was formed as an alternative to the collusionist Conservatives. In Somoza's own party, Ramiro Sacasa led a splinter movement called the Constitutionalist Movement (MC). The small but increasingly influential Christian Democratic movement and the new archbishop of Managua, Miguel Obando Y Bravo, also opposed the triumvirate (termed the "Junta of the Three Little Pigs"). In May 1972 the junta officially assumed power, but the archbishop boycotted the ceremony and a joint pastoral letter of the Nicaraguan bishops called for "a completely new order."[25] Thus, joining the traditional Conservative opposition, the influential Nicaraguan Catholic Church entered the struggle against the Somoza dynasty.

Major opposition groups, including elements of BANIC and BANAMERICA, middle-class entrepreneurs, and local organizations, boycotted the presidential elections in September 1974 with the slogan "There is no one to vote for."[26] Opposed officially only by the Conservative candidate Edmundo Paguagua, Somoza won an easy victory for a term that would end in 1981. To punish the opposition for the crime of "inciting to electoral abstentionism" (almost 50 percent of the eligible voters abstained), Somoza had "the Twenty-Seven" (the twenty-seven major opposition leaders) brought to trial, deprived of civil rights for six months, and barred from traveling.[27]

With Somoza's "election" the multi-class, ideologically pluralistic opposition formed a coalition called the Democratic Liberation Union (UDEL) under the leadership of Somoza's long-time adversary Pedro Joaquín Chamorro. Though the United States failed to recognize the opportunity it presented, UDEL offered a moderate, liberal, capitalist alternative to Somoza that, if successful, would have preempted the revolutionary efforts of the FSLN. As one writer perceptively concludes, "There can be no doubt . . . that in Nicaragua the bourgeois opposition itself opened up the crisis of the Somoza regime and actually led the first phase of the revolution. *It was only at the end of the process, with the help of Somoza's intransigence, that the FSLN captured the leadership of the struggle.*"[28] Had the United States taken this opportunity to support a moderate political alternative (and had it done so in 1972 or even 1977 in El Salvador [see below]), it is very possible that bloody civil wars in those nations could have been averted.

The mobilization and reorganization of political opposition to Somoza from 1970 to 1974 coincided with socioeconomic changes and natural catastrophes that gradually eroded the dynasty's hold on the country. From 1970 to 1972 a drought seriously disrupted agricultural production and export earnings, thereby exacerbating the country's balance of payments problem. Simultaneous inflation, rise in food prices, and unemployment generated student and worker protests.[29] While Somoza and Agüero worked out the details of the triumvirate pact, foreign investment stimulated the modernization of agribusiness, disrupted rural Nicaraguan society, and served as a prelude to the crisis of the late 1970s.

Still, Somoza managed these problems in the early 1970s directly and firmly through repression of his adversaries by the Guardia. Internal control of the Guardia itself depended on family members in key positions, frequent rotation of field commanders, and lucrative opportunities for graft or special privileges at almost all levels. Significantly, even with the economic difficulties of the early 1970s, Somoza attempted to buttress his position during the triumvirate (1971–74) with substantial pay increases of 50 to 150 percent for Guardia personnel.

Just as Somoza seemed to be succeeding in retaining dynastic control through the triumvirate junta, an earthquake struck Managua on December 23, 1972, reducing the center city to rubble and leaving an estimated 10,000 dead, thousands more injured, and 50,000 homeless. Although the city's suburban industrial infrastructure was largely unaffected, the earthquake destroyed almost 80 percent of the commercial establishments.[30]

The Somoza government's response to this disaster destroyed all remaining vestiges of its legitimacy, credibility, or moral authority.

In the aftermath of the earthquake the *Guardia Nacional* actually disintegrated. Most soldiers left their posts to take care of their families or to try to salvage personal belongings. Others, often led by officers, occupied themselves with massive looting, at times using *Guardia* vehicles to remove the stock from damaged stores. For nearly two days, Somoza was unable to muster even a company of troops. As a result, his prestige and that of the *Guardia* had sunk to an all-time low and the nation seemed on the verge of anarchy. . . .

As the work of reconstruction progressed, the Somozas and higher-ranking officers increasingly found ways to use the disaster as a means of increasing their own wealth. Bribes for guarding damaged property, for issuing new construction permits, or for obtaining import licenses, or even for obtaining food, the distribution of which was for a time a government monopoly, all offered lucrative possibilities.[31]

The extent of Somoza's venality is suggested by Pablo Joaquín Chamorro's report on "Operation Vampire" in *La Prensa*: "The emergency assistance included thousands of liters of plasma, more than the available medical teams and hospitals could use. Somoza sent the surplus to the United States, pocketing the profits. This transaction was so lucrative that during the period of reconstruction that followed the earthquake, he created a commercial blood bank through an intermediary . . . and began to buy Nicaraguan blood for pennies, process it, and send it to the United States, where it became dollars."[32]

Somoza and his clique formed demolition companies, real estate firms, and construction enterprises to profit from the reconstruction. His seemingly unlimited avarice, in the words of two analysts, "became the most efficacious promoter of Socialism in Nicaragua, while his brutal repressive campaigns became the most effective device for recruiting new insurrectionists for the FSLN."[33]

During this period the FSLN adopted a much lower profile in Nicaraguan politics. After the military setback in Zinica in 1970, the Sandinistas decided to abandon guerrilla operations in the countryside temporarily and to emphasize instead urban and rural political work and urban "military" actions. Oscar Turcios Chavarría, second-in-command of the unsuccessful Pancasán *foco*, returned from Cuba to replace the slain Julio Buitrago as head of the FSLN urban directorate. Almost all the other principal FSLN leaders remained imprisoned or outside the country.

Focusing on mobilization of FSLN-oriented students in the FER and creating alliances with the newly formed Catholic student group, the Christian Revolutionary Movement (MCR), the FSLN sought to broaden the social and ideological base of the anti-Somoza forces. Protests against hikes in gasoline and food prices, the distribution of propaganda leaflets, the organization of neighborhood committees, and work among labor organizations provided for an indirect Sandinista presence even though military activity was essentially dormant. This clandestine political work and the forging of links to the rising Catholic student and worker groups would prove invaluable in the late 1970s.

Nevertheless, occasional confrontations with the Guardia or local constables produced casualties and newspaper headlines. In 1973 the Guardia captured, then killed, Oscar Turcios and Ricardo Morales, leaving the FSLN without any of its national directorate in the country. Quickly, however, new cadres took the place of those fallen; the Sandinistas continued political work in the major towns and the "accumulation of forces" in the rural areas.[34] According to Humberto Ortega, Nicaraguan minister of defense in the early 1980s: "In the period 1970–74, with greater political-organizational work among the masses, and with a considerable development of the vanguard's internal structures in the mountains, the city and the countryside, the Sandinist war took great leaps forward in the accumulation of political, organizational, material and military [force]."[35]

At the end of 1974 the FSLN carried out the first of a series of spectacular operations that reinforced their heroic image, embarrassed the Somoza regime, and discredited Somoza with many of his own Guardia hardliners. On December 27, 1974, an FSLN commando team crashed a party at the home of José María Castillo Quant, killed Castillo and several guards, and took prisoner a number of celebrities that included Somoza's brother-in-law Guillermo Sevilla Sacasa, his cousin Noel Pallais Debayle, a number of government ministers, and the Chilean ambassador. In response, Somoza imposed martial law, suspended constitutional rights, and ordered the detention of hundreds of suspected FSLN sympathizers.

Ultimately Somoza gave in to the Sandinistas' demands: freedom for a number of political prisoners, including Daniel Ortega, a ransom of one million dollars (originally the FSLN commandos asked for five million), free passage to Cuba, and the dissemination of a long Sandinista communiqué over radio and in the press. As the victorious commandos headed toward the airport with the archbishop of Managua, and the ambassadors of Mexico and Spain as "volunteer hostages," crowds along the route shouted their support and anti-Somoza slogans. Again, the dictator responded in the only way he knew: with intensified repression and counterinsurgency.

Despite their success in the raid, the FSLN cadres still numbered less than three hundred. By 1975 seemingly minor ideological and strategic differences of the sort experienced by guerrilla movements earlier in the rest of Latin America fragmented the organization into three splinter movements: the proletarian wing; the advocates of a "prolonged people's war" (GPP); and the "third force" insurrectional group, Terceristas, which included many Catholic and non-Marxist revolutionaries.[36] The fragmentation of the FSLN allowed the Guardia to attack successfully both guerrilla cadres and numerous front groups among students and neighborhood committees. FSLN militant Dulce María Guillén writes, "The response of the dictatorship was stronger than we had anticipated; in some cases it did us serious structural damage. It was a very difficult period, above all in relation to the masses. The masses became dispirited. . . . They captured many of our people working in clandestinity . . . [and] destroyed some mass organizations . . . entirely that had previously confronted the *Guardia*. . . . Entire families disappeared."[37]

Encounters between the FSLN guerrillas and the Guardia brought mixed results in 1975 and 1976 but generally proved unfavorable to the rebels. In March 1975, guerrillas raided an outpost at Río Blanco and occupied the town for six hours. Somoza reacted by making Río Blanco a headquarters for counterinsurgency operations in the north and by initiating operation "Aguila VI," during which whole villages suspected of sympathizing with the rebels or providing supplies were subjected to wanton, senseless brutalization and massacre. Protests by Catholic priests—whose denunciations reached the U.S. Congress—and the natural hostility of the population created more and more enemies of the dynasty and a growing tide of unfavorable publicity in the United States.

Nevertheless, Aguila VI did eliminate a number of FSLN leaders. In November 1976, Eduardo Contreras, leader of the commando unit that attacked the Castillo house in 1974, died in a firefight and the next day the Guardia killed FSLN founder Carlos Fonseca Amador. One authority suggests that by the time the operation ended, only a few dozen FSLN militants survived.[38] Once again Somoza seemed to have defeated the Sandinistas; the widely read periodical *Latin America* declared the Sandinistas "virtually eliminated as a threat."[39]

Even if the FSLN still lacked political or military strength, however, the increased activity of UDEL, widespread popular resistance to the repression, and a shift in U.S. foreign policy all combined to undermine Somoza's position. U.S. economic and military support had long been the bulwark of the Somoza dynasty. Military assistance from 1974 to 1976 exceeded support in real terms (corrected for inflation) for the period 1962–66 by 67 percent.[40] Under the human rights emphasis of the Carter administration's foreign policy, aid to the Somoza regime declined dramatically.[41] John Booth reports that economic assistance for 1977–78 declined by 75 percent in real terms and military aid by almost 45 percent.[42]

Somoza's supporters in the U.S. Congress could not overcome the growing media attacks (including Jack Anderson's scathing columns) or the testimony to Congress of Nicaraguan priests and political opponents of the dynasty.[43] Badly damaged by Ambassador Turner Shelton's departure in 1975 (under mounting criticism for his obsequious relationship with the dictator), the Somoza regime began to lose the single most important source of its power: unconditional support by the United States for Somoza's "anti-Communism."[44] From exile in 1980, Somoza bitterly denounced President Carter and his policies, making crystal clear the overwhelming significance he accorded to the shift in U.S. foreign policy from 1976 to 1979: "When it comes to Cuba and Fidel Castro, Mr. Carter and his State Department have consistently used blindfolds and earplugs. I told the proper U.S. authorities on many occasions that Cuba was our common enemy. . . . The reaction was always the same—one of expressed disbelief or non-interest. I wanted the United States to understand that in Cuba we both faced a mortal enemy and that Cuba wanted, and if unopposed would ultimately get, far more than Nicaragua."[45]

Even as President Carter's new foreign policy pressed Somoza to lift the state of siege imposed after the FSLN attack on the Castillo house in 1974, Anastasio Somoza II suffered a heart attack on July 28, 1977. Flown to Miami for treatment, he could not return home until September 10. Shortly after his return, Somoza lifted the state of siege in hopes of regaining U.S. support, and legal opposition political activity resumed immediately. The FSLN Tercerista group responded quickly, attacking Guardia installations in Ocotal, Masaya, and San Carlos, near the border with Costa Rica. At about the same time a prominent group of anti-Somozans called *Los Doce* ("The Twelve") issued a proclamation calling for a popular uprising against Somoza. This group included respected businessmen, an international banker, Catholic priests, a corporation lawyer, an architect, an economist, and the owner of a supermarket chain. Although some of The Twelve had ties to FSLN Terceristas, the composition of this group clearly demonstrated that the Nicaraguan bourgeoisie had chosen to oppose the Somoza dictatorship.

Members of affluent families now engaged actively in the

anti-Somoza struggle; a minority joined the Sandinistas. The UDEL escalated its demands for Somoza's departure and Pedro Joaquín Chamorro's *La Prensa* savagely denounced Somoza's abuses. In November 1977, *La Prensa* published a full-page appeal by "The Twelve" for a democratic alternative to Somoza. Significantly, this appeal, as well as proclamations by the UDEL, now included a place for the FSLN in any new government. In response, Somoza had "The Twelve" tried in absentia and sentenced to prison terms. Two months later hired killers assassinated Pedro Joaquín Chamorro after *La Prensa* published an exposé of Somoza's blood plasma export business described above.[46]

This murder incited public outrage throughout the country. It galvanized the anti-Somoza opposition as business, labor organizations, the Catholic Church, UDEL, and the FSLN demanded Somoza's resignation. In Managua, thousands of people took to the streets in sometimes violent demonstrations; two weeks later a general strike began that practically paralyzed the country for a month. After U.S. Ambassador Mauricio Solaún's mediation brought a temporary restoration of "normality," the U.S. diplomatic mission continued its efforts to engineer a transition to a centrist civilian government but vacillated about forcing Somoza out of office. The Somoza lobby and supporters in Congress reiterated their fears of a "Communist takeover," preventing the U.S. from moving quickly to try to avoid the bloody insurrection and civil war that would engulf Nicaragua for the next eighteen months.

In February 1978 the people of Monimbó, an Indian community in Masaya, planned a celebration to rename a plaza in honor of the murdered Pedro Joaquín Chamorro. Harassed by the Guardia, the crowd attacked them, barricaded the town, and declared it a free territory. After a period of skirmishing, the Guardia, commanded by Somoza's oldest son, Anastasio III, mounted a fierce assault supported by heavy weapons and aerial attacks and retook the town. Although there were more than two hundred civilian casualties, new spontaneous uprisings occurred at Subtiava and Diriamba, with a similar response from the Guardia. These events were followed in April by massive student strikes. More and more young people and women joined the armed popular insurrection in the capital and provincial towns. Though the FSLN claimed no direct leadership of these popular uprisings, Somoza flatly stated that, in his view, all such opposition was Communist-inspired and his response would be military suppression. Pedro Joaquín Chamorro's assassination had ignited the spark of insurrection throughout the country, but the general strike in early 1978 failed to end the dynasty. In the government paper, *Novedades,* Somoza proclaimed, "As my father said, I will not go, neither will they force me to go."[47] For their part, the non-Marxist, non-FSLN opposition lacked military force and organization, and the U.S. refused to (or could not) oust Somoza directly. Thus, no choice remained but armed insurrection, and only the FSLN had the capabilities and experience to direct a military struggle against the Guardia. Somoza confirmed tragically Che Guevara's prediction: a human tragedy of immense proportions and bitter civil war would be required to end the dynasty.

In July 1978 the non-Marxist movements created an expanded political group called the Broad Opposition Front (FAO), uniting Alfonso Robelo's Nicaraguan Democratic Movement, "The Twelve" (and therefore the FSLN Terceristas), the Social Christian party, and Conservative splinter groups in a more complex anti-Somoza coalition.[48] The FSLN also mobilized a new coalition of student, worker, and neighborhood groups, but rejected any compromise that would install "Somozaism without Somoza."

Then, on August 22, 1978, another spectacular FSLN operation further undermined the Somoza regime. A guerrilla commando group led by Tercerista "Comandante Cero," Edén Pastora, seized the national palace, and captured approximately 1,500 people, including 49 deputies and several close friends and relatives of Somoza. Naming the raid "Operation Pigsty," the Sandinistas had symbolically captured the government of Nicaragua. Worldwide press coverage allowed the Sandinistas to broadcast a lengthy communiqué that ended with a call for "democratic and revolutionary forces" to fight for a democratic and popular government in Nicaragua. Once again playing a key role in a Sandinista victory, Archbishop Obando y Bravo negotiated the following conditions: release of a number of political prisoners (including Tomás Borge), payment of a large cash ransom, repeated broadcasts and publication of FSLN statements calling for Somoza's ouster and preparation for the "final offensive," accession of the government to strike demands of hospital workers, and Mexican, Panamanian or Venezuelan planes to take the guerrillas out of the country.[49]

Despite this agreement, Somoza's elite commanders bitterly resisted giving in to the FSLN demands. A U.S. mercenary leader of an elite group, Michael Echanis, commented: "We could have taken the building in eighteen minutes. I figured maybe two hundred to three hundred would be killed. The plan was to shock the building with tank fire and blow the doors with recoilless rifles. I was going to helicopter in with my commandos and drop down through the roof hatches. The old man wouldn't buy it and the only reason was they held Papa Chepe's [José Somoza's] son. My guys were unhappy."[50] Rejecting a bloody military attack, Somoza caved in—as he had in 1974. The image of the heroic, daring Sandinistas was perpetuated and they became legendary throughout Latin America.

Less than a month later, the FSLN opened a new military offensive that coincided with a growing number of spontaneous uprisings like that in Monimbó, first in Matagalpa, and then in León, Masaya, Chinadega, and Managua itself. Somoza responded with bombing raids on the town and villages where resistance occurred, and as the Guardia forced the FSLN to withdraw, civilians were treated as a hostile force. Increasing numbers of people, motivated in part by self-preservation, joined the FSLN or followed them out of the besieged towns. The September offensive resulted in more than 5,000 dead, thousands more wounded, and more than 50,000 refugees seeking asylum in neighboring countries.[51] However, what seemed a series of military victories for Somoza represented, in reality, the final stage of the dictatorship: full-scale war by Somoza and the Guardia on the Nicaraguan people.

The Broad Opposition Front and the United States still sought a negotiated settlement, but Somoza refused to transfer power. In late 1978 a realignment of anti-Somoza student groups, political parties, neighborhood committees, professionals, and front groups formed the United People's Movement (MPU), a mass-based alternative to the more moderate FAO. This increased popular armed mobilization, together with the casualties of 1978, reinforced the FSLN's determination to win a *political* and military victory that would preclude the installation of "Somozaism without Somoza." As the war continued, the moderate FAO gradually lost credibility and the Sandinistas emerged as the clear vanguard of the anti-Somoza struggle. To solidify their position, the Sandinistas invited anti-imperialist, anti-dictatorship forces to join them in a coordinated National Patriotic Front (FPN) with their immediate objective the destruction of the Somoza regime. The FPN, to the displeasure of the United States, gradually replaced the FAO as the most visible and viable alternative to Somoza.[52]

Remarkably, many units of the Guardia continued to protect the dynasty. Unlike Batista's Cuban army in 1958–59, the Nicaraguan Guardia fought fiercely to the end and even defeated the anti-Somoza forces in some encounters. Thus, by February or March 1979 the FSLN military force represented the only viable instrument to overthrow Somoza. It meant that Somoza's defeat would cost up to 50,000 dead, hundreds of thousands of wounded, and the destruction of the country's major towns and economic infrastructure.

In March 1979 the three FSLN splinter groups reunited, setting up a joint command with three members from each faction.[53] This joint command at last combined the rural organizational efforts of the GPP, the work in urban mass organization of the *proletarios,* and the politico-military leadership of the *Terceristas,* thereby providing a distinctive version of Che Guevara's *foco*-based revolution. From its first military initiatives in the early 1960s the FSLN had suffered defeat after defeat; yet, as Che Guevara had predicted, the politico-military struggle was gradually being won.

The Guardia waged war on the Nicaraguan population from March to July 1979, while at the same time attempting to defend itself against mounting FSLN attacks on installations throughout the country. When the war reached Managua in May and June, Somoza turned his rightist death squads on FAO leaders as well as on suspected Sandinistas. On June 4 the FSLN called for a general strike to topple the regime; sixteen days later U.S. television viewers witnessed the callous murder of ABC newsman William Stewart—a murder that cost Somoza the last of his public support in the United States.

Still not willing to admit defeat, Somoza ordered his tanks, planes, and helicopters to attack the FSLN in the suburban shanty towns of Managua. Historian Thomas P. Anderson, who was in Managua shortly after, "was reminded of photos of the destruction of Hiroshima. . . . Only a few businesses appeared to have escaped destruction and these were watched over by cold-eyed *Guardia.* These, I was told, were spared because Somoza owned an interest in them. . . . No exact casualty statistics were kept by either side, but estimates of the dead ranged from 40,000 to 50,000. Even accepting the lowest figure, this represented a higher casualty rate than that in the U.S. Civil War. Another 100,000 had been wounded, and lay, often without proper medical attention, in makeshift hospitals about the country; 40,000 children had been orphaned and 8,000 tons of emergency food relief were needed every day to prevent famine."[54]

Finally, on the night of July 16, 1979, U.S. ambassador Lawrence Pezullo convinced Somoza that the war was lost, and the next day Anastasio II left Nicaragua and eventually sought sanctuary in Paraguay. Fourteen months later he was assassinated in Asunción.

The Sandinista victory represented a contradictory reaffirmation of Che Guevara's message. A guerrilla *foco,* or rather, many guerrilla *focos,* sowed seeds that took almost twenty years to bear fruit. Instead of a quick Cuban-like victory, the Nicaraguan *foco* ultimately gave rise, after years of military defeat, to a multiclass popular insurrection that plunged the country into bloody civil war.

The Nicaraguan experience had proven Che Guevara to be both right and wrong. First, only armed struggle proved sufficient to overthrow Somoza's version of Caribbean dictatorship but only protracted warfare combined with years of *political* organization and mobilization brought the *foco*'s aspirations to fruition. Second, this mobilization required the incorporation of significant numbers of entrepreneurs, clerics, workers, and traditional political elites to oust the dictator. Third, even this politico-military alliance would likely have failed without extensive assistance from foreign nations, especially Costa Rica, Venezuela, Panama, Mexico, and Cuba.[55] Finally, as in Cuba, the withdrawal of U.S. support from the Nicaraguan dictatorship allowed domestic civil opposition to coalesce around the less numerous FSLN cadres and defeat Somoza. If the Sandinistas inherited Che Guevara's most important legacy—the inspiration to challenge the dictatorship through armed struggle—they were also forced to modify profoundly the tactical, strategic, and political implications of *foquismo* in order to prevail.

POSTSCRIPT: NICARAGUA AFTER SOMOZA

In the first five years after defeating Somoza, the FSLN dedicated itself to consolidating political power, attempting to reconstruct the economy, and moving Nicaragua in the direction of a socialist society. Inheriting an economy left in shambles by civil war and Somoza's last-minute theft of foreign reserves, the Sandinistas faced overwhelming difficulties in bettering the lot of the Nicaraguan people. In addition, the Sandinistas' socialist orientation and close ties with Cuba both alienated many of the entrepreneurial and non-Marxist groups that had joined the anti-Somoza coalition from 1976 to 1979 and provoked U.S. military and economic attacks from 1981 to 1984. Toward the end of 1983 the Sandinista government was threatened by a growing number of guerrilla raids from U.S.-supported units based in Costa Rica and Honduras.

Historical ironies could not be ignored as the counterrevolutionary guerrillas forced the Sandinistas to threaten "hot pursuit" into Costa Rica and Honduras—just as had Somoza in the 1970s. In late October 1983 the U.S. military invasion of Grenada made all too clear to the Sandinistas that the covert U.S. assistance to anti-government rebels could, if circumstances presented themselves, become more direct, overt, and menacing. The CIA-financed and -directed mining of Nicaraguan ports and sabotage of factories and farms, and the Reagan administration's requests for increased funding for the *contras* (opposition forces) based in Honduras underlined the U.S.

commitment to destabilizing or destroying the Sandinista government, despite a surprise visit to Nicaragua by the U.S. secretary of state in early June 1984.

Internal opposition to the Sandinista government from sectors of the Catholic Church, entrepreneurs, and supporters of a more traditional pluralist polity slowed the movement to a one-party socialist system. Far from having consolidated the revolutionary regime in power, the Sandinistas attempted to mobilize popular support against both internal and external adversaries. With joint U.S.-Honduran military exercises on the Nicaraguan frontier in 1984 and the expansion of the U.S. military presence in Central America, the Sandinistas faced considerable political, economic, and military difficulties in attempting to reconstruct the devastated Nicaraguan economy and stabilize the political situation within the country. Somoza was gone, but Nicaragua's future remained enmeshed in superpower cold war politics that denied the legitimacy, or even the possibility, of efforts at autonomous national development.[56]

NOTES

1. For background on nineteenth- and twentieth-century Nicaragua, see Ralph Lee Woodward, Jr., *Central America: A Nation Divided* (New York: Oxford University Press, 1976); Richard Millett, *Guardians of the Dynasty* (New York: Orbis, 1977); Jaime Wheelock Román, *Nicaragua: Imperialisimo y dictadura* (Havana, Cuba: Editorial de Ciencias Sociales, 1980); Henri Weber, *Nicaragua: The Sandinist Revolution,* trans. Patrick Camiller (London: Verso Editions, 1981); John Booth, *The End and the Beginning: The Nicaraguan Revolution* (Boulder, Colo.: Westview Press, 1982); Thomas Walker, ed., *Nicaragua in Revolution* (New York: Praeger, 1982); Thomas P. Anderson, *Politics in Central America: Guatemala, El Salvador, Honduras, and Nicaragua* (New York: Praeger, 1982); Claribel Alegría and D. J. Flakoll, *Nicaragua: La revolución Sandinista, una crónica política 1855–1979* (Mexico, D.F.: Ediciones Era, 1982); Walter Lafeber, *Inevitable Revolutions: The United States in Central America* (New York and London: Norton, 1983); Peter Rosset and John Vandermeer, eds., *The Nicaraguan Reader* (New York: Grove Press, 1983).

2. On Sandino, the guerrilla leader, see Neill Macaulay, *The Sandino Affair* (Chicago: Quadrangle Books, 1971); Gregorio Selser, *Sandino general de hombres libres* (San José, Costa Rica: Editorial Universitaria Centro Americana, 1979); Carlos Fonseca, ed., *Ideario político de Augusto César Sandino* (Managua: Secretaría de Propaganda y Educación Política, FSLN, 1980); Humberto Oretega Saavedra, *50 años de lucha sandinista* (México, D.F.: Editorial Diógenes, 1979); United States Department of State, *A Brief History of the Relations between the United States and Nicaragua, 1909–1928* (Washington, D.C.: Government Printing Office, 1928).

3. See Dana G. Munro, *Intervention and Dollar Diplomacy in the Caribbean, 1900–1921* (Princeton: Princeton University Press, 1964).

4. Cited in Millett, *Guardians,* p. 52.

5. See NACLA, "Nicaragua," *Latin America and Empire Report* 10, no. 2 (February 1976): 26–27, 31–32; Bernard Diederich, *Somoza and the Legacy of U.S. Involvement in Central America* (New York: E. P. Dutton, 1981), p. 57.

6. Cited in Diederich, *Somoza,* p. 57.

7. In retrospect certain Sandinista leaders have made clear their Marxist inspiration and have even attempted to recast Sandino himself as a "solid anti-imperialist fighter," though recognizing Sandino's nationalist rather than Marxist-Leninist orientation. See Tomás Borge, "El FSLN y la Revolución Nicaragüense," special separate of *Cuadernos del Tercer Mundo* 6, no. 63 (August 1983).

8. James Nelson Goodsell, "Nicaragua," in Robert Wesson, ed., *Communism in Central America and the Caribbean* (Stanford: Hoover Institution Press, 1982), pp. 52–53; James Wilkie, ed., *Statistical Abstract of Latin America* (Los Angeles: UCLA Latin America Center, 1976); Alain Birou, *Fuerzas campesinas y políticas agrarias en América Latina* (Madrid: I.E.P.A.C., 1971), p. 35.

9. Alegría and Flakoll, *Nicaragua,* pp. 148–53; Millett, *Guardians,* p. 225.

10. Millett, *Guardians,* p. 224; Diederich, *Somoza,* pp. 57–60; Pedro Joaquín Chamorro, *Estirpe sangrienta: Los Somoza,* 2d ed. (Mexico, D.F.: Editorial Diógenes, 1980).

11. *New York Times,* November 18, 1960, p. 1, cited in Millett, *Guardians,* p. 225.

12. Doris Tijerino, *Inside the Nicaraguan Revolution* (as told to Margaret Randall), trans. Elinor Randall (Vancouver: New Star Books, 1978), p. 52; see also Booth, *The End,* pp. 138–40.

13. Diederich, *Somoza*, pp. 60–61.
14. Alegría and Flakoll, *Nicaragua*, p. 168.
15. Weber, *Nicaragua*, pp. 35–36.
16. See interview with Tomás Borge in *El Día*, Mexico City, September 9, 1979, cited in Diederich, *Somoza*, p. 70.
17. Interview in *El Día*, Mexico City, September 18, 1979, cited in Diederich, *Somoza*, p. 70.
18. Interview, Sepember 9, 1979, cited in Diederich, *Somoza*, p. 69.
19. Alegría and Flakoll, *Nicaragua*, p. 184.
20. Interview in *El Día*, Mexico City, April 4, 1979, cited in Diederich, *Somoza*, p. 84.
21. Cited in Diederich, *Somoza*, p. 85.
22. Ibid., pp. 87–88.
23. Anderson, *Politics*, p. 154, citing "Nicaragua de las armas al poder: La familia Somoza," *Cuadernos de Amanta* (Lima), no. 1 (August 1979): 15, and "No me voy," *The Economist*, September 2, 1978, pp. 66–67.
24. Diederich, *Somoza*, p. 89.
25. Millett, *Guardians*, pp. 235–36.
26. *La Prensa*, June 24, 1974, cited in Diederich, *Somoza*, p. 101.
27. Diederich, *Somoza*, p. 102.
28. Weber, *Nicaragua*, p. 33.
29. Ibid., p. 38; Weber, citing official statistics, points to average inflation rates before 1970 of 1.7% per year, compared with 9.7% per year from 1971 to 1975 and 11% in 1977. See also Alegría and Flakoll, *Nicaragua*, p. 218.
30. Millett, *Guardians*, pp. 236–37; Alegría and Flakoll, *Nicaragua*, pp. 219–20; Diederich, *Somoza*, pp. 93–105.
31. Millett, *Guardians*, pp. 238–40.
32. Cited in and translated from Alegría and Flakoll, *Nicaragua*, p. 221.
33. Alegría and Flakoll, *Nicaragua*, p. 222.
34. Henry Ruíz, in *Nicaragua*, May–June 1980, pp. 18–19, cited in Alegría and Flakoll, *Nicaragua*, p. 227.
35. Humberto Ortega, *50 Años*, pp. 120–21.
36. See Booth, *The End*, pp. 143–44, for a description of the ideological differences between these FSLN fragments. A slightly different characterization of the three splinters of the FSLN is that of Weber, *Nicaragua*, pp. 53–55; see also Ricardo E. Chavarría, "The Nicaraguan Insurrection: An Appraisal of Its Originality," in Walker, *Nicaragua*, pp. 29–30.
37. Interview with Dulce María Guillén, November 1979, cited in Alegría and Flakoll, *Nicaragua*, p. 235.

38. Weber, *Nicaragua*, p. 53.
39. *Latin America* (weekly published in London), November 1976.
40. Booth, *The End*, p. 128.
41. John Booth (*The End*, p. 129) cites Somoza's supporter in the Liberal Nationalist party as follows: "[Jimmy Carter's] foreign policy, supposedly in favor of human rights, was a cynical instrument of pressure applied selectively to Nicaragua, which has no oil." Bernard Diederich (*Somoza*, p. 117) notes that "although Jimmy Carter would later receive most of the credit for the United States' tough human rights policy, it was the 1973–74 Congress which acted first to prohibit military and developmental assistance to gross violators of human rights, unless there were extraordinary circumstances justifying such assistance." See also William M. Leogrande, "The United States and the Revolution," in Walker, *Nicaragua*, pp. 63–70.
42. Booth, *The End*, p. 128.
43. This refers particularly to Representative Charles Wilson (D-Texas), John Murphy (D-New York), and Jim Wright (majority leader, D-Texas). For the attacks by Jack Anderson, see Jack Anderson and Les Whitten in the *New York Post*, August 18, 19, and 22, 1975; see also Alan Riding in the *Financial Times* (London), August 13, 1975, and *New York Times*, August 6, 1975.
44. James Cheek, political officer in the Managua embassy, was given the State Department's Rivkin Award in recognition of his reports through the department's Dissent Channel that contradicted the rosy reports of Ambassador Shelton. Cheek had described Somoza's post-earthquake policies in harsh terms and clearly favored a shift in U.S. policy; see Diederich, *Somoza*, pp. 104–6, and Millett, *Guardians*, p. 241.
45. Somoza and Cox, *Nicaragua Betrayed*, pp. 296–97, 301. For support by American intellectuals for Somoza's anti-Communism, see Council on American Affairs, *Nicaragua: An Ally under Siege* (Washington, D.C., 1978).
46. See Diederich, *Somoza*, pp. 155–56. Almost all Nicaraguans blamed Somoza for Chamorro's assassination. Some accounts charge that his son, Anastasio III, led the attack. Others merely state that "guardsmen" killed Chamorro. Somoza claimed the murder resulted from the anger of the blood bank owner over Chamorro's article in *La Prensa*. See Anderson, *Politics*, p. 157; Booth, *The End*, pp. 157–58; Chavarría, "The Nicaraguan Insurrection," p. 30. The Chamorro family had been one of the most politically influential in Nicaragua from the time they provided the country's first president (1853–55). Other Chamorros had been president of

Nicaragua in 1875–79, 1917–21, 1921–33, and 1926. Thus the assassination of the leader of the aristocratic opposition to Somoza left no one safe from the dictator.

47. Ibid., p. 160.

48. Booth, *The End,* p. 153; Weber, *Nicaragua,* p. 41.

49. Diederich, *Somoza,* pp. 176–88; Chavarría, "The Nicaraguan Insurrection," p. 31.

50. Tom Fenton, Associated Press, September 9, 1978, cited in Diederich, *Somoza,* p. 180.

51. Alegría and Flakoll, *Nicaragua,* pp. 344–71; Anderson, *Politics,* pp. 160–62; Chavarría, "The Nicaraguan Insurrection," pp. 32–34.

52. Alegría and Flakoll, *Nicaragua,* pp. 379–82.

53. Ibid., pp. 387–89; Weber, *Nicaragua,* p. 58.

54. Anderson, *Politics,* pp. 161–62, 165.

55. See Diederich, *Somoza,* p. 217, for description of the worldwide collaboration against Somoza.

56. See NACLA, "Target Nicaragua," *Report on the Americas* 16, no. 1 (January–February 1982): 2–45; Susanne Jonas, "The Nicaraguan Revolution and the Reemerging World War," in Walker, *Nicaragua,* pp. 375–89; Anderson, *Politics,* pp. 183–93; Booth, *The End,* pp. 222–27; Weber, *Nicaragua,* pp. 86–144; William M. LeoGrande, "Revolution in Nicaragua: Another Cuba?" *Foreign Affairs* 58 (1979): 28–50; James Petras, "Whither the Nicaraguan Revolution?" *Monthly Review* 31 (1979): 1–22.

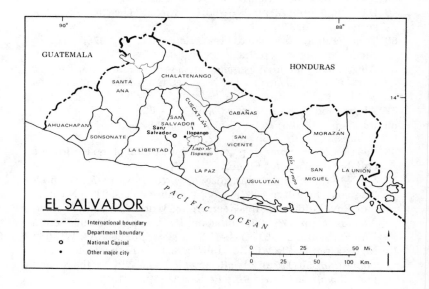

EL SALVADOR

- – - – International boundary
- ─── Department boundary
- ⊙ National Capital
- • Other major city

El Salvador

POLITICAL CHRONOLOGY

1931–44 Dictatorship of General Maximiliano Hernández Martínez. *La Matanza* (1932) massacre of thousands of Indians, peasants, and "subversives"; repression of labor and opposition political movements.

1944 Popular uprising, student strikes, May–October; internal coup in October 1944, followed by elections.

1945–48 Administration of General Salvador Casteneda Castro. Amnesty for opposition; mild reforms opposed by Conservative oligarchy and most of military; labor activism and political protests resurge. Elections of 1948 preempted by "progressive" coup in December 1948.

1948–50 Major Oscar Osorio emerges as strongman of new military government. New election law (1949) outlaws political parties based on religion, sex, class, foreign financial support, or Communist affiliation. Osorio forms new official party (PRUD) to maintain military control.

1950–56 Administration of Colonel Oscar Osorio. PRUD administration emphasizes economic modernization, public works programs, and political continuity. Moderate reforms of labor law permit some legal union activity as regime seeks a popular base.

1956–60 Administration of Colonel José María Lemus. Economic recession cripples public works programs; political unrest increases, with small but vocal pro-Cuban forces emerging in 1959–60. Regime resorts to repression and incarceration of opposition but cannot forestall a military coup.

1960   New junta with three civilian members seeks to "open" the political system; amnesty for exiles and political prisoners. Some junta members voice support for the Cuban revolution.

1961   U.S. supports counter-coup headed by Colonel Julio Adalberto Rivera; interim civilian-military directorate governs until elections in April 1961. New official party, PCN, emerges.

1962–67   Administration of Colonel Adalberto Rivera. Close ties with U.S. and participation in Alliance for Progress and Central American Common Market. Growing strength of populist and Christian Democratic political movements; strong economic growth and modernization.

1967–72   Administration of General Fidel Sánchez Hernández. Continuation of mid-1960s reforms and economic programs; economic recession dampens support for PCN. "Soccer War" against Honduras (1969) provides nationalist impetus but growing political opposition threatens PCN dominance. National Opposition Union challenges regime in 1972 elections; Colonel Arturo Armando Molina elected through fraud and intimidation.

1972–77   Administration of Colonel Arturo Armando Molina. With electoral option eliminated, some of opposition turns to armed struggle; FPL initiates military activity; ERP goes into combat (1971–72); FARN and FAPU emerge as "non-Marxist" politico-military alternatives. PCN candidate wins elections in 1977.

1977–79   Administration of General Carlos Roberto Romero, faces massive opposition to electoral fraud and continuation of PCN regime. Violence and political opposition increase, as does guerrilla activity against the government. Break with Carter administration over human rights issue. Coup ousts Romero.

October
1979   U.S. supports coup against Romero in hopes of installing a more acceptable administration and gaining popular support to defeat guerrillas.

1979–84   Political instability; succession of juntas and presidents amid a worsening political, economic, and military situation. By 1981–82 country submerged in civil war with growing U.S. commitment to "military solution." Military operations by government and guerrillas intensified at the end of 1983 and beginning of 1984.

1984   José Napoleón Duarte elected president. The military struggle continued as the United States increased its support for the new government.

BACKGROUND

The political and economic history of El Salvador, like that of most Latin American countries, is the story of agricultural boom and bust tied to a monocrop export trade that depends on extreme exploitation of the indigenous population and rural poor. Balsam trees, cacao, cochineal dye, indigo, coffee, henequen, cotton, and sugar have provided the basis of wealth and power for several hundred families who controlled the colony, the nineteenth-century republic, and the twentieth-century nation-state. Each of the export booms intensified the misery of the rural labor force and appropriated increasing amounts of the communal lands, small holds, and tenancies into the hacienda-plantation economy of the rural oligarchy. Finally, in the 1970s, the most recent cycle of agricultural modernization and proletarianization of the rural work force provided the social context for revolutionary civil war.[1]

Maintaining a colonial type of economy and social structure into the late twentieth century, El Salvador has experienced, in all its history, only the briefest interlude of "political opening"—the optimistic era following World War I. This interlude, coinciding as it did with the export-induced prosperity of the 1920s, ended with the international economic collapse of the Great Depression in the 1930s, a collapse that would ultimately lead in 1932 to the loss of the modest political reforms enjoyed by the nation's small urban population.

In early 1932 the dictatorship of Maximiliano Hernández Martínez responded to an abortive rural insurrection, which had been encouraged by the country's Communist party, with the brutal and indiscriminate massacre of thousands of Indians and campesinos. This massacre, called, literally, *La*

Matanza, (The Massacre), is the benchmark for modern Salvadoran history in the same way that the counterrevolution of 1954 is the benchmark for modern Guatemalan history.[2]

After the *Matanza,* the government outlawed worker organizations, fiercely repressed the Communist party, and restricted freedom of press, assembly, and general political activity. The dictatorship executed Augustín Farabundo Martí, a founder of the Communist party and a militant in the guerrilla forces of Sandino in Nicaragua in the late 1920s, along with other Communist leaders. Martí's name and the example of his revolutionary endeavors became, in the late 1970s, the symbol of the politico-military organizations that brought revolutionary guerrilla warfare to El Salvador—a country bypassed by the wave of guerrilla movements in the late 1960s.

From the time of *La Matanza* to the present, the small Salvadoran oligarchy, with wealth based on coffee, cattle, cotton, sugar, and agribusiness, allied with selected military leaders to maintain firm control of the nation. Despite some important divisions within the elite class based on personalist, ideological, and economic differences, basic agreement existed on the need to preserve social and political order. A dramatic mythology surrounding the peasant insurrection of 1932 buttressed the oligarchy's determination to prevent a repetition of the "subversion" and the threat to "Western Christian values" by the "great unwashed hordes" of Indians and campesinos who made up the majority of the population. This threat "justified" a permanent vigilance by security forces and national guardsmen in the rural areas.

From 1932 to 1944, the dictatorship of Maximiliano Hernández Martínez paralleled the repressive regime of Ubico in Guatemala. Until 1941, vocal supporters of the fascist governments of Europe occupied important government posts in El Salvador. Bizarre, mystical, and brutal, Hernández Martínez later served as the model for the tyrannical dictator in Gabriel García Márquez's brilliant novel *Autumn of the Patriarch.*[3] Popularly called *el brujo* (the warlock), the dictator reportedly responded to a measles epidemic by ordering that street lights be wrapped in colored cellophane to purify the air and wipe out the pestilence, while at the same time refusing to adopt the measures recommended by international health experts. He expressed his views in homilies such as "It is good that children go barefoot. That way they can better receive the beneficial effluvia of the planet, the vibrations of the earth" and "It is a greater crime to kill an ant than a man, because a man who dies is reincarnated while an ant dies forever."[4] Surveying the Salvadoran scene in the year before the *Matanza*, a U.S. military attaché to Central America, A. R. Harris, wrote:

> About the first thing one observes when he goes to San Salvador is the number of expensive automobiles on the streets. There seems to be nothing but Packards and Pierce Arrows about. There appears to be nothing between these high priced cars and the oxcart with its barefooted attendant. There is practically no middle class between the very rich and the very poor. . . .
>
> The situation is ripe for Communism and the Communists seem to have found that out. On the first of December 1931, there was in the Post Office in San Salvador over 3,000 pounds of Communist literature emanating from New York City, which had been confiscated by the postal authorities during the previous month.
>
> The authorities seem to realize that the situation is dangerous and are quite alert in their fight against Communistic influences. One thing in their favor is that the people never go hungry. The poor can always get fruit and vegetables for nothing and they can steal fire wood. . . . Also, since they never had anything, they do not feel the want very acutely of things they have never had. . . .
>
> A socialistic or Communistic revolution in El Salvador may be delayed for several years, ten or even twenty, but when it comes it will be a bloody one.[5]

Not until fifty years later would Major Harris's predictions be tragically confirmed.

The wave of liberalization that swept Latin America toward the end of World War II ended the reign of most Central American dictators. Student protests, popular unrest, and political pressure from the American embassy over the death of a wealthy American's son finally pushed the dictator of El Salvador into a hasty resignation and flight from the country in 1944. Shortly thereafter, the country experienced its first labor strikes in twelve years and a brief upsurge of political activity by reformist movements. The threat of the spread of the reformist process from Guatemala and increased worker militancy destabilized the "elected" government of General Salvador Casteneda Castro (1945–48). Convinced of the need for economic modernization, development, and diversification to stave off radical reforms, elements of the Salvadoran military and segments of the ruling oligarchy supported a military coup.

In 1948, Colonel Oscar Osorio, leader of a military faction favoring modernization of the Salvadoran polity and of the economic infrastructure, came to power in a coup, followed two years later by "elections" to legitimize the new administration. Modernization meant building a small industrial base; government investment in roads, dams, and power facilities; and encouragement of export growth in cotton and cattle. A new constitution recognized limited rights of organization for urban labor and adopted social and labor legislation reminiscent of that incorporated into the Mexican Constitution of 1917. El Salvador was only several decades behind times. Colonel Osorio even attempted to create a military-dominated political party (Revolutionary Party of Democratic Unification, PRUD) modeled on the successful Mexican ruling party, the Institutionalized Revolutionary Party.

Economic modernization provided some new opportunities for professionals and middle-class entrepreneurs; it also allowed for the expansion of the government apparatus and the beginnings of a clientelistic political organization, similar to that of Mexico. A small minority of urban workers and migrants found jobs in a nascent manufacturing sector. For the majority of peasants and most of the rural labor force, however, modernization meant a continuation of the process of proletarianization: loss of land, loss of employment opportunities, loss of hope for a future in the countryside.[6]

In 1956, Colonel Osorio gave way to his hand-picked successor, the official candidate of the PRUD, Colonel José María Lemus. The effort to replicate Mexico's successful dominant-party system failed, however, as the military proved unable to respond effectively to economic recession, rising unemployment, and popular protests. When the Cuban revolution inspired new hope in Salvador's weak and fragmented leftist and reformist movements, Lemus reacted swiftly, filling the jails with political prisoners and directing the military to suppress forcefully the increasing manifestations of student and worker discontent. Even moderate political opposition was accused of Communist connections, and the torture and beating of some prisoners angered even certain elements of the oligarchy.

Though organized labor, opposition political movements, and the revolutionary organizations of El Salvador were weak, even by the standards of Central America, the political and social ferment of the early 1960s seemed, in some ways, to conform to Che Guevara's analysis in *Guerrilla Warfare*. Certain features of the Salvadoran situation, however, would allow the entire decade of the 1960s to pass without the creation of any significant revolutionary guerrilla movement in the countryside. Thus, in terms of the conditions enumerated by Che Guevara and reviewed in the cases above, El Salvador, notwithstanding important similarities, exhibited some significant idiosyncrasies.

1. El Salvador lacked any semblance or history of real liberal democracy, or even distant memories of a substantive reformist era (e.g., Guatemala, 1944–54; Venezuela, 1945–48). The general population lacked any positive identification with the political system. However, there also existed no prototypical Caribbean dictatorship by 1960 to serve as an archetypal enemy for revolutionary campaigns of popular mobilization.

Like Guatemala, El Salvador lacked an effective political party system or significant centrist parties before 1960. Indeed, in this respect, El Salvador might have been even further removed from a modern party system than Guatemala. Labor organizations, student movements, and other popular organizations were extraordinarily weak, thereby further reducing the likelihood that liberal democracy and pluralism would develop.

In contrast to the Guatemala case, the military-civilian party, PRUD (later PCN, Party of National Reconciliation), constituted a real electoral machine that also distributed patronage, favors, government contracts, and career opportunities to selected civilians and military officers. At its lowest levels, PRUD/PCN even incorporated lower-middle-class and working-class militants, thereby creating a clientelistic network that provided some support for the regime.

This made the political system somewhat more complex and less vulnerable than a typical personalist Caribbean dictatorship (e.g., Somoza's in Nicaragua).

2. The physical terrain of El Salvador offered little in the way of isolated hinterland where guerrilla *focos* could establish safe training and staging areas or consolidated bases. Notwithstanding some mountainous and volcanic territory, the density of El Salvador's population and the very small size of the country provided few of the geographic advantages enjoyed by guerrillas in the other nations treated herein.

By the late 1970s and early 1980s the revolutionary movements of El Salvador claimed to have made the people their mountains. Realistically, however, the physical terrain of El Salvador imposed significant limitations on the development of the sort of guerrilla operations envisaged by Che Guevara in *Guerrilla Warfare.*

3. As in Guatemala, Colombia, and Peru, the "agrarian question" in El Salvador was of primary economic and political importance to large numbers of the population. Most of the country's foreign exchange in 1960 derived from agricultural exports, and over 60 percent of the population still sought to earn a living in the countryside. The recent and continuing loss of peasant lands to capitalist agriculture (1940–60) created conditions of rural proletarianization reminiscent, in some ways, of pre-revolutionary Mexico at the turn of the century.

In these respects, opportunities to gain political support with appeals for agrarian reform corresponded closely to Che Guevara's prescriptions. Moreover, the high degree of concentration of good agricultural land (in 1961 less than 10 percent of agricultural units controlled almost 80 percent of the land), the close relationship between the landowners and security forces, and the overt and systematic political and economic exploitation of the peasantry and rural labor made the objective conditions of the countryside ideal for those revolutionary movements inspired by the message of Che Guevara.

These conditions also meant that the elites of El Salvador would fiercely resist any efforts at agrarian reform, opposing even the type of palliative reforms or colonization of new lands that has occurred in Venezuela, Colombia, Peru, and even Guatemala.

4. El Salvador's revolutionary Marxist tradition was relatively young and very weak. After the *Matanza* of 1932, the Communist party was all but destroyed and was outlawed. Rural labor organizations were illegal and only limited organizing occurred even in urban areas before the 1960s. Indian *confradías* of the sort that participated in the 1932 insurrection offered a potential model for clandestine resistance,[7] but before the early 1970s no effective political opposition forces operated in the countryside.

These conditions meant that a strictly *foco* approach to guerrilla warfare and revolution would confront the dilemma of a largely unorganized and politically unsophisticated population that was intimidated by the presence of national guard and security force units. Only long, hard political-organizing efforts could even secure a safe staging area for a guerrilla operation. Without a Sierra Maestra and without a strong revolutionary organizational linkage to the rural population (unlike the Communists in Cuba, for example), any Salvadoran guerrilla movement faced a difficult task in creating the subjective conditions needed for revolution.[8]

EL SALVADOR IN THE 1960s

Colonel Lemus's government did not survive the socioeconomic ferment of 1960. In October 1960, junior officers and civilian professionals overturned the PRUD administration in a move characterized as a "progressive" coup. Promising genuine elections, a literacy campaign in the countryside, and economic reform, the new junta lasted only three months; fearful of "another Cuba," the United States orchestrated a "stabilizing coup" by a group of colonels headed by Julio Adalberto Rivera. To emphasize the U.S. commitment, President John Kennedy declared: "Governments of the civil-military type of El Salvador are the most effective in containing Communist penetration in Latin America."[9]

In 1962, in a move to "legitimize" his administration, Colonel Rivera resigned from the junta, created the Party of National Conciliation, and "won" the presidential election.[10] The PCN supported a government-controlled labor movement (Confederación General de Sindicatos, CGS) which, in turn, received funding, training, and anti-Marxist ideology from the American Institute for Free Labor Development (AIFLD). With this labor confederation as a center piece, the PCN government created a populist image and a façade of political liberalization. Relying heavily on U.S. economic assistance, President Rivera chose the clasped hands of the Alliance for Progress as the logo for the new ruling party and attempted to give a veneer of democracy to the PCN-military regime. Although Rivera and his successor, General Fidel Sánchez Hernández (1967–72), accepted the rhetoric of civic action, as well as funding for irrigation projects, schools, roads, and food subsidy programs, neither they nor the Salvadoran oligarchy compromised on the most critical issue of all: agrarian reform. Moreover, in an effort to extend PCN influence and control in the countryside, the governments of the mid-1960s supported the creation of the Organización Democrática Nacionalista, or Orden. Orden had no formal budget and no formal link to the state apparatus, yet the director of the Guardia, General José Alberto "Chele" Medrano, dispersed government patronage, credit, land, jobs, and access to services to thousands of PCN supporters in the countryside.

This clientelistic system included at its core some ten thousand paramilitary working-class and peasant auxiliaries to buttress the military-political apparatus of the PCN and to serve as part of the counterinsurgency operations in the countryside. Under mounting U.S. pressure to conform to the objectives of the Alliance for Progress, the Rivera administration combined its civic action operations with a slight liberalization of the political process. A new electoral law provided for proportional representation, thereby bringing opposition political parties and movements into the formal arena of political debate. In accord with the times, the Salvadoran leadership attempted to give the country's political institutions a democratic façade. The nascent Christian Democratic party (founded in 1960), though weaker than its sister parties in Venezuela, Guatemala, Costa Rica, Peru, and Chile, managed to grow quickly and by 1968 challenged the PCN for control of the national legislature and elected mayors in the country's principal cities.

The "political opening" coincided with an economic boom based on the expanding volume and value of agricultural exports and even a certain growth in industrial output as El Salvador participated in the Central American Common Market. This boom also implied further proletarianization of the peasantry and concomitant migration to the urban areas and to neighboring Honduras. From 1961 to 1975, the proportion of the rural population that was landless increased from 12 percent to 41 percent.[11] In this sense the economic upturn contained the seeds of future discontent when the export market softened and El Salvador temporarily lost access to the markets of Honduras because of the so-called Soccer War of 1969.[12]

The war resulted, in large part, from the fact that neighboring Honduras also faced U.S. pressure to enact agrarian reforms and to comply with the charter of the Alliance for Progress. Resentful of the asymmetry of Honduran–El Salvador economic relations and looking for a politically palatable manner of implementing some land redistribution without challenging its own rural oligarchy, the Honduran government notified many of the 300,000 Salvadoran residents that they had thirty days to leave their land and jobs in Honduras. In June 1969, Honduras ended its open border policy, closing the frontier to Salvadoran immigrants. El Salvador attempted to block the reentry of its citizens, fearing the effects of hundreds of thousands of returning peasants and workers, and protested to the Inter-American Commission on Human Rights. A month later, Salvadoran military forces entered Honduras, defeated Honduran ground forces, and cut the roads to Nicaragua and Guatemala. Only U.S. threats of economic sanctions against El Salvador persuaded that country's government to end the conflict.

The military victory over its larger neighbor temporarily diverted attention from the growing socioeconomic crisis in El Salvador. But the ultimate repatriation of the majority of the peasants from Honduras so intensified the pressure for land that General Sánchez Hernández proposed a "democratic program" of agrarian reform.[13] In January 1970 a National

Agrarian Reform Congress declared land concentration a major barrier to the country's development and also urged recognition of the right of rural labor to organize unions. For the first time, progressive members of the Catholic Church in El Salvador took a strong public stand favoring agrarian reform. Right-wing terrorists retaliated, anticipating the frequent torture and murder of progressive priests and nuns in El Salvador later in the decade. With modest beginnings, a new "popular church" of "base communities" and politically oriented clerics pushed for reforms and social justice. Just a few years later, following the example of Camilo Torres in Colombia, priests and religious workers died as combatants in the guerrilla struggle or as victims of right-wing death squads.

In spite of this new national focus on the agrarian question and mounting Catholic pressure for social reform, the Salvadoran oligarchy remained intransigent. They were ultimately successful when a rightist-*oficialista* victory in the legislative elections of 1970 guaranteed that the proposals for agrarian reform and for limitations on the political power of the landowners in the countryside would be placed on the back burner.

Meanwhile, two new progressive political organizations had joined the Christian Democrats in opposition: the Revolutionary National Movement (MNR), a social democratic type of movement, led by Guillermo Ungo,[14] and the Democratic Nationalist Union (UDN), in reality a legal front group for the outlawed Communist party. In September 1971, anticipating the upcoming legislative, mayoral, and presidential elections, the Christian Democrats, the MNR, and the UDN created a united National Opposition Union (UNO). Subjecting this opposition to harassment, physical violence, and, finally, "disqualification," the official PCN presidential candidate, Colonel Arturo Armando Molina, secured victory only through electoral fraud and administrative irregularities. After further fraud in the legislative election of March 1972, Colonel Benjamín Mejía, commander of the Zapote barracks, led an abortive coup supported by the Christian Democratic leader Napoleón Duarte. The Salvadoran air force bombed the rebel barracks to defend the PCN "victory," while the U.S.-supported CONDECA (Central American Defense Council) forces of Guatemala and Nicaragua flew arms and equipment to San Miguel to support the regime. Hundreds of deaths, numerous arrests, and the imposition of martial law confirmed the PCN "electoral" victory.

Thus, the "political opening" of the 1960s proved to be a mirage. Encouragement of political opposition and elections did not mean that the oligarchy and their allies in the armed forces were willing to accept a real transfer of power through elections or even military-directed programs of progressive modernization. The ruling elites of El Salvador, unlike those of Venezuela, Colombia, and Peru, demonstrated convincingly that no alternative to violence and revolution existed if significant reforms were to occur. Colonel Molina's "electoral" victory destroyed the opportunity to make a transition to a regime of moderate civilian reformers, and set the stage for revolutionary guerrilla movements whose leaders had learned many lessons from the military failures of their brethren in other Latin American nations in the 1960s.

ORIGINS OF THE GUERRILLAS AND POLITICO-MILITARY ORGANIZATIONS

The tendency toward fragmentation and sectarianism of the political left, so common in Latin America, proved extreme in El Salvador, even though a small country with a small population. From the founding of the first politico-military organization by dissidents of the country's Communist party (as in Venezuela, Guatemala, and Colombia), a confusing array of revolutionary organizations evolved to challenge the status quo from 1970 through the mid-1980s.

In 1970 the secretary general of the Communist party, Salvador Cayetano Carpio, rejected the official political line of his party. Breaking with the party and its legal front, UDN, Cayetano Carpio and his compatriots formed the Popular Liberation Forces (FPL).[15] Years of struggle in the labor movement and within the ranks of the Communist party had convinced Cayetano Carpio that a literalist application of Che Guevara's *foco* thesis would not succeed. Nevertheless, he and the FPL "armed commandos" attempted to initiate the armed struggle without a vanguard party, planning instead to build, over time, a political vanguard forged in the fires of combat. In Cayetano Carpio's own words:

> The initial group started virtually from zero. We lacked logistics, infrastructure, funds, arms and, if that weren't enough, we lacked military know-how. But at the same time, the people needed to be shown that on the strength of their own forces, they could and should take up arms against their enemies. . . . So we had to choose between putting off the solution of that necessity and offering the people organizations that were incomplete and had already shown their inefficacy as all around means of struggle or else form armed commandos. We chose the latter course. . . .
>
> In all honesty, we can state that, from the start, we ruled out the guerrilla *foco* theory. . . .
>
> In that regard, we were helped a great deal by the experience of some guerrilla movements in South America and in other countries that were removed from the people, that failed to reach out to them to organize them and that succumbed to militaristic designs. . . . After building support groups, we attained a certain degree of influence among the working class and the student movement. . . .
>
> Therefore, it would appear that we travelled unorthodox paths. . . . But in fact, we set out to create the conditions which, in turn, created the Marxist working class party.[16]

For two years the FPL placed primary emphasis on building a political and military base. After the fraudulent elections of 1972, the organization moved into visible military-guerrilla operations. From 1972 to the present (1984), the FPL has remained one of the most important revolutionary, military, and political organizations in El Salvador, continuing the struggle against succeeding military-civilian governments and juntas, even after Cayetano Carpio took his own life in April 1983 when he learned that Melida Araya Montes, his second-in-command, had been assassinated by supposed revolutionary comrades.

A second politico-military organization, the Peoples' Revolutionary Army (ERP), emerged in 1971–72 as an alliance of young Communists (Juventud Comunista), radical Christian Democratic youth, intellectuals, and professionals. Initially more narrowly committed to the military struggle than the FPL, ERP urban operations, such as bombings and bank robberies or kidnapings to raise funds for military operations, drew more attention than the quieter political work of the FPL. Though it rejected a literalist *foquista* line, the ERP emphasized guerrilla-inspired insurrection rather than protracted popular war, thereby following closely the spirit of the Cuban experience. Driven by personalist and ideological divisions, however, the ERP fragmented into several distinct factions; at one point in 1975 internal strife even led to the assassination of the revolutionary poet Roque Dalton. Moreover, in the view of one writer, the ERP's early actions had many negative effects on all Salvadoran revolutionary forces—effects that were only partially ameliorated in the late 1970s:

The line regarding short-term victory generated military conceptions and solutions for every type of activity or problem and reflected a profound underestimation, even scorn, for the revolutionary movement of the Salvadorean masses, channeled through different methods, forms and means of struggle.

Militarism for its part not only isolated the ERP from the people but from the very development of the political process in El Salvador. Because it expected a rapid denounment of class contradictions and spent its time preparing the instruments of war, the ERP was unable to influence the forces that were developing in the critical phases of the social movement.

As a logical consequence of the foregoing, the ERP underwent even greater division. . . .[17]

Joaquín Villalobos, a principal leader of the ERP, recognized some of the errors in the ERP's tactics, in particular the excessive emphasis on strictly military solutions and the lack of attention to creating the subjective conditions for revolution. To correct this deficiency, the ERP created in 1978 a movement for the masses, the 28th of February Popular Leagues (LP-28), and in 1980 a new revolutionary political party, the Party of the Salvadoran Revolution (PRS), to which, in theory, the military arm, the ERP, would be subordinate.

As a result of the internal divisions in the ERP and the assassination of Roque Dalton for "treason" (not accepting the militarist line), there arose a third politico-military organization, the National Resistance Party (RN), and its military arm, the Armed Forces of National Resistance (FARN). In 1974 the

National Resistance was linked, in turn, to a heterogeneous political movement, the United Popular Action Front (FAPU), that drew together many of the Catholic reformers and revolutionaries who had joined the struggle against the incumbent regime. Urging the establishment of a democratic and revolutionary government, FARN leaders also emphasized the possibility of attracting middle-class and "patriotic" military officer support—as had the guerrilla movements in Venezuela, Colombia, and Guatemala.

The RN and its military arm, the FARN, rejected the "popular armed insurrection" approach of the ERP as well as a narrow *foquista* line. Instead, the RN emphasized political work and military resistance to government and rightist attacks. This resistance included a number of highly publicized kidnapings of businessmen and managers of multinational corporations and even the assassination of the Israeli consul in El Salvador.

Between 1975 and 1979 the various revolutionary military organizations and political movements placed mounting pressure on the nation's military governments. In 1979 the Communist party of El Salvador (PCS) finally joined the military struggle officially after decades of electoral and organizational alliances with opposition parties. Party leader Schafik Jorge Handal explains the party's decision:

> After the February 20, 1977, ballot-box fraud, large-scale battles took place in the country. It was a week of insurrections, and the PCS played the role of the principal leader in the eyes of the people. It was precisely after those events that the majority of the people began to support armed struggle.
>
> Then, the PCS also changed, with a Political Commission decision in April 1977. However, eleven years of legal struggle and electoral participation had left their mark upon us as well. Over 87 percent of the PCS membership in February 1977 had joined the Party during that period and had been educated in that form of struggle. The time-honored Leninist thesis on the need to be prepared for all forms of struggle to be able to switch from one to another is not easy to apply, as we certainly found out in practice.
>
> . . . Two years behind the times, we took the step in the direction of armed forms of struggle. . . .
>
> From the start, we were well aware that the ballot box was not the

way to take power, but we were also convinced that it was necessary
to lead the people to learn for themselves, in the school of experience. . . .

The Salvadorean people and their candidates running on the ticket
of the National Opposition Union (UNO) won the 1972 and 1977 presidential elections by a comfortable margin, but the ballot was not
respected.[18]

During 1979 the PCS began to create armed militias, adopting the name of Armed Forces of Liberation (FAL). Shortly
thereafter, the old UDN joined other mass organizations in the
Revolutionary Coordination of the Masses (CRM), thereby
committing the major Communist front organization to participation in the revolutionary struggle.

Still another revolutionary military organization took shape
in 1979, the Revolutionary Party of Central American Workers
(PRTC). Basing its political program on the objective of regional revolution and the defeat of imperialism, the PRTC split in
late 1980, with its more "nationalist" elements focusing on the
Salvadoran reality. Drawing leaders from the old (1972) ERP
and Communist labor organizations, the PRTC remained a
minor, though dedicated, force in the revolutionary left.

Thus, by 1980 the variety of politico-military organizations
in El Salvador presented a confusing alphabet soup of revolutionary activity. The table below, adapted from Liisa North's
study of El Salvador, synthesizes the evolution of organizations on the revolutionary left into the early 1980s.[19]

Despite the extreme fragmentation of the revolutionary
forces in El Salvador, the victory of the Sandinistas in Nicaragua in 1979 provided immense encouragement to the various
insurrectionary movements. "If Nicaragua was victorious, so
too will be El Salvador" became a new slogan of the guerrilla
armies and political organizations. Increasing political agitation, protests, strikes, and opposition violence pushed the
Romero government into even more brutal repression. With
the apparent approval of the U.S. embassy and more progressive military officers, General Romero was ousted in a blood-
less coup in October 1979. Civilian politicians, including Guillermo Ungo, Héctor Dada, Rubén and Mario Zamora, and
Ramón Mayorga attempted to form a reformist junta but were

Guerrilla Organizations, Associated Popular Organizations, and Political Directorates

Guerrilla Organization	Popular or Mass Organization	Political Directorate or Party
Popular Forces of Liberation— Farabundo Marti (FPL-FM) (1970)	Popular Revolutionary Bloc (BPR) (1975)	FPL-FM (1970)
Popular Revolutionary Army (ERP) (1971)	Popular Leagues – 28th of February (LP-28) (1977)	Party of the Salvadoran Revolution (1977)
Armed Forces of National Resistance (FARN) (1975)	United Popular Action Front (FAPU) (1974)	National Resistance (RN) (1975)
Revolutionary Party of Central American Workers (PRTC) (1979)	Popular Liberation Movement (MLP) (1979)	PRTC (1976)
Armed Forces of Liberation (FAL) (1979)	Various labor and front organizations, including UDN (1967)	Communist Party of El Salvador (PCS) (1930)
The first three, in combination with the Communist Party in El Salvador (PCS), formed the Unified Revolutionary Directorate (DRU) in January 1980 to coordinate action. The PRTC joined	The first three, in combination with the Democratic Nationalist Union), signed a declaration of unity establishing the Movement for Popular Unity (MUP) on January 11, 1980.	

later. In October 1980, the command structures were unified and the Farabundo Marti National Liberation Front (FMLN) was established.

The Revolutionary Coordination of the Masses (the Coordinadora) was established, composed of the top leadership of the various organizations. Somewhat later, the MUP also entered the Coordinadora. The MUP was joined by the social democratic Revolutionary National Movement (MNR), the Popular Social Christian Movement (MPSC, a split from the Christian Democratic Party), and a number of associations and unions to form the Democratic Revolutionary Front (FDR) on April 18, 1980.

SOURCES: Liisa North, *Bitter Grounds: Roots of Revolt in El Salvador* (Toronto: Between the Lines, 1981); Cynthia Arnson, *Background Information on the Security Forces in El Salvador and U.S. Military Assistance* (Washington, D.C., Institute for Policy Studies, 1980); Ricardo Sol, *Para Entender El Salvador* (San José, Costa Rica, Departamento Ecuménico de Investigaciones, 1980); Tommie Sue Montgomery, *Revolution in El Salvador* (Boulder, Colo.: Westview Press, 1982).

unable to bring the military establishment under political control. A subsequent junta in which the Christian Democrats participated also failed to resolve the fundamental contradictions of the Salvadoran civil war.

In the meantime, the committed revolutionary politico-military organizations refused to place any faith in reformist juntas or nonmilitary solutions. The enthusiasm generated by the revolutionary victory in Nicaragua led, in the short term, both to further political unification (the foundation of the Democratic Revolutionary Front [FDR], in April 1980), and to an overly optimistic announcement in January 1981 of a "final offensive" that would bring the revolutionaries to power. After a relatively successful general strike in mid-1980, the "final offensive" inflicted some damage on government installations and intensified pressure on the declining economy. It failed, however, to achieve its principal objective: military victory. Recognizing the failure of *triunfalismo* (a strategy of quick victory), the revolutionaries retrenched and continued the war.

With a new presidential administration in the United States, El Salvador received prime billing as the "front-line" of the "Soviet-Cuban-U.S. confrontation" that highlighted the foreign policy agenda of the Reagan administration.[20] In the meantime, the polarization of the political-military conflict in El Salvador engendered new levels of ferocity. The year before President Reagan's electoral victory in the U.S., the number of political assassinations in El Salvador increased greatly, including as their victims leaders of the Christian Democratic party, student leaders, and Archbishop Oscar Arnulfo Romero, who had enraged army officers by calling on Salvadoran soldiers to obey God's law and to refuse to kill their brothers. From January through October 1980, numerous beatings, shootings, and atrocities on Church personnel and property made clear the regime's intolerance of Catholic reformism and calls for social justice. By the end of the year the administrator of the country's Human Rights Commission, six of the FDR's executive committee members, and four American missionaries had joined the thousands of victims of civil war and rightist violence.[21]

Notwithstanding the growing evidence of terrorism on the regime's part, outgoing president Carter authorized renewed military aid to the "centrist" Salvadoran junta in January 1981 and lifted the arms embargo imposed earlier in his administration. At the same time, Cuba and Nicaragua increased their support for the Salvadoran revolutionaries with the formation of the United Revolutionary Directorate (DRU) in May 1980 to coordinate the military activities of the various politico-military organizations. The indigenous origins of the revolutionary organizations now seemed overshadowed by the extent to which the Salvadoran conflict took on regional and international meaning for the United States, the Soviet Union, Cuba, Nicaragua, and the other nations of the Western Hemisphere.

POLITICO-MILITARY EVOLUTION OF THE GUERRILLAS IN THE 1980s

From 1980 to 1984 the revolutionary Salvadoran politico-military organizations were prevented from achieving military victory only by increasing levels of U.S. military and economic assistance, military training, and massive U.S. intervention in Salvadoran politics. Even though centrist reformers and progressive military officers were shunted aside after December 1981, U.S. officials continued to orchestrate and finance elections in an effort to legitimize the succession of juntas and "presidents." In addition, the U.S. embassy, in a desperate attempt to shore up the old order, encouraged agrarian reform programs modeled on the "pacification" operations carried out in South Vietnam, as well as a variety of civic action–public works projects.[22]

Commenting on these efforts, a former U.S. ambassador to El Salvador, Robert E. White, predicted that "the United States now can only postpone the inevitable day of reckoning when the Right exacts its price, and that price is either the elimination or the total neutralization of the Christian Democrats. That day is coming. Whether it will be in two months or six months, I don't know."[23]

From the time the Reagan administration released the so-called white paper on El Salvador in early 1981, it was clear that that nation had become "the place to draw the line" against revolution in the hemisphere. Just as the U.S. administrations of the 1960s had sought to prevent "more Cubas," the Reagan administration intended to prevent "more Nicaraguas" in Central America. But U.S. military advisers, economic and military assistance, and a hemispheric diplomatic offensive against "Communist subversion" could not create either a willingness among the Salvadoran military to fight or political legitimacy for makeshift governments.

Even the large turnout in the national elections of March 1982 (which some observers estimated at 102 percent) served ultimately to reinforce rightist political movements because the left and the FDR/FMLN refused to participate, and the Christian Democrats lost ground to a coalition of rightist and military forces.

Since U.S. policy makers had hoped that a Christian Democratic victory would both consolidate the authority of José Napoleón Duarte and symbolize the moderate-reformist face the U.S. wished to paint on the Salvadoran government, the victorious alliance of Robert D'Aubuisson's ARENA with other rightist forces represented a serious defeat for U.S. policy. ARENA's campaign slogan promised that El Salvador would be the tomb of the "reds," and D'Aubuisson, former director of the National Guard's Intelligence Service, had even promised to prosecute leading Christian Democrats for treason.

Divisions within the Christian Democratic party from 1980 to 1984, along with the assassination of scores of mayors and party cadres, even while Duarte ostensibly headed the governing junta (March 1981), eroded even the façade of a moderate-reformist administration. In short, there was no viable political center in El Salvador. In the words of the leaders of the FMLN to President Reagan in December 1982: "To pretend that the solution to the Salvadorean conflict is the March elections, is . . . outside reality. How can a democratic process be guaranteed in the context of indiscriminate repression? If you can decide the destiny of the United States, it is because you hold your office by virtue of free elections. North Americans went to elections in peace, and this is the indisputable condition in order for a people to elect their governors.[24]

This letter convinced the Reagan administration only of the

need to step up the military campaign against the guerrillas and their political movements. By the fall of 1983, Americans asked the question, Is El Salvador another Vietnam? For the people of El Salvador—those who supported the counterinsurgency programs, those who wished only for peace, and those who supported or joined the opposition politicomilitary organizations—the accuracy of Che Guevara's prediction of regional confrontation between the United States and revolutionary guerrilla movements was little consolation for the widespread death, devastation, and suffering they experienced.

In the course of 1982 and 1983 the various revolutionary armed forces wreaked havoc on the Salvadoran economy, destroying bridges, electric installations, and even 70 percent of the Salvadoran air force at the Illopango Air Force Base in an attack in January 1982. Their frequent occupation of regional urban centers and towns embarrassed both the government and the United States. Moreover, the government's response to the guerrilla operations vastly increased the death toll among combatants and civilians. By early 1983, U.S. policy makers publicly recognized the fragility of the Salvadoran government; massive increases in military assistance, training, and U.S. operations in neighboring Honduras underscored the real military success of the revolutionaries and the political failure of the Salvadoran junta. Nevertheless, by September 1983 this large U.S. commitment and more aggressive military tactics seemed to reverse the military tide somewhat and to provide temporary breathing room for the incumbent government. U.S. naval maneuvers and amphibious invasion exercises, as well as open support for an army of Nicaraguan counterrevolutionaries based in Honduras, emphasized both the threat against Nicaragua and the determination to defeat the Salvadoran revolutionary forces.

Again in March 1984 the United States promoted elections as a democratic solution to the Salvadoran conflict. The guerrilla organizations refused to participate and called upon their followers to continue the armed struggle. A runoff election in May 1984 made Christian Democrat José Napoleón Duarte president of El Salvador. The Reagan administration, which supported the victor's candidacy with covert CIA funding and aid programs, declared that El Salvador was making progress toward true democracy. The leftist opposition, however, remained skeptical and the civil war continued.

In contrast to the Colombian, Venezuelan, Peruvian, and Guatemalan military, the Salvadoran armed forces proved incapable, in the early 1980s, of carrying out effective antiguerrilla operations. In 1983 and 1984, U.S. civilian and military personnel for all practical purposes directed, supplied, and managed the counterinsurgency operations of the Salvadoran government and guaranteed, for a while at least, the survival of the regime. These developments contrasted markedly with events in the rest of Latin America. Neither Cuban nor Nicaraguan revolutionary forces had faced an explicit U.S. politico-military commitment to the incumbent regime; indeed, quite the contrary was true. President Carter's abandonment of the Somoza dynasty after 1977 paralleled the Eisenhower administration's lack of support for Fulgencio Batista throughout 1958. Thus in 1984 it was clear that the fragmented revolutionary forces of tiny El Salvador were confronting a far more difficult international and military situation than had the Cubans and Nicaraguans.

As this book goes to press, the war continues in El Salvador, its outcome uncertain but the likelihood of establishing the liberal democracy that the United States proclaims as its objective seemingly more remote than at any other time in the country's twentieth-century history. As the best publicized case of insurrectionary warfare in Latin America in the 1980s, El Salvador became the bloodiest confirmation of Che Guevara's predictions of U.S. and oligarchical response to revolution. El Salvador also became a tragic example of how the regionalization of cold war policies and perceptions challenged the course of social, economic, and political change in Latin America.

NOTES

1. The literature in English on El Salvador is much less extensive than that on Venezuela, Colombia, Peru, or even Guatemala. Nevertheless, a limited number of studies provide useful over-

views of twentieth-century Salvadoran socioeconomic and political development. See Thomas P. Anderson, *Matanza: El Salvador's Communist Revolt of 1932* (Lincoln: University of Nebraska Press, 1971); idem, *The War of the Dispossessed: Honduras and El Salvador, 1969* (Lincoln: University of Nebraska Press, 1981): and idem, *Politics in Central America: Guatemala, El Salvador, Honduras, Nicaragua* (New York: Praeger, 1982). See also Robert Armstrong and Janet Shenk, *El Salvador: The Face of Revolution* (Boston: South End Press, 1982); Enrique Baloyra, *El Salvador in Transition* (Chapel Hill: University of North Carolina Press, 1982); David Browning, *El Salvador: Landscape and Society* (Oxford: Clarenden Press, 1971); James Dunkerley, *The Long War: Dictatorship and Revolution in El Salvador* (London: Junction Books, 1982); William H. Durham, *Scarcity and Survival in Central America: Ecological Origins of the Soccer War* (Stanford: Stanford University Press, 1979); Marvin E. Gettleman et al., eds., *El Salvador: Central America in the New Cold War* (New York: Grove Press, 1981); Tommie Sue Montgomery, *Revolution in El Salvador* (Boulder, Colo.: Westview Press, 1982); Liisa North, *Bitter Grounds: Roots of Revolt in El Salvador* (Toronto: Between the Lines, 1981); Stephen Webre, *Napoleón Duarte and the Christian Democratic Party in Salvadoran Politics, 1960–1972* (Baton Rouge: Louisiana State University Press, 1979); Alistair White, *El Salvador* (New York: Praeger, 1973); Ralph Lee Woodward, Jr., *Central America, A Nation Divided* (New York: Oxford University Press, 1976).

2. The best-known analysis of the massacre of 1932 is Anderson's *Matanza*. See also Armstrong and Shenk, *El Salvador*, pp. 16–32; North, *Bitter Grounds*, pp. 34–41; Rafael Menjivar, *Formación y lucha del proletariado industrial Salvadoreño* (San Salvador: UCA, 1979).

3. Gabriel García Márquez, *El otoño del patriarca*, translated as *The Autumn of the Patriarch* by Gregory Rabassa (New York: Avon Books, 1976).

4. Roque Dalton, *Las historias prohibidas del pulgarcito* (Mexico City: Siglo XXI, 1974), pp. 125–26, cited in Armstrong and Shenk, *El Salvador*, p. 26.

5. Cited in Armstrong and Shenk, *El Salvador*, pp. 26–27.

6. For data on the expansion of export agriculture and concentration of ownership of farmland in El Salvador, see Dunkerley, *The Long War*, pp. 59–66.

7. For a discussion of the *cofradías*, Catholic brotherhoods with dis-

tinctive Indian characteristics, see North, *Bitter Grounds*, pp. 36–38, and William L. Wipfler, "El Salvador: Reform as a Cover for Repression," *Christianity and Crisis* 40, no. 8 (May 11, 1980).

8. Salvador Cayetano Carpio, a long-time Communist and then guerrilla leader, recognized these problems explicitly in interviews published, before his death, in Mario Menéndez Rodríguez's *Voices from El Salvador* (San Francisco: Solidarity Publications, 1983), pp. 11–45.

9. Anderson, *Matanza*, p. 157.

10. In this election, AGEUS, the university student organization, offered a donkey as an opposition candidate, "the only candidate worthy to compete against officialism." Tommie Sue Montgomery, *Revolution*, p. 74, citing Webre, *Duarte*, p. 47.

11. Dunkerley, *The Long War*, p. 83, citing T. J. Downing, "Agricultural Modernization in El Salvador, Central America," Centre for Latin American Studies, University of Cambridge, occasional paper no. 32 (1978).

12. The four-day war betwen El Salvador and Honduras was called the Soccer War by the media because it broke out after the two countries' soccer teams had met in the qualifying rounds for the 1969 World Cup. See William H. Durham, *Scarcity and Survival in Central America* (Stanford: Stanford University Press, 1979); Thomas P. Anderson, *The War of the Dispossessed*; Mary Jane Reid Martz, *The Central American Soccer War: Historial Patterns and Internal Dynamics of OAS Settlement Procedures* (Athens: Ohio University Center for International Studies, 1978).

13. Montgomery, *Revolution*, p. 82.

14. By the fall of 1983 Guillermo Ungo became a principal leader of the political directorate of the allied revolutionary forces (FDR) in El Salvador, after earlier attempting to create a reformist alternative to revolution in the country. Ungo's father had been a founder of the Christian Democratic party.

15. The founding and evolution of the FPL is described by Salvador Cayetano Carpio in Mario Menéndez Rodríguez's *Voices*, pp. 13–25.

16. Ibid., pp. 35, 37–38.

17. Ibid., pp. 90–91.

18. Ibid., pp. 118–19; the translator has rendered PCS into CPS for English readers.

19. North, *Bitter Grounds*, p. 79; Montgomery, *Revolution*, p. 124.

20. For strong support of the Reagan administration's "new Cold War" policies, see Mark Falcoff, "The El Salvador White Paper and Its Critics," *Foreign Policy and Defense Review* 4, no. 2

(1982): 18–24. For a critical view of U.S. policy toward El Salvador, see Arnon Hadar, *The United States and El Salvador: Political and Military Involvement* (Berkeley: U.S.–El Salvador Research and Information Center, 1981); Jenny Pearce, *Under the Eagle: U.S. Intervention in Central America and the Caribbean* (Boston: South End Press, 1982), pp. 205–78.

21. For a chronology of political violence from 1977 to 1981, see appendix 1 in North, *Bitter Grounds,* pp. v–xviii.

22. See Montgomery, *Revolution,* p. 177, for a chronology of the elimination of the progressive officers, headed by Colonel Adolfo Majano, and the civilian reformists from the governing junta in 1981. For a justification of U.S. policy in El Salvador and Central America, see Thomas O. Enders, "The Central American Challenge," *Foreign Policy and Defense Review* 4, no. 2 (1982): 8–17; an unusual insight into "special operations" and training programs can be found in Rafael Lima, "Combat Surf: The Last Expedition to El Salvador," *Surfer* 24, no. 10 (October 1983): 72–81.

23. Gettleman et al., *El Salvador,* p. 356.

24. Cited in Montgomery, *Revolution,* p. 187.

POSTSCRIPT

GUERRILLA WARFARE AND THE CRISIS
OF THE 1980s

Since the end of World War II, U.S. foreign policy toward Latin America has been dominated by global cold war concerns. Policy makers justified economic and military assistance to Latin American nations as responses to the threat of "Soviet imperialism [which] constituted a mortal threat to our own national existence."[1] From the first CIA–covert military operation in 1954 through mid-1984, U.S. officials regularly justified Latin American policy in terms of superpower confrontations.

Even as U.S. concerns for Latin America focused on Soviet-inspired Communist influence, the peoples of Latin America underwent profound socioeconomic change that intensified the already extreme inequities in the distribution of wealth, income, and opportunities throughout the region. The modernization of export agriculture, increased industrialization, and massive urbanization altered the demographic and occupational structure of the hemisphere. These changes placed even more pressure on the fragile yet often repressive governments of the region.

The old order in Latin America offered little hope for the vast majority of the region's people. Without land to till, adequate nutrition or jobs, housing, health care, or educational opportunities, the majority of Latin Americans cared little about superpower cold war conflicts. The shibboleth of "Communism vs. Capitalism" and the notion of Soviet threats to hemispheric security meant nothing to the poor and malnourished as they toiled to provide for their daily subsistence. Yet as the region's rulers routinely and cynically labeled political opponents of all sorts as "Communists," U.S. policy makers, with few exceptions, identified with the old order against "subversion." The "logic" of cold war tended to blind U.S. policy makers to the internal conditions that demanded reform or necessitated revolution.

After 1959, the Cuban revolutionaries' ideological and political confrontation with the U.S., as well as their proclaimed intent to stimulate and support "anti-imperialist" (anti-U.S.) revolutions, exacerbated the United States' opposition to autonomous political change in the region. Cuban, Soviet, and U.S. international machinations overshadowed the underlying polarization of social, ethnic, race, and class struggle that characterized the period 1959–84. The drama of Latin America, the immense tragedy of repression and despair, appeared to Americans as a minor subplot to the center-stage theater of world politics.

In this context, Che Guevara's *Guerrilla Warfare* represented a dramatic challenge. His initial call for a handful of "brave and dedicated men" in each nation to spark the struggle that would oust the Caribbean-style dictatorships quickly evolved into a call for continental and international struggle against imperialism. Guevara's inspiration, combined with the ideological underpinnings of the revolutionary struggles he promoted, contaminated, in the eyes of U.S. policy makers, the battle for social, economic, and political justice in Latin America. The cycles of insurgency and counterinsurgency that followed tore the fabric of Latin America apart.

In much of Latin America, this struggle replaced the old oligarchs and Caribbean-style dictatorships with "modernizing" military regimes. Increasingly, the progressive elements in Latin America, whether Christian, Marxist, or social democratic, viewed U.S. policy as a principal obstacle to the creation of a more humane, egalitarian society in the region. More and more, the anti-imperialist vision promoted by Che Guevara became the dominant view of large sectors of non-Marxist Latin Americans.

Ironically, Che Guevara's original formulations in *Guerrilla Warfare* offered authentic reformers and U.S. foreign policy makers hope for the future. Che's original insistence that the guerrilla struggle could not be germinated successfully where "the possibilities of peaceful struggle have not yet been exhausted" proved highly accurate. Only where local elites, bolstered by U.S. policy, destroyed beliefs in a democratic alternative have guerrilla and revolutionary politico-military movements achieved notable success. In Nicaragua, El Salvador, and Guatemala, farcical elections and repressive dictatorships made "peaceful struggle" a dangerous, often fatal charade. In contrast, in Venezuela, and even in Colombia and Peru, the appearance of alternatives to armed struggle, and the existence of real—if not profound—reformist programs offered precisely the obstacles to widespread popular support of guerrilla movements that Che Guevara predicted.

Che Guevara's modification, in "Guerrilla Warfare: A Method," of his original thesis urged that the guerrilla method—armed struggle led by the guerrilla *foco*—be used against the formal democracies ("oligarchic dictatorships") of the region. To the obvious targets, such as Somoza, were added the reformers and moderates such as Betancourt in Venezuela or Belaúnde in Peru. The mistaken broadening of the original thesis alienated nationalists, reformists, and democratic forces and legitimized increased U.S. military assistance programs in Latin America. Defending the reforms of Acción Democrática in Venezuela or even the fragile efforts of President Belaúnde in Peru could not be equated in the U.S. Congress or in U.S. public opinion with support for Somoza in Nicaragua or the Guatemalan military dictators.

But as Guevara failed to limit the applicability of the guerrilla method to the targets indicated in *Guerrilla Warfare,* so the United States failed to limit its military assistance and political support to the formal democratic regimes most able to resist guerrilla warfare and least likely to engage in institutionalized torture and terrorism. Neither Che Guevara, nor his Latin

American disciples, nor the policy makers of the United States recognized the legitimacy of truly *national* reformist or revolutionary movements that refused to identify with international socialism or the "western bloc." The overwhelming influence of cold war ideological and security concerns in United States–Latin American relations, and in Guevara's modifications of *Guerrilla Warfare,* contributed to a quarter century of political polarization, tragedy, and death in Latin America. As these lines are written, this legacy continues to govern the U.S.-supported attacks on the Sandinista government in Nicaragua and U.S. support for military terror in El Salvador, Guatemala, Chile, and Uruguay. It also inspires hard-line Marxist-Leninist contempt for, and opposition to, authentic, democratic efforts to transform Latin American nations into more humane, egalitarian, and free societies.

INDEX